Evidence for Faith

THE CORNELL SYMPOSIUM ON EVIDENTIAL APOLOGETICS
Ithaca, New York
29 August–7 September 1986

Evidence for Faith

Deciding the
God Question

Edited by
John Warwick
Montgomery

PROBE
Books

DISTRIBUTED BY WORD PUBLISHING

DALLAS LONDON VANCOUVER MELBOURNE

Copyright © 1991 by Probe Ministries International

Library of Congress Cataloging-in-Publication Data
Evidence for faith : deciding the God question / edited by John Warwick Montgomery.
    p.   cm.
    Includes bibliographical references and index.
    1. Apologetics—20th century. I. Montgomery, John Warwick.
    BT1102.E46   1991   91-8917
    239—dc20   CIP

ISBN 0-945241-15-1

Place of Printing Printed in the United States of America.

Editor Louis D. Whitworth

Associate Editor Meisje L. Johntz Connor

Consulting Editor Rich Milne

Cover Design by John M. Henderson III/JMHIII Designs Lagoon Nebula photograph by U.S. Naval Observatory. Reproduced by permission of National Aeronautics and Space Administration.

98 97 96 95 94 93   5 4 3 2

For

Herman John Eckelmann

from a generation of disciples
who still remember Cayuga's waters
and whose lives were permanently impacted
by his concern for the lost

Table of Contents

Preface

THIS IS A BOOK FOR BELIEVERS AND FOR UNBELIEVERS. Its authors—many of them scientists and all of them trained at secular universities—became and remain Christians because the evidence for the truth of Christianity overwhelmingly outweighs competing religious claims and secular world views.

This volume is literally capable of changing lives, and the lives of more than one of its contributors were in fact turned upside down by the force of the evidences here set forth. The Editor himself is in that category, and his tale is worth retelling, for it will help to set this book in perspective.

I arrived at Cornell University as a callow freshman in 1948. I commenced a double major in philosophy and classics. My religious position—if it can be so dignified—was liberal-to-secular. As with many freshmen I found myself in the Navy barracks-style dormitories erected at the end of the Second World War to accommodate the glut of students of that generation. Incredibly, an upperclassman—in electrical engineering—had chosen to forego the Neo-Gothic beauty and convenience of the permanent dormitories to remain with the lowly frosh as a barracks-dorm counselor: Herman John Eckelmann was his name, and evangelism was his game.

But not the mindless evangelism of today's electronic church nor the relationalism of modern churchmanship; rather, his was a thoroughgoing *apologetic* evangelism, in the tradition of the Apostle Paul among the philosophers at Athens. Eckelmann asked the penetrating, Socratic questions: *Why* are you at University? What do you think life is all about? Where will you spend eternity? Have you considered the claims of Jesus Christ and the evidence for these claims?

He would not let you go. He would not tolerate sloppy thinking. His minuscule room was stuffed with the best of classic and contemporary apologetic literature. You had an objection? Eckelmann had a book— generally more than one—on that point, and it was often a book just off the press.

The answers were invariably better than the questions. In my case, he gave me, shortly after their publication, Wilbur Smith's *Therefore Stand,* Edward John Carnell's *Introduction to Christian Apologetics,* and C. S. Lewis's early writings in defense of the faith. And he kept pressing me to a decision: "If the evidence is that good—and you know it is—*what are you going to do about it?*" One night in my dormitory room, on my knees before the God of heaven and earth who had assuredly died to redeem me, I did something about it. The following day, the world had become a different place, and my life has never been the same since.

This scenario is by no means unique. Eckelmann was at it hammer and tongs in the 1940s, and he is still at it hammer and tongs today. After completing his engineering degree, he went to theological seminary, principally to master the biblical languages under the impeccable instruction of Dr. Allen A. MacRae (another contributor to this volume). The seminary years were his only break with Cornell. He returned there to serve until retirement at the Cornell Radiophysics and Space Center, ultimately as its chief photographer and designer of a color stereo close-up camera for U.S. manned lunar landings. While at the Space Center, Eckelmann simultaneously pastored the Faith Bible Church in Ithaca, providing an oasis of serious, apologetic preaching in a desert of flaccid cultural religiosity.

And always he has engaged in personal evangelism, with a particular eye for the student with the capacities to replicate such an apologetic witness elsewhere. He has regularly sent such students—often after they obtained Ph.D.'s in the rigorous scientific disciplines—on to seminary. The result: scholars who know both theology and the secular mindset, and who are concerned to present the lifechanging evidence for Christian truth.

This volume puts together their thinking. We call it the Cornell Symposium on Evidential Apologetics. This name is appropriate because (1) the arguments given for the existence of God are concerned with evidence, not with philosophical or theological presuppositionalism; (2) the papers were presented "far above Cayuga's waters," in earshot of the carillon that still plays the evensong at twilight, on the twenty-fifth anniversary of

Eckelmann's congregation; and (3) Cornell has served as a *locus sacrissimus* for most of the contributors. Indeed, this book may be said without exaggeration to benefit both from a holy place (Cornell University) and from a tutelary spirit (Herman John Eckelmann)!

The fervent desire of the Editor and the contributors is to take the reader on an intellectual and existential pilgrimage. Consider well the evidence this volume presents to your mind and heart. Then act on it. You won't regret it—either in time or in eternity.

Strasbourg, France   JOHN WARWICK MONTGOMERY
The Feast of the Epiphany
6 January 1991

Part 1

A Hard Look
at Evidence

1.1

The Value of an Evidential Approach

William J. Cairney

IN 1951, KEN TAYLOR, FAMOUS IN CHRISTIAN CIRCLES for his translational-paraphrase work on The Living Bible, wrote a very interesting little booklet for InterVarsity Christian Fellowship. The booklet, entitled *Is Christianity Credible?* opens with a familiar scene. Professor Jones, a courteous, patient college professor is addressing a group of new freshmen. Professor Jones is a sincere straight-talker, and very likeable. His claim to fame is that in the previous academic year, he had influenced all but about 15 percent of his incoming evangelical Christian freshmen to renounce totally their commitment to a Christian perspective.

His method was simple. He talked straight from the shoulder and from his heart to the group of freshmen students before him. . . . He enjoyed his life work of helping students rethink their religion so that they would come to understand that historic Christianity is unacceptable to a thinking person.[1]

As we enter Professor Jones's class through the insights (and possible recollections) of Ken Taylor, we find Jones challenging his students to get beyond immature thinking and welcome their opportunity for intellectual maturation. Jones holds forth on element after element of the Christian belief and systematically dissects each one. Inerrancy of the Scriptures, devils, angels, miracles, virgin birth, bodily resurrection of Jesus Christ, the creation account in Genesis, the Mosaic laws—on and on. Jones asks these students to "face these matters squarely as men and women in college rather than as children."[2] He even quotes the Apostle Paul in exhorting the students to "put away childish things."[3]

As Taylor related more and more of Jones's arguments, methods, and results, I found myself reliving a chapter of my own life. Perhaps many of you, also, can place yourselves right in that freshman class. As a prelude to the series ahead, I would like to share some autobiographical data as a way of keynoting a theme that I wish to develop—the value of an evidential approach to a knowledge of God.

Having been born into a Christian home, my early church experience could best be described as "positive." The local congregation was the focal point for our family's social activities, and people related to one another in an attitude of mutual encouragement and support. Moreover, the Bible was taught systematically and memorized extensively. The congregation was composed largely of Scottish and Irish immigrant families who had settled in this New York City urban community as a result of family ties or availability of certain kinds of work (mostly trades). The educational level was generally low by American standards with high school graduation common, but lesser educational levels also common, especially among people who had come in from the "Old Country," as it was generally known. Except for a rare two or three younger folks, university education was not even represented. Because the congregation had such a commitment to biblical knowledge, this lack of formal education was not especially apparent, nor was it an issue.

The church also had a serious commitment to evangelism and put a special premium on children's ministry. As a result of those efforts, as an elementary schooler I took what I consider to this day to have been a deliberate, conscious step of faith in Jesus Christ in response to the Apostle Paul's counsel to the jailor at Philippi in Acts 16:30–31. Following a serious earthquake resulting in major damage to the prison and life-threatening circumstances for the jailor, the man asked Paul (and Silas, Paul's companion), "'Sirs, what must I do to be saved?' They replied, 'Believe in the Lord Jesus, and you will be saved—you and your household.'"[4] From that point on I considered myself a "Christian" according to the biblical criteria for that title and committed myself to "grow in the faith." I was active in the high school group later on and participated extensively in the music ministry playing piano and organ and leading congregational singing. This involvement and activity level continued through college at the same church with the same people. A model young believer . . . or was I?

The crisis for me occurred in my college years. It was a quiet crisis, probably unrecognizable to most people. It began in "seed" form in the very first class of my freshman year, in Biology 101. The professor, also the Biology Department Head, stated emphatically, "Evolution is a fact. It has been proven and no competent biologist disagrees with it. You may believe in a Creator if you wish, but that is your private belief and not a matter of the science we will deal with here!" In my conservative church congregation, evolution (which most people pronounced "ēvolution") was anathema. This professor turned out also to be my academic advisor. He listened to my ideas with interest and a great deal of amusement. In that I had once done a presentation to our high school youth group on the impossibilities of "ēvolution," I came to him on several occasions armed with what I considered irresistible ammunition against this notion. My best arguments were no arguments at all in that, as he pointed out, they had all been dealt with by people competent in the science and found to be of no consequence.

Junior year in college—and enter my own "Professor Jones." I had decided to double major in biology and chemistry with a goal of medical school or graduate school in the biomedical sciences. (I especially liked cellular physiology.) "Jones" taught a capstone course in cellular biology. He was a very likable, credible man. He was warm, dynamic, enjoyed an excellent professional reputation, was a devout Unitarian and one of the most organized teachers I have ever encountered (to this day). He proceeded to show, systematically and plausibly, the sequence of molecular evolution from basic building block molecules to biologically meaningful macro-molecules to cells to complex multi-tissued organisms. In addition to his factual data, he commented on the philosophical implications of it all in a polished and persuasive manner. His impact on me was immense. For the next two years, I was truly his disciple in the strongest sense of the word.

In addition to "Jones," several other influences combined with maximum effect. For one, the known campus Christians were generally regarded as "out of it." They were somewhat undynamic, a little bit tacky in dress and manner, and (with minor exceptions) were not the best students. In short, no one wanted to be like them. In contrast, the students who did have their acts together tended to think along the lines of "Jones." They were clear-thinking, goal-oriented, well-dressed, pre-professional people. Most were professed agnostics, and they were not afraid to defend their world view.

I recall a conversation I had in the science library with a young woman who eventually graduated number one in our class. She expressed the conviction she had that "agnosticism is the only intellectually defensible position." This, from her, was like a mental tidal wave.

In attempting to get help for this intellectual challenge I sought counsel from people who had been my mentors in spiritual matters, members of my local church. While the responses varied from person to person, the theme was nevertheless the same: "In matters of science versus Scripture, the University is wrong." I can't begin to describe the credibility gap that began to develop. To think, a person with an eighth-grade education telling a Ph.D. molecular biologist that he was wrong in his own field. At that point, after multiple tries at answers, I made an assumption. That assumption was wrong in retrospect; but it guided my mindset for several years. I assumed—because these conscientious folks (with a strong commitment to the Bible but with limited scientific training) couldn't give me answers—that there were no answers.

The overall effect of my experiences and assumptions was to force me to try to live a dichotomy, to try to be comfortable in both worlds, jumping from one to another, as needed . . . but with the burning conviction that those worlds were incompatible and irreconcilable. This all came to a head one Sunday morning as I was participating in communion at our church. The Apostle Paul strongly exhorts the church at Corinth,

Therefore, whoever eats the [communion] bread or drinks the cup of the Lord in an unworthy manner will be guilty of sinning against the body and blood of the Lord. A man ought to examine himself before he eats of the bread and drinks of the cup.[5]

I was unexamined, unconvicted, unworthy, and becoming more than skeptical. I felt myself to be the biggest hypocrite on the face of the earth—song leader, pianist, organist, youthful Christian mouthpiece, outward model. One person whose reactions I remember and appreciate to this day was my father. He was an elder in the church and his grasp of Scripture was considerable. He was also interested in science, especially biology. I would share my thoughts with him, yet he couldn't answer my technical questions either. But, he listened, and he came back with thoughtful replies. I appreciated his patience. I'm sure he thought I was working it out because he got lots of outward signs from me to warrant that conclusion.

Graduating with a brand-new bachelor's degree, I had still not resolved the basic conflicts. Linnea and I were married right at college graduation time; she graduated as a nurse, I as a fledgling microbiologist. We immediately moved to Cornell University ("Jones's" graduate alma mater) to begin graduate school. I had initially hoped to follow in "Jones's" footsteps and have his former major professor and mentor on my graduate committee and perhaps as my committee chairman if things worked out. (They didn't.)

Our initial church experience in the Ithaca area was terrible (not sparing the most descriptive term). We had been given a lead on this particular congregation from our church back home. It seemed to us that this church had accumulated, under one roof, every negative evangelical stereotype we had ever seen or known. I was becoming very comfortable in a naturalistic Neo-Darwinist mold, able to defend naturalistic organic evolution very well, and becoming less and less content with the dichotomy. Our church attendance dwindled to nothing by the end of our first Cornell year. It was really all over, I felt. Time to own up. Time to make a break with the family heritage. I was tired of trying to live a Christian world view with a large part of my intellect on a shelf marked "non-functional."

But . . . I was not entirely convinced that the God of the Bible wasn't "there." So I thought that a challenge to Him might be in order (a "reverent" challenge . . . just in case). My challenge went somewhat like this: "God . . . if you are truly there . . . show me that the biblical Christian model is acceptable to a thinking person. Show me that there is sound evidence that even a scientific mind can accept, that the Bible is the actual Word of God, that it is accurate and authoritative in its assertions . . . or I am going to kick over the whole works!" I found as a result of that prayer that the God who really is there does not take such challenges lying down!

Soon after that challenge (certainly not more than two weeks), Linnea and I were made aware of a little church group that was meeting in a home about a five-minute ride from where we were living at the time. We were told that the man pastoring this fledgling church had a seminary degree and was also a research associate at Cornell. That sounded interesting, so we visited.

I can't begin to describe the experience. We came to the back door of a home in which perhaps forty-five to fifty people were gathered in a crowded family room which somehow also housed a piano and a double-manual, full-pedalboard Allen organ! And all elements of this milieu were contributing to a sound level I can best describe as "tangible." The singing really was fun. The people were happy and friendly to a degree that I interpreted as "not for real."

The pastor of the congregation was one Herman J. Eckelmann, a graduate of Faith Seminary in Philadelphia and, indeed, a research associate in astrophysics at the Cornell University Space Center. Significant is the fact that the subject of the series was "Evidence from Science for the Authenticity and Authority of the Christian Bible." Call that "coincidence" if you will.

For the next full year at Cornell, we systematically reviewed and analyzed historical, archaeological, cosmological, and even biomedical evidence that the Bible was written by the very God who claims to be its Author. We discovered that the Author of the biblical text had left a massive body of internal and external evidence to validate His claims to authorship, evidence that could be examined and tested.

This was especially important, because as we look at the world around us, we see countless systems which people are following. These "models for truth" or "approaches to God" are largely untested by their adherents.

College and university campuses provide students and faculty with a veritable smorgasbord of "isms." Christianity in its various denominations and sects, Buddhism, B'Hai, Islam, Hinduism, Shintoism, Hare Krishna, New Age, etc., ad infinitum, all compete for attention and allegiance. What an expansive list of choices!

Suppose we had no family biases, no ethnic biases, no creedal biases of any sort and were confronted by this assemblage of systems in our attempt to discover God. We certainly would be tempted to ask, "How can I know which system, if any, is really an approach to a knowledge of God?" Individuals and groups have responded to this problem in numerous ways. Some have considered feelings as their personal means of verification. If it feels good for me, it must be "right." But, people have felt good about "bad" systems as well as "good" ones. Nazism, Communism, and the cult of Jim Jones all began with good feelings.

Closely allied to good feelings is the notion of the positive influence on society claimed by numerous systems and cults. "Our teenagers don't turn to drugs." "We keep our families together." "Our moral standards are the highest in the nation." "Our divorce rate is the lowest in the Western world." And the claims, of course, imply that God is obviously blessing this or that "ism" and that therefore it is "the true way to God."

Overall acceptance is another common verification point. A certain "ism" engulfs a whole region of the United States, affects institutions, permeates every corner of the culture, produces scholars, advocates, and apologists, and becomes a power to be reckoned with. An individual living within that system would easily be led to think that its scholars had worked out the details and that a system accepted by so many important and gifted people couldn't possibly be wrong. Again, Nazism and Communism both capitalized on waves of popular acceptance.

But what about "isms" that claim "faith" as their point of verification? And here we begin to tread on interesting ground, because the Christian Bible indeed places great importance on faith in the development of a personal relationship with God. In fact, a verse quoted over and over by "isms" and by mainline orthodox Christianity alike is "And without faith it is impossible to please God, because anyone who comes to him must believe that he exists and that he rewards those who earnestly seek him."[6]

"So," says the well-dressed person at the door, "our prophet is bringing a new revelation from God to the world, and God asks that you accept this revelation by faith and act upon it by joining our church." When confronted by such a challenge, I have a standard reply: "Why should I accept your system of faith? What evidence can you give me that the God of the universe inspired either the Bible or the words of your prophet?" That strategy has certainly produced some memorable discussions!

But what about the possibility of evidence? Maybe evidence is available to validate one of the many systems which claims to be an approach or the approach to God. We might actually expect that to be so, if an almighty God has designed a channel by which mankind could come to the fullest possible knowledge of Himself. But what "evidence" would we look for? What would constitute "evidence"? Could I suggest a few possibilities?

History Written in Advance. We can all write history in retrospect, but an almighty, omnipotent Creator would not be bound by our notions of space and time, and would thus be able to write history before it occurs. Suppose that we encountered a sourcebook that contained page after page of history written in advance with such accuracy and in such detail that good guessing would be completely ruled out.

Prescience. Suppose that in this same sourcebook, we were able to find accurate statements written ages ago demonstrating scientific knowledge and concepts far before mankind had developed the technological base necessary for discovering that knowledge or those concepts. Perhaps an almighty God would be trying to get our attention with such fore-knowledge.

Historical Evidence. Suppose that in this same sourcebook, we were to find historical assertions that time after time were verified as true as historical scholarship continued. And closely allied to that . . .

Archaeological Evidence. Suppose that in this same sourcebook, statements that are difficult to verify are made about people and places, but as archaeology "unearths" more knowledge of the past, time after time the sourcebook is seen to be true in its assertions.

Philosophical And Logical Coherence. Suppose that this same source-book, even though written piecemeal over thousands of years, contains well-developed common themes and is internally consistent.

And suppose all of these evidences hang together without internal contradiction or literary stress within the same anthology. Collectively, we could not take these evidences lightly.

And so, we start the journey . . .

Notes

[1] Kenneth N. Taylor, *Is Christianity Credible?* (Downers Grove, Ill.: Inter-Varsity Press, 1951), 4.

[2] Ibid., 7–8.

[3] 1 Cor. 13:11, King James Version.

[4] Acts 16:30–31. This and all subsequent Scripture references in this chapter are from the New International Version of the Holy Bible, copyright 1978 by the New York International Bible Society.

[5] 1 Cor. 11:27–28.

[6] Heb. 11:6.

1.2

An Evidential Approach to Biblical Christianity

Herman J. Eckelmann

FIVE BLIND MEN INVESTIGATED AN ELEPHANT. The first felt the trunk and said, "An elephant is like a large hose." The second one touched the tail and stated, "An elephant is like a rope." Still another encountered an ear and exclaimed, "An elephant is like canvas." The fourth one examined a leg and said, "Elephants are like trees." Finally, the fifth one, who felt a side, said emphatically, "Elephants are actually houses!" Each thought clearly of the elephant in terms of his own too-limited data.

Though this illustration is an old one, it points out an ageless and important truth: Incomplete evidence or faulty methodology results in contradictions that are more apparent than real. This is important for us because some of the conflicts between science and Christianity are based on similar misrepresentations. It is important to appreciate how badly such misconceptions affect both scientific and Christian claims if we are to find the truth about God, man, the world today, and the world to come.

One person may say, "Science is a developing body of truth; it contradicts the Bible, therefore the Bible cannot be accepted." Another may say, "Science does not actually contradict the Bible; this allegation is only the claim of certain non-Christians who want to seem to have nearly infallible support for their preferences. Actually, the data of science do not contradict the data taught in the Scriptures." Can the correct viewpoint be discovered? For that matter, is it all that important? Not much is at stake in the case of religions which say all will be well finally, no matter what one does. Those religions which say man will have another chance in the next life or that there is no next life also need not worry anyone greatly. On the other hand, a religion which teaches that the stakes involved in our present choices are almost infinitely high in the next life ought to be investigated early and carefully, if it has even the slightest chance of being true. We, therefore, propose to examine the data and truth claims at the interface between science and the Bible.

The Function of a Scientist

The function of a scientist is that of observing, theorizing, and then testing his theories (or hypotheses). Recently, the spinning of theories has been called "model making." Good illustrations of this function can be found in Joss and Salpeter's "Models for Carbon-Rich Stars with Helium Envelopes," John Warwick Montgomery's "The Theologian's Craft," and J. D. Watson's *The Double Helix.*[1] Certain "facts" seem to be causally related (cause and effect). A mental model is constructed in an attempt to fit the facts together in a systematic way. The purpose is to relate adequately past data and enable the model maker and others to predict more successfully what will happen in the future, given similar circumstances. The data or evidence used in the model-construction process may come from all of experience, not just from a laboratory. The data may be the kind that can be modeled mathematically and thus processed to some degree in a computer.

The Nature of Model Making

Model making is necessarily a process of successive approximations, since a model usually cannot reliably go any farther than the limited data (and accuracy) available at the moment. And, because we do not have infinite, total, or exhaustive knowledge, we cannot be absolutely certain we have all the pertinent data necessary to make a "final" model. Models are always subject to revision, fine tuning, or even abandonment when new inputs necessitate changes to provide for total integration of an enlarged body of data. Therefore a finite human cannot claim total, infinite, absolute, or final knowledge about anything. Can we then have a working certitude about anything? Do we ever come to the place where we are morally obligated to go with the best data at hand? If not, how could anyone ever be justly regarded as blameworthy on Judgment Day and judged for any actions or crimes?[2]

The Nature of Data

The term *data* has commonly been defined as facts taken for use as a basis for reasoning. More recently, it is being recognized that so-called facts are actually conclusions we hold in our minds after "interpreting" one or more sense experiences or feelings within ourselves. The conclusions actually are mini-models which we have made unconsciously. Thus, what we frequently call *facts* are actually models with the propensities for fallibility already mentioned. Data are what we have before conclusions are drawn. Data are the sense and/or psychological experiences that come to the mind for arranging into possible models, one of which is chosen for the needs of the situation.

Possibilities in the Handling of Data and Models

The information content of the data, for a logical person, predestines the conclusion, just as a computer's output is predetermined by its inputs ("garbage in, garbage out"). Skewing the incoming data or excluding some of it from our thinking produces models which differ from what they ought to be. Ignorance of available pertinent data tends inevitably to result in unnecessarily imprecise, untruthful, and even dangerous models. What we are saying when we claim to understand something is that we have a mental model that connects the data points in a way intellectually satisfying to us. The points may be connected with anything from straight lines to all kinds of curves and loops, producing a simplest possible model, or an infinite variety of more or less arbitrary models. We should restrict our model's form to the minimum required by the available data. Anything else is blind faith.

The systematic exclusion of certain data from the model-making process by preselecting only part of what is available is an immoral exercise of the mind. It may be done unconsciously or subconsciously to maintain the appearance of respectable rationality for what may actually be a matter of personal prejudice. Thus a person may become willfully blind, deliberately limiting his input data, thus apparently justifying the making of a defective model. Such self-will, when practiced on a large collective scale, can lead to tragic errors of judgment on the part of individuals and even nations. We are morally obligated to proceed on the basis of the best data available as decisions are necessitated.

We seek, therefore, to fit together our input data more or less smoothly into small models. These small models are the parts that go into the overall model or philosophy of reality (Weltanschauung) which each person constructs. Supposedly, this determines his outlook or philosophy of life. Actually his outlook or philosophy also largely determines the initial small models as well, and they in turn the larger one. The circular feedback naturally occurring can pose an almost insuperable obstacle to the correction of one part of the total mass that does not fit new data. The strain on intellectual honesty can be severe.

Becoming A Christian

The Mistaken Way of Blind Faith

The Bible never said there were three wise men. Neither did it say Eve gave Adam an apple or that God made the universe out of nothing. These are traditions, and, like most traditions, they should be questioned. Christians are people of the Book, which means real Christianity is not some mystery religion practiced in a cave, but rather that its actual content is fully set down. It can be studied, checked, and rechecked objectively. "Sola Scriptura," the motto of the Great Reformation, is a statement of the fact that the Book is the Christian's ultimate standard of reality and living. No one has the right to call his pizza-inspired dreams an authoritative addition to that base line.

On the other hand, to get a lock on people's minds, cultists (and other power-trippers) frequently demand a blind faith in some other basic doctrine or teaching. Once evidence and reason are thus shrewdly by-passed, they are not likely to be used consistently in further thinking either. The absolute blind-faith starting position is held to be totally authoritative and determines all that follows. This is not the teaching of the Book. Therefore, it is not the teaching of genuine (biblical) Christianity. The exercise of blind faith is essential to cultic religions because, in principle, it is the end of all argument; any possible future re-examination is headed off before getting started.

A typical unfortunate scenario might begin with someone who calls himself (or herself) a prophet. In essence he says God gave him a message mankind needs today. Perhaps he claims to have been given some gold tablets with the initial message already engraved on them in an unknown language, which only the prophet is able to translate. Then the tablets conveniently disappear. Or, the prophet is simply "inspired" to directly speak and/or write what is to be followed. We are told this is the way the Christian Scriptures were given, and this new prophet is in the same line or tradition. He, therefore, should be similarly honored and obeyed. Others may want to join him as additional prophets, sharing authority over people. Competition is not usually welcomed, so new prophets tend to come one by one as old ones die off. Sometimes later revelations are difficult to harmonize with what was previously given. When this happens, an important new doctrine would naturally state that the most recent revelations supersede all previous "inspired" material, especially when contradictions are perceived. Thus, mistakes can be made to become virtues. Allegedly, followers are being continuously and advantageously supplied with changing truth for changing times.

Things can get a bit sticky when several "prophets" claim simultaneously they are being led in certain ways or given special revelations that do not harmonize well with each other. An accommodation may be reached, where, having supposedly been given new truth by God, they feel it necessary or wise to call a meeting to take a human vote on it all before propagation for all to honor and obey as God's Word. Whatever they may call themselves, their primary purpose is to obtain power over people, preferably in large numbers. Everything, then, depends on persuading these people to commit themselves early on to a blind faith in some basic proposition that later will make them follow as unquestioningly as possible. The Koran, for example, doesn't even attempt to give any reason for belief in its religio-ethical system (i.e., any solid evidence strong enough to rationally support its command/reward structure). Rather, it claims, essentially, one will know it is true if one's heart is in the right place. Evidently there are people who can be successfully programmed, by just such a simple statement, to "experience" the required feeling. Everything down the line depends upon accepting the imposition of an early, essentially blind decision. Pride later hinders re-examination of the rightness of this starting point. The belief that this erroneous starting point is the Christian position allows many to take the leap in the dark, to make the basic commitment that predestines all future compliance.

Soon after the individual's commitment is made, the burden of building and using beautiful cathedrals is often imposed, for this psychologically imprints an authentication of the original blind faith decision more and more firmly. Thus, the road downhill gets steeper and more difficult to retrace. The way is paved for the revelations to be claimed to be self-authenticating, or to be believed solely on the authority of "the Church." In time, antiquity is invoked, and the cult is thus further psychologically clothed with believability and consequent authority over people. It may then gain the further respectability of being called a church, then a denomination.

Finite Man and His Finite Knowledge

Finite man cannot and does not possess exhaustive knowledge; therefore he usually has to learn on the basis of probabilities inherent in data gathering and the model-assembling process. If he had exhaustive or infinite knowledge he would not need to learn anything. Some have said finite knowledge of an infinite Being would be an infinitesimal percentage of the totality, and, therefore, man cannot say anything significant about God. However, in simple math we know the general equation for a straight line in a two-coordinate system is $y = mx + b$. Even though the line is infinitely long in both directions, and we are finite, we can and do say certain very significant truths about it in the equation. So also, the God who lives is infinite in certain definable attributes. (For a good discussion of this, I recommend J. Oliver Buswell's *Systematic Theology of the Christian Religion.*[3])

Thus we must recognize that we can know certain truths about God. In orthodox Christianity the Holy Spirit works to open one's mind to truth. Then new facts, fresh insight about God or the nature of reality, the influence of the Word of God, or changes in circumstances act upon a person's mind, spirit, and world view. A new openness to Christian evidences begins to develop. This type of evidence is discussed in such books as Urquhart's *The Wonders of Prophecy,* Stoner and Newman's *Science Speaks,* Newman's *The Evidence of Prophecy* and *Genesis One and the Origin of the Earth,* and Josh McDowell's *Evidence that Demands a Verdict.*[4] Then an honest examination reveals truth, and an explanation is required for the unfailing accuracy of the Scriptures in recording history far in advance of its occurrence and scientific knowledge far in advance of its discovery. Then the closed system or giant model previously held is not adequate to integrate the new data, and an agonizing reappraisal is indicated; a choice is required to deal fairly no matter what the ego cost. Fearing the taunts and reprisals of colleagues and friends, some do not make this choice. Others, grasping the overall significance and moral imperative of receiving this new data at any cost, find they embrace not only data, but also as a logical consequence, a Person—Jesus Christ. Much is involved when this happens. In the light of moral standards revealed in the Bible to be inherent in the nature of the Lord, a reassessment of one's life transpires. Also a new attitude toward things contrary to His nature occurs. Sin begins to be called sin, and though it was once a thing desired, progressive dislike for it now becomes natural. Answers to prayer occur which are not easily explained away statistically. Reasons for living a particular kind of life with otherworldly goals are discovered, and a peace is experienced which far transcends previous transient and deceptive pleasures. A startling result of the emerging new nature is a growing satisfaction in fulfilling one's responsibilities to the Lord. The habit of erecting false models of convenience lessens as appreciation for truth deepens. The certitude required for life's decisions is adequately transmitted, in His providence, by the supplied data.

Looking Back

Christians, looking back over their past, feel certain things characterized them and the world out of which they came. Most important is that the world's model has been warped by carefully preselecting certain data, i.e., excluding that which would lead to submission to the living God as He has presented Himself in the Scriptures.

For example, the "faith" that miracles cannot have happened is the result of unfounded arbitrary assumptions plus partial data exclusion. Heaven, hell, and a final judgment are said to be unbelievable. Actually, the unbelievability is the result of thinking within the confines of an arbitrary model that permits only horizontal conceptualization. Such a thinker scarcely looks at data that would expand his ability to integrate the sensory experience of a large body of mankind. After becoming Christians, we recognize that we once ignored large areas of evidence that threatened our model with change. "Facts" were used to rationalize our unwillingness to submit to revealed responsibilities. Our model was inhospitable; it was skewed by self-will for temporary "freedom" or autonomy.

This intellectualization of nonsubmission to the Lord is a misuse of the mind. It is an action that must be forsaken in this life, or the person will be held permanently responsible. To reject data provided for our enlightenment is a permitted freedom, but the abandonment of this available light is an invitation to Him to justly abandon us. It is wise to recall that He does not need us; we need Him. Thus, refusal to accept instruction to repent of sin, and the consequent rationalization of this refusal, via model warping and data exclusion, is permanently contrary to a person's own best interests. Hell is real and deserved, we are informed.

The individual's reaction is either to actually become a Bible-reading Christian, or to turn away, twisting and neglecting the data ever more assiduously and systematically in an effort to create and maintain feelings of security. Failure to perfect this seductive dream model permits recurring feelings of insecurity, even paranoia. There is a need for more and more assurances that "all is well." Hence many flock to hear ever more clever and dogmatic agnostic, atheistic, or cultic speakers to bolster their failing rationalizations.

Preliminary Conclusions

These issues supposedly lie within the field of epistemology (the study of how we know, the theory of knowledge). Actually, for many, epistemological errors are only the symptoms of a deeper corruption, the tendency to choose one's model for ego reasons, and then justify it by tampering with the data.

The worst thing that can happen to an individual is for God to let that person have his own way. That is, to allow him to remain within his fantasy, an illusion that corresponds only with the data chosen to steer him away from the greatest reality, from his responsibility as a creature to his Creator, and from becoming and eternally enjoying that for which he was created.

Model Making, Selection, And Revision

Let us imagine how a new baby girl might begin to think. We will collapse time so that her experiences begin at birth with a smoothly working pair of eyes. A picture comes to her mind by means of her eyes. An unfamiliar cold-wet feeling comes as well. In her mind she thinks and observes an arm move and receives certain feedback-feeling from the arm and the body on which it was resting. Our baby does this several times and concludes that she exists, that the external world observed by her eyes and which interacts with her really exists, and, incidentally, that her senses are essentially reliable. The same sort of experiences with the rest of her body in interacting first with the medical world and then with her mother, convince her that the world external to her has a structure, can be interacted with, and is predictable, at least in part. She has thus acquired certain illumination which serves her in all subsequent rational thought. (John 1:9 illustrates that this is providentially supplied.) It is important to notice that these basic "presuppositions" are testable rather than being beyond verification or falsification. They are not a priori. Fred Hoyle, speaking on the necessity of using models that can be tested, said:

Herbert Dingle has quite correctly warned us recently against promoting a theory simply because we happen to like it. . . . The grounds for a serious discussion of a theory lie in the possibility of subjecting it to observational test. . . . Gold has expressed this most aptly by saying that "for a theory to be of any value it must be vulnerable." Vulnerability supplies the conditions for success or failure in accordance with observational tests, and it is on this that science, and indeed all rational argument, is based.[5]

Now let us imagine a baby grown into adulthood. Data come to this person's mind. Mental images, or perhaps analogs, are invented to string the data together. Then a working model is adopted by a process of selection, governed ideally by consideration of probabilities pro and con (i.e., which model is the simplest, and fits the data with the least forcing or blind faith). The varying degrees of accuracy and reliability of the data also enter into the decision-making process.

Ralph Bates, a good friend of mine, told the following story to illustrate the process. During a bombing run in World War II, the four-engine bomber he was piloting had two engines knocked out on the same wing. Reduced air speed prevented him from keeping up with the return flight so he limped along as best he could, taking cover at an altitude that had solid cloud cover both below and above his plane. Thus, he was not apt to be seen from the ground while over enemy territory, nor from any altitude other than his own. Meanwhile, his fellow pilots, keeping radio silence, landed at their home base, and three other friends took off in fighter planes to meet him as quickly as possible and protect him from enemy fighter attack the rest of the way back. These were good friends, and so they decided to kid him along. Just before their estimated time of interception they turned their planes over and flew upside down in formation into Ralph's view, hoping to make him think he had vertigo, that his senses were playing tricks on him, and that he actually was the one flying a weakened plane in a dangerous inverted position. The trick worked. Captain Bates was convinced. But before doing anything he checked his instruments. They said he was right side up. Nevertheless, he was still convinced and accounted for their "error" on the basis of flak damage. He had learned, however, to make one further observation. The co-pilot had a duplicate set of sensors. He looked at them and again was told his plane was right side up. But vertigo is so convincing that the feel of the seat belt means nothing. Ralph thus began to believe he was upside down and was about to "right" his badly damaged plane, when he resolutely decided that the testimonies of both attitude sensors were more reliable than his inner convictions. Only with the exercise of great self-control was he able to keep from turning the plane over. No doubt he reflected on his friends' sense of humor as well. In any case, he chose the right model because he weighed the reliability of his friends' data suggesting another model and considered the probabilities wisely before making his final decision.

Bringing other relevant data into the model-making process before reaching firmer conclusions is both illustrated and commanded in Scripture:

And we have a more sure prophetic word [than Peter's sole testimony] to which you do well taking heed as to a lamp shining in a dark place . . . knowing this first, that no prophecy of Scripture is to be unraveled by itself [in isolation from the rest of the Scriptures] because prophecy was not brought at any time by the will of man, but holy men spoke, being borne along by the Holy Spirit.[6]

The Lord tells us here that arriving at the correct model or interpretation of any passage is more apt to be done by thoughtful exegesis that takes into account all the other Scriptures. This is the prescribed method for discovering or closely approximating the thought intended to be conveyed. It is an intellectual responsibility commanded by the Lord for our own good. Since God does not give gifts to be thrown away or wasted, it follows that we are responsible to develop and exercise all the care of which we are capable in the model-making, selection, and revision process required in the study of the Scriptures.

Having spoken of what should happen ideally, let me now discuss what frequently happens in reality. Paul, borne along by the Holy Spirit, says of a certain people that they had "a zeal for God, but not according to knowledge."[7] That is, self will (thinking of themselves more highly than they ought) and perhaps a desire to "draw away disciples after them"[8] led them to choose the wrong model of uprightness. But they are held responsible for this wrong choice. How could they be held responsible but that their decision was made in a culpable or blameworthy willingness to substitute a less probable for a more probable model indicated by a sufficiently clear body of teaching in the Word of God? Therefore, the weighing of probabilities is required of all gifted with thinking ability.

Again, in Matthew 16:1–4a we see:

The Pharisees and Sadducees came to Jesus and tested him by asking him to show them a sign from heaven.

He replied, "When evening comes, you say 'It will be fair weather, for the sky is red,' and in the morning, 'Today it will be stormy, for the sky is red and overcast.' You know how to interpret the appearance of the sky, but you cannot interpret the signs of the times. A wicked and adulterous generation looks for a miraculous sign."

Thus the Lord points out to us that an attachment for sin is what lies behind the fact that some people never have enough evidence to conclude they ought to repent and trust Him with all they have.

The model-making process and the weighing of probabilities is corrupted proportionately to the tolerance of sin in a person's life. Sinful man tends to give preference to models that excuse his autistic, self-willed, lawless spirit, his self-centered desire for absolute self-sovereignty, rather than decide only on the basis of intrinsic probabilities. The perceived clarity is considerably lower because conflict is higher in a sinful mind. This the Lord characterizes as hypocrisy, thus guaranteeing, apart from repentance and conversion in this life, a moving, Divine-human encounter in the Day of Judgment.[10]

If the fact of a universal probabilism actually means we don't know anything with absolute certainty and therefore can't say we know adequately what is right, then how will God judge the world, something we know He will do?[11] Wrongly weighing one model over another to accommodate or excuse a self-willed life is an irresponsible use of the gift of mind and leads finally to severe judgment. We should instead lower our unjustified resistance by exercising self-examination and repentance as frequently and regularly as necessary to prepare our minds for uncluttered study to do what is right, i.e. to obey His inscripturated Word. The Lord said, "The heart is deceitful . . . and desperately wicked."[12] He also said it is our responsibility to "break up" the "fallow ground" of our minds in order not to sow God's word "among thorns."[13] Surely an unencumbered mind is necessary to evaluate, for example, whether a particular passage is figurative, and if so, how to unravel the figure in the light of the rest of the Scriptures. Also, the negative effects of sin on the mind should not be ignored in translating or, for that matter, in the developing of a best possible resultant Greek and Hebrew text from accumulated archaeological information.

There are other interesting passages on model generation and selection. The statement "In the multitude of counselors there is safety"[14] suggests the use of many people to insure the generation of a large enough number of models to allow for one or several being close enough to provide for right decisions if selected. Also, the Lord said in John 5:44, "How can you believe, who welcome glory one from another, and seek not the honor that comes from God only?"[15] Wanting to have disciples, the uppermost seats, and to avoid the stigma of being known as a believer in Christ will clog the ability of an otherwise willing person to identify certain kinds of essential truth, and of course, a person will not succeed in hiding behind jiggered weighting of models on Judgment Day.[16] For Christians who are well-informed and possess academic degrees, there is also the warning, "Knowledge puffs up, but love edifies."[17]

During the time when the Jewish people return to their land and rebuild their temple, we are told to expect a rejection of the teaching of the return of the Lord Jesus Christ on the grounds of an alleged absolute uniformity and continuity of the laws of nature. More specifically, we are informed that the mockers mentioned in 2 Peter 3:3–8 will usually be characterized by lives conducted in accordance with their lusts or cravings. We should therefore not be overly impressed by their airs of certitude.

Revelation of a Further Epistemological System

There is evident in the Scriptures a prescience in matters of science and history, especially history. Three times in Isaiah 40–49 the claim is made that Jehovah is the only God who knows "the end from the beginning."[18] False religionists are challenged to show where their gods have predicted previously and the predictions have reliably come to pass. They are called to do so, and, from the fact that they cannot do so reliably, repeatedly, and in detail,[19] the conclusion is given that they are just "wind and confusion."[20]

The subject is in need of further development but is introduced in McMillen's *None of These Diseases,* Newman's *The Evidence of Prophecy,* Stoner and Newman's *Science Speaks,* and Urquhart's *The Wonders of Prophecy.*[21] The scriptural claims in the light of this type of evidence are well discussed in Machen's *What Is Faith?, Christianity and Liberalism,* and *The Christian Faith in the Modern World.*[22] Also worthy of further study is Warfield's *Inspiration and Authority of the Bible,* and his brief article, "Inspiration," in the *International Standard Bible Encyclopedia.*[23] Among the more recent works is Packer's "Biblical Authority, Hermeneutics, and Inerrancy" in the *IFES Journal.*[24]

Beyond the epistemological system noted above, which should lead us to the Scriptures, there are passages like Romans 2:14–15:

> For when the Gentiles, who have not the law, do by nature the things contained in the law, these, having not the law, are a law unto themselves: who show the work of the law written in their hearts, their conscience also bearing witness, and their thoughts the mean while accusing or else excusing one another.[25]

John 1:9 says that the Lord Jesus is the light that "illuminates every man that comes into the world."[26] This passage tells us that, by some means not specified, a certain illumination concerning the Lord's existence and moral rectitude[27] and man's deservedness of His judgment[28] is implanted in every person. Thus we see an enormous advantage in recognizing the teaching authority and reliability of the Scriptures which give us these insights, otherwise obscured by the lawless spirit (*anomia*) characterizing so much of our lives and clouding our minds.

Mysticism: A Data Source?

The ground for assessing the nature and validity (or lack of it) of mysticism is obtained by first recognizing the evidences for the origin, authority, and reliability of the Scriptures. The Scriptures themselves indicate that two-way conversation between the Lord and human beings is, with very rare exceptions, confined to prophets.[29] "The Lord told me this and that yesterday" is not an experience to be expected, but rather suspected. Even the experienced prophet Jeremiah did not give credence to a particular vision of his own until the rather detailed prophecy in it came to pass.[30] Nor is there any scriptural basis for believing any inner feeling, conviction, or sense of peace is the voice of God. Paul never wrote in any of his corrective epistles, "If you people had only gotten on your knees and followed the inner leading of the Holy Spirit you would not have gone wrong." Nor did any biblical author ever suggest we should sit down and empty our minds of all thoughts and invite a spirit, even the Holy Spirit, to come in and take control of our lives, minds, or mouths. Instead, the Apostle Paul said, in effect, "The Scriptures say this and you have been doing that—why?" Leading-by-feelings, however, is a doctrine for some. Such an important source of guidance, if right, would be taught in several extended passages of Scripture, but it is not. Instead we are told there is frequently an epistemological link between humans and demons.[31] This is the morass of the occult, which we are carefully to avoid.[32]

It is the popular thing in some circles to claim that it is the leading of the Holy Spirit for Christians to join or remain in ecumenical fellowship with those who long to be a part of what chapters 17 and 18 of Revelation describe as abominable and from which the Lord calls His people out.[33] Those claiming such special spirituality and leading of the Holy Spirit should acknowledge that the Spirit has already spoken in 2 Corinthians 6:14, 1 Corinthians 10:21, and Revelation 18:4–5, commanding us to stay out of that which is religious but apostate. Any inner voice which speaks to the contrary cannot be that of the Holy Spirit. The claim to have the gift of tongues that frequently accompanies such disobedience only suggests more strongly a different source for the tongue-speaking.

Misleading Miracles

God teaches us in His word that miracles are not all of divine origin.[34] Some are merely human tricks; others are of demonic origin, permitted by the Lord to test us.[35] God warns us to not be gullible but to try or test every spirit first.[36] It is easy to see that the person who understands and maintains the proper place of study of the Scriptures in his daily life is going to be forewarned and forearmed against being used or made merchandise of by the great Enemy.[37] However, there are some fitting the Lord's description (through Peter) who, encountering in the Scriptures "things difficult to understand," and being "unlearned" and/or "unstable," will "twist them . . . to their own destruction."[38]

What people think determines what they are and do. Harmful belief and authority systems thrive on uncertainty about the existence of the God of the Bible. How to rely on the Lord's self-disclosure is caricatured in the media. Everyone should have a reasonable opportunity to know how to know the truth and avoid traps set around such important terms as *evidence, probability, certitude,* and *faith.* Man-made arguments have failed because they are not scriptural, and the belief that there is nothing but slippery subjectivism plagues the world. Nevertheless, justifiable certitude is possible for the finite, imperfect, thinking person willing to obey Scripture.

Repentance from sin and reliance on the Word of the Lord lead to a certain clarity of mind and an improved ability to discern these important matters. What a blessing that He, having paid the awful price of our redemption on the cross, should invite a simple, sincere repentance and then promise needed daily help![39]

Notes

[1]Paul C. Joss and Edwin E. Salpeter, "Models for Carbon-Rich Stars with Helium Envelopes," in *The Astrophysical Journal,* 181 (1973): 393 and 409; John Warwick Montgomery, "The Theologian's Craft: A Discussion of Theory Formation and Theory Testing in Theology," in his *The Suicide of Christian Theology* (Minneapolis, Minn.: Bethany Fellowship, 1970); J. D. Watson, *The Double Helix* (New York: Antheneum, 1968; reprint, New York: Mentor Books, 1969).

[2]Rom. 2:12–16; 3:6.

[3]J. Oliver Buswell, *Systematic Theology of the Christian Religion,* 2 vols. (Grand Rapids, Mich.: Zondervan, 1962), 1:36ff.

[4]John Urquhart, *The Wonders of Prophecy* (Harrisburg, Pa.: Christian Publications, 1925); Peter W. Stoner and Robert C. Newman, *Science Speaks,* 4th ed. (Chicago: Moody, 1976); Robert C. Newman, ed., *The Evidence of Prophecy* (Hatfield, Pa.: Interdisciplinary Biblical Research Institute, 1988); idem, *Genesis One and the Origin of the Earth* (Downers Grove, Ill.: InterVarsity Press, 1977); Josh McDowell, *Evidence that Demands a Verdict* (San Bernardino, Calif.: Here's Life Publishers, 1972).

[5]Fred Hoyle, *Frontiers of Astronomy* (New York: Mentor Books, 1960), 312.

[6]2 Pet. 1:19–21. Author's translation.

[7]Rom. 10:2–3. This and subsequent quotations from the Scriptures will be in the authorized King James Version of the Bible unless indicated otherwise.

[8]Acts 20:30.

[9]Matt. 16:1–4a. This quotation from the Scriptures is from the New International Version of the Bible, copyright 1978 by the New York International Bible Society.

[10]Rom. 14:9–12; 2 Cor. 5:10.

[11]Rom. 3:6.

[12]Jer. 17:9.

[13]Jer. 4:3.

[14]Prov. 11:14.

[15]John 5:44. Author's translation.

[16]John 3:18–21.

[17]1 Cor. 8:1b. Author's paraphrase.

[18]Isa. 41:26–29; 44:6–7; 46:9–10. See also 45:21.

[19]Inerrancy is the biblical standard for predictive reliability (see Deut. 18:20–22).

[20]Isa. 41:29.

[21]S. I. McMillen, *None of these Diseases* (Old Tappan, N.J.: Fleming H. Revell Co., 1972); Newman, *The Evidence of Prophecy;* Stoner and Newman, *Science Speaks;* Urquhart, *Wonders of Prophecy.*

[22]J. Gresham Machen, *What Is Faith?* (Grand Rapids, Mich.: Eerdmans, 1969); idem, *Christianity and Liberalism* (1923; reprint, Grand Rapids, Mich.: Eerdmanns, 1974);

idem, *The Christian Faith in the Modern World* (1936; reprint, Grand Rapids, Mich.: Eerdmanns, 1974).

[23]B. B. Warfield, *Inspiration and Authority of the Bible* (Philadelphia, Pa.: Presbyterian and Reformed Publishing Co., 1970); *International Standard Bible Encyclopedia*, 2d ed. (Grand Rapids, Mich.: Eerdmans, 1982), s.v. "Inspiration" by B. B. Warfield.

[24]J. I. Packer, "Biblical Authority, Hermaneutics, and Inerrancy," in *IFES Journal*.

[25]Rom. 2:14–15. Slightly paraphrased.

[26]John 1:9. Slightly paraphrased.

[27]Rom. 1:18–31.

[28]Rom. 1:32; 2:12–16.

[29]1 John 4:1.

[30]Jer. 32:6-8.

[31]See 1 Tim. 4:1–6; Rev. 12:9.

[32]1 John 4:1–3.

[33]Rev. 18:4–5.

[34]See Exod. 7:11–12, 22; 8:7, 18–19; Matt. 24:24; Rev. 13:11–18.

[35]Deut. 13:1–11; Matt. 24:23–27; 2 Thess. 2:8–10; Rev. 13:13–14; 16:14; 19–20.

[36]2 Cor. 11:13–15; 1 Tim. 4:1–5; 1 John 4:1–3.

[37]2 Cor. 11:13–15; 2 Pet. 2:1–3; 1 John 4:1–3.

[38]2 Pet. 3:16. Author's translation.

[39]Rom. 5–8; Gal. 5:16–26; Heb. 4:15–16.

Part 2

God and Scientific Cosmology

2.1

A Theistic Approach
to Science

Garret Vanderkooi

THE PURPOSE OF THESE PAGES is to point out some of the shortcomings of the prevalent naturalistic world view, and to show how a better understanding of reality can be achieved by an approach which acknowledges the actions of God in the world. The development of the naturalistic world view will be briefly surveyed, after which the inability of this view to account for observations in two general areas will be discussed. The first general area deals with determinism, prophecy, providence and miracles, and prayer. The second area relates to the origin of life. It will be shown that these areas can be accounted for if the biblical world view is accepted.

Philosophy of Science: Historical Development

Dualism

Plato described earthly objects as the imperfect representations of ideal forms located somewhere in the heavenlies. Aquinas spoke of nature and grace; nature was the physical world, and grace concerned God, the soul, and other spiritual beings. For both Plato and Aquinas, the immaterial or spiritual was more important than the material or physical. This other-worldly attitude persisted throughout the medieval era, as evidenced by the almost exclusive selection of religious subjects for paintings and other types of art work. Nature was not purposefully studied to any degree, and while there were probably many reasons for this, including the generally poor economic conditions, the underlying notion that nature was of little value certainly discouraged its study and appreciation.

This pervasive low view of nature began to change in the sixteenth century, in part as a result of the Protestant Reformation and the translation of the Bible into the common languages. Students of the Bible realized that nature had value because God made it, and therefore that it is also appropriate to study God's handiwork and to praise Him for His marvelous creation. It was for just this purpose that the prestigious Royal Society of London was founded in the seventeenth century. The charter of the Society stated that the studies of its members should be directed "to the glory of God and the benefit of the human race."[1] At that time the Society consisted largely of Puritan Calvinists and included such well-known names as Isaac Newton and Robert Boyle, from whom we get Newton's laws of motion and Boyle's gas laws. The lively interest which was shown in natural science in the seventeenth century once and for all broke the former emphasis on things spiritual. Descartes, in the early part of that century, explicitly developed the concept of the dualism of matter and mind. The external world, including all of physical reality, was placed on the side of matter, while mind was defined as "unextended thinking substance." Descartes thereby inadvertently laid the groundwork for the eventual dismissal of "mind" (and with it the immaterial or spiritual realms) as having any real substance or importance.

Natural Laws

The seventeenth-century scientists of the Royal Society saw nature as God's creation. It was evident to them that nature is orderly rather than chaotic, and they considered this order to be the result of purposeful design by a rational God. Science therefore had the lofty motivations of "thinking God's thoughts after Him" and "discovering the laws by which God runs the universe." They believed that what they called laws of nature were just that, a set of rules imposed by God which nature is constrained to obey. The "laws" (e.g., the laws of motion) were mathematical relationships which described a variety of experimental observations, but these scientists were bold, and rather presumptuously gave them metaphysical significance. The early scientists undoubtedly overextended their case by claiming a supernatural meaning for their laws, but their belief in an intelligent and rational Creator gave them a firm metaphysical foundation upon which to build their science; that is, they had an a priori basis for assuming that nature is orderly and susceptible to rational interpretation. The later naturalistic empiricists, on the other hand, had no such basis upon which to work. When they ruled out metaphysical constructs and belief in a Creator God in order to be strictly rational or "scientific," they also lost the basis for belief in an orderly universe, which is an essential prerequisite for rational scientific investigation. (The concept that nature is comprehensible and orderly is not necessarily self-evident from observation; a case can be made that apparent order only exists under the carefully controlled and simplified conditions of the laboratory.) The progressive movement away from the theistic (or deistic) view of science held in the seventeenth century to the largely atheistic view of the nineteenth and twentieth centuries resulted in the eventual abandonment of the dualistic world view which had existed in one form or another since Plato, and the substitution of a monistic world view in which only physical reality is recognized.

The efforts of the seventeenth-century scientists are to be applauded not only because of their outstanding contributions to the development of modern science, but also because they gave credit to God for what they discovered. At that time it was quite acceptable to include references to the Maker in scientific papers, something which today is strictly out of order. A critical flaw developed in their system, however. As more laws were discovered (laws by which God supposedly ran the universe), there became less need to include God Himself in one's reckonings. If the laws God made could effectively control everything, God could retire from the scene and let the whole show run according to the laws, and only intervene now and then when something went wrong. This gave rise to the Divine Clockmaker view of God proposed by Robert Boyle. God was understood to have designed and made the universe with great wisdom, and once it started running, it would go through its paces following the laws laid out for it. The discovery of the laws of motion by Newton had much to do with the development of this concept. Newton found that the orbits of the planets in the solar system could be accounted for by a set of simple mathematical relationships. It was observed, however, that there were some deviations from these predicted orbits, and Newton thought that the deviations would be cumulative and would eventually cause a critical instability in the system. Being a God-fearing man, he invoked the hand of God to correct them. Thus the role of God in running the universe was maintained, albeit as a clock repairman.

It was perhaps inevitable, given this background, that God would eventually be left out of the picture altogether. The great French mathematician Laplace, in the eighteenth century, carried Newton's

studies of celestial mechanics a step further and showed that the orbital
deviations which concerned Newton were simply the result of three-body
interactions among the planets, and that these would damp themselves out
rather than cause a catastrophe if uncorrected. Hence the corrective
actions presumed necessary by Newton were no longer needed. There is a
story that when Laplace presented a copy of his major book on mechanics
to Napoleon, that Napoleon replied, "Monsieur Laplace, they tell me you
have written this large book on the system of the universe, and have never
mentioned its Creator." Laplace is reported to have answered, "I have no
need of that hypothesis."[2] Thus the Creator God of the Bible who was
believed in and worshipped a century earlier by the founders of the Royal
Society, had become a debatable or unnecessary hypothesis. It seemed that
nature with its governing laws was sufficient unto itself, and it was
assumed that all of nature, including man himself, could be explained in
terms of known or at least knowable natural laws. God was at most the
clock manufacturer, but not the clock repairman, because the clock did not
need any repairs. God, if He existed, was irrelevant.

Empiricism and Logical Positivism

Now if God is irrelevant or nonexistent, what happens to natural laws?
According to the eighteenth-century philosopher David Hume, who
formally developed the concepts of empiricism, the only way of obtaining
reliable knowledge is by sense impressions, i.e., by empirical observations. Any ideas not ultimately based on sense impressions are considered
to be meaningless. This position ruled out metaphysical concepts, and the
mathematical relationships which had formerly been granted metaphysical status as laws of nature could now only be considered as correlations
between observables. The practical philosophical basis of natural science
has not changed significantly since Hume. Empiricism and its twentieth-
century counterpart, logical positivism, continue to serve as guiding
principles for working scientists, even though these formalisms appear to
have fallen out of favor with professional philosophers of science.
Logical positivism defines two main categories of statements: meaningful
and meaningless statements. Meaningful statements have been variously
defined as those which are verifiable, falsifiable, or confirmable by
empirical observation. All other statements are labeled as meaningless
(except, of course, analytic statements which are true by definition).
Hence any ideas or concepts which do not have what would loosely be
called a scientific (i.e., verifiable) basis are considered meaningless. The
logical positivist abhors unprovable, metaphysical assumptions, just as
the empiricist did. While positivism provides a good set of principles for
the scientist to follow, in that it tells him not to accept anything which

cannot be supported by verifiable data, positivism as an all-encompassing theory of knowledge has proved inadequate.[3]

It is interesting to note that natural science developed and flourished in the Western Hemisphere during a period of time when belief in a supreme Creator God was widespread. No comparable development took place in the Eastern animistic or Hindu cultures where natural events are often given magical explanations. It is also worth considering that the current decline of Western science may indeed be due in part to the general disbelief in God as the Creator and hence to the loss of a basis for belief in the foundational principle of order, upon which science was based.

Courses in the philosophy of science are usually omitted from typical college science curricula. This is quite unfortunate; the result is that most working scientists do their research without having any clear conception of the philosophical underpinnings (or lack thereof) of their scientific endeavor.

Relativism, Linguistic Analysis, and Neoorthodoxy

From Plato onward, there has been an underlying tension over the relative importance of the material versus the immaterial realms of existence, with the balance first being in favor of the immaterial, and later shifting toward the material. For a brief period in the seventeenth century, it appeared that this tension was being overcome in the work of the Puritan Calvinists of the Royal Society, who considered both the material and the immaterial to be important. But in the ensuing years the great success of natural science and the disinclination of many individuals to acknowledge God resulted in the apparent elimination of the tension, not by establishing a balance but by the total rejection of the immaterial realm. For Hume and the empiricists, there was only one category of true knowledge, that which could be attained by scientific observation. This unfortunately left out several areas of human experience which many people consider important. Immanuel Kant, in the eighteenth century, attempted to overcome this problem by defining two categories of knowledge (thereby reintroducing dualism): the phenomenal realm of observational science and the noumenal realm of universals, intangibles, and experimentally unverifiable concepts. This effort still did not provide an adequate basis for a unified view of the world, however, and after Kant came thinkers who gave up trying to find a basis for knowledge, concluding that all is relative. The hope was abandoned that absolute truth can be found or even exists. (Francis Schaeffer, in his books *The God Who Is There*[4] and *Escape From Reason*,[5] provides a helpful overview of the development of modern relativistic concepts.)

The linguistic analysis school of philosophy of the present century tried to circumvent the problem of meaningless statements presented by the logical positivists in much the same way that Kant attempted to circumvent the empiricists, but within the framework of relativism. According to linguistic analysis, language has diverse and quite possibly nonoverlapping usages.[6] For example, science and religion are both considered to be legitimate areas of concern, but their languages and domains of interest are so different that the methods and results of science should not be applied to religion, or vice versa. Philosophers from the school of linguistic analysis believe that since science deals with nature, and religion concerns itself with such intangibles as morality, God, and the supernatural, these are two entirely different realms and are to be kept apart and not confused.

The neoorthodox theology of Karl Barth has parallels with the dualistic thinking just described. Religious statements concerning God, the soul, and salvation are in one category, while areas in which empirical observation is possible, including science and history, are in another compartment. It is often said that "the Bible is not a scientific textbook" and that the purpose of the Bible is to teach men about things spiritual, not about nature or history.

This widely held philosophical and theological belief has several practical consequences. Many people think that it is impossible for a good scientist to be a religious person. Scientists are supposed to be empiricists or positivists, and positivists are expected to reject the subjective mystical type of knowledge which, it is alleged, is found in the religious category. Numerous scientists are Christians, however, and in particular many are orthodox biblical Christians who reject this neoorthodox concept of split categories. The attractiveness of biblical Christianity to scientists arises from the fact that the information in the Bible is presented as being real and, where possible, testable or confirmable; thus they approach the Bible in the same frame of mind as they approach scientific research. In spite of this, if a scientist or theologian publicly tries to cross the line of division between the science and religion categories, there is likely to be resistance. A case in point is the matter of evolution and creation. Evolution is put in the domain of science, and creation in the supposedly untestable religious category. It is no wonder that even the name of an organization which attempts to study creation scientifically, "The Institute for Creation Research," causes irritation in many circles; one is not supposed to be able to do research on "religious" subjects.

The Unseen Realm

A way out of the dilemma of split categories of knowledge is to return to the biblical view in which the real existence of both the physical and spiritual realms is acknowledged. This was the position held by the physicist and astronomer Sir Arthur Eddington, Fellow of the Royal Society, as stated in a little book called *Science and the Unseen World.*[7] He speaks of the "seen" and "unseen" realms; the unseen realm of God, the soul, and other spiritual beings is understood to be just as real as the seen world of nature. The fundamental difference between this view and the dualistic approach to knowledge of Kant, or the split categories of the neoorthodox, is that interaction between the seen and unseen realms is considered to be possible. God is not the "wholly other," as Barth would say, but rather is real and must be reckoned with in the events of this world. If there is interaction between the two realms, then the possibility exists that there are observable effects in the seen world for which the causes should rightly be attributed to the unseen world. This, of course, has been claimed all along by the biblical writers, but it is assumed to be impossible by the naturalistic philosophers.

If it is true that there are causes originating in the unseen realm for effects observable in the physical world, might there not be some cases where a reasonable argument can be given for their occurrence? In suggesting this, one immediately becomes open to the charge of invoking a "God of the gaps." But just because some past "gaps" have since been filled by natural explanations does not mean that all gaps will eventually be so filled. That is the naturalistic assumption, which is explicitly rejected in the position being put forward here. In the following sections, two areas will be described in which God's active role in the world seems evident; one of these is the fulfillment of prophecy and the related areas of providence and miracles, and the other is the origin of life.

Determinism, Prophecy, Providence and Miracles, and Prayer

Determinism Versus Uncertainty

The universe of Laplace was deterministic. By his understanding of physical reality, if one were able to specify precisely the positions and momenta of all the particles in the universe at a given instant in time and possessed proper knowledge of all the forces acting between these particles, one should be able to predict the future with complete accuracy, given a sufficiently powerful calculating machine. This conclusion was once widely accepted as an inevitable consequence of the assured results of science, but it no longer has scientific support. It is now known, as a result of the quantum revolution in physics which occurred during the 1920s, that it is not possible even in principle to simultaneously specify the precise position and momenta of small particles such as atoms and electrons. This is a result of the Heisenberg Uncertainty Principle,[8] which is an integral part of the modern view of the nature of physical reality.

Laplace based his deterministic conclusions on the fallacious assumption that all bodies, large and small, would behave in the same manner as the planets of the solar system, but this extrapolation of the principles of celestial mechanics to the atomic domain is not valid.

This deterministic science was compatible with the philosophic determinism or fatalism taught by various of the world's religions; and it was even claimed by some Christian theologians to be in agreement with biblical doctrines. This is evident from the following statement by Boettner:

As far as the material universe apart from mind is concerned, we have no trouble at all to believe in absolute Predestination. The course of events which would follow was, in a very strict sense, immutably determined when God created the world and implanted the natural laws of gravity, light, magnetism, chemical affinity, electrical phenomena, etc. Apart from the interference of mind or miracle, the course of nature is uniform and predictable. This has not only been admitted but dogmatically held and asserted by many of the greatest scientists.[9]

This was published in 1932, after the revolution in physics which led to the downfall of determinism as a physical principle, but knowledge of that event had not as yet penetrated theological circles. The view of nature held by Boettner differed little from the earlier deistic concept of the Clockmaker God, i.e., the view that the world would follow its predetermined course except for interference from human mind or divine miracle.

Now, as a result of quantum mechanics, absolute determinism is no longer supported by science; only an approximate causality is supported which permits the general but not the absolute predictability of nature. The mathematical relationships which apply to atomic or subatomic particles are expressed as statistical probability statements. Given a large number of particles or events, one can reliably predict the average behavior of the group, but prediction of the behavior of individual particles or of single events is impossible, in principle as well as in practice. The determinism of Laplace was based on the premise that the positions and momenta of all particles, large and small, could be specified; but quantum mechanics says that the positions and momenta of small particles cannot be simultaneously specified with unlimited accuracy. Thus the deduction of Laplace concerning absolute predictability was incorrect if viewed from the present state of knowledge. The present is not rigorously determined by the past, nor the future by the present. Not everyone accepts this probabilistic view of the universe. Einstein for one never accepted chance as a fundamental principal of reality, but rather considered it to be an acknowledgment of our own ignorance, as he expressed in an oft-quoted statement, "God does not throw dice" (a pregnant assertion even though Einstein's God could hardly be considered an equivalent of the God of the Bible). But while one is free to adopt a belief in determinism for whatever religious or philosophic reason, the position cannot be supported by appeal to scientific observation.

Prophecy

There are some rather profound theological consequences of the uncertainty principle. Consider the case of prophecy. A prophecy is a statement in which some future event is described beforehand in sufficient detail that it can be recognized when and if it occurs. In the biblical context, prophecies are understood to originate from God. Under the old deterministic system a prophetic statement could be considered as an example of God's foreknowledge, based on His ability to *predict* the future. Assuming the right initial conditions were set up at the time of the Creation, the whole future development of the universe was supposedly determined (as described in the preceding quotation from Boettner), and thus the all-knowing Creator could also tell what would happen at any given future time. Now, however, according to the modern view of physical reality, it is not possible to attribute God's foreknowledge to the predictability of nature, because nature by its very essence is not absolutely predictable. Now, for prophecies to be possible, we must conclude that the One who gives the prophecies must also be in a position to carry them out. A prophecy can no longer be viewed as a prediction of future events, but rather as a declaration of what God is going to make happen in the future. This is in fact also the biblical position, as stated in Isaiah 46:9–11:

"I am God, and there is none like me. I make known the end from the beginning, from ancient times what is still to come. I say: My purpose will stand, and I will do all that I please. . . . What I have said, that will I bring about; what I have planned, that will I do."[10]

There is not even a hint of prediction here; rather, God is saying through Isaiah that He is actively involved in the world and will do what He says He will do. This does not sound like the Clockmaker God of the seventeenth century; His action in the world is not an occasional corrective role but a very active guiding hand.

But how, one might ask, can God, who is a Spirit and not of material essence, cause things to happen in the world in order to make prophecies come true? This question concerns the nature of providence.

Providence and Miracles

Providence refers to God's beneficent guidance and control of the world and of our lives, whereas miracles are usually considered to be special events which differ from the way things usually happen. In scientific terms, miracles might be defined as events which have a vanishingly small probability of happening, or which contradict one of the conventionally accepted "laws of nature." While providence is often thought of as God working within the scope of natural laws, not all miraculous events necessarily violate natural laws, as they may be the result of seemingly fortuitous (but improbable) convergences of events at a particular time and place. Thus no clear distinction can be made between the providential and the miraculous, other than that the latter may tend to be more dramatic than the former.

Pollard discusses the relationship of natural law to providence in his book *Chance and Providence.*[11] He emphasizes that natural laws, as now understood, are really probability statements which give the expected behavior for large numbers of events, but which say little about individual occurrences. He explains God's providence as being His control of the individual events of which real history consists. These are guided by God to cause to happen what He wants to happen, without upsetting the overall probabilities for multiple events. For example, it may be predicted how many people will die in car accidents in a given holiday weekend, but who actually dies is in God's hand. Miracles, on the other hand, cannot simply be explained as the adjustment of the probabilities within the scope of natural laws.

There is a most interesting story recorded in the Old Testament in which there was no apparent violation of any natural law, but a special sequence of events which resulted in the miraculous fulfillment of a prophecy made a short time before. This is the case of the words of Micaiah to King Ahab, which are recorded in 1 Kings 22. In verse 28 we read that "Micaiah declared, 'If you [Ahab] ever return safely, the Lord has not spoken through me.'" Then a little farther on, in verse 34, the text says "But someone drew his bow at random and hit the king of Israel between the sections of his armor." The random arrow would have been considered a freak accident were it not prophesied beforehand that ill would befall the king; in this context, it must be seen as evidence of God's control over events in such a way as to cause the fulfillment of His prophecies. (I am sure that some will reject this interpretation and will claim that God simply "knew" this would happen to Ahab, but I think it is more consistent with the scriptural context to say that God made it happen.)

Consider a few of the miracles of Jesus. When He turned the water into wine (John 2:1–10), there must have been a transformation or creation of matter in order to provide the kinds of molecules which are present in wine but not in water. Hence the "law" of conservation of matter was violated. If there is any doubt about this in the case of the wine, then consider the feeding of the five thousand (John 6:5–14). Jesus started with five loaves and two fish, but after feeding everyone, there was more left over than He started with. Again, when Jesus walked on water (John 6:16–21), the law of gravity was overridden. As for the many healings and the raisings of the dead, it is worth considering all the molecular rearrangements which must occur to make dead or damaged cells be restored to life. All of these examples show that our so-called laws of conservation of matter and energy are not inviolate.

It is not my purpose to try to prove to anyone that miracles can happen. Many people, especially scientists and liberal theologians, simply do not accept the possibility, and no amount of argument or evidence will convince them otherwise. If one's presuppositions say that the fundamental natural "laws" can never be broken, then one is forced to reject the evidence for miracles and to consider the reports of such to be the products of naive observation, or worse, of artful deception. I am thoroughly convinced in my own mind, however, that miracles actually do happen in the present time as well as in biblical times, having witnessed some miracles myself as well as having heard many firsthand reports of such from others. This present-day evidence for miracles makes it easier to believe (but admittedly not easier to understand) the miracles recorded in the Bible. If we accept that miracles are indeed part of reality, it is incumbent upon us to attempt to integrate this phenomenon into our overall world view. This may not be an easy task, considering that naturalistic presuppositions permeate the society in which we have been raised and educated.

Miracles, as well as providence, might be described in terms of the seen and unseen realms of Eddington. We are accustomed to thinking in terms of cause and effect; a force, for example, acting on an object is said to be the cause of the accelerating motion of the object, which is the effect. Usually another physical body provides the force. In a miraculous event, the force might be said to originate on the other side of the invisible partition between the seen and unseen realms; hence the motion of the object would have no observable cause. God and other (created) spiritual beings evidently have the power to bring about physical effects within the world, even though we presume that these spiritual beings do not themselves consist of physical substance.

Belief in the supernatural, but not necessarily in God, has become much more widespread in Western culture in the course of the last one or two decades than it has been for a long time. This is evidenced by the rapid rise in popularity of the New Age movement, which has much in common with ancient Hinduism. It is as if the pendulum of Western world views, which had been stuck for the last two or three centuries on naturalism, is now rapidly swinging toward the other extreme of an animistic and pantheistic world view, replete with a panoply of spiritual beings. Holders of such a view are likely to conclude that the natural world is capricious and unintelligible, due to the actions of these beings, just as animists in primitive cultures have always believed. The biblical description of reality contradicts both of these world views. The Bible clearly teaches that there is one God who is eternal and who is the Creator of all else that exists. It also teaches that there are angels (good spiritual beings), demons (bad spiritual beings), and souls of men. Thus the biblical world view contradicts Western naturalism, since the latter altogether rejects the existence of real non-physical beings. Those in the Eastern Hinduistic and animistic cultures, on the other hand, know full well (experientially) that many spiritual beings exist, most of whom are thought to be bad, but they do not know that one God created everything and that He is more powerful than all of the other spiritual beings; or, further, that this God is good in His very essence.

Prayer

If we make room in our view of the world for the providential and miraculous acts of God, we can also more readily believe in the efficacy of prayer. How could we think that prayers can have any meaning or effect in the world if everything is absolutely predetermined anyway? (This is a problem I struggled with for a number of years.) But now we see that everything is not absolutely predetermined. God must be in a dynamic, day-by-day control of the world in order to carry out His declared and undeclared purposes. Is it not, therefore, to be expected that He has both the freedom and the power to respond, in real time, to the requests of those who pray to Him? In the long run, God will surely bring about whatever He has promised; but in the short term there may be many possible routes, all of which can achieve the declared ultimate objectives. The route which is actually followed may be influenced by prayer.

Evolution and Creation

In considering evolution and the problem of origins, it is essential to keep in mind the distinction between microevolution and macroevolution. Microevolution refers to the evolutionary variation and adaptation of existing species, whereas macroevolution is the grand concept that all of life developed and proliferated in a process lasting millions or billions of years, starting with inanimate matter and ending with man. There is not, or should not be, any conflict over microevolution. Variation and adaptation are observed both in nature and in the laboratory, and several biochemical mechanisms are known by which these can occur. The question may legitimately be asked, however, just how extensive are the changes which can be brought about by these mechanisms; can there be variation only within species, or can new species or perhaps even genera or families develop by these means? This is not known. Those who believe in macroevolution assume that the mechanisms of microevolution provide a basis for understanding the development of all life forms, but this is an unproven hypothesis, based on a long extrapolation from the available data.

The real evolution-creation controversy concerns macroevolution, and it is most clearly focused in the question of the origin of life. This is essentially the question of how the first living, replicating cells came into existence, starting from nonliving material. The two answers that are seriously proposed for this event are that it happened in a series of small steps spread over a long period of time or else all at once in a creative act. The first but not the second of these proposed mechanisms can be evaluated in scientific terms. This will be done after the basic assumptions of the proponents of the two schools of thought have been examined.

A creative mechanism for the origin of life entails the assumptions that God exists and that He can do things in the world. The presupposition of naturalistic evolution, on the other hand, is that everything that happens in the world is explainable in natural terms; a logical consequence of this postulate is that life must have developed by natural means, since life has not always existed. Jacques Monod is an articulate proponent of naturalistic evolution. His basic assumption, given in the following quotation from his book *Chance and Necessity*,[12] is stated in such dogmatic terms as to give the impression it is an established fact rather than a presupposition: "Chance alone is at the source of every innovation, of all creation in the biosphere. Pure chance, absolutely free and blind, is at the root of the stupendous edifice of evolution." For evolutionists like Monod, there is no such thing as design or purpose in nature, whereas for the believer in creation, design and purpose permeate the biosphere. For an evolutionist who is an atheist, there is no possibility of his ever being swayed from the evolutionary position by logical argument, since no other options are open to him.

The supposed validity of the evolutionary model is simply assumed by the writers of many scientific textbooks; in others, mechanisms for the origin of life which involve supernatural acts may be mentioned but are summarily rejected as being "unscientific." (What these writers do not seem to realize, however, is that just because a concept or a theory is not amenable to scientific experiment does not necessarily mean it is wrong.) Many people who are not in a position to judge for themselves have been persuaded by science teachers and textbook writers that evolution is a "proven fact of science." The following paragraphs are intended to show that this is not the case; macroevolution not only is not a proven fact of science but in scientific terms must be labeled as well-nigh impossible.

Biochemical Evolution

The early steps in a hypothetical evolutionary scheme for the development of life are necessarily of a chemical or biochemical nature. This problem is discussed by Lehninger in his textbook *Biochemistry*.[13] (This text [1975] was chosen for purposes of citation because it is written in especially clear terms; similar assumptions and proposed mechanisms are also found in the most recent biochemistry texts.) Lehninger gives a set of what he calls "working assumptions" for the development of life:

1. The first cells were much simpler than present-day bacteria.
2. They arose as a result of a long chain of single events.
3. Each stage in their evolution developed from the preceding one by only a very small change.
4. Each step must have had a reasonably high probability of happening in terms of the laws of physics and chemistry.[14]

Given these basic assumptions, the following steps may be envisioned as part of a developmental pathway:

Atoms → Molecules → Macromolecules → Cells → Proliferation of Species → Man

It is worthwhile to consider the steps in this pathway, keeping in mind especially the fourth "working assumption," which is basically the naturalistic assumption. The first step, from atoms to simple molecules, does not present any problem. Many simple molecules would have formed spontaneously under assumed primitive earth conditions. Even amino acids and the aromatic bases found in nucleic acids could have formed under those conditions, as shown by scientists in the 1950s. They subjected mixtures of methane, ammonia, and water to electrical discharges or ultraviolet light, and found that biomolecules were produced.[15]

The production of macromolecules in the second step of the pathway refers to the formation of polyamino acids (long chains of amino acids, also called proteins) from the monomeric amino acids, and the formation of polynucleotides (DNA and RNA) from nucleotides. This is a much more difficult problem than the first step. Sidney Fox has carried out many experiments attempting to show that polyamino acids could have formed under prebiotic conditions.[16] It is not possible to generate such chains in aqueous solution under presumed prebiotic conditions, since the free energy change in water is positive for the formation of the peptide bonds which join the amino acids together, i.e., the natural tendency is for these bonds to break rather than to be formed. Fox therefore tried heating mixtures of dry amino acids to high temperatures. He found that protein-like chains were made, which he called *proteinoids*. These proteinoids must necessarily have a random sequence of amino acids, considering their nonspecific method of synthesis. By contrast, real proteins of biological origin have precisely specified amino acid sequences. The sequence, in turn, determines the three-dimensional structure which is required for its enzymatic activity. Each different kind of protein has its own specific sequence and structure. A living cell stores the information specifying the sequences of all the proteins which it is able to make in its DNA, and this information is passed from generation to generation through the replication of the DNA.

The probability of synthesizing any of the specific sequences of amino acids which are found in naturally occurring proteins is essentially zero if random synthesis methods are employed. (Random methods must be assumed for the prebiotic environment, given the naturalistic assumptions.) This can be demonstrated by calculating the possible number of permutations on the ways in which the twenty naturally occurring amino acids can be arranged in a chain having the length of a typical protein. A calculation of this type was included by Dixon and Webb in the first edition of *The Enzymes*.[17] They considered a sequence of five hundred amino acids, which would have a molecular mass of about sixty thousand daltons; this is the size of an average protein such as hemoglobin. If each of the five hundred positions can be any one of the twenty amino acids, then there are 20^{500} possible sequences, which equals 10^{650} (i.e., 1 with 650 zeroes after it). They then state that an amount of such a protein equal in mass to that of the earth would contain 6×10^{46} molecules. Thus in that mass of protein the chance of finding a particular sequence is ($6 \times 10^{46}/1 \times 10^{650}$), or about one chance in 10^{603}. Dixon and Webb conclude that "the simultaneous formation of two or more molecules of any given enzyme purely by chance is extremely improbable."[18]

Some may object to the preceding argument by proposing that given enough time, the improbable may become probable. Perhaps so, but it is almost universally accepted that the earth has a finite age, which is on the order of five billion years. That sounds like a long time, but actually is less than 10^{18} seconds. If the sequence of each of the protein molecules in the above example could be permuted one thousand times per second, then there would be a total of 10^{67} protein sequences which could be generated in the presumed five billion year age of the earth. This is still a very small number compared to the total number of possible sequences. Hence it is not possible to get around the sequence problem by invoking long time periods.

In living cells, the nucleotide sequence of DNA provides the information for the protein sequences. Once a good strand of DNA exists, together with the complex molecular machinery necessary to replicate it, it is possible to get variations in the progeny as a result of changes in the sequence. Pieces of DNA can also be transferred from one organism to another, thereby conferring new characteristics to the recipient. Mechanisms such as these are involved in the observed variations and adaptations of microevolution and are becoming progressively better understood as a result of the rapid progress being made in molecular genetics and molecular biology. Thus once life exists, variation is possible. But no plausible mechanism has been proposed by which a first meaningful strand of DNA (or of protein) could have been formed under abiotic conditions.

The third stage in the hypothesized evolutionary pathway for the origin of life is the macromolecule-to-cell transition. One of Lehninger's working assumptions is that the evolutionary development took place in a long series of small steps, each of which had a reasonably high probability of occurrence. It is very difficult to see, however, how the macromolecule-to-cell transition could be made by a series of small steps; everything must be present in a cell at the same time and in the correct three-dimensional arrangement for a cell to be functional. What makes this problem so difficult is that the fundamental biochemical outline of cellular metabolism is cyclical rather than linear; it is an interdependent scheme with no starting or stopping point, just like the proverbial chicken and the egg. Figure 2.1 gives its essential features:

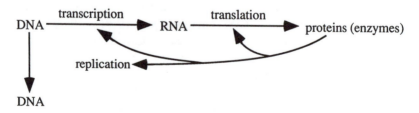

Figure 2.1

The primary carrier of genetic information is DNA; the process of transcription yields RNA, and translation gives the proteins. Replication results in the formation of new identical strands of DNA. All three of these processes—transcription, translation, and replication—require the presence of many enzymes which are themselves the product of the translation step. More than a hundred different enzymes are involved at the translation step alone. Thus while DNA contains the sequence information for the proteins, other copies of the same proteins must already be present in order for the information stored in the DNA to be used. This basic scheme is found in all cells which are capable of reproducing themselves, from the simplest to the most complex. To suppose, as Lehninger does, that simpler cells existed in the past is idle speculation. There is no good reason to believe that fundamentally simpler cells are even possible.

Lehninger acknowledges the conceptual difficulties of the macromolecule-to-cell transition. He writes, "It is this stage in chemical evolution that is most difficult to understand, since there are few if any modern nonbiological prototypes of self-organizing, self-replicating molecular systems."[19] Green and Goldberger, in their book *Molecular Insights into the Living Process*,[20] are more forthright in their evaluation of this problem. They state: "The macromolecule to cell transition is a jump of fantastic dimensions, which lies beyond the range of testable hypothesis. In this area all is conjecture." Both of these writers were prominent biochemists. Each knew what the writers of most biology texts apparently do not know, that the scientific foundation for the proposed evolutionary origin of life is very weak at best and contains holes which even speculation proves inadequate to fill.

Evaluation of the Evolutionary Hypothesis

Why do writers such as Lehninger and Monod (a molecular biologist) subscribe to the proposed evolutionary origin of life, while the problems outlined in the previous paragraphs are well known to them? Monod's strong assertion that life arose by chance is not based on scientific observation, though since he speaks with the voice of a scientist one is led to believe that such is the case. Rather, these writers as well as many others arbitrarily rule out even the possibility of a supernatural origin for life and hence are forced to the conclusion that evolution happened, although they do not know how, and in spite of the evidence which says it is impossible.

Anyone who observes nature must admit that it has the appearance of being the product of design rather than chance. This is the case regardless of whether one's observations are made at the level of field biology or of molecular biology. If there is no designer, however, then it cannot have been designed, and any indication of such is only apparent and not real. That is the position of Monod. But why should one not accept the appearance of design at face value, and take this as supporting evidence for belief in a wise Designer, i.e., God? Doing so opens a whole new range of possibilities for understanding how life came into existence.

Creation

The idea of design and a Designer is wholly compatible with the biblical position that God created life. The role of God as Creator is a concept which is found throughout the Old and New Testaments; it is not restricted to Genesis, although the greatest amount of detail is given there. Unfortunately, the meaning of the Genesis account has been the subject of much controversy which tends to obscure the essential message. Some theologians, especially those of the neoorthodox persuasion, label the first several chapters of Genesis as allegorical stories from which no factual information on the history of the earth can be obtained. For those who consider the Bible as the inspired, infallible Word of God, on the other hand, Genesis is considered to be a historical record, but again there is disagreement over how it should be interpreted. One group holds to what is often called the six-day, six-thousand-year position, while another sees the "days" as ages or periods of time and accepts the scientific evidence that the earth is a good deal older than six-thousand years. It is all too easy for the essential concepts of creation to be totally overlooked as a result of the debates over these interpretations.

It should be understood that there is a close relationship between miracles and creation. If one accepts the evidence that miracles actually happen and are supernatural events, then it should not be difficult to accept the idea of divine creation, which was also the result of supernatural acts. Conversely, if one believes in creation, one can hardly rule out the possibility that God can still do creative, miraculous acts in the world today. Regardless of whether we are talking about creation or miracles, we are dealing with events that cannot be accounted for by naturalistic presuppositions. In some of Jesus' miracles, matter was evidently created out of nothing, just as it was at Creation. In others of His miracles, dead tissue was reorganized and brought back to life, which again must have been similar or analogous to what happened at the time of the original creation of life.

The watershed issue with which one must deal in thinking about creation and miracles is whether one accepts the idea that God can do things in the world and that He is not bound to abide by the principles which the seventeenth-century scientists called the "laws by which God ran the universe." If this is accepted, then the seemingly diverse issues discussed in this paper, i.e., prophecy, miracles, answers to prayer, and Creation, are all within the realm of the possible and should not cause surprise or disbelief when and if they occur. Similarly, the watershed question about Creation does not concern the length of the days, or whether it was progressive, or to what extent microevolution was used as a mechanism, but whether one's own world view even allows God to carry out creative acts. If one's answer to this question is in the affirmative, then one is free to weigh and consider the biblical texts and the various aspects of biblical interpretation, as well as the valid results of scientific investigation, in order to arrive at a provisional history of life which may include both natural and supernatural processes.

Summary and Conclusions

The dualistic view of reality has been traced from the time when the immaterial aspect was considered to be most important, through the period in which the physical realm was emphasized but without the exclusion of the spiritual realm, and from there to the stage in which the dualistic world view was altogether abandoned in favor of a naturalistic, monistic world view. Now it is necessary for us explicitly to recognize and admit that this last step was a gross error, and we must again attempt to reconstruct a theistic world view in which the dual (physical and spiritual) nature of reality is accepted, and in which the two aspects are held in a properly integrated and interrelated balance.

The scientific method, as elaborated in the principles of logical positivism, has proved itself to be an efficient way of learning about the physical universe. Its results, however, are necessarily limited. I propose that we should go beyond it by adopting a theistic approach. The theistic approach to nature and science gives a substantial basis for believing that there is design and order in nature. Without this confidence, true science is not possible, and science (to know) is reduced to technology (to control or manipulate). If we accept the theistic approach, nature takes on meaning and value because it is the handiwork of God, and when we see beauty, we can freely give the credit to the One to whom it is due.

Notes

[1] I. G. Barbour, *Issues in Science and Religion* (Englewood Cliffs, N.J.: Prentice-Hall, 1966), 37.

[2] Ibid., 58.

[3] Cf. E. A. Burtt, *The Metaphysical Foundations of Modern Science* (Garden City, N.Y.: Doubleday, 1954); T. A. Kuhn, *The Structure of Scientific Revolutions* (Chicago: University of Chicago Press, 1962).

[4] Francis Schaeffer, *The God Who Is There* (Downers Grove, Ill.: InterVarsity Press, 1968).

[5] Francis Schaeffer, *Escape From Reason,* (Downers Grove, Ill.: InterVarsity Press, 1968).

[6]Barbour, *Issues,* chap. 9.

[7]Arthur Eddington, *Science and the Unseen World* (New York: Macmillan, 1930).

[8]H. Margenau, *The Nature of Physical Reality* (New York: McGraw-Hill, 1950).

[9]Loraine Boettner, *The Reformed Doctrine of Predestination* (Grand Rapids, Mich.: Eerdmans, 1932), 313.

[10]This and all subsequent Scripture references in this chapter, unless otherwise noted, are from the New International Version of the Bible, copyright 1978 by the New York International Bible Society.

[11]W. G. Pollard, *Chance and Providence* (New York: Scribner, 1958).

[12]Jacques Monod, *Chance and Necessity,* trans. Austryn Wainhouse (New York: Random House, 1972), 112.

[13]A. L. Lehninger, *Biochemistry,* 2d ed. (New York: Worth Publishers, 1975), 1034.

[14]Ibid.

[15]Ibid., 23.

[16]Ibid., chap. 37.

[17]M. Dixon and E. C. Webb, *The Enzymes* (New York: Academic Press, 1958), 668.

[18]Ibid.

[19]Lehninger, *Biochemistry,* 1035.

[20]D. E. Green and R. W. Goldberger, *Molecular Insights into the Living Process* (New York: Academic Press, 1967), 407.

2.2

Inanimate Design as a Problem for Nontheistic Worldviews

Robert C. Newman

WHEN THE APOSTLE PAUL PRESENTED THE GOSPEL to people unfamiliar with Scripture,[1] he appealed to nature as evidence for the existence of God. Similar arguments for God from design in nature continued to be popular for centuries.[2] However, they were generally abandoned about a century ago under the impact of Darwin's *Origin of Species*. Since then many have felt Darwin's "survival of the fittest" is the source of this design rather than God.

In recent years, however, serious questions have been raised regarding the sufficiency of evolution as an explanation for the origin of life and of its diversity.[3] To the extent that evolution itself is in trouble, it will hardly serve as a replacement for God in explaining design in living things.

In any case, biological evolution can hardly explain design in the non-living part of nature. And it is here that recent advances in science have uncovered far more evidence for a designer than was known in Darwin's time or even ten years ago. Let us look at some of this evidence here.

Life depends upon the more basic substratum which we study in chemistry and physics. Behind all life on earth stands the right chemistry, the right environment, and the right universe. Consider first the right chemistry.

The Right Chemistry

All life on earth depends on the operation of very complex biochemicals containing thousands or even millions of atoms. These include DNA and RNA (which store and transmit the information on how living cells operate) and proteins (which provide most of the structure of living things and cause the necessary chemical reactions to occur at rates sufficiently rapid for plants and animals to be able to respond to changes in their environments). All these molecules possess enormous complexity and very specific structures to carry out particular, specialized tasks. Such specific organizational complexity itself presents a serious challenge to anyone who thinks that life arose by random processes rather than by design, but that is not the subject of this discussion.[4]

On a much simpler level, the properties of carbon, phosphorus, and water suggest that life didn't just happen. Carbon is the only element in existence which will form chains of almost unlimited length, such as are needed for the complex molecules of DNA, RNA, and protein that occur in living things. All the carbon in our universe was apparently formed inside stars, and then scattered over space when the largest stars ran out of fuel and exploded.[5] Yet only by two coordinated "quirks" in nature is carbon a common element rather than a very rare one. Carbon is formed in stars by a rare collision of three helium nuclei. Were it not for the fact that the temperature inside stars is right at the energy level of a "resonance" for carbon, little would be formed. That is, the energy level of helium nuclei inside stars is just right for these nuclei to stick together for a unusually long time. If this resonance energy were only 4 percent lower, carbon would be very rare. On the other hand, carbon easily combines with another helium nucleus to form oxygen, but it just so happens that the temperature in stars is slightly above the oxygen resonance. If this resonance were only one-half of 1 percent higher, nearly all carbon would convert to oxygen. In either case, carbon would be very rare and life itself would be rare or nonexistent not only on earth, but anywhere in the universe.[6]

Phosphorus is unique among the chemical elements in that it forms certain compounds which can store large amounts of energy. Without these compounds, there would be no higher animal life, since higher animals need such an efficient method of energy storage to function. Yet only phosphorus, of all the elements, has this capability. It almost looks as if phosphorus was designed for this purpose.

The familiar chemical we call water is at least as unusual as carbon or phosphorus. It is a very small molecule (a combination of two hydrogen atoms and one oxygen), lighter than molecules of nitrogen or oxygen. It should thus be gaseous at temperatures suitable for life. However, water forms itself into polymers, combinations of two or three water molecules loosely joined together, so that in fact it is a liquid at these temperatures. As a liquid it is a very important component of the blood of animals, the sap of trees, and the fluid in living cells. Yet when water evaporates, it no longer forms polymers. This allows it to disperse in the atmosphere so it doesn't stifle life by lying on the earth's surface as an unbreathable gas. No other substance has this property.

Water is also a universal solvent, carrying the many necessary solid chemicals which circulate in the bloodstream, in plant sap, and in living cells. All other liquids which can dissolve a comparable number of chemicals are highly corrosive and deadly to living things.

Water is unusual in its ability to absorb a large amount of heat for a given change in temperature. As a result it moderates the climate of the earth and helps to stabilize the body temperature of animals. Like few other substances, it expands rather than contracting on freezing. This means that ice floats on water rather than sinking, so that lakes and oceans will not freeze all the way to the bottom, which would kill all marine life. It also means that water aids in the formation of soil by splitting up rocks. Truly water is a most amazing substance. Like a thirsty traveler on a hot day, the chemist can say, "There's nothing like it."[7]

Thus the universe had just the right chemistry to support life, and this depends on certain physical constants being just the right size and on some unique chemicals for which there are no substitutes. Is this an accident? Is it merely an accident of observation? That is, is this true only because if it weren't, we wouldn't be here to talk about it? We will return to these questions later, but not until we have considered the evidence of design in our environment and in the basic forces which operate in our universe as a whole.

The Right Environment

Environmentally, our earth is unique in the solar system and at least very rare in our galaxy. The temperature at the earth's surface varies substantially from pole to equator, from summer to winter, and from the Dead Sea to Mt. Everest. Yet it never exceeds the boiling point of water except in the vicinity of volcanoes, hydrothermal vents, and geysers. Temperatures below freezing are much more common, occurring on high mountains even at the equator, at moderate latitudes in the winter, and year-round at the poles. Yet our oceans never freeze up completely even in arctic regions, because of our proximity to the sun, internal heat from the earth, and a peculiar property of water. By contrast, the average temperature on Venus, our nearest neighbor sunward, is about 900 degrees Fahrenheit! On Mars, the next planet further away, temperatures barely rise above freezing even in midsummer at the equator. So far as we know, earth alone has the right temperature range for life: warm enough for water to be liquid, cool enough that complex biomolecules are not destroyed.

A substantial amount of water is also needed in the environment to support life though a few organisms have special techniques for preserving water so they can live in arid conditions. For the earth as a whole (center to surface), the fraction of terrestrial water is small. But this is all concentrated at the surface, so that our globe is two-thirds covered by water at an average depth of three miles. The amount of water on Venus and Mars is infinitesimal by contrast.

Earth also has the right atmosphere. Consider merely its oxygen content. If there were much less oxygen in our atmosphere, animals would not have enough to breathe. If there were much more, plant life would be burnt up. Free oxygen, so necessary to most kinds of life, is virtually absent on Mars and Venus.

Earth's gravity is also just right. If the earth were only one-fourth as massive as it is, the atmospheric pressure would be too small to support life. If the earth were twice as massive, the atmosphere would be thick enough to work like a greenhouse in summer, raising the temperature high enough to kill us all.

Earth has the right kind of sun. A sun only 20 percent larger would burn up its fuel in only four billion years. By now, such a sun would have expanded into its "red giant" stage, and the earth would have burned up as it became enveloped by the sun's atmosphere. On the other hand, if our sun were only 20 percent smaller, the earth would have to be much closer in to get enough heat, and the additional tidal friction from the sun would slow the earth's rotation and produce unacceptably long days and nights with their consequent broiling and freezing temperatures. In addition, a smaller sun would not produce enough blue light for plants to be able to make sugar and oxygen. Both sugar and oxygen are needed by animals to live, and they can produce neither themselves.[8]

The right kind of sun cannot vary much in brightness or life will not survive. In fact, our sun's luminosity already has varied "too much" over the past four billion years, increasing in brightness by some 25 percent. But the creation of plant life was timed just right to save the day! As the sun got hotter, plants removed carbon dioxide from the atmosphere and replaced it by oxygen at just the right rate to turn down the greenhouse effect and keep temperatures on earth in the range safe for life.[9]

This trick performed by the plants only worked because the earth was at the right distance from the sun. If it had been 5 percent closer, the greenhouse effect would have been too strong early in earth history, the plants would never have gotten started, and earth would now be a furnace like Venus. But if the earth had been only 1 percent further from the sun,[10] the cooler temperatures about two billion years ago would have produced a runaway ice age, and the earth would now be like Antarctica everywhere.[11]

Thus the earth has just the right environment. Can we reasonably explain all this away as accidental and claim there is really no Designer behind our universe? Let us save this question for discussion until we have considered the evidence of design in the basic forces of our universe.

The Right Universe

Not only do we live in a universe having the right chemistry to support life, and on a planet with the right environment for life, it also turns out that the basic forces in our universe are just right. Without the precise balance which exists among these primary forces, life would be impossible anywhere in our universe.

There are just four basic forces presently known to mankind: gravity, electromagnetism, and the strong and weak nuclear forces. The weakest of these is gravity, which is some 10^{40} times weaker than the strongest, the so-called strong interaction. Gravity dominates at large distances because the other three forces act only over short distances or cancel out. The electromagnetic force is the most familiar of these other forces. It is responsible for electricity, for magnetism, for holding the electrons of an atom to its nucleus, and for holding together matter to form solids. It is much stronger than gravity and like gravity can act over long distances. However, the electromagnetic force is produced by charged particles which may have either negative or positive charges. The like charges repel one another and the opposite charges attract, canceling each other out and decreasing the resulting force. By contrast, gravity has only positive charges (called *mass*); these attract one another rather than repelling and add together to increase the total force.

The strong nuclear force holds together the neutrons and protons that make up the nucleus. It acts strongly, but only over very short distances, about 10^{-13} centimeters, the radius of a typical nucleus. The weak nuclear force, as the name implies, is weaker (by one hundred thousand times) than the strong force, though much stronger than gravity (by about 10^{34}). It also acts over short distances and is involved in a number of less familiar activities such as the decay of a neutron into a proton, electron, and neutrino.[12]

As suggested above, the balances that exist among these forces in our universe are precise, making possible life as we know it. Consider first of all the delicate balance between gravity and the expansion speed of our universe. Since the 1920s it has been apparent that our universe is expanding, apparently from an event known as the "big bang" which occurred some fifteen to twenty billion years ago. Whether our universe is expanding fast enough to continue to do so forever, or whether it will eventually stop expanding and start collapsing, are alternatives still hotly debated among cosmologists. The evidence at present favors a permanent expansion. In any case, it is obvious that the actual density of matter in our universe is within a factor of ten of the so-called critical density, the point of exact balance between permanent expansion and eventual contraction. But for the density to be even so close to this critical density after some twenty billion years of expansion, it must have been very precisely tuned in the earliest moments of the big bang. At 10^{-43} seconds after the big bang, for instance—the so-called Planck time—the density must have been equal to the critical density to an accuracy of one part in 10^{55}. The practical effects of this fine tuning are two. If the density had been ever so slightly higher, then the universe would have collapsed quickly instead of lasting some twenty billion years, and there would never have been any opportunity for life to form. On the other hand, had the density been ever so slightly smaller, the universe would have expanded much more rapidly than it did, and no galaxies, stars, or planets would have formed. Again, no life. Life is the result of fine tuning the density of matter-energy at the Planck time to one part in 10^{55}.[13]

Life depends on the existence of a number of the heavier chemical elements, especially carbon, nitrogen, and oxygen. Only hydrogen, helium, and a few of the very lightest elements would be formed in the big bang itself. The rest are formed inside stars. It is the behavior of the strong and weak nuclear forces that controls how stars operate. If the strong force were much weaker than it is, there would be few stable elements. For instance, if it were only 50 percent weaker, not even iron and carbon would be stable, and without these elements there could be no life as we know it. But if the strong force were only 5 percent weaker, the element deuterium would not exist, and stars could not burn as they do. On the other hand, if the strong force were only a few percent stronger, the diproton would be stable, protons could combine by the strong interaction to form deuterium, and stars would burn catastrophically! The strong interaction has to be just the right strength to have stable stars and stable elements necessary for life.

But the weak nuclear force is important, too. As mentioned above, the heavier elements are formed in the interiors of stars as a part of their aging process. Stars first "burn" hydrogen to form helium. The helium is combined to form carbon, nitrogen, and oxygen. These in turn are burned in the centers of aging stars to form the even heavier elements such as silicon, iron, lead, and uranium. But were it not for the weak force, all these elements would remain trapped inside the stars where they would be of no use for life. However, when a star has used up most of its nuclear fuel, it begins to collapse. It becomes very hot inside and begins producing large numbers of neutrinos. As the neutrinos escape from the star (because the weak force is just the right strength) they grasp on to the outer layers of the star, causing the star to explode as a supernova and scatter its heavy elements all over the neighborhood. These elements will later become part of the next generation of stars and form planets which accompany such stars. As a result the earth has the heavy elements so necessary for life. If the weak force were much smaller than it is, the neutrinos would escape quietly, not interacting sufficiently with the outer layers of the star. Thus the star would not explode, and no heavy elements would escape. If, on the other hand, the weak force were much stronger, the neutrinos themselves would not be able to escape from the star, we would again have no explosion, and no heavy elements outside the star. Thus if the weak force were much different than it is, there would be no heavy elements outside of stars. And without heavy elements, there would be no chemically-based life.

There is one more crucial balance we need to discuss. Gravity is much weaker than electromagnetism (10^{37}), yet gravity dominates in the realm of astronomical distances. Why is this so? Both gravity and electromagnetism are long distance forces, both decreasing inversely with the square of the distance. Why should not electromagnetism be more important than gravity in controlling the movements of planets, stars, and galaxies? The reason is that electromagnetism is produced by two kinds of charges, negative and positive, and that these occur in equal numbers, so that at large distances they cancel each other out. But why is this? Why should there be exactly equal numbers of positive and negative charges? Scientists don't know. The main negative charge is the electron, which is a very small particle compared to the proton, the main positive charge. In modern cosmological theory, as the universe cooled down from the big bang, protons would have "frozen out" much earlier than electrons, and there is no obvious reason why the two should be equal in number.[14]

In fact, it is not obvious why there should even be any positively charged protons since it is assumed that earlier in the history of the universe there were enormous numbers of positive protons and negative antiprotons, and these annihilated each other when the universe cooled down below the temperature necessary to produce proton-antiproton pairs. But apparently there were a few more protons than antiprotons, so these were left over when all the antiprotons were used up. Much later, the universe cooled down enough so as to no longer produce electron-antielectron pairs, and again, almost exactly the same number of electrons were left over to balance out the positive charge of the leftover protons! The number of electrons and the number of protons left over must have been the same to much better than one part in 10^{37}. If this had not happened, our universe would be dominated by electromagnetism instead of gravity.

What would this mean? We don't know all the ramifications of such a situation. At least, there would be no galaxies, stars, or planets, since these structures are all dominated by gravity. It is doubtful that a stable universe of any sort could exist for the billions of years needed for life on earth in such circumstances. Recall our discussion above on the balance between gravity and expansion. Likewise, it is unlikely that radiation could travel long distances in a universe where electromagnetism dominates, in which case one could not have a pleasantly warm planet getting heat from a hot, distant sun.

In view of all these carefully tuned balances between the forces in our universe, it becomes obvious that with very slight changes in the strength or balance of these forces, we get a universe which will not support life as we know it or can imagine it. What are we to make of this? The simplest explanation is that we live in a designed universe.

The Anthropic Principle

Scientists have been discussing this problem for several years now. As Stephen Hawking has pointed out,

The odds against a universe like ours emerging out of something like the Big Bang are enormous. . . . I think there are clearly religious implications whenever you start to discuss the origins of the universe. There must be religious overtones. But I think most scientists prefer to shy away from the religious side of it.[15]

In shying away from religious explanations, some have suggested that this apparent design is merely an "accident of observation." Admittedly, life would be impossible unless all the factors discussed above came out just right. But if life were impossible, then we wouldn't be here ourselves, and there would be no one to observe such a universe! Conversely, there will only be observers in a universe where all these factors work out just right. This explanation, that the order in our universe is just an accident of observation, is called the *anthropic principle* (more precisely, the *weak anthropic principle*).

The anthropic principle is certainly a clever explanation, and it is undeniably true in some sense. Yet it still leaves us with the existing universe as a fluke of vanishingly small probability. As an explanation, it is methodologically much inferior to any theory in which a universe such as ours would be a likely result. But if such a being as the God of the Bible exists, then an apparently designed universe such as ours would be a likely result rather than such a surprise as we have in an accidental universe.

Not all who espouse the anthropic principle are satisfied with the so-called weak form sketched above. Some have moved into Eastern mysticism, pantheism, or something equally esoteric to propose a strong anthropic principle. In this view, man himself has somehow caused the world to be just right to allow life and humanity to exist in it, whether this be done by man being a part of god who is everything, or by some theory which allows physical causes to produce effects backward in time. Such suggestions attempt to provide a model in which the special order found in the universe has some adequate cause. Such views range far beyond the scientific evidence discussed here and also beyond the scope of this paper. To answer such suggestions, we must consider how the evidence for the existence of the God of the Bible compares with that adduced for the particular worldview espoused. I merely comment that I am unaware of any evidence for such positions comparable to that for the God of the Bible.

To return to the weak anthropic principle, however, some are hopeful that further investigation will reveal that our universe had to be the way it is, that it is merely the logical result of laws that lie behind it. This is doubtless one motivation of physicists who are seeking to explain all four basic forces in our universe as merely varied manifestations of one single force, or *superforce*. We must continue to remind ourselves that the dream of finding such a superforce has not yet materialized and may never do so.[16] Many research programs of great promise have never panned out. Even if a superforce is discovered, this will not explain the evidence of design found in the various laws themselves.[17]

But even if it should turn out that some such superforce lies behind the four basic forces, the problem of design will not be so easily solved. As Paul Davies says:

Should we conclude that the universe is a product of design? The new physics and the new cosmology hold out a tantalizing promise: that we might be able to explain how all the physical structures in the universe have come to exist, automatically, as a result of natural processes. We would then no longer have need for a Creator in the traditional sense. Nevertheless, though science may explain the world, we still have to explain science. The laws which enable the universe to come into being spontaneously seem themselves to be the product of exceedingly ingenious design. If physics is the product of design, the universe must have a purpose, and the evidence of modern physics suggests strongly to me that the purpose includes us.[18]

Notes

[1]See, e.g., Acts 14:15–17.

[2]This line of argumentation reached its height in William Paley, *Natural Theology* (1802); and Thomas Chalmers et al., *The Bridgewater Treatises,* 12 vols., 1833–40.

[3]See, e.g., Michael Denton, *Evolution: A Theory in Crisis* (Bethesda, Md.: Adler and Adler, 1985); Gordon Rattray Taylor, *The Great Evolution Mystery* (Newark: Harper and Row, 1983); Charles B. Thaxton, Walter L. Bradley, and Roger L. Olson, *The Mystery of Life's Origin* (New York: Philosophical Library, 1984).

[4]Besides the items in note 3, above, see also Fred Hoyle and Chandra Wickramasinghe, *Evolution From Space: A Theory of Cosmic Creationism* (New York: Simon and Schuster, 1981); Phillip E. Johnson, *Darwin on Trial* (Washington, D.C.: Regnery Gateway, 1991).

[5]See, e.g., *McGraw-Hill Encyclopedia of Astronomy* (1983), s.v. "Elements and nuclides, origin of."

[6]Fred Hoyle, *Galaxies, Nuclei and Quasars* (New York: Harper and Row, 1965), 147–50.

[7]For further information on these topics, see Alan Hayward, *God Is* (Nashville, Tenn.: Thomas Nelson, 1980).

[8]Michael H. Hart, "Atmospheric Evolution," in *Extraterrestrials: Where Are They?* ed. Michael H. Hart and Ben Zuckerman (New York: Pergamon, 1982), 156. See also note 9.

[9]Owen Gingerich, "Let There Be Light: Modern Cosmogony and Biblical Creation," in *Is God a Creationist?* ed. Roland Mushat Frye (New York: Charles Scribner's Sons, 1983), 132–33.

[10]Recent literature claims that one can go out 20 percent further if the greenhouse effect is sufficiently strong, but this runs into other problems with such atmospheres.

[11]Michael H. Hart, "Habitable Zones about Main Sequence Stars," *Icarus* 37 (1979): 351–57.

[12]*McGraw-Hill Encyclopedia of Physics* (1983), s.v. "Fundamental Interactions" by Abdus Salam.

[13]Most of the points in this section are discussed in Paul C. W. Davies, *The Accidental Universe* (Cambridge: Cambridge University Press, 1982); more briefly in John Boslough, *Stephen Hawking's Universe* (New York: William Morrow, 1985), chap. 9. See also John D. Barrow and Frank J. Tipler, *The Anthropic Cosmological Principle* (New York: Oxford University Press, 1986).

[14]On the formation of the various elementary particles as the universe cools down from the big bang, see Steven Weinberg, *The First Three Minutes* (New York: Bantam, 1979).

[15]Boslough, *Stephen Hawking's Universe,* 121.

[16]Stephen Hawking, *A Brief History of Time* (New York: Bantam, 1988), chap. 10; more detail in Paul Davies, *Superforce: The Search for a Grand Unified Theory of Nature* (New York: Simon and Schuster, 1984).

[17]See the last paragraph in Davies, *Superforce.*

[18]Davies, *Superforce,* 243.

2.3

The Evidence
of Cosmology

Robert C. Newman

COSMOLOGY IS THE STUDY OF THE KNOWN PARTS of the universe in an attempt to describe the universe as a whole. It interprets the information presently reaching the earth in order to reconstruct the history of the entire cosmos. Given such limitations, we should not be surprised that cosmology often involves speculation (though large parts of cosmology are not speculative) and that many cosmological models are still being proposed and defended.

With physicist Hannes Alfven, we may wish to throw up our hands and dismiss cosmology as a waste of time.[1] Yet some of the questions it seeks to answer may be too important to be safely ignored. The Bible warns us that the universe is created and that its Creator will one day call us to account for our every thought and deed.[2] However unlikely we may think it that the Bible is really a message from God, as mathematician Blaise Pascal has pointed out, the stakes are so high and the disaster so great if we are mistaken that it would be foolish for us to live as though the universe is eternal without carefully examining whatever data may bear on the subject.[3]

Not only may cosmological questions have ultimate personal importance, the scientific materials available to answer such questions are more extensive today than ever before. With the development of ever-larger optical telescopes, the invention of radio telescopes since World War II, and, most recently, of artificial satellites to make observations above our obscuring atmosphere, we now have an enormous amount of new data. In addition, earthbound work in physics has given us greatly increased understanding of the atom, its nucleus, elementary particles, and the basic forces at work in the universe.

In this paper, we shall sketch the scientific data relevant to cosmology, including such items as the nature of stars and their distances from us, galaxies and their redshifts, Olber's paradox, cosmic distance scales, quasars, and the so-called three-degree blackbody radiation. At convenient points in this discussion, we shall examine a number of cosmological models, some proposed by secular scientists, others by various Bible-believers. In the end, we shall summarize our findings and propose a best model on the basis of present scientific knowledge.

The Nature of Stars

Although astronomers in general are also interested in planets, asteroids, and comets, cosmologists tend to confine their study to stars and galaxies, since these alone have as yet been observed beyond our solar system.[4] Let us first consider stars.

What is a star? We have one nearby to study—the sun—about ninety-three million miles (or eight light-minutes)[5] away. The rest of the stars are at least four light-years away, over a quarter of a million times further. Our sun is a huge ball of gas, mostly hydrogen, held together by its own gravity. The temperature at its visible "surface" is several thousand degrees. Calculating the temperature inward from the surface, we find that it rises to about ten million degrees at the center. As a result, the sun is a gas all the way through in spite of enormous densities deep within. At such a high central temperature, hydrogen experiences a nuclear reaction which converts it to helium, releasing enormous amounts of energy. This energy, equivalent for our sun to the explosion of about two billion fifty-megaton hydrogen bombs per second,[6] provides all our sunlight and keeps the sun from collapsing under the force of its own gravity. A mass of hydrogen equal to that of the sun should be able to keep burning by this reaction for some ten billion years.

In brief, that is what the sun is like. Why do we believe the sun is a star, or that the stars are suns? There are several reasons.

In the first place, we can measure distances to about a thousand of the nearest stars by a rather direct method of triangulation we call *parallax*. You may easily demonstrate this method by holding your finger up at arm's length and looking at it first with one eye and then with the other. Your finger will appear to jump back and forth against its background even though you hold it quite still. In astronomy, your finger corresponds to a nearby star, the background to the more distant stars. Your eyes correspond to photos taken six months apart at opposite ends of the earth's orbit around the sun, about 185 million miles apart instead of the couple inches between your eyes. Measuring the amount of "jump" for each star, we find that the nearest stars are about four light-years (twenty-five trillion miles) away, and that for stars beyond about one hundred light-years, the jumps get too small to measure. Only about a thousand of the billions of stars visible in our telescopes show measurable jumps.

What does this have to do with whether or not the stars are suns? Well, when we allow for the geometrical dimming of light due to distance, we find that our sun is about the same brightness as stars of the same color. Bluer stars tend to be brighter; red ones dimmer. We can even make a graph, plotting star brightness against star color, and show that most of these stars lie near a single line (called the *main sequence*) and that the sun lies near it too.

A second reason to believe that the stars are suns comes from weighing them. This we can do whenever stars occur in pairs or groups (called *binary* or *multiple* stars) which rotate around one another. If we know the size of the orbit and the time it takes to circle each other once, we can immediately calculate the sum of the masses of the stars in the group. Main sequence stars, those with the same color as our sun, turn out to have the same mass. Bluer stars are heavier; redder ones are lighter.

In these and many other ways, stars show themselves to be the same kind of objects as our sun. Of course, stars differ considerably among themselves. Some are one hundred times heavier than our sun; some one hundred times lighter. Some have surface temperatures ten times hotter; others twice as cool. Some expend their hydrogen fuel a million times faster; others a million times slower. However, there does appear to be a minimum size for stars. Observations agree with calculations that for an object less than about 8 percent of the sun's mass, the central temperature will not be high enough to have a nuclear fusion reaction. As a result, the object will be a large planet rather like Jupiter instead of a star.

Camping's Physically Small Universe

At this point we are ready to consider the proposal of radio-preacher Harold Camping, that the whole universe is really quite small, only a few light-years across.[7] Camping argues that the parallax method described above merely shows us that the thousand nearest stars are a few light-years away and closer than the background stars, but it doesn't tell us how far away the background is. All distance measurements used on the background stars are unreliable, he says, being based on false assumptions. Instead, these background stars lie in a thin spherical shell only a short distance further away!

This view is mistaken, as can be shown by some simple arguments based on geometrical proportions, each of which is no less reliable than the parallax method itself. For instance, we can measure the motion of stars toward or away from us by a shift in the frequency of light coming from them, a technique much like that used in police radar for catching speeders. Considering pairs of binary stars that are far enough apart to appear as separate stars in our telescopes, we measure the angular size of their orbits and the speed at which the two stars move around each other. If these stars were only a few light-years away, then the physical size of the orbits must be relatively small, and stars moving at the speeds measured should complete their roundtrips in just a few days. In fact, however, many such stars take years to make a circuit, and are therefore many hundreds of light-years away.

Second, according to Camping's view, the dimmer main sequence stars must appear to be dim because they are very small rather than very far away. For the billions of dim stars which we observe in large telescopes, these would be so small that gravity could not hold them together.

Third, these dimmer stars often form clusters. If we make a separate graph for each cluster, plotting star brightness against star color, we find that each cluster produces a pattern similar to that of the thousand nearby stars. Each graph has a main sequence line. If we assume the main sequence in each cluster has the same actual brightness for each color as does the main sequence in our nearby stars, then these clusters are much further away from us, some a hundred light-years, some a thousand, some much further. This assumption is very reasonable, since computer calculations of star structure show that stars on the main sequence are merely those which get their energy by turning hydrogen into helium, in contrast (say) to red giant stars, which have used up their hydrogen and now are turning helium into carbon, nitrogen, and oxygen. Thus the view that the universe is much larger than a few light-years across is able to explain the energy source of stars in clusters by the same mechanism that explains the energy source of the sun and nearby stars.

Such examples could be multiplied easily. They show us that Camping's physically small universe does not fit the data. The universe really is much bigger than the distances to the nearest stars.

Galaxies

As we look out into the universe, we see that most stars occur in clusters of hundreds or thousands of stars. These clusters in turn, together with much gas and dust, form larger collections we call *galaxies*. The most familiar galaxy is the Milky Way, known for its immense milky white band of stars. Named by the ancient Greeks, this galaxy is the one in which we live. Our sun and the nearby stars are also a part of this galaxy, even though they seem separate to us because we are among them. This is just like the lights in a large city viewed from in town, where the nearby lights seem distinct from the glow of the more distant parts.

Our galaxy is thought to have some one hundred to two hundred billion stars. It is shaped like a pinwheel as viewed from above, or like a pair of marching-band cymbals placed face-to-face. The whole galaxy is some one hundred thousand light-years across, and we are located in the place of the galaxy about two-thirds of the way out from the center. Nearby are two small irregularly-shaped galaxies, which we call the *Magellanic clouds* since they were discovered (for Europeans) by Ferdinand Magellan on his voyage around the world. They cannot be seen from latitudes as far north as the U.S. The nearest galaxy bigger than ours is the Andromeda galaxy, containing some two hundred to three hundred billion stars and located about two million light-years away. Many galaxies are spirals like the Milky Way and Andromeda. Some are elliptical, like Andromeda's small companions. Others are irregular, like the Magellanic clouds. The smaller galaxies have hundreds of millions of stars; the larger, hundreds of billions.

How do we know the distances to other galaxies? Obviously not by parallax, since this method only works for the thousand or so nearest stars, all well within our own galaxy. The answer is that astronomers have developed a number of longer-range techniques for measuring distance. Each longer-range method is calibrated by using a technique which is good for shorter distances but which overlaps the range of the other. Techniques good over the same range are also checked against one another.

What are these distance-measuring techniques? Most of them depend on some way of calculating the actual or absolute brightness of stars, clusters, or galaxies. Then the apparent brightness of the object is observed. Since apparent brightness decreases geometrically with the square of the distance from object to observer, the distance of the object can then be calculated. We have already looked at one method for determining absolute brightness, namely, the fact that main sequence stars of the same color have the same brightness. Certain types of variable stars also have a definite average brightness which is related to the rate at which they fluctuate. Main sequence stars and variable stars are used to measure distances within our galaxy and to several nearby galaxies, out to a few million light-years. In nearby galaxies, we notice that the brightest stars in a cluster and the brightest globular clusters tend to have a certain specific brightness. Using these, we can measure distances out to some hundred million light-years. Beyond this distance, measurements are less certain, though it appears that the brightest galaxies in large galaxy-clusters have a similar brightness. This provides very rough distance measurements out to the most distant known galaxies, over a billion light-years away.

Moon and Spencer's Optically Small Universe

Two secular scientists, Parry Moon and Domina Spencer,[8] have proposed that certain phenomena of binary stars usually explained by Einstein's theory of relativity can be explained without relativity if we assume that light travels in circles of radius five light-years rather than in straight lines. In such a cosmos, the universe may be arbitrarily large in actuality, but an observer could never see objects more than ten light-years away. Light from more distant sources would curve back on itself before reaching us. Though there are only a dozen or so stars within ten light-years, these might be understood as appearing to us as billions of stars as we see their light on its first, second, third, or even millionth circuit around the heavens.

This suggestion has attracted little interest in secular circles, but a number of young-earth creationists have spoken favorably of it.[9] These creationists see in such a model a possible explanation for how light from apparently distant objects could reach us in just a few years. This explanation avoids the so-called apparent-age problem of having God create light already on its way to us from objects more than a few thousand light-years away.

Unfortunately, the cosmology of Moon and Spencer will not solve this problem, and it is hardly likely to be the actual state of affairs in any case.

In the first place, the model does not solve the problem of light travel-time. Even though the brightest stars might be those we are seeing directly, and the dimmer stars might be starlight which has made many trips around these alleged circles, this dimmer light must still have traveled a long way and taken a long time to do so. Only the light from the first, direct images of the stars would reach us in less than fifteen years. The second-image light would have to make an additional circuit, arriving about thirty years later.[10] Light which by dimness or other distance-measuring technique appears to have come from more than ten thousand light years away would have actually made several hundred circuits and taken over ten thousand years to do so. The optically-small universe of Moon and Spencer is therefore of no help to young-earth creationists.

Nor is the model at all likely to be true. Since the radius of curvature for light rays in this model is five light-years, we would see nothing that is actually further away from us than ten light-years, i.e., on the opposite side of the circle. This would mean that our sky has only a handful of really distinct stars, all the rest of the star images being multiple "reflections" of these. This would be similar to looking into one of those "wrap-around" mirrors found in clothing stores, in which we see multiple images of ourselves. A few minutes study of actual astronomical photographs should convince most of us that we are not merely looking at multiple reflections. The images of globular clusters and galaxies, for instance, are too coherent—having centers, rotational motion, and such—to be multiple images of only a dozen stars! Then too, there are far more than a dozen different star colors, sizes, and densities which we observe.

Galactic Redshifts

Since the 1920s we have known that the light coming to us from all but the closest galaxies is redshifted. The spectrum of light from each galaxy contains dark lines where chemical elements in the outer atmospheres of stars have absorbed light coming out from the star. These lines are located at longer wavelengths (corresponding to redder light) in the spectra of these galaxies than they are for the same elements in a laboratory on earth. Not only is the light redshifted, but the amount of shift is larger for more distant galaxies, increasing in an approximately linear way with distance.

There are only three known mechanisms that redden light: (1) scattering by dust and gas, (2) gravity reddening, and (3) motion reddening. The first of these mechanisms causes the sun to look red near sunset when its light passes through many more miles of atmosphere to reach us than it does at midday. For galaxies, though, this reddening would be due to gas and dust in space between us and the galaxy. Such reddening would increase with distance like the redshift does, but it would not shift the spectral lines since it only scatters more blue light than red. This cannot be the proper explanation of the galactic redshift.

Gravity reddening is due to the energy lost by light as it fights its way outward from a strong gravitational field. It does shift spectral lines toward the red, but there is no reason why it should produce more reddening for more distant galaxies. This explanation, too, is inadequate to explain the galactic redshifts.

Motion reddening is a shift in light's apparent frequency or wavelength due to the movement of the light source and observer away from one another. More commonly known as the Doppler shift, it also allows for blueshifts when source and observer are approaching one another. Most of us have observed the Doppler shift of sound waves when we noticed the change in pitch of a train whistle, auto horn, or siren when the vehicle passed us. The tone is higher pitched as the vehicle approaches, but suddenly drops as it passes, and is lower as it moves away. For light waves, it is color rather than pitch which we observe; the color seems bluer for approaching objects and redder for receding ones. This effect is not noticeable at ordinary speeds without special equipment (though police radar works on this principle), and we do not ordinarily see objects traveling at an appreciable fraction of the speed of light, since light is only appreciably redshifted at speeds close to the speed of light. Motion reddening will explain the observed galactic redshifts if we assume that all galaxies except a few in our local group are moving away from us. This assumption, known as the expansion of the universe, is generally accepted by cosmologists today.

A Static "Tired-Light" Universe

A few cosmologists have preferred to postulate some unknown mechanism to produce the galactic redshifts rather than accept the strange idea that all the galaxies are moving apart. Cosmologies which deny an expanding universe are called *static universes,* not to be confused with the *steady-state universe* we shall discuss later. The various mechanisms proposed for reddening are usually called *tired-light theories.*

French physicist Jean-Pierre Vigier,[11] for instance, proposes that an otherwise unknown lightweight elementary particle exists, which scatters light in such a way as to redshift the spectral lines in proportion to the distance the light travels. This does not fit recent calculations regarding the frequency dependence of tired light.[12]

In addition, if one proposes a static universe which is uncreated and therefore eternal, several other problems arise. Since gravity is only an attractive force, such a universe would not remain static unless another unknown force is postulated to balance that of gravity. This is what Einstein proposed in adding his "cosmological constant" to his equations for general relativity to avoid an expanding or contracting universe. Einstein was unwilling to have a universe with a beginning.[13] He would later see this as the greatest mistake of his career.

A second problem for a static universe involves the fact that individual stars have only a finite amount of hydrogen fuel and a substantial rate at which they use it up. Thus no star burns forever. Since stars are obviously still burning today, proponents of an eternal static universe must postulate some unknown mechanism to "recycle" fuel. Such a process would presumably use considerable energy itself or violate the law of entropy by which energy tends to disperse.

Eternal static universes of infinite size are also troubled by Olber's paradox. Named for a nineteeth-century astronomer, this paradox arises from the obvious fact that the sky is relatively dark at night. An eternal universe filled with stars should have a very bright sky. Why is that? In an infinite universe, with an infinite number of stars, we should be able to see the light from all of them. Our sky would be solid starlight!

A more technical explanation is that the apparent brightness of a light diminishes as the square of our distance from its source. If we divide up the universe into spherical shells of equal thickness centered on ourselves, each shell increases in volume as the square of the distance from us, exactly canceling the diminishing of the light. Therefore if each shell has the same density of stars, it will provide us with the same amount of light no matter how far away it is! For an infinite universe, the sky should be infinitely bright, or, allowing stars to block the light from stars behind them, as bright as the surface of an average star! Even residents of such bright-sky cities as New York can see that this is not the case.

The paradox can be avoided only if one of the following is true:

1. The universe is finite in size, so there is no light from shells beyond a certain distance.
2. The universe is finite in age, so that no light has yet reached us from shells beyond a certain distance.
3. The universe is expanding in such a way that stars beyond a certain distance are traveling away from us at speeds faster than that of light, so their light will never reach us.
4. The arrangement of stars in the universe is hierarchical, so that more distant shells have fewer stars in such a way that the sky appears relatively dark.

Only the last of these four alternatives allows an infinite, eternal static universe. This is such a peculiar case that few are willing to defend it, and it does not fit recent observations of distant objects in the universe.[14] It still fails to solve the problems of gravity and fuel that trouble all static cosmologies. Thus we conclude that a static universe, eternal or not, really doesn't fit the known scientific data.

A Young "Created-Light" Universe

Many young-earth creationists believe that our universe is very large (whether static or expanding) but very young, no more than about ten thousand years old. But most of the objects visible in our larger telescopes give every indication of being more than ten thousand light-years away, a distance still well inside our Milky Way galaxy. Consequently, many young-earth creationists claim the light from these distant objects never really was emitted from them, but was created on its way to us.[15]

Such a view is defended on the ground that God created objects with apparent age: that Adam looked full-grown only a moment after he was created; that newly-created trees had growth rings in them; that the wine Jesus created at Cana tasted like it had been grown on vines and aged. No doubt there is some merit to the idea that objects brought suddenly into existence will appear to have a fictitious age. However, not being present, we can only speculate on whether such an apparent age would be indistinguishable from actual age. Would newly-created trees really have growth rings? Would Adam have a navel, though he was never born? Would he have toughened or baby-soft skin? We don't know, though the Bible repeatedly says that God does not lie (e.g., Titus 1:2) and that the record of nature is trustworthy (e.g., Ps. 19:1–4).

But this view, when applied to cosmology, must take an additional and substantial step, from apparent age to fictitious history. How is that? When we look out into space with a telescope, we are actually looking back into the past since light takes time to travel. Looking at the sun, we see events that happened on its surface about eight minutes ago since we are about eight light-minutes away. When we observe the star Alpha Centauri (about four light-years away), we see what was happening there four years ago. Similarly for more distant stars; we see their radiation, flares, variation, rotation, position, etc.—i.e., the events occurring on them—at the time the light left them, whether ten, one hundred, or one thousand years ago.

But according to the theory of a young "created-light" universe, when we reach (say) a distance of ten thousand light-years, we suddenly shift from real history to fictitious history, though there is no evidence of any seam (say, some sort of flash or discontinuity) to indicate that anything unusual has happened. In this view the phenomena we see in the Andromeda galaxy, for example, represent merely the galactic rotation, stellar positions, stellar explosions, expanding gas clouds, etc., that would have happened if the galaxy had existed two million years ago. But these events didn't actually happen because none of these things existed. Such a view bristles with both scientific and theological problems far more severe than the suggestion that the Bible does not narrate a recent creation.

A less theologically troublesome way to have a large, young universe is to assume that the speed of light was very high or infinite at creation, so that light from the most distant parts of the universe reached the earth immediately or soon after creation. Thereafter the speed of light decreased to its present value. This proposal is entertained with some favor by Paul Steidl and advocated very strongly by Barry Setterfield.[16] Unless the speed of light dropped immediately after creation to its present value, however, it should appear to be higher as we look back into the past, that is, as we look at more distant objects.

But several important constants occurring in spectroscopy involve the speed of light, e.g., the fine-structure constant and the proton magneton, which relates to hyperfine structure.[17] If this proposal is correct, we should be able to test it by observing the fine and hyperfine structure in the spectra of stars and interstellar gas. This would be difficult at optical wavelengths because the detail gets lost in the motions of the gas. But at radio wavelengths the radiation itself is often due to transitions between fine or hyperfine energy levels. Thus the so-called twenty-one centimeter spectral line of hydrogen involves a hyperfine transition, yet it gives no evidence for a change in the speed of light as far out as we can detect it (several million light-years so far).[18]

Actually, Setterfield has based his theory on a predetermined result he is aiming for, an infinite speed of light at about 4000 B.C. He thus extends only about three hundred years of actual measurements to predict six thousand, and does this by making his curve rise sharply in a way not implied by the data. Even these last three hundred years of information on the speed of light include early work with primitive instruments, and most of the change Setterfield finds comes from the two earliest measurements (Roemer in 1675 and Bradley in 1728). Yet according to British physicist Alan Hayward,[19] Setterfield has misreported the results of Roemer and Bradley, which would give an increasing speed of light according to their figures as reported in the 1973 *Encyclopaedia Britannica*.

The idea that the speed of light has changed radically in the past few thousand years has little to recommend it.

The Isotropic Radio Background

Let us return to our discussion of cosmological data. The development of radio telescopes (powerful radio receivers with giant antennas) after World War II led to the discovery by Arno Penzias and Robert Wilson in 1965 of the isotropic radio background. Simply stated, they found that at radio wavelengths the sky is not black but gray, that radiation is coming to us uniformly from all directions. This radiation does not vary in strength daily or seasonally. Thus it does not originate in our solar system, galaxy, or even galaxy cluster, as we are located off-center in each of these and should therefore experience daily and seasonal variation.

The spectrum of this radiation has now been measured over a wide range of wavelengths, from just under a meter to well under a millimeter, more than five hundred times the range of our visible spectrum. Throughout this range, the spectrum conforms nicely to that of a so-called blackbody at a temperature of about three degrees above absolute zero (3°K). *Blackbody*, incidentally, is a technical term for an object that absorbs all radiation striking it and emits radiation in a spectrum that depends only on the object's temperature. This isotropic (equal from all directions) radio radiation is thus commonly known as the *three-degree blackbody radiation*.

The spectrum and isotropic nature of this radiation fit very nicely into the scheme of "big bang" cosmologies to be discussed later. In these views the radiation is seen as the remnant of radiation from the universe as a whole at a time shortly after the big bang, this radiation having subsequently cooled down due to the expansion of the universe. Physicist George Gamow predicted such radiation as a consequence of a big bang cosmology some twenty years before it was actually discovered.

Quasars

Early in the 1960s, radio-astronomer Maarten Schmidt and colleagues discovered a new class of astronomical objects which they called *quasi-stellar radio sources*, or *quasars* for short. The longer name tells us a bit about them: the objects look like stars through an optical telescope, and they probably would never have been noticed were it not for their unusual brightness at radio wavelengths.

It is the spectrum of quasars that reveals their significance for cosmology. Quasars have redshifts which are greater than those of the most distant known galaxies. If these redshifts are due to the expansion of the universe, and if the expansion rate is linear with distance, then the farthest known quasars are more than ten billion light-years away. Furthermore, if quasars are as far away as their redshifts indicate, then they are the most powerful objects in the sky, challenging our imagination to dream up energy sources for them. Present proposals to explain their energy include matter-annihilation, stellar collisions, and enormous black holes.

Of course, it is possible that quasars are not really so far away, but that their redshifts have another explanation. Astronomer Halton Arp has suggested that quasars are fragments blown off by exploding galaxies. So far, however, he has been unable to locate any blueshifted quasars to represent fragments blown toward us. This is a serious problem for his view. Moreover, a number of quasars show secondary, smaller redshifts in their spectra, suggesting that some of their light has been absorbed by gas clouds between us and them. Since these smaller redshifts are still quite large, it looks as though the quasars really are at the enormous distances that their redshifts indicate.

The Steady-State Universe

Shortly after the end of World War II, the English cosmologists Hermann Bondi, Thomas Gold, and Fred Hoyle proposed what has come to be known as the *steady-state cosmology*. Accepting the evidence (sketched above) for stars of finite lifetime and a universe which is expanding, they yet claimed that the universe had always existed. Instead of being static or changing with time, this model saw the universe in a dynamic "steady state" in which the density of matter was kept constant by the expedient of adding new matter as the old matter moves away. This new matter is continually being added by a kind of creation, not the supernatural act of God but the natural working of an impersonal force. The new matter also serves to fuel new stars which are continually forming. Thus the stars we now see are only a few billion years old. The debris from older, burnt-out stars does not clog up the cosmos because the universal expansion carries it away. Thus at any time in the past (no matter how far back), there have always been stars burning.

Bondi, Gold, and Hoyle claimed their cosmology was philosophically more satisfying than cosmologies with a beginning (such as the big bang cosmologies we will discuss below). Their theory not only satisfied the Cosmological Principle, that the universe (viewed on a sufficiently large scale) looks the same in all places and directions, it also satisfied the more rigorous Perfect Cosmological Principle, that the universe looks the same at all times.

The steady-state cosmology came to enjoy a considerable vogue for some years, in spite of the fact that it postulated the violation of nearly every conservation law in physics (though all on a scale too small to be observed locally). But in the middle-1960s new observations began to press it severely. The most important of these observations were: (1) the three-degree blackbody radiation described above, which was predicted by big bang cosmologies but a surprise for the steady-state theory; (2) the higher density of quasars at great distances (that is, far back in the past) rather than nearby (that is, recently), violating the Perfect Cosmological Principle; (3) the finite and similar ages of all galaxies at about fourteen billion years.

Since 1965 Hoyle has retreated to a modification of the steady-state theory which is beyond empirical test: we are in an expanding part of a universe that is steady-state on a scale so vast that we will never be able to observe it; some other parts of the universe are collapsing, so the average density remains constant.[20] With such untestable modifications, few cosmologists are enthusiastic about the steady-state theory today.

Varieties of the Big Bang Universe

Since the mid-sixties, big bang cosmologies have held the field as best fitting the available data. They have continued to look better still in recent years with the application of high-energy physics to events following the big bang.[21] Yet the big bang theory is actually a group of several alternative theories: (1) the oscillating cosmology, (2) the single-bounce (or full-cycle) big bang, and (3) the no-bounce (or half-cycle) big bang. All proponents of this theory agree that the universe is presently expanding from an event which occurred ten to twenty billion years ago—the big bang. At that time the universe began to expand from a state of extremely high density and temperature (perhaps both were infinite). Since then the universe has continued expanding and cooling. The quasars are some sort of object (possibly a particular type of galaxy) that existed early in the history of the expansion. The blackbody radiation arises even earlier than quasars, a remnant of the fireball at the time radiation and matter separated and the universe became relatively transparent.

The three varieties of the big bang cosmology differ on the nature of the big bang and what happened before it. The no-bounce big bang was proposed in the 1920s by George Lemaitre, a Belgian Roman Catholic astronomer, who apparently saw the big bang as the creation event. George Gamow later removed creation by suggesting that the big bang was really a "big bounce." His one-bounce big bang model proposed that the universe was initially a thin hydrogen gas from eternity past which gradually pulled itself together, finally bouncing at the big bang; it has been expanding ever since and will continue to do so forever. Gamow's theory was later modified into the oscillating big bang model, which sees the universe as alternately expanding and contracting, with a big bang every hundred billion years or so. This last form of the big bang theory was most popular until very recently, both among cosmologists and in the media, with Carl Sagan and Isaac Asimov active in promoting it. But in 1983 it was shown that the universe cannot bounce, and cosmologists have moved toward universes having some sort of beginning at the big bang. Let us examine each of these varieties in reverse order.

Problems with the Oscillating Cosmology

The oscillating cosmology sees the universe as alternately expanding and contracting forever. Its problems, naturally enough, involve: (1) making an expanding universe stop expanding and begin contracting, (2) making a contracting universe stop contracting and begin expanding, and (3) doing both forever. As Gamow's one-bounce big bang shares problem (2) with the oscillating cosmology, let us look at the other problems first.

Of course, forever is a long time indeed! If there is any process which causes our universe to lose energy at a non-zero rate, then an oscillating universe would have run out of energy (and so ceased to oscillate) long ago. This rules out any oscillating universe which has only a finite amount of matter embedded in an infinite space, as it will continually lose energy by radiation into the empty space. If we imagine that the radiation is trapped in our universe by having our whole three-dimensional space expanding and contracting inside a larger space of (say) four dimensions, we must also assume that no energy "leaks out" into this four-dimensional space either. This is a very unlikely assumption, as we have no examples of energy confined to a point, line, or surface which do not have leakage into their surroundings. We might suppose that our universe is infinite, so that there is nowhere the universe is not, and therefore nowhere for the radiation to escape. Could we have such a universe that existed and oscillated forever? Perhaps. But getting an infinite amount of matter which is spread over an infinite volume of space to coordinate its activities so as to expand and contract in unison seems to be a tall order for natural laws to accomplish. And if we postulate a Coordinator, we might as well have a Creator.

So much for problem (3). Problem (1) is easily solved theoretically; all the cosmos needs is a sufficient density of matter for its self-gravity eventually to overcome the expansion and turn it into a contraction. This is like throwing a ball up in the air and waiting until gravity pulls it back to earth. On earth, however, we have plenty of gravity but not much velocity for a hand-thrown ball. Naturally the ball soon stops rising and begins to fall. If, however, we increase the ball's velocity sufficiently by (say) shooting it upward in a rocket at more than seven miles per second, it won't come back. Alternatively, if we throw the ball up from the surface of a small enough planet (say, at seventy miles per hour from an asteroid less than twenty miles in diameter), the gravity won't be strong enough to stop a ball moving even that slowly.

What is the case for our universe? Is the matter density high enough relative to its expansion speed to stop the expansion eventually or not? At present the answer appears to be no. We have only been able to locate something like 10 percent of the density needed to stop the expansion, and the astronomers have already counted the mass from visible stars, the total mass around galaxies, and the invisible gas between galaxies. About the only candidates left to supply the missing mass are black holes between galaxies, brown dwarfs, dark matter that does not radiate, and the possibility that some of the elementary particles called neutrinos are not actually massless as previously thought. Even with this list of candidates, observational constraints for a universe dominated by cold, dark matter seem to rule out a universe that will one day collapse.

For the oscillating cosmology, then, problem (1) may be solvable, but it looks very bad at present. Problem (2) kills any possibility of an oscillating cosmology. Problem (3) looks insolvable without making very special and unlikely assumptions. As Jastrow suggests, the favor that the oscillating cosmology presently enjoys is probably more the result of a "religious" motivation—a desire to eliminate creation—than to any evidential merit of the theory itself.[22]

Problems with the One-Bounce Cosmology

Gamow's one-bounce cosmology postulates that the universe has always existed. From eternity past to some ten to twenty billion years ago it was rather dull: a mass of hydrogen gas gradually pulling itself together by means of its own gravity. At the big bang it bounced, and since then it has been expanding, forming galaxies, stars, planets, life, etc. All of this will one day die, though the universe will continue to expand forever as a collection of dark and lifeless cinders. This theory has not been nearly so popular as the oscillating model, though perhaps it is reflected in T. S. Eliot's poem about the world ending "not with a bang but a whimper."

The one-bounce theory avoids the oscillating cosmology's problem (3) with energy loss, as no eternally repeating cycle is required. It does have a problem of its own with eternity. It also avoids problem (1), as the one-bounce universe never stops expanding once it starts. It does share problem (2) with the oscillating cosmology, and we will examine this in a bit.

First, however, let us look at the one-bounce theory's problem with eternity. Gamow postulates that for an infinite period of time the universe is contracting towards the big bounce. This involves a contraction rate that is zero at eternity past and gradually increases in just such a way as to take an infinite time to accomplish a finite action. Mathematically, this is easily arranged by means of an asymptotic function. For instance, the function $f = 2^x$ gets closer and closer to zero as x becomes more and more negative, f approaching zero as x approaches minus infinity. Physically, however, it is questionable whether this could ever be arranged without a supernatural Arranger. The slightest non-uniformity in the mass distribution of the gas will produce local contraction at a substantial rate instead.

On to problem (2). Can a contracting universe "bounce" so as to begin expanding? More seriously, can a universe which must contract to such high temperatures and densities as characterize the big bang fireball subsequently bounce? The cosmological equations of Einstein and Friedmann[23] have a mathematical singularity at the hoped-for bounce point, indicating that the temperature and density would go to infinity. Is this over-idealized? Attempts to avoid this problem by introducing irregularity do not appear to work.[24] This agrees with our present knowledge of physical forces, where at very high densities the force of gravity (which only attracts but does not repel) overpowers the repelling tendencies in the nuclear and electromagnetic forces, pulling everything into a black hole from which there is no escape. Asimov would like to think that our whole universe is even now a black hole, but he has still not succeeded in explaining why its matter should bounce when highly compressed.[25]

Of course one can postulate some unknown force that saves the theory (just in the nick of time!) by introducing a repulsion sufficient to overcome gravity, and which comes into play only at densities or temperatures high enough to produce the big bang fireball. Jastrow, however, argues that even this is insufficient.[26] Such a repulsive force, he says, will have an equivalent potential energy E. This energy, by Einstein's mass-energy equivalence formula, $E = mc^2$, will behave like a mass m. This additional mass, added to the mass of the matter already present, will strengthen the gravitational force enough to overcome the repulsive force, so that the universe will still collapse into a black hole! Thus big bang cosmologies employing a bounce seem to be fatally flawed unless one postulates a (very special) repulsive force that does not obey Einstein's mass-energy equivalence principle.

Lemaitre's No-Bounce Cosmology

The original form of the big bang theory, suitably modified to take into account discoveries since Lemaitre's day, avoids the problems discussed above. By having creation of mass-energy at the big bang, the problems of contraction and bounce are avoided. The theory has enough flexibility to fit an ever-expanding universe or one which eventually contracts. Eternal activity is transferred "outside" the universe to God the Creator rather than remaining in the physical laws and causing the problems faced by the various non-supernatural cosmologies we have discussed.

As a matter of fact, recent experimental and theoretical work in the area of high energy particle physics has been used to reconstruct the events following the big bang, extrapolating back to well within one second of the event itself.[27] Some findings of this research point strongly to a Designer, as we suggest elsewhere in this book. The power of such extrapolation to explain the microstructure of our existing universe suggests that the universe really did experience such enormous densities and temperatures early in its history, and that it may have even started at a singularity of infinite density and temperature.

Several attempts have recently been made to finesse such an absolute beginning of the universe at a finite time in the past. French physicist Levy-Leblond wants to redefine time so as to put the big bang at an infinite time in the past.[28] Stephen Hawking wants to say that the universe popped into existence by itself (no help from God needed), but that time is not defined before the Big Bang, so we must not talk about what was before.[29] Others wish to use Heisenberg's Uncertainty Principle to claim that before the Planck time (10^{-43} seconds after the big bang) the universe was just a spongy conglomeration of space-time with no beginning. These all look like attempts to suppress the truth at the first opportunity when data fail, of refusing to extrapolate when consequences are unpleasant. The consistency and order of our universe appear to follow nicely from the big bang. Why try to explain away the big bang by claiming humans are limited from further direct investigation? The only reason must be because it seems to point to a Creator, as do the other evidences investigated in this book.

Conclusions

We have now completed our rather sketchy survey of the data and theories of modern cosmology. What can we say in conclusion?

1. It is fair to say that we know too little observationally and theoretically to be able to specify a single scientific model for the nature of the universe.
2. Yet the universe is certainly large. There is little reason to deny that some of its objects are more than a billion light-years away from us, even ten billion light-years if the quasar redshifts are cosmological.
3. The universe gives every appearance of being old but of finite age, probably in the range of ten to twenty billion years.[30] Alternative proposals—that the universe is eternal or only a few thousand years old—are controlled by other considerations than scientific data, and they interpret the data to fit.
4. The universe is most naturally understood as created. The no-bounce big bang theory of Lemaitre gives the best fit to the presently known data.

But shouldn't scientists prefer a natural and non-personal cause for the universe over a supernatural and personal one? Isn't the former the simpler hypothesis? Two remarks are in order here, the first concerning definitions of science, the second concerning simplest hypotheses. What is science? Is it a game to see if we can "explain" everything without recourse to the supernatural, or is it an attempt to find out how things really are? If it is the former, then of course we prefer a natural or non-personal cause; but science itself is then somewhat trivialized, as it may have nothing to do with what actually is. If science is an attempt to find out how things really are, then we should prefer the hypothesis that has the best evidence and ability to explain.

What does it mean to choose the simplest hypothesis? Surely, not to choose one so simple that it doesn't fit the data. And the data of cosmology cannot finally exclude the fact that the universe we actually inhabit contains life, and mankind, and the Bible. The evidence of extremely complex design found in living things[31] (especially in the mind of man) and the evidence of a moral sphere in man[32] argue that a power that is more like a mind than a force controls the universe. Though well outside the scope of this paper, there is quite adequate evidence to suggest that this mind is the God of the Bible.[33]

How do our conclusions square with the Bible? Like the cosmological evidence, the Bible pictures the universe as immeasurably large,[34] but apparently finite.[35] It describes the universe as the creation of the infinite, personal God of the Bible.[36] The major problem regards the age of the universe. The Bible has been traditionally understood to teach a rather recent creation, on the order of a few thousand years ago. This is the main reason for the current strength of the young-earth creationist movement in evangelical circles. Yet it is imperative that we realize the Bible itself nowhere explicitly indicates the earth is young, that the days of Genesis 1 are literal and consecutive, or that the genealogies of Genesis 5 and 11 should be added up to give a complete chronology. As I have sought to deal with these matters in my book *Genesis One and the Origin of the Earth*, I refer the reader there for a more detailed discussion. Though an earth and universe some billions of years old is certainly not taught explicitly in the Bible, I believe it is not in disagreement with a fair and reasonable interpretation of the Genesis account.

Notes

[1]Hannes Alfven, "Cosmology: Myth or Science?" in *Cosmology, History and Theology*, ed. Wolfgang Yougrau and Allen D. Breck (New York: Plenum, 1977), 12–13.

[2]Rom. 2:15–16; Rev. 20:11–15.

[3]Blaise Pascal, *Pensees* (1670), sec. 3, esp. par. 233. Pascal's works are most accessible in English in the Modern Library edition (New York: Random House, 1941) and in

Great Books of the Western World (Chicago: Encyclopaedia Britannica, 1952), vol. 33. An updating of the wager in terms of game theory is given in Robert C. Newman, "Pascal's Wager Re-examined," *Bulletin of the Evangelical Philosophical Society* 4 (1981): 61–67.

[4]Excepting luminous gas—which occurs in galaxies—and quasars, which may or may not be galaxies.

[5]A light-minute is the distance light travels in a minute, about eleven million miles. A more common unit for measuring distances in astronomy is the light-year, about six trillion miles.

[6]The explosive power of nuclear weapons is measured by the equivalent weight of the World War II explosive TNT needed to produce an equal explosion. A megaton is one million tons.

[7]Harold Camping, *What is the Size of the Universe?* (Oakland, Calif.: Family Radio, 1981).

[8]Parry Moon and Domina E. Spencer, "Binary Stars and the Velocity of Light," *Journal of the Optical Society of America* 43 (1953): 639.

[9]Harold Slusher, *Science and Scripture* (March/April 1971), 22; John C. Whitcomb, Jr. and Henry M. Morris, *The Genesis Flood* (Philadelphia, Pa.: Presbyterian and Reformed, 1961), 369–70; Robert E. Kofahl and Kelly L. Seagraves, *The Creation Explanation* (Wheaton, Ill.: Harold Shaw, 1975), 154.

[10]The circumference of a circle with radius five light-years is about thirty light-years.

[11]Jean-Pierre Vigier, "Cosmological Implications of Non-Velocity Redshifts—A Tired-Light Mechanism," in Yougrau and Breck, *Cosmology, History and Theology,* 141–57.

[12]Charles W. Misner, Kip S. Thorne, and John A. Wheeler, *Gravitation* (San Francisco: W. H. Freeman, 1973), 775.

[13]Robert Jastrow, *God and the Astronomers* (New York: Norton, 1978), 27–28.

[14]Robert C. Newman, "Hierarchical Cosmologies: A New Trend?" *Journal of the American Scientific Affiliation* 24 (1972): 4–8. Judging from the years since this article appeared, the answer to the title question is "no."

[15]Whitcomb and Morris, *Genesis Flood,* 369; Henry M. Morris, *The Genesis Record* (Grand Rapids, Mich.: Baker Book House, 1976), 65–66. The problems here are discussed in Kofahl and Seagraves, *Creation Explanation,* 154; and in Paul M. Steidl, *The Earth, the Stars and the Bible* (Phillipsburg, N.J.: Presbyterian and Reformed, 1979), 222–23.

[16]Steidl, *Earth, Stars and Bible,* 223–24; Trevor Norman and Barry Setterfield, *The Atomic Constants: Light and Time* (Menlo Park, Calif.: Stanford Research Institute International, 1987).

[17]Donald H. Menzel, *Fundamental Formulas of Physics* (New York: Dover, 1960), 1:149, 151; 2:454, 460, 545.

[18]See Fred Hoyle, *Astronomy and Cosmology* (San Francisco: Freeman, 1975), 586–87.

[19]Alan Hayward, *Creation and Evolution* (London: Triangle Books, 1985), 139–42.

[20]Fred Hoyle, *Galaxies, Nuclei and Quasars* (New York: Harper and Row, 1965).

[21]If one believes the popular press, some top scientists have begun to move away from the big bang. Actually, according to Hugh Ross (Ph.D., astronomy), the exact opposite is the case. For example, in *Facts & Faith* (vol. 4, no. 4 [winter 1990–91], 2), Ross states

that five astrophysicists recently got a lot of attention by their article in *Nature* (346 [1990], 807–12). What escaped the notice of many was that the arguments presented were simply a rehash of the same arguments they had used against the big bang in the 1960s. Ross goes on to state that these five (and perhaps none other than these five) hang on to the steady state theory. For more information write Reasons to Believe, P.O. Box 5978, Pasadena, CA 91117, and ask about their quarterly newsletter, *Facts & Faith*.

[22]Jastrow, *God and the Astronomers*, 27–28; 111–16.

[23]See Stephen Hawking, *A Brief History of Time* (New York: Bantam, 1988), chap. 3; G. Siegfried Kutter, *The Universe and Life* (Boston: Jones and Bartlett, 1987), 62–65.

[24]Robert H. Dicke, *Gravitation and the Universe* (Philadelphia, Pa.: American Philosophical Society, 1970), 66–67.

[25]Isaac Asimov, *A Choice of Catastrophes* (New York: Simon and Schuster, 1979), 68–69. Recent articles by Alan Guth and Marc Sher (*Nature* 302 [1983]: 505–7) and by Sidney Bludman (*Nature* 308 [1984]: 319–22) indicate that the universe has far too much entropy to bounce.

[26]Robert Jastrow, *Until the Sun Dies* (New York: Norton, 1977), 28–29.

[27]See, e.g., Steven Weinberg, *The First Three Minutes* (New York: Bantam, 1979); and John Boslough, *Stephen Hawking's Universe* (New York: William Morrow, 1985).

[28]Jean-Marc Levy-Leblond, "The Unbegun Big Bang," *Nature* 343 (2 November 1989): 23.

[29]Stephen Hawking, *Brief History of Time*, chap. 8.

[30]Some of the considerations for a detailed age are discussed in chapter 1 of Robert C. Newman and Herman J. Eckelmann, *Genesis One and the Origin of the Earth*, 2d ed. (Grand Rapids, Mich.: Baker Book House, 1981).

[31]E.g., *Encyclopaedia Britannica* (1970), s.v. "Life" by Carl Sagan. Sagan notes that the information content of the simplest living cell is equivalent to 100 million pages of that encyclopedia. See discussions in Michael Denton, *Evolution: A Theory in Crisis* (Bethesda, Md.: Adler and Adler, 1985); Charles B. Thaxton, Walter L. Bradley, and Roger L. Olson, *The Mystery of Life's Origin* (New York: Philosophical Library, 1984).

[32]On brain complexity, see the concessions by Sagan in Carl Sagan, *Dragons of Eden* (New York: Random House, 1977), 46, 212; on the moral sphere in man, see C. S. Lewis, *Mere Christianity* (New York: Macmillan, 1953), bk. 1.

[33]See, e.g., Josh McDowell, *Evidence That Demands a Verdict* (Arrowhead Springs, Calif.: Campus Crusade, 1972); Peter W. Stoner and Robert C. Newman, *Science Speaks*, 4th ed. (Chicago: Moody, 1976); John Urquhart, *The Wonders of Prophecy* (Harrisburg, Pa.: Christian Publications, 1925); John Warwick Montgomery, ed., *Christianity for the Tough-Minded* (Minneapolis, Minn.: Bethany, 1973).

[34]Jer. 31:37; 33:22; Ps. 8:3–4.

[35]Ps. 147:4.

[36]Gen. 1:1 and elsewhere.

2.4

Cosmogony, Genesis 1, and the Origin of the Earth

Robert C. Newman

To MANY MODERNS, one of the main stumbling blocks to accepting the Bible as God's word is the apparent conflict they see between the findings of modern science and the account of creation narrated in the first two chapters of Genesis. Science is seen as postulating a universe which has always existed, or at least one which is billions of years old. By contrast, they see the Bible as picturing a universe which is created and only a few thousand years old. Science is viewed as describing a universe which developed slowly, with life and its diversity arising and evolving by natural processes. The Bible, however, is seen as describing the origin of the universe and all its life in the space of one literal week, less than two hundred hours.

Reactions to this problem have been varied. Some people have dismissed the Bible as merely the guesswork (mythology) of ancient man and moved on to atheism, agnosticism, or some other religion.[1] Others, feeling that there is more to Christianity or Judaism than ancient guesses, have claimed that God used the mistaken ideas of antiquity as a vehicle by which to transmit His messages to mankind.[2] Still others have denied that the Genesis account is even trying to tell us anything about science, that it is answering only religious questions about origins.[3]

None of these solutions seems adequate in view of the evidence sketched elsewhere in this book. That the universe has an origin; that it is designed; that the origin of man is not explicable by natural processes; that the Bible is more than the work of ancient men; that the Author of the Bible is the controller of history; that Jesus is the promised Messiah and that His resurrection is a historical fact—all these point to the existence of the God of the Bible and that the Bible does not just give religious truths but cosmological and historical ones as well.

But if the God described in the Bible exists, then it is a mistake to reject what He has to say about origins—whether one dismisses what God says in the Bible (as do those mentioned above) or what He says in His world (as young-earth creationists often do). In this paper, we suggest that a fair treatment of both the biblical data and the scientific data concerning origins results in harmony, though each source provides information that the other does not. There are, in fact, some striking correlations between the two. As one trained in astrophysics and biblical studies, I will basically confine my discussion to the origin and early history of the earth, concentrating on planetary physics and geophysics and leaving biology to others.

The Age of the Earth

In the area of origins the major point of dispute among evangelical Christians today is probably the age of the earth. Is our planet only a few thousand years old, as most people think the Bible teaches? Or is it some billions of years old, as most people think science teaches?

In handling the data relevant to this problem, young-earth creationists tend to construct their models on origins from the Bible alone, and then interpret scientific data within this framework. Theistic evolutionists tend to construct their models from science alone, and then interpret the biblical data within this framework. As an old-earth creationist, I suggest we should construct our models using both sets of data taken together. Occam's razor—the principle that phenomena should be explained using the minimum number of features possible—should not be applied to choose the simplest model when science or Scripture alone has been used as the data source.

My reason for this suggestion involves a distinction made in Scripture between two kinds of revelation, traditionally called *special revelation* and *general revelation*. Special revelation is God's disclosure to mankind of Himself, His world, His plans for mankind, etc., by means of direct (or supernatural) information, usually in verbal form. This information was conveyed to His prophets and subsequently written down in the Bible.[4] General revelation is God's disclosure to mankind of Himself, His world, and the nature of mankind itself by means of indirect (i.e., providential or nonsupernatural), nonverbal information. This information is conveyed to all mankind, both externally through the universe and internally through human conscience.[5] Questions regarding origins involve information from both general and special revelation. Therefore both should be used together in constructing accurate models of what happened.

How are both of these to be used to produce such models? I believe they should be harmonized (both coming as they do from the same God), in a way similar to that which we use in harmonizing different biblical accounts of the same event. An example of such harmonization within special revelation may help. I count myself among those who accept the Bible as an accurate, inerrant revelation from the God who cannot lie. Therefore, when I see apparently divergent accounts in the Bible of what seems to be the same incident, I proceed as follows. First of all I consider whether the accounts do indeed record the same event. If after investigation I am satisfied that the accounts refer to the same incident, I then interpret the accounts in such a way as to harmonize with one another, yet trying not to ignore or twist what either account says.

For instance, accounts of Jesus casting out demons into a herd of swine are recorded in Matthew 8, Mark 5, and Luke 8. In each Gospel this incident occurs after Jesus stills a storm. All record that it took place east of the Sea of Galilee; that the demon-possessed lived in tombs; that the demons recognized Jesus as Son of God; that they sought permission to enter the swine; that the swine all drowned; that the herdsmen fled to the city; and that the people begged Jesus to leave the area. It is therefore most likely that the same incident is in view.

This being so, I attempt to harmonize the apparent discrepancies regarding the number of demoniacs (two in Matthew, one in Mark and Luke) and the location of the event (Gadara, Gerasa). In this particular case, I suggest that there were actually two demoniacs, but that one was either less seriously possessed than the other or took less part in the dialogue. Mark and Luke, in constructing a condensed account, eliminated reference to him. The location I take to be on the east shore of the Sea, slightly north of the middle, at a geographically suitable site known today as Kursi. The name *Gerasa* is probably intended to represent this place rather than the distant Decapolis city of that name forty miles southeast. The reference to Gadara, about ten miles away, may indicate that Kursi was in the territory controlled by Gadara. More likely, this was the nearest town Mark and Luke thought their Gentile readers would be familiar with.

In this chapter we will not consider the scientific evidence for an old earth and a long period of creative activity. A number of helpful works treating this subject have been written by evangelical Christians.[6] I agree that science gives every indication that we live in a universe some ten to twenty billion years old on a planet some four to five billion years old. Instead I intend to cover the biblical evidence regarding the age of the earth.

Does the Bible really teach that the earth is only a few thousand years old and only a few days older than mankind? This is the prima facie view, but it overlooks biblical evidence that points in another direction.

First of all, there are hints in Scripture that the period from Jesus' ascension to His second coming is very short on a time scale that takes all of history into account. For instance, the book of Revelation speaks of His return as "soon."[7] Peter,[8] Paul,[9] and Jude[10] consider themselves to be already in the "last days" or "last time." John even says we are in "the last hour,"[11] though it has now been nearly two thousand years since he penned these words. Suppose the figure of speech John is using is an analogy. Then if he is viewing human history as a day, we are carried back far beyond Ussher's 4004 B.C. to something like 20,000 B.C. If we view his reference to the "last hour" as part of a year, we increase this period to hundreds of thousands of years. On such time scales, the second coming of Christ will indeed be soon, even should it not occur for several thousand years more.

Something of the same sort appears in several references to God's view of time. He sees a thousand years as a day[12] or even as a watch in the night.[13] Suppose we ask, Against the background of what larger unit of time are we to view these figures? Some suggest they are to be viewed against a week (so one traditional view, with human history lasting only seven thousand years). But the timespan most prominent in Psalm 90 is not the creation week (though creation is mentioned) but the human lifespan since the fall, never more than a thousand years, and by Moses' time reduced to seventy or eighty years. In this context, we could say that God's "lifespan" since the fall is seventy or eighty years of thousand-year days, i.e., twenty or thirty million years. If instead a watch in the night corresponds to a thousand years (three per night, or six in twenty-four hours), this increases the span by a factor of six, to about one hundred million years. If we take God's "lifespan" as that of the primeval patriarchs (about a thousand years), then the time back to creation would scale up to half a billion to several billion years, depending on whether the unit representing a thousand of our years is a day or a watch.

Something similar results from Psalm 102:25–27, where the decay of heaven and earth is compared to the wearing out of God's garment.[14] The point here is not that we can calculate the time of creation from these figures. Rather, they warn us not to be so sure that the Bible requires a young earth. And they hint that the biblical teaching is compatible with an old earth.

There are other such hints. The last plague of Revelation is a great earthquake. "No earthquake like it has ever occurred since man has been on earth, so tremendous was the quake."[15] Why does the writer use the qualification "since man has been on earth" instead of "since the earth was created" or no qualification at all? May it not be because there have been worse earthquakes earlier in earth's history, before man came on the scene?

Did the events of creation occupy only one week as we humans measure time? This is the traditional view of the matter, but here again, the text provides hints which point in a different direction.

The most obvious of these hints involves the enormous activity that must have taken place on the sixth day of creation according to the traditional scheme. This scheme assigns all activities mentioned between the references to day five and day six to the latter of these. Thus the events of day six are described in Genesis 1:24–31.

According to the traditional scheme, Genesis 1 teaches that the land animals and mankind (male and female) were created on the sixth day. In the more detailed description of creation in Genesis 2, we see that the events of this day would involve the following: (1) God creates the land animals; (2) God creates man; (3) God puts man in a garden which He has grown for him, with instructions to take care of it; (4) God brings before man all the birds and land animals in order for Adam to name them; (5) Adam names them all, finding no helper suitable for himself; (6) God puts Adam to sleep; (7) God makes Eve from Adam's side; (8) Adam awakes, sees Eve, and says, "At last! This is bone of my bones and flesh of my flesh!"

Now many of these things were done by God and therefore might occupy Him for as much or little time as He pleased. Even so, the use of the term "caused to grow"[16] suggests some longer period of time than a day for God's activity. But Adam, being neither all-powerful nor all-knowing, needed considerable time to name the animals, particularly since names were not arbitrary in ancient biblical culture but told something about the one named. Thus Adam would not rattle off a series of nonsense syllables; he would observe each kind of animal to choose an appropriate descriptive name. It is hardly likely that there were so few kinds of animals created that Adam could study and name them in just one day.

In addition, we get the impression, both from God's statement that it is not good for man to live alone, and from Adam's "at last!" (the literal force of the Hebrew word happá'am in 2:23), that Adam had lived a sufficient time to become lonely before the creation of Eve.[17] All this indicates that the events of Genesis 1:24–31 took longer than one day. If so, either the days of creation are longer than regular earthdays, or the days are separated by long periods of time.[18] This latter alternative is my own personal preference.

In addition to all this, the Bible intimates that the seventh day either has not yet occurred or is still in progress, neither of which is consistent with the data that the days of creation were earthdays immediately following one another. In the letter to the Hebrews, chapters 3 and 4, we are told that at the time of David and in the first century A.D. (and presumably, still today) it was possible to enter into God's rest, which is identified[19] as the seventh-day rest of Genesis 2:2. Apparently the seventh day is either still going on or hasn't yet started.[20]

Thus the Bible provides numerous hints that the creation account is not to be read simply as narrating a recent event occurring some few thousand years ago which lasted no more than a week of our time. Instead, using the same procedures of harmonization between general revelation and special revelation that evangelicals commonly use within special revelation, we obtain an old-earth view in which God intervened at various points to prepare our earth, the whole activity covering a span of time consistent with the generally accepted findings of modern science. In fact, a stronger correlation between Genesis and science is obtained by this procedure than by the interpretations of either young-earth creationists or theistic evolutionists.

A Scientific Model for the Origin of the Earth

Before we begin to look at Genesis 1 as it may be understood if the earth is very old, let us first consider the standard scientific model for the origin of the earth that has been developed in recent years. Basically, science today views the origin of planets as a natural byproduct of the formation of a star as it condenses from a cloud of interstellar gas and dust. This model was first proposed by Immanuel Kant and Pierre Laplace almost two centuries ago. Suitably modified to take account of advances in both observation and theory, this model is advocated by most investigators today.[21]

We shall discuss in some detail the particular view of Thomas Gold and Fred Hoyle[22] (suitably updated), as it seems to fit the whole range of data better than its competitors. The principal difference between this model and other star-formation models is the part played by magnetic fields in solving the angular momentum problem.

Gravity has the longest range among known forces. Its strength decreases inversely with the square of the distance between the masses involved. Unlike the electromagnetic force, gravity cannot be neutralized; it is produced by a quantity called *mass* which is only positive. By contrast, electric charges are either positive or negative and may cancel each other out. Thus gravity is the dominant force in the behavior of astronomical objects of substantial size.

Even if one supposes that negative masses are lurking somewhere in the depths of space, the electric and gravitational forces are still not analogous, for like charges repel whereas like masses attract. Systems of objects dominated by the force of gravity are thus unstable and tend to contract, whereas systems dominated by electric forces tend to form stable solids.

As we look out into the space between stars, we find no strict vacuum there even though we cannot produce a better vacuum on earth. Instead space is filled with thin clouds of gas and dust, some so diffuse as to be invisible, others thick enough to scatter or even completely absorb light from stars lying behind them.

No matter how low the density of such a gas cloud, if it is cool and massive enough, the mutual attraction of its gas particles will overcome its outward gas pressure and the cloud will begin to contract. The higher the average density of the cloud, the less mass it need have to collapse. External forces, such as magnetic fields or shock waves, may also aid in starting such a collapse.[23]

According to the big bang cosmology, which at present seems best to fit observations, the universe itself began with matter and energy expanding from a state of high temperature and density. As soon as the general expansion cooled the universe to a sufficiently low temperature, self-gravitation overcame the expansion locally. This would occur first only for very large volumes, so that large-scale clouds would be formed. But as these became denser due to their own contraction, each large cloud would split into smaller ones. These, after further contraction, would in turn split into even smaller clouds.[24] In this way, apparently, the observed hierarchical structure of the universe was formed—stars occur in clusters, clusters in galaxies, and galaxies themselves are grouped in galaxy-clusters and superclusters.

Turning now to the relatively small cloud which would eventually contract to form our sun and its planets, let us consider the forces which are at work in the cloud. First and strongest is the inwardly directed gravitational force which produces the contraction. The strength of this force depends on the distribution of gas and dust within the cloud.

Resisting this gravitational contraction is the gas pressure, which depends on the temperature and density of the gas at each point in the cloud. As the cloud contracts, both temperature and density rise due to compression. The cloud loses energy by radiation, however, so that the temperature does not rise fast enough to stop the contraction. Only the sudden onset of nuclear fusion, when the cloud reaches about ten million degrees at its center, provides a heat source powerful enough to stop the contraction and thereby produce a star.[25]

Returning to earlier stages of the contraction, let us consider in more detail what is happening. The gas cloud or protosun would initially have been thin enough to be transparent. A hypothetical observer inside the cloud would be able to see out of it without difficulty. Any stars in existence at that time (the sun appears to be at least a second-generation star)[26] would be visible. As the contraction proceeds, however, the gas and dust would eventually become dense enough to block light from outside, so that the cloud becomes dark within.

Other processes are going on as the cloud contracts. Collisions between gas atoms or molecules tend to cancel out all but two of the large-scale motions: (1) the linear movement of the cloud through space, and (2) its rotation. Of these two, the latter will be more significant for the further development of the cloud unless it collides with another cloud or a star.

The continued contraction of the cloud tends to amplify the cloud's rotation in much the same way that a figure skater increases her spin rate by drawing in her arms. Both cases demonstrate the conservation of angular momentum. But this rotation introduces a third force in addition to gravitation and gas pressure, namely the centrifugal force, which is directed outward and is strongest at the "equator" of the cloud's rotation. As a result, the cloud collapses more slowly near its equator than near its poles, and its shape becomes flatter. If this effect were not eventually hindered by magnetic effects, the cloud would become pancake-shaped.

The collapse of a gas cloud to form a star involves an enormous contraction. The cloud is typically on the order of a light-year (several trillion miles) across when it breaks away from the surrounding clouds, but the final star is only about a million miles across, a contraction by a factor of a million or so. If the angular momentum normally present in the original cloud were concentrated in the final star it would split apart. Therefore, few stars could form without shedding some of their angular momentum.

Some clouds split into pieces due to high angular momentum and go on to form multiple star systems. In such cases, the formation of planets is less likely because multiple stars allow for few stable planetary orbits. Our sun, however, is a single star, so it must have shed its angular momentum by some other process, as we shall see below.

Meanwhile the temperature of the contracting gas cloud rises as potential energy is converted into heat as well as radiation.[27] As the cloud gets hotter, the wavelength of this radiation becomes shorter until eventually the cloud begins to glow visibly. At this point, our hypothetical observer inside the cloud would see everything around him glowing. It appears that this transition from darkness to light would occur in a matter of months, very quickly on the astronomical time-scale.

The glowing of our gas cloud also signals the beginning of substantial ionization. At temperatures of several thousand degrees, the collision of atoms in the cloud becomes sufficiently violent to rip off electrons, changing the gas into an ionized plasma, sometimes considered a fourth state of matter distinct from solid, liquid, or gas.[28]

The appearance of ionization introduces a fourth force, electromagnetism, to complicate the interaction of the previous three. Up to this point, the struggle between gravity and gas pressure would have produced a roughly spherical cloud. The presence of rotation, however, gradually flattened the cloud into an oblate spheroid (less technically, the shape of an M&M candy, non-peanut type). Now, however, this spheroid becomes a plasma filled with a tangle of magnetic fields, produced by the movement of the positively charged ions and negatively charged electrons. These fields, which behave somewhat like rubber bands, resist stretching. With the plasma densities and linear dimensions involved here, the magnetic fields are said to be "frozen in," so that plasma and fields move in concert.[29]

Now the inner part of the cloud, being more dense than the outer part, is rotating more rapidly than the outside. Any magnetic fields connecting inside and outside will thus tend to get stretched. Resisting this stretching, the magnetic fields will speed up the rotation of the outer part. As a result, the inner region gives up some of its angular momentum and centrifugal force to the outer part and begins to collapse more rapidly and resume a more spherical shape. The outer region receives the additional centrifugal force and becomes more flattened.

In fact, the combination of gas pressure and increased centrifugal force near the cloud's equator now conspire to overcome the inward pull of gravity. As a result, the flattened outer region now begins to move outward in the equatorial plane of the cloud, so that the whole cloud begins to look something like Saturn with its rings. In this way, angular momentum is transferred from the central mass of the cloud, which will eventually form our sun, to a flat disk of ionized gas and dust rotating in the same direction as the cloud, which will later form the planets.

As this outward-moving ring of material gets away from the glowing central gas cloud, it begins to cool off and become de-ionized. The small fraction of heavier, less volatile elements and compounds in the ring becomes un-ionized relatively close to the cloud, whereas the lighter, more volatile materials do not regain their electrical neutrality until they have moved farther out. When the material is no longer ionized, it unhooks from the magnetic field, ceases to move outward, and takes up circular orbits around the protosun. The gas cloud/protosun continues to collapse, perhaps repeating several times the process of throwing off angular momentum by means of a ring of material. Such rings and the protosun will have slightly different planes of rotation due to small differences in the detailed distribution of mass, momentum, and magnetic field in the collapsing cloud.

Finally, the cloud has collapsed sufficiently for the temperature at its center to start a nuclear reaction. This reaction converts hydrogen to helium, producing sufficient heat to raise the gas pressure enough to balance gravity and stop the cloud's collapse. The cloud thus becomes a star, and is now stable against gravitational collapse so long as it has hydrogen fuel to keep the reaction going.

Meanwhile, back in the equatorial rings, the less volatile materials have condensed into small solid particles with various liquids and gases adsorbed on their surfaces. Because this material lies in a rather thin disk, it conglomerates fairly quickly into planet-sized objects, perhaps in as little as ten thousand years.[30] Contrary to earlier views, in which each planet was thought to have been a large individual gas cloud which cooled to a molten ball and then solidified, it now appears that each planet was formed cold, from the collision of solid dust particles.[31]

Near the end of this process, there would be a number of rather violent collisions, as the larger competitors in each orbital area fought it out for final control. The presence of massive Jupiter seems to have interfered with the formation of a planet in the present asteroid belt. And it probably captured considerable material which would otherwise have gone to form Mars. These collisions would also be responsible for the disorder observed in the small-scale motions of the solar system, such as the rotation of planets on their axes. Asteroid-sized objects colliding with nearly full-sized planets could easily produce planetary rotations tilted from the plane of the solar system as a whole.[32]

Focusing now on the newly-formed earth, we would find a lifeless sphere of conglomerated nonvolatile compounds, with hydrates, liquids, and gases loosely attached. There would be no oceans nor any atmosphere to speak of. The interior, though rather warm due to the high pressure of overlying materials, would probably not be nearly as hot as it is at present.[33]

But radioactive elements with short half-lives would soon begin to heat the interior. Since the earth is a rather good insulator, the internal temperature would rise, melting some of the materials, breaking down some of the compounds, and driving off the hydrates and absorbed liquids and gases. Lighter materials such as water and various gases would seek the surface, whereas the heavier materials such as iron and nickel would flow downward to form the core. Gradually the earth would develop the various interior layers it has today.[34]

As the water and gases reached the surface, an atmosphere and an ocean would be formed. If the gases spewed out by volcanoes today[35] and the atmospheres of Venus and Mars provide reliable clues,[36] then the early terrestrial atmosphere would have had little or no free oxygen. Instead, its oxygen would have been locked up in carbon dioxide, and the atmosphere would have been much more effective in trapping heat from the sun. This trapping, the so-called greenhouse effect, would have made the surface temperature higher, vaporized more water, and produced a heavier cloud cover than we have today. But pictures of the earth taken from space show that only a moderate increase in our present cloud cover would be necessary to make it complete; in that case, it would be impossible to see any astronomical objects, even though a large amount of diffuse sunlight might reach the surface.

Sometime later in the earth's history, the atmosphere was oxygenated. Apparently early plant life on earth replaced most of the carbon dioxide with oxygen.[37] This would have decreased the greenhouse effect, lowered the temperature, precipitated much of the water vapor, and cleared the atmosphere.

Our oceans presently contain enough water to cover the earth's surface to a depth of two miles, were it not for the fact that the land is not flat. The earth has enough heights and depths to confine this water to deep basins covering two-thirds of the earth's surface. But today's large relief (variations in altitude) is apparently the result of continental drift or (more accurately) the movement of crustal plates. This plate movement is responsible for the formation of mountains and the opening of the ocean basins.[38] Since most areas of the earth contain marine fossils and all the earliest fossils are marine life, this suggests the surface relief of the earth was once small enough for a single ocean to cover the entire planet.

Volcanic action such as we see forming islands in the Atlantic and Pacific (but on a larger scale) would eventually have formed large islands, called continental shields. Continued erosion and metamorphosis of these islands would have separated heavier, more soluble simatic material (dominated by silicon and magnesium) from the lighter, less soluble sialic materials (dominated by silicon and aluminum), so that the latter would be left to form the bulk of the continents we observe today.[39]

Genesis 1 on Earth's Origin

Having surveyed briefly the standard scientific model for the origin of the earth, we now turn to look at the biblical data. Our basic source of information is the first two chapters of Genesis. For our more restricted concern with the non-biological aspects, the first nineteen verses of Genesis 1 are primary. We will here sketch these verses in order, noting something of what the Hebrew text says, what range of interpretation this allows, and how it fits with the scientific model sketched above.

Genesis 1:1

In the beginning God created the heavens and the earth.

Some have seen this as merely a summary of the creation account to follow, but such a view leaves Genesis without any account of the origin of the earth, the existence of which is assumed in verse two. Others have translated verse 1: "In the beginning when God created the heavens and the earth, the earth was without form." This is grammatically possible, but invokes an unusual Hebrew construction and disagrees with the ancient translation of the Bible into Greek.[40] It seems more natural to the context to understand Genesis 1:1 as the first event in the creation sequence. God first created the heavens and the earth, and then continued in verse 2 and following to form and fill them.

What is meant here by *heavens* and *earth?* The former word is used in three senses in the Bible: (1) the unseen abode of God, (2) the place where the stars are (outer space), and (3) the place where the birds fly (the air or atmosphere).[41] Here in Genesis 1:1, the word is apparently used in senses (2) or (3), or more broadly, like our word *sky,* to cover both.

The word *earth* in Hebrew is also used several ways: (1) the whole world (planet Earth), (2) the dry land, and (3) a country or region.[42] The first sense is probably meant here, as the seas have not yet been mentioned, and the account is more universal in scope than befits a single country.

I suggest that Genesis 1:1 refers to the creation of the material which is to make up heaven and earth, whether the whole universe or just the planet is in view. The following verses then describe God's activity in forming this material into various finished products. In these verses the planet Earth, rather than the whole cosmos, receives nearly all the attention.

Because Hebrew is generally agreed to be less abstract or more concrete than ancient Greek or modern English,[43] I suggest the rest of our passage narrates the creation by describing what it would look like to a human observer had one been present, just as the author of a narrative often describes what the reader would have seen if present at the event. In several places below, the observer appears to be earthbound, even before the earth exists as a solid planet. We will develop this idea as we proceed.

Genesis 1:2

And the earth was formless and void, and darkness was over the surface of the deep; and the Spirit of God was moving over the surface of the waters.

Both *tohu* (formless) and *bohu* (void) occur only rarely in the Bible; their meanings are thus somewhat difficult to pin down. The standard dictionaries give for *tohu:* "formlessness, confusion, unreality, emptiness"[44] and "wasteland, nothingness, nonentity."[45] For *bohu,* they give "emptiness"[46] and "void, waste."[47]

Many interpreters view the earth as already a solid planet at this point in the account, so they translate *tohu* and *bohu* as "waste" and "empty," meaning that its surface is not yet habitable. On the other hand, the ancient

Jews who translated Genesis into Greek some two centuries before the time of Christ rendered these two words by *aoratos* (invisible) and *akataskeuastos* (unprepared, unfurnished).[48] In agreement with this ancient translation and most modern translations, we suggest that the earth at this point in the narrative is not yet a solid body but is shapeless and empty, perhaps even invisible. This is an excellent non-technical description of the gas cloud which eventually forms the earth in the standard scientific model.

The second clause of Genesis 1:2 suggests the earth is in darkness. Whether this has been true from creation to this point (the usual interpretation) or whether the earth became dark subsequent to its creation is not stated. We suggest the latter—that the earth, a shapeless, empty cloud, becomes dark as contraction raises its density enough to block starlight.

The words *tehom* (deep) and *mayim* (waters) in the third clause naturally suggest the sea, though both have broader uses. The former is also used of depths of the earth.[49] The ancient Septuagint translation of Genesis into Greek uses *abyssos* here, meaning "abyss, bottomless, unfathomable." A good fit with the scientific model proposed above may be had if this is understood as a description of the gas cloud, which has now contracted to a dark, unfathomable mass. Likewise *mayim,* though nearly always translated "waters," is also used for other fluids[50] and for the frozen and vapor states of water.[51] Scientifically, we now know that water is found in extraterrestrial gas clouds such as that which formed the earth.[52]

Genesis 1:3–4

Then God said, "Let there be light"; and there was light. And God saw that the light was good; and God separated the light from the darkness.

Now after darkness comes light. This is certainly in agreement with the standard scientific model. The contracting gas cloud, having first become dark within, now heats up to the point where it begins to glow.

But this is a strange sort of light, for we are explicitly told that God by an additional act separates it from the darkness. Taking these clauses to be ordered chronological developments rather than further descriptions of a static state, our hypothetical observer first sees darkness everywhere, then light everywhere, then some of both after they are separated. But if our observer is riding along with the material which will later become the earth, this is just what he would see in the scientific model! Inside the cloud during its dark state, he sees only darkness. Then the cloud begins to glow, and he sees only light all around him. Finally, he is pushed outside the cloud along with the equatorial disk that will form the earth, and he then sees both light and darkness at once.

Genesis 1:5

And God called the light day, and the darkness He called night. And there was evening and there was morning, one day.

Here the words *day* and *night* occur for the first time. In Hebrew, as in English, *darkness* and *night* are not synonymous, nor are *light* and *day*. Rather "night" is a particular subclass of "darkness," which we now know occurs when our side of the planet Earth is facing away from the sun. "Day" is an analogous subclass of "light" for our side facing toward the sun. Notice it is just at this point in our scientific model, when the planet Earth condenses out of the equatorial disk of dust, that it is proper to identify light with day and darkness with night. We suggest, then, that it is here in the Genesis account that the planet Earth becomes a solid body and not before.

The second sentence of Genesis 1:5, with similar passages throughout the account, has traditionally been taken to teach that the events of creation took place in six consecutive twenty-four-hour days. Others have pointed out that *day* can sometimes mean a much longer period of time.[53] I suggest that the "days" of Genesis 1 are twenty-four-hour days; that they are sequential but not consecutive; and that the creative activity occurs largely between days rather than on them. Each Genesis day introduces a new creative period and was selected out of the eons of time actually taken by God's creative activity in order for mankind to commemorate creation in the seven-day week.[54]

Genesis 1:6–8

Then God said, "Let there be an expanse in the midst of the waters, and let it separate the waters from the waters." And God made the expanse, and separated the waters which were below the expanse from the waters which were above the expanse; and it was so. And God called the expanse heaven. And there was evening and there was morning, a second day.

The word *raqiah,* here translated *expanse (firmament* in the King James Version), means something spread out. It is most commonly used for the object created here in the Genesis account. All scholars associate it with the sky, but some see it as a huge dome, others as the atmosphere.

For several reasons it appears to be the atmosphere. (1) Nothing is said of any space between the firmament and the lower waters, nor of the firmament moving to separate the waters. Thus the firmament seems to fill the space between upper and lower waters, as the atmosphere does and a domed sky does not. (2) The birds are said (literal Hebrew) to "fly *upon* the face" of the firmament.[55] The preposition *'al* used here means "upon, above," not "below," suggesting the birds are flying upon the air, not beneath a dome. (3) The Hebrews were well aware that the air supported water in the form of clouds, and the phrase "waters which were above the expanse" is actually broad enough in Hebrew to describe clouds floating in the sky.[56]

Given this understanding of the expanse or firmament, Genesis is here describing the formation of the atmosphere, after the earth has become a solid body. The presence of water is indicated in the text, so the sea is already present or is formed at the same time as the atmosphere. Job here fills in a gap not narrated in Genesis—the formation of the seas—in a poetic use of birth imagery:

> Or who enclosed the sea with doors,
> When, bursting forth, it went out from the womb;
> When I made a cloud its garment,
> And thick darkness its swaddling band.[57]

The context of Job 38 connects this event with confining the seas to their designated locations, which is also the subject of Genesis 1:9–10, immediately following. Thus the sea is in existence no later than Genesis 1:8, but not earlier than its "mother" the solid earth, according to Job. That Job calls the clouds the garment with which God wrapped His "baby," the ocean, suggests that the atmosphere was present when the sea was formed. To reconcile Genesis and Job, we suggest that the sea "burst forth from its womb" at the same time that the "firmament was dividing water from water." Likewise in our scientific model, the sea and atmosphere were formed simultaneously by outgassing from the earth's interior, exactly the same picture!

Genesis 1:9–10

Then God said, "Let the waters below the heavens be gathered into one place, and let the dry land appear"; and it was so. And God called the dry land earth, and the gathering of the waters He called seas: and God saw that it was good.

According to Genesis, the earth was once totally covered by water, after which dry land appeared. As pointed out in our discussion of the scientific model, this seems to fit the evidence from geology: (1) there is enough water to cover the earth to a depth of two miles if the dry land were perfectly smooth, and (2) neither of the two types of crust presently covering the earth would alone provide enough relief for dry land to exist, but the action of plate movement has opened the ocean basins and built up mountains. This plate movement will not begin until the earth's interior heats up enough for the outgassing mentioned in Genesis 1:6–8.

Genesis 1:11–13

Then God said, "Let the earth sprout vegetation, plants yielding seed, and fruit trees bearing fruit after their kind, with their seed in them, on the earth"; and it was so. And the earth brought forth vegetation, plants yielding seed after their kind; and God saw that it was good. And there was evening and there was morning, a third day.

With the appearance of dry land, the Genesis account first mentions life, namely land vegetation. This need not mean there was no life before this time, but only that our hypothetical observer would not begin to see life of a size and type for which there were words in ancient Hebrew.

Following the scheme previously suggested for the Genesis 1 days— twenty-four-hour days which introduce new creative periods—we need not suppose that the fruit trees of this passage were created before any kind of animal life whatever. Rather, we assume that the creative period involving land vegetation began before the creative periods of sea, air, and land animals of sorts big enough to be noticed by an average human observer. In any case, since vegetation is mentioned only once in the entire creation account, it is possible that all vegetation is lumped together for economy of expression, or to indicate its significance as part of the foundation on which animal and human life is built. A recent evolutionary educational film follows this same pattern,[58] though it can hardly be urged that evolutionists believe all vegetation developed before the animals. Occasionally biblical historical narratives will shift from strict chronology to a topical approach, later shifting back. Some scholars see this in the Gospel of Matthew, for instance.

Genesis 1:14–19

Then God said, "Let there be lights in the expanse of the heavens to separate the day from the night, and let them be for signs, and for seasons, and for days and years; and let them be for lights in the expanse of the heavens to give light on the earth"; and it was so. And God made the two great lights, the greater light to govern the day, and the lesser light to govern the night; He made the stars also. And God placed them in the expanse of the heavens to give light on the earth, and to govern the day and the night, and to separate the light from the darkness; and God saw that it was good. And there was evening and there was morning, a fourth day.

The traditional interpretation of this passage assumes that the sun, moon, and stars did not exist until this point in the narrative, in obvious contradiction with the present scientific consensus. This view is still maintained by young-earth creationists. However, in view of our modern knowledge that the day-night sequence is a result of sunlight and the earth's rotation, it seems gratuitous to suppose that God here creates the sun to replace some other unspecified source of light previously created in Genesis 1:3, all without any statement to this effect. Since the Genesis account has already mentioned atmospheric water, and since Job 38:9 speaks of clouds and "thick darkness" covering the seas, it seems more reasonable to suppose that Genesis 1:14–19 describes the first appearance of the sun, moon, and stars to our hypothetical observer on the occasion of the breakup of the earth's cloud cover. This loss of cloud cover would be the result of plant life oxygenating the atmosphere.

If this is the proper understanding of Genesis 1:14–19, then the sequence of the Genesis account is striking indeed. The author has delayed mentioning one important aspect of the physical environment—the final clearing and preparation of the atmosphere in its present breathable form—until after he has mentioned the plants. From a literary point of view, this event appears to be out of order, as the rest of the Genesis account would lead us to expect that the preparation of the physical environment would be concluded before the creation of life begins. Instead the creation of the plants is narrated before the appearance of the heavenly bodies. Yet according to our scientific model, vegetation was the immediate cause of both the oxygenation of atmosphere and the removal of its heavy cloud cover!

Conclusions

We have now provided a brief survey of scientific materials regarding the origin of the earth and the contents of Genesis 1. We suggest a detailed correlation exists between them on the basis of a few simple interpretive assumptions. We tabulate this correlation in table 2.4.

Is this just a coincidence? The result of clever manipulation of the biblical text? Or does this indicate that the Creator is also the author of Genesis 1? It is interesting that this correlation is more detailed than that argued by liberal theologians for the similarities between the Babylonian creation account and Genesis 1, on the basis of which many scholars have concluded that the writer of Genesis used the Babylonian account.[59] Heidel gives such a table of correlations, though he does not believe that Genesis used the Babylonian account. His list includes only seven items, several of which he admits are questionable; ours includes twelve. The fact is, there is a better correlation between Genesis and modern science than between Genesis and ancient pagan creation accounts. If you dismiss the Genesis account as merely the guesswork of ancient men, you are on less solid ground than if you accept it as an ancient communication from God, telling us in simple language how He actually did it.

Biblical Material	Scientific Theory
1. In the beginning God created the heavens and the earth	1. A beginning; big bang?
2. Earth is without form, void	2. Earth is amorphous, tenuous nebula
3. Darkness is on the face of the deep	3. After some contraction, cloud becomes dark within
4. Spirit of God moves on the face of the waters	4. (Providential oversight with occasional intervention)
5. "Let there be light"	5. Further contraction causes cloud to glow
6. Light is divided from darkness	6. Planetary material thrust outside glowing cloud
7. Light equals day, darkness equals night	7. Planet condenses from planetesimals; sun, rotation give day/night sequence
8. Waters burst forth from the womb of the earth (Job 38); the firmament appears	8. Earth is heated within by pressure and radioactivity, driving out water and gases to produce atmosphere and oceans
9. Waters are divided above and below the firmament	9. Presence of atmosphere allows both surface and atmospheric water
10. Waters are gathered; dry land appears	10. Continental material develops from sub-oceanic by vulcanism and erosion
11. Earth brings forth vegetation	11. Land vegetation appears
12. Lights appear in the sky to mark off days and seasons; sun dominates day; moon dominates night	12. Photosynthesis by vegetation replaces carbon dioxide with oxygen, clearing atmosphere so sun, moon, stars visible; also prepares atmosphere for animals, man

Table 2.4

Notes

[1]Isaac Asimov, *Asimov's Guide to the Bible: The Old Testament* (New York: Avon, 1971).

[2]M. Conrad Hyers, *The Meaning of Creation* (Atlanta: John Knox, 1984).

[3]Howard J. Van Till, *The Fourth Day* (Grand Rapids, Mich.: Eerdmans, 1986).

[4]See, e.g., Deut. 18:14–22; Ps. 19:7–11; 119; 2 Tim. 3:14–17.

[5]See, e.g., Ps. 19:1–6; Rom. 1:18–2:16. The biblical wisdom literature (Job, Proverbs, Ecclesiastes) seems to deal heavily with general revelation in the form of human observations and inferences regarding nature and humanity.

[6]Daniel E. Wonderly, *God's Time-Records in Ancient Sediments* (Flint, Mich.: Crystal Press, 1977); idem, *Neglect of Geologic Data: Sedimentary Strata Compared with Young-Earth Creationist Writings* (Hatfield, Pa.: Interdisciplinary Biblical Research Institute, 1987); see also Robert C. Newman and Herman J. Eckelmann, *Genesis One and the Origin of the Earth* (Hatfield, Pa.: Interdisciplinary Biblical Research Institute, 1989); Davis A. Young, *Christianity and the Age of the Earth* (Grand Rapids, Mich.: Zondervan, 1982); and Alan Hayward, *Creation and Evolution: The Facts and the Fallacies* (London: SPCK, 1985).

[7]Rev. 1:1; 3:11; 22:7, 12, 20.

[8]Acts 2:17.

[9]2 Tim. 3:1.

[10]Jude 18.

[11]1 John 2:18.

[12]Ps. 90:4; 2 Pet. 3:8.

[13]Ps. 90:4.

[14]Note that the Bible does not consider the heavens a permanent, changeless realm, though this idea came into medieval Christian theology from Greek thought.

[15]Rev. 16:18. This quotation is from the New International Version of the Bible, copyright 1978 by the New York International Bible Society.

[16]Gen. 2:9. This and all subsequent Scripture quotations in this chapter, unless otherwise noted, are from the New American Standard Bible, copyright 1971 by the Lockman Foundation.

[17]For a more detailed treatment of this argument, see R. John Snow, "How Long is the Sixth Day?" appendix 3 in Newman and Eckelmann, *Genesis One,* 125–35.

[18]Christians have debated a great deal about the length of the Genesis days and whether or not there are gaps in the genealogies of Genesis 5 and 11. For long or intermittent days, see Newman and Eckelmann, *Genesis One.* For the possibility of large gaps, see William Henry Green, "Primeval Chronology," *Bibliotheca Sacra* 47 (1890): 283–303, reprinted in Newman and Eckelmann, *Genesis One,* app. 2. For short days and short (or no) gaps, see John C. Whitcomb, Jr., *The Early Earth* (Grand Rapids, Mich.: Baker Book House, 1972); and Henry M. Morris, *The Genesis Record* (Grand Rapids, Mich.: Baker Book House, 1976). A number of points relevant to the early chapters of Genesis are argued by various proponents in Ronald Youngblood, ed., *The Genesis Debate: Persistent Questions About Creation and the Flood* (Nashville, Tenn.: Thomas Nelson, 1986). A large number of works on these subjects are described in Tom McIver, *Anti-Evolution: An Annotated Bibliography* (Jefferson, N.C.: McFarland, 1988). Dallas E. Cain has supplied a chart of views of Genesis 1 in "Let There Be Light: Spectrum of Creation Theories," *Eternity* 33, no. 5 (1982): 20–21.

[19]Heb. 4:4.

[20]Further developed in Newman and Eckelmann, *Genesis One,* 65–66, 85.

[21]E. V. P. Smith and K. Jacobs, *Introductory Astronomy and Astrophysics* (Philadelphia, Pa.: Saunders, 1973), 108–9; William K. Hartmann, *Moons and Planets: An Introduction to Planetary Science* (Belmont, Calif.: Wadsworth, 1973), chap. 4–6; G. Siegfried Kutter, *The Universe and Life* (Boston: Jones and Bartlett, 1987), chap. 3 and 5; Joseph F. Baugher, *The Space-Age Solar System* (New York: Wiley, 1988), chap. 20.

[22]Fred Hoyle, *Frontiers of Astronomy* (New York: Mentor, 1957), chap. 6; idem, *Astronomy* (New York: Crescent Books, 1962), 269–73.

[23]See Bart J. Bok, "The Birth of Stars," in *New Frontiers in Astronomy,* ed. Owen Gingerich (San Francisco: Freeman, 1975), 127–40.

[24]J. A. Wood, *Meteorites and the Origin of Planets* (New York: McGraw-Hill, 1968), 88–90.

[25]George Abell, *Exploration of the Universe* (New York: Holt, Rinehart and Winston, 1964), 558; F. W. Cole, *Fundamental Astronomy* (New York: Wiley, 1974), 332; Robert Jastrow and M. H. Thompson, *Astronomy: Fundamentals and Frontiers* (New York: Wiley, 1972), 171–72.

[26]Abell, *Exploration of the Universe,* 586–87; L. Motz and A. Duveen, *Essentials of Astronomy* (Belmont, Calif.: Wadsworth, 1966), 406.

[27]Abell, *Exploration of the Universe,* 556-57. A more technical discussion is given by M. Harwit, *Astrophysical Concepts* (New York: Wiley, 1973), 95–97.

[28]See, e.g., Konrad B. Krauskopf and Arthur Beiser, *Fundamentals of Physical Science,* 6th ed. (New York: McGraw-Hill, 1971), 129–30.

[29]T. G. Cowling, *Magnetophydrodynamics* (New York: Interscience, 1957), 6–8.

[30]R. A. Lyttelton, "On the Formation of Planets from a Solar Nebula," *Monthly Notices of the Royal Astronomical* 158 (1972): 463, 473, 482.

[31]Wood, *Meteorites,* 109; Jastrow and Thompson, *Astronomy,* 340–41.

[32]Berlage (H. P. Berlage, *Origin of the Solar System* [Oxford: Pergamon, 1968], sec. 56–74) has a number of interesting suggestions in this area; see also Hartmann, *Moons and Planets,* 119–20.

[33]Jastrow and Thompson, *Astronomy,* 365–66; Hartmann, *Moons and Planets,* 256–62.

[34]Jastrow and Thompson, *Astronomy,* 366–67; Hartmann, *Moons and Planets,* 217–21.

[35]Hartmann, *Moons and Planets,* 336.

[36]Von R. Eshleman, "The Atmospheres of Mars and Venus," in *Frontiers of Astronomy,* ed. Owen Gingerich (San Francisco: Freeman, 1970), 48–58.

[37]Ibid., 48, 58; Hartmann, *Moons and Planets,* 336.

[38]Continental drift is discussed in any recent geology text, e.g., Richard F. Flint and Brian J. Skinner, *Physical Geology* (New York: Wiley, 1977), chap. 18. For more detailed discussions, see P. J. Wylie, *The Dynamic Earth* (New York: Wiley, 1971); or A. Hallam, *A Revolution in Earth Sciences* (Oxford: Clarendon, 1973).

[39]Hartmann, *Moons and Planets,* 275, 279; Flint and Skinner, *Physical Geology,* 360–66.

[40]For a more detailed response to this alternative, see Edward J. Young, *Studies in Genesis One* (Philadelphia, Pa.: Presbyterian and Reformed, 1964).

[41]Robert C. Newman, "The Biblical Teaching on the Firmament" (S.T.M. thesis, Biblical Theological Seminary, 1972); Francis Brown, S. R. Driver, and Charles A. Briggs, *A*

Hebrew and English Lexicon of the Old Testament (Oxford: Clarendon, 1907), 1029–30; R. Laird Harris, Gleason L. Archer, Jr., and Bruce K. Waltke, *Theological Wordbook of the Old Testament* (Chicago: Moody Press, 1980), 935–36.

[42]Brown, Driver, and Briggs, *Hebrew and English Lexicon*, 75–76.

[43]*Zondervan Pictorial Encyclopedia of the Bible* (Grand Rapids, Mich: Zondervan, 1975), s.v. "Hebrew Language" by Gleason L. Archer; *International Standard Bible Encyclopedia* (1939), s.v. "Language of the Old Testament" by T. H. Weir.

[44]Brown, Driver, and Briggs, *Hebrew and English Lexicon*, 1062.

[45]William L. Holladay, *A Concise Hebrew and Aramaic Lexicon of the Old Testament* (Grand Rapids, Mich.: Eerdmans, 1971), 386.

[46]Brown, Driver, and Briggs, *Hebrew and English Lexicon*, 96.

[47]Holladay, *Hebrew and Aramaic Lexicon*, 34.

[48]Alfred Rahlfs, ed., *Septuaginta*, 7th ed. (Stuttgart: Wuerttembergische Bibelanstalt, 1962), ad loc.

[49]Gen. 49:25; Deut. 33:13; Ps. 71:20; Ezek. 31:4.

[50]2 Kings 18:27.

[51]2 Sam. 22:5; Job 26:8; 36:27–28; 37:10; 38:30; Jer. 51:16.

[52]Bok, "Birth of Stars," 130.

[53]Ps. 90:4; 2 Pet. 3:8.

[54]This is discussed in further detail in Newman and Eckelmann, *Genesis One,* 64–66, 83–88. See also Hayward, *Creation and Evolution,* chap. 10; Dallas E. Cain, "Creation and Captron's Explanatory Interpretation (ca. 1902): A Literature Search," *IBRI Research Report* 27 (1986).

[55]Gen. 1:20.

[56]For a more detailed treatment, see Newman, "Biblical Teaching."

[57]Job 38:8–9.

[58]*Evolution and the Origin of Life* (Del Mar, Calif: CRM Educational Films, 1973).

[59]Alexander Heidel, *The Babylonian Genesis,* 2d ed. (Chicago: Phoenix, 1963), 129. Heidel's correlation follows:

Genesis	Babylonian
1. Divine spirit creates cosmic matter and exists independently of it	1. Divine spirit and cosmic matter are coexistent and coeternal
2. The earth a desolate waste, with darkness covering the deep	2. Primeval chaos; goddess Tiâmat enveloped in darkness
3. The creation of the firmament	3. The creation of the firmament
4. The creation of dry land	4. The creation of dry land
5. The creation of the luminaries	5. The creation of the luminaries
6. The creation of man	6. The creation of man
7. God rests and sanctifies the seventh day	7. The gods rest and celebrate

Part 3

Revelatory
Biology

3.1

What Is Life and Why Ask the Question?
A Biologist's Perspective

William J. Cairney

As an opener in my undergraduate honors biology class, I present the students with a practical problem. I ask them to envision themselves fifteen to twenty years down the road. They have completed doctoral level work in some area of the biological sciences, and they are establishing themselves as achievers in their biological careers. They are approached by NASA representatives and asked to direct this nation's next set of efforts to detect the presence of life in near space. As they are mentally trying on this role for size, I ask them a series of related questions. "How would you recognize 'life' if you bumped into it?" "How would you know it was 'life'?" "What would 'life' look like and what would it be doing?"

This gets us immediately into a discussion of the characteristics of systems we generally agree are "living" and usually provokes a very stimulating discussion of "What is life?" We go to the opening pages of our undergraduate biology texts and find that the authors cover essentially the same ground, regardless of what text we examine. A "living thing" is generally described as a "system" in some sort of "dynamic equilibrium" with its environment. This brings up the question of what happens in this "dynamic equilibrium." We then begin to list the features we observe in living things as we know them. Some of the characteristics we agree on are:

1. Metabolism—the use of an energy source to perform some kind of work with the release of a waste product or by-product. In life as we know it, this would include activities such as digestion, absorption, respiration, excretion, synthesis of materials, etc.
2. Growth—the amount of material that is made a part of the system is greater than the amount of material which is eliminated and results in an increase in the mass of the system. (Note: Some non-living systems exhibit this characteristic. For instance, crystals "grow.")
3. Reproduction—ability to produce another of its own kind. (Crystals can also "reproduce.")
4. Irritability—ability to respond to stimuli or to environmental change.

If the class agrees with this concept of life, I put up an overhead slide, and, for a while, allow them to look at it without comment.

"Congratulations class, you have just described . . . a *bus!*"

While they are smirking and wondering how anyone could mistake a bus for a living system, I describe a "college classroom" of beings from another solar system. The "professor" is asking the question: "Class, if you were in charge of an effort to detect 'life' in a nearby solar system, how would you recognize it if you bumped into it?" Time passes and an enterprising young space creature designs an unmanned probe which intercepts Earth and sends back data. The probe records and returns the following:

Have identified yellow oblong forms that exhibit characteristics of living systems according to following criteria:

Metabolism—oblong forms use chemical energy known as "petroleum" to produce internal chemical changes, movement, H_2O, CO_2, and hydrocarbon waste products.

Growth—traced origin of oblong forms to place known as "Detroit" . . . observed assembly of parts . . . amount of material incorporated into system is greater than amount eliminated.

Reproduction—many associated organisms known as "humans" (which also seem to be dynamic systems) facilitate increases in number of oblong forms. [Note: We all view humans as "living." Humans also have what might be viewed as "associated organisms," spermatozoa and eggs, which facilitate an increase in numbers of humans. Are spermatozoa "living things"? In our requirements for life we haven't demanded a certain *mechanism* of reproduction. We have just required the *phenomenon* of reproduction.]

Irritability—oblong forms respond to stimuli and changes in environment . . . when liquid H_2O hits big square eyes of creatures, two thin appendages wipe it away . . . when environment becomes very cold, oblong forms generate their own internal heat . . . when associated organisms (same organisms involved in reproduction) position themselves at certain places and wave two of their four appendages, oblong forms stop and ingest these organisms, carry them to remote locations, and egest them unaltered (suggests some sort of symbiosis) . . . during planet's night hours, oblong forms emit light from anterior surfaces.

At this point you think "the analogy is ridiculous." Not so! As extraterrestrials we are approaching something—a bus—that we've never seen before. We have no preconceived notions about buses, and, according to our criteria, the phenomena we observe *could* indicate "life."

I also realize this is very subjective . . . but I ask you as a reader to be brutally honest at this point. Don't all of you have experience with automobiles that display *personality?* I have had two dramatic examples of such creatures. Our family had a two-door Toyota coupe for many years. It had a personality much like a bright but aging medium-size dog. It was very faithful, required periodic feeding plus a little praise now and again. It was somewhat reluctant to go out in cold weather, although it ran very well in warm weather with a clear sense of well-being. We also had a Dodge mini-motorhome. Its personality approximated that of a thoroughbred Clydesdale horse, very elegant-looking, but ponderous and not very graceful. It enjoyed showing people how powerful it was, but it was not overly intelligent. Even the most objective scientist among you will fully relate to what I have just described.

The whole point of enjoying ourselves with this imaginative mental meandering is that our concept of life is based not only on criteria we may erect, but also on pre-conceived notions. Our concept of life is also based upon familiar and recognizable patterns, and we tend to insist on these as we imagine what life should be outside of our direct experience.

Suppose I project a stick figure on a screen and allow my students to observe it for a minute. I then turn off the projector light and remove the acetate sheet from the machine. I wait another minute to allow everyone to savor the experience. ("Now what?" they think!)

I then place a clean acetate sheet on the projector and turn on the light. I ask someone to come forward and with a few strokes of a marker to reconstruct the stick figure. Within a couple of seconds, it emerges.

Question: When I turned off the projector and the figure was no longer visible, did it cease to exist? No, even if I had destroyed my original acetate sheet, the pattern existed as an organized pattern of neuronal responses within the primary visual cortex of each individual viewing the screen. Neurophysiologist David Hubel is actively investigating these complicated pathways and is mapping an "intricate edifice of orderly columns" of cells in the brain responding to visual patterns. The mind integrates all of the data, and the person redraws the figure at will.[1]

Let's go a step further. On television this very evening, you watch *The Tonight Show* starring Johnny Carson. In his Burbank studio Carson sits there in the flesh. The audience can observe and admire this complex molecular pattern known as "Johnny." This pattern is picked up by a videocamera in the room and carried by rearranged electrons to a transmitter which loads it on a carrier wave. Modulations of this carrier wave carry this same complex pattern out from the studio. The encoded wave is picked up thousands of miles away by a receiver which decodes it and displays it on a screen where a certain distribution of light, dark, and color faithfully shows the features of "Johnny." The pattern is recognizable to us only in the studio and on the screen. But was the pattern not just as detailed within the videocamera as on the light that was reflected off Carson? Was the pattern not just as detailed, just as real within the transmitter? Was the pattern not just as complex on the carrier wave and within the receiver? Could we, standing and watching, detect it within the sending and receiving sets or in wave form? No, but just because we couldn't detect it, did that mean that it didn't exist or didn't represent a patterned extension of something living yet not immediately seeable by us? If, in our attempt to detect life outside of our world or in defiance of the limits of our preconceived notions, could there be wave patterns or molecular patterns that represent life and extensions of life and evidences of life that we miss totally, just because our technology can't decode them?

One of the best summaries of this nebulous area of what really constitutes and heralds life was stated by microbiologist Philip L. Carpenter: "The definition of life is essentially a philosophic matter that cannot be settled by argument, although discussion serves the useful purpose of focusing attention on the complexity of the problem."[2]

Cornell astronomer Carl Sagan reflects similar thoughts in his writings on the search for extraterrestrial life. "I cannot tell you what an extraterrestrial being would be like. I am terribly limited by the fact that I know only one kind of life, life on Earth."[3]

We as humans spend considerable time evaluating the possibility of evolution of life . . . *as we know it.* When we send probes to distant planets, we have set up those probes to detect life *as we know it,* feeling that life *as we know it,* would at least be recognizable to us if we bumped into it.

Are there other worlds that contain life, *as we know it?* The outlook for the solar system looks pretty bleak. What about life on other solar systems? We can make predictions if we like, but what hard evidence is there? None really. Not yet.

What about life in other forms? We look out there, and we say, "Well, I can't imagine what those forms would look like or consist of." And that's honest. We are *locked in* to our notions of what life *must* be like and that all expressions of it or evidences of it must be molecular. That creates the further impression in us that what we're seeing out there is a big expanse of universe where we don't detect other creatures and beings. We are tempted to admit frustration that we could *ever* detect them, and we even conclude that "other forms" don't exist.

Humankind, over the centuries, has often concluded the same thing about the God of the Bible. Can't see Him . . . hmmm . . . can't detect Him with our current technological capabilities . . . hmmm . . . must not be there. If He existed, He must be composed of *something* . . . and the only thing we detect out there is vast space with dynamic islands of matter . . . but no God, no angels, no devils . . . hmmm . . . must not exist. Remember the Russian cosmonauts who returned from space and said, "No, no God up there! We looked for Him. No evidence." And, having been among the handful of humanity to have gone there, they are certainly experts on space. And heaven! Where could that be? "Far beyond the starry sky," as the familiar fundamentalist hymn says. It must be at least that far away, because we can't see anything out there that fits the description. What a long trip it would be to get there! How many billions of light years for the journey? Incredible! We'd spend eternity just getting to it.

But, let's interrupt this line of conjecture for now and develop yet another idea.

Mathematicians (and many others) for over one hundred years have read and enjoyed a book published in 1884. In that year, Dr. Edwin A. Abbott published his second and revised edition of a book bearing the title, *Flatland: A Romance of Many Dimensions*. Anyone who has taken even a high school course in plane geometry will enjoy the thrust of this imaginative little volume.

Dr. Abbott pictures intelligent beings whose whole experience is confined to a plane, or . . . space of two dimensions, who have no faculties by which they can become conscious of anything outside that space and no means of moving off the surface on which they live.[4]

Please place *yourself* in that situation. You are living very much like a character in a comic strip on a two-dimensional page, and you are confined to it. To the two-dimensional comic strip character, the only detectable things are the things on that page (plane). Comic strip artists capitalize on this concept routinely by having a living three-dimensional person appear to jump into a comic strip, whereupon that person is then noticeable to that comic character and can interact with him. Dr. Abbott asks his readers, who have the consciousness of the third dimension, to imagine

a sphere descending upon the plane of Flatland and passing through it. How will the inhabitants regard this phenomenon? They will not see the approaching sphere and will have no conception of its solidity. They will only be conscious of the circle in which it cuts their plane. This circle, at first a point, will gradually increase in diameter, driving the inhabitants of Flatland outwards from its circumference, and this will go on until half the sphere has passed through the plane, when the circle will gradually contract to a point and then vanish, leaving the Flatlanders in undisturbed possession of their country. . . . Their experience will be that of a circular obstacle gradually expanding or growing, and then contracting, and they will attribute to *growth in time* what the external observer in three dimensions assigns to motion in the third dimension.[5]

It is fun to take other three-dimensional shapes and allow them to impinge on Flatland. How about a cylinder? When the cylinder has approached Flatland to the point that it is one millimeter away, what do the Flatlanders perceive? Nothing! Suppose the cylinder impinges end-on. What do they perceive? They see the sudden appearance of a circle in their plane. Suppose it impinges on its side. They would then see the appearance of a line with a rectangle increasing in width growing from it. As the cylinder continued to pass through Flatland, the width of the rectangle would narrow to a line and would disappear. In any case, are the Flatlanders ever capable of perceiving the true nature of the cylinder? No. They can only describe it as their sensory abilities, their experiences, and their limitations will allow. When the cylinder is lifted out of Flatland, does it cease to exist? Not at all. All we can say is that that particular *pattern,* that *shape,* no longer impinges on Flatland, even though it may be only one millimeter away and even though an observer sitting on the rim of our cylinder could be fully aware of things going on in Flatland.

In his "Introduction" to *Flatland,* scholar William Garnett, for the purpose of encouraging *Flatland* readers to think of implications, postulates the existence of a *fourth* spatial dimension. He says,

Transfer this analogy to a movement of the fourth dimension through three-dimensional space. Assume the past and future of the universe to be all depicted in four-dimensional space and visible to any being who has consciousness of the fourth dimension. If there is motion of a three-dimensional space relative to the fourth dimension, all changes we experience and assign to the flow of time will be due simply to this movement, the whole of the future as well as the past always existing in the fourth dimension.[6]

Here we are getting into some of the most fundamental mysteries of science, the concepts of space and time (or should I say the single concept of space-time). On the basis of this imagery, let us deal with a few loaded questions and their implications, that is, if we can shed our comfortable three-dimensional thinking for a moment and admit the *possibility* of such a fourth spatial dimension:

Is "life" just matter? Or is it a *pattern superimposed upon matter* as Carson's pattern is superimposed upon the carrier wave? If a particular life form is a pattern superimposed upon matter in our three-dimensional space, what happens to a person when he dies? Does he cease to exist? Or do we merely witness the dissolution of a three-dimensional "pattern" in our three-dimensional space? And suppose that pattern were to be removed from our three-dimensional world. Would that person (pattern) need to be billions of miles away to be in "heaven" . . . or just one millimeter?

Does the Christian Bible say anything which leads the reader to the notion that there may be a fourth spatial dimension? And, a related question, since we are dealing with definitions of "life" and possibilities for life elsewhere: does the Bible say anything about the existence of actual life forms which are non-recognizable or non-detectable by so-called "ordinary" senses? A few suggestions:

(1) In the New Testament, the Bible specifically states that the God of the Hebrews and the Christians (who claims to stand above our three-dimensional space-time) has created what He calls "principalities and powers" composed of beings (i.e., life forms) who possess intelligence and whose forms are not directly detectable by our ordinary senses. These beings apparently are able to impinge in some way on the lives and experiences of humankind.[7] This would probably be very hard for them to do if they lived at the far edges of our three-dimensional universe, billions of light years away.

(2) There is a story that Jesus tells about a certain rich man and Lazarus, a beggar. As the account goes, both men died, and both are immediately pictured as fully aware in an existence just "removed" from the one they had left. The rich man believed (rightly or wrongly) that Lazarus could interact with persons in the life that the rich man had just left. He said, "Abraham, could you please send Lazarus to my brothers in 'Flatland' and tell them they need to be aware of this place."[8]

(3) A dialogue is recorded between a dying Christ and a criminal being executed on a cross to Christ's right. Jesus says, "You will be with me in paradise this very day." The plain meaning was that *without extensive travel time,* the two would be with one another in a condition other than dead.[9] Their "patterns" would persist and be as functional and interactive as they had been in their three-dimensional arena.

(4) There are several New Testament references to Jesus being able to appear instantly, at will, and in person, following His resurrection.[10]

(5) In one of his letters to the Corinthian Christians, Paul describes the experiences of a man (perhaps Paul himself) caught up into what Paul describes as the "third heaven." The man returns to "Flatland" and is totally unable to communicate his experience there in any meaningful sense.[11]

(6) In another letter to Corinth, Paul looks forward to an inexpressible quality of life when he inhabits the place where God dwells and is no longer confined to "Flatland." He also indicates that God has revealed a glimpse of this to us.[12]

(7) The writer of the letter to the Hebrews spends an entire chapter discussing the dynamics of Christian faith and examples of biblical characters who exemplified it.[13] In the very next chapter, he begins with a thought construction that could be strictly viewed as a figure of speech, but which is at least "very interesting" in the light of our analogies. "Wherefore, seeing *we also* are *compassed about* with so great a cloud of *witnesses* . . . let us [run the race of life in like manner]."[14] It is an interesting figure of speech, isn't it?

In a few words, what does all of this have to do with the existence of the God of the Bible and the recorded accounts of how He works and His alleged interactions with humans? It has everything to do with it! Again, if we acknowledge at least the *possibility* of such a being standing above our definitions of life and our concepts of space and time, we (as inhabitants of three-dimensional space) would have the experience of a man observing and experiencing a chemical reaction from *inside* the reaction vessel. He observes that certain things happen in certain ways and with a certain degree of predictability. This allows him to predict, on the basis of observation and the knowledge of process, what the nature of the reactants might have been twenty, thirty, or sixty minutes ago, at least before he was able to watch it directly. He might also postulate what might be the purpose of the person outside the test tube who is conducting the experiment. Based on data he observes and data reported to him by the Experimenter, he might even have some feel for the big picture, although not have exhaustive knowledge of *all* that the Experimenter might have in mind. The one thing that is obvious to our observer-in-the-tube is that *the Experimenter can change the reaction whenever He wishes,* to slow it, accelerate it, stop it, restart it, or alter it in any way He wishes to accomplish His purpose. The Experimenter seems to enjoy the fact that we (the observers) are fascinated by the reaction and want to know more about it. So He feeds us information, which further increases our fascination and answers *some* of our questions. The information also heightens the mystery so that we want to know more as we become increasingly fascinated with the Experimenter Himself and His interaction and with the dialogue He is maintaining with us.

The world of science and mathematics does not totally confine its activity to investigation and description of our three-dimensional world. Some of the most fascinating seminars and presentations I have ever attended have been ones given by mainstream scientists at mainstream universities on mathematics (especially geometries) that describe our space. In some of these, the presenters have gone beyond the geometry of "our space" to discuss the features of space-time of fourth and higher dimensions and have concluded that while we apparently cannot direct energy into those dimensions, their existence is fully plausible. It is also interesting that in question-and-answer sessions following these talks, presenters and listeners alike engage in the most imaginative interchanges in this vein until someone raises the implication that these ideas provide the undergirding, the veritable grass roots, for the existence of the theological plane. At that point either discussion ceases or those theological dimensions are summarily dismissed.

But what if the God of the Bible is "up there"? Suppose He desires to communicate to observers in the vessel. What if He had actually written His words in a book to us in "Flatland"? What might we expect to find? Prescience perhaps? It appears in the Christian Bible in phenomenal detail and with incredible accuracy. History written in advance, perhaps? It is there in the Christian Bible in such detail as to rule out even remarkably good guessing.

Well then, does humankind have a responsibility or is responsibility optional? Given the nature of the message and its stated scope ("to every creature"), it does not appear optional.

In a recent book, famous British author and speaker Major Ian Thomas describes the experiences of Moses as he travels the desert on a humdrum day and encounters the burning bush. Here is a phenomenon that defies explanation: the fire burns vigorously, yet the bush is not consumed. Moses acts responsibly by "making intelligent inquiry" and discovering "holy ground."[15] A profound knowledge of the Experimenter grows from that initial experience as he continues his intelligent inquiry for the next forty or so years. Our responsibility? "Intelligent inquiry," and, as Thomas records, "any burning bush will do!"[16]

Notes

[1] Doug Stewart, "Interview—David Hubel," *OMNI* 12, no. 5 (1990): 74–110.

[2] Philip L. Carpenter, *Microbiology*, 4th ed. (Philadelphia, Pa.: W. B. Saunders, 1977), 4.

[3] Carl Sagan, *Cosmos* (New York: Random House, 1980), 40.

[4] William Garnett, "Introduction" to *Flatland: A Romance of Many Dimensions,* by Edwin A. Abbott, 5th ed. (1884; Oxford: Basil Blackwell, 1950), iv.

[5] Ibid., v.

[6] Ibid.

[7] Eph. 6:12; Col. 1:16; 2:10–15.

[8] Luke 16:19–31. (Author's paraphrase.)

[9] Luke 23:43. (Author's paraphrase.)

[10] Mark 16:14; Luke 24:36; John 20:14, 19.

[11] 2 Cor. 12:2–4.

[12] 1 Cor. 2:9.

[13] Heb. 11.

[14] Heb. 12:1. (King James Version followed by author's paraphrase. Author's emphasis.)

[15] Ian Thomas, *The Saving Life of Christ* (Grand Rapids, Mich.: Zondervan, 1969), 66.

[16] Ibid., 70.

3.2

Biomedical Prescience 1
Hebrew Dietary Laws

William J. Cairney

DURING MY GRADUATE STUDENT DAYS at Cornell University, a number of us met in a university classroom each afternoon from 4:45 to 5:15, a brief half-hour. The location of the room was publicized on posters located at prominent sites around campus. The title of this official Cornell club was the "Cornell Bible Research Group" or CBRG. The purpose of the organization at that time was to provide a forum for open discussion of issues such as evidence for the existence of God, evidence for the authenticity of Christian Scripture, and related topics. The group was composed of people representing many disciplines. Some (not all) were Christians. Some were individuals curious to find out what in the world we were doing. Some were skeptics. Some were out-and-out antagonists. After a couple of years of this daily exercise, I came away with a definite feeling for how Christians are perceived by non-Christians in an academic community. The Christian stereotype is often not a positive one, for a number of reasons, some legitimate. I also came away with a feeling for the training and the mindset that a Christian must have to share his or her faith in the academic arena.

As someone who had been raised in a Christian home and who had to struggle over serious challenges from the academic community, I found myself identifying with people who came to CBRG searching for foundations and answers. A number of these folk had been raised in a fairly formal Christian or Jewish format and had come to the same basic point in their lives. They had come to feel that the Judeo-Christian position was completely *without foundation* and that a person with "religious" leanings was committing a tremendous leap of blind faith based on bias and emotion. Hear it again, many felt that the Christian position was *without foundation*. Fortunately, at CBRG, often for the first time in their lives, many of these people were confronted with hard, solid evidence for the validity of the Christian model, evidence that could be examined critically and tested against rigorous criteria.

Reactions to these evidences were varied. Some did not want to hear any more. It made them nervous. Some reacted emotionally and became angry. Some got hooked on it and wanted to hear more. Some were argumentative in very academic intonations. Some believed and became Christians as a result of it.

Of the Christians who attended regularly, there were individuals who were versed in evidences from many separate disciplines. Some, for instance, handled prophetic evidence very well. Others presented historical and archaeological evidence. Still others were experts in philosophy and apologetics. A few were able to present compelling instances of prescience in Scripture from the various areas of natural science.

Of all of the evidences available for examination, prescience has been the area which has impressed me most. By *prescience* we mean the occurrence, in Scripture, of accurate statements reflecting an in-depth knowledge of scientific concepts *far* before mankind had laid the technological base for such things to be known.

Credibility is an important part of interpersonal communication in the academic arena. Thus, I would like to present significant examples of prescience in Scripture from my own professional field, evidence which continues to impress me more and more, evidence that won't quit, even as I dig deeper and deeper.

One additional point before we begin formally—the proper perspective for this sort of material. We do not examine this sort of evidence as an end in itself. We study evidences to enhance our overall knowledge and appreciation of Scripture as a foundation for a proper knowledge of God. We can memorize volumes of evidential material and if it serves as nothing but an intellectual exercise, it is not serving its rightful purpose. Also, Peter exhorts the Christian to "be ready always to give an answer to anyone who asks you a reason of the hope that is in you, with meekness and fear."[1] In the academic community, the individuals before whom we must consistently and firmly present our Christian case are usually well-informed skeptics. Are we armed with sufficient information to present our case with credibility and conviction to such persons? Will we be able to anticipate the responses of such persons? Or, by opening our mouths, will we make ourselves appear inadequate, hence make the entire Christian model appear inadequate as well?

If we find ourselves constantly exposed to well-educated, well-read, and well-spoken people, if that is the sphere in which God has placed us, the need may truly exist for us to have a certain armamentarium of material at our fingertips to enable Scripture to become credible for those people. To be able to deal with *evidences within one's own field of expertise and demonstrated competence* becomes extremely important. In that spirit I would like to hazard a paraphrase of 1 Peter 3:15: "If a person asks you about the hope that is in you, be ready to give a *meaningful answer,* an answer appropriate to that person's level of understanding. And do it firmly, humbly, and respectfully."

This is the first of three chapters on the general topic of prescience in the area of health science demonstrated in the Christian Bible. In exploring this topic it will become evident that prescience in this area is not just occasional, but is present in abundance, especially in the Old Testament, but also in the New Testament. As a basic reference I'd like to suggest you read *None of These Diseases* by S. I. McMillen, M.D.[2] For many years Dr. McMillen was college physician at Houghton College, Houghton, New York. In our discussion of prescience, we will use some of his material directly or use a basic idea in *None of These Diseases* for further amplification. When we are through, we will only have whetted appetites. The evidence is vast!

The Rise of Biomedical Technology

In order to appreciate what we're getting into here, we need to establish a historical base for some technological discoveries. In the field of pathogenic microbiology, instrumentation is critical to research and discovery. X-ray crystallography, mass spectrometry, chromatography in all of its various forms, transmission and scanning electron microscopy, flow cytometry, and computerized cell image analysis techniques are all used extensively to increase our superstructure of knowledge. Nearly all of these technologies would have been completely unknown to the biomedical community at the beginning of this century. Perhaps the most important of all microbiological tools, however, is the basic light microscope. It is *the* "foundation instrument."

The microscope was invented and somewhat popularized in the seventeenth century. Galileo probably invented the first usable microscope around 1610. He did not do much with his microscopes, though, as he was much more interested in exploring the heavens with his telescopes. Robert Hooke, an Englishman, was the first to use the microscope extensively. He also constructed a compound microscope capable of greater magnification than those made by Galileo. As Curator of the Royal Society of London in 1662, he had to prepare microscopy demonstrations for public display. His work, *Micrographia,* a collection of his observations, is considered a benchmark publication in microbiology.[3]

Anton van Leeuwenhoek was nearly a contemporary of Robert Hooke. Van Leeuwenhoek was not the first person to make a microscope, but was one of the first (along with Hooke) to support his observations with accurate reporting and illustration. Leeuwenhoek was a Dutch drapery merchant who sold buttons and ribbons for a living. He swept out the town hall as janitor for extra money. His microscopy work was strictly a hobby, but one he pursued vigorously. He ground lenses in his basement, and over his lifetime he constructed over 250 microscopes. Leeuwenhoek made public his records of observations in a series of letters to the British Royal Society written over many years.

We know from Leeuwenhoek's descriptions that he saw protozoa, fungi, and bacteria. He viewed them as a curiosity. We have no record of anyone (other than Hooke and possibly Galileo) having seen these organisms earlier or even having been aware of their existence. Even in Leeuwenhoek's day, these creatures were not linked with disease. In fact, it wasn't until over two hundred years later, that the German physician Robert Koch published the famous "Koch's Postulates" and clearly linked *Bacillus anthracis* with the development of anthrax in cattle.[4] Indeed, the entire technological base for knowledge of the microbial basis for disease, including transmissibility factors, insect vectors, and host-pathogen relationships is barely one hundred years old.

When were viruses directly observed? Not until the advent of a functional electron microscope in the middle of the twentieth century, although some clues to viral structure were obtained through the use of x-ray techniques as early as the 1930s. Again, we are dealing with a very recent technology.

Armed with these facts, I have a question: Did these elements of applied microbiological knowledge ever appear before? Yes! In fact, not only had such material appeared in history, but it appeared in such a way as to be usable for the prevention of disease in an entire nation. It appeared in written form in a document dating from approximately 1400 to 1500 B.C.

Prescience in the Hebrew Scriptures

Let's then make a long historical jump of about thirty-five hundred years to a band of Semites migrating across the Sinai Peninsula led by a chieftain named Moses. This band, the Hebrews, had a notion that there was one true God and that He revealed Himself through prophets who passed on His very commands, and, in many cases, wrote them down as sacred guidance for the nation.

The chieftain, Moses, was one such spokesman for this deity named Jehovah, and the first five books of the Hebrew Scriptures are ascribed to him. Moses indicates over and over that Jehovah was the source of the words he was writing. Moses' writings contain an account of the creation of the universe, including earth and the biosphere, as well as historical notes on the first humans to inhabit the planet, a cataclysmic flood that ended human life except for a select few, and the descent of the Hebrew nation from one Chaldean patriarch named Abraham.

Clean and Unclean Animals

In addition to serving as a historical record, Moses' written works preserve the civil and religious guidance Jehovah provided for the Hebrews. In the record are page after page of rules the Hebrews were to observe in the realms of social practice, religious observance, custom, and diet. The dietary rules, with which we are primarily concerned here, are spelled out very clearly in Leviticus, Moses' third book. Leviticus describes in detail what the tribe could and could not eat. Several times in Leviticus, and in other books entitled Exodus, Numbers, and Deuteronomy, Jehovah is reported as saying, "If you follow these rules, it will go well with you. You will be healthy and you will prosper in every way."

Summarizing the laws and specific examples that Moses gives, the available animal food sources are divided into two categories, clean and unclean.[5] The "clean" (edible) animals included all members of the cattle family; sheep (domestic and wild); goats (domestic and wild); and all members of the deer family.

The chief criteria for being clean were that these animals had split hoofs and were cud-chewers. Both criteria had to be met in order for an animal to be considered clean. Also on the "clean" list were fowl (domestic and wild) and fish with fins and scales.

The "unclean" list included *any animal that did not both chew the cud and have split hoofs,* hence swine, horses, and camels; *any animal "going on paws,"* hence cats (domestic and wild) and dogs (domestic and wild); *any aquatic or marine creature without both fins and scales,* hence shellfish, crustaceans (e.g., lobster, crab, crayfish, shrimp), and catfish; *birds of prey,* hence eagles, hawks, owls, and falcons; *reptiles and amphibians,* hence snakes, turtles, lizards, and frogs; and *rodents,* hence mice, rats, and rabbits.

It is certainly interesting here that Jehovah's counsel to the Hebrews called not only for not eating the animals in question but also for *not even touching the carcasses.* The thrust of Leviticus 11:24–28 is (in my free but accurate paraphrase),

If you find one of these unclean animals lying on the roadside, don't touch it, don't try to stuff it for posterity or display, don't try to resuscitate it, *leave it!* And if you absolutely have to carry it away, you must wash yourself and your clothes immediately and not touch any other person until the sun sets on that day.

While the "unclean" list may contain many of our modern-day favorites, the "clean" list still contains a reasonable variety of meat sources, certainly enough variety to prevent dietary boredom! I would like to single out just a few of the animals on the "unclean" list for special mention.

Swine. Swine were very available to the Hebrews. The surrounding peoples raised swine. The meat was tender, tasty, and must have been a big temptation. The problem is that swine harbor several disease-producing microorganisms easily transmissible to man.

Tapeworm cysts, for example, occur in swine worldwide. Tapeworms remain in the intestinal tract of the host and deprive the host of its nourishment. They are contracted by eating poorly cooked meat or by ingesting crushed fleas and lice from the live bodies or carcasses.[6]

Trichinosis is caused by *Trichinella spiralis.* This is a worm whose larval forms encyst in striated (voluntary) muscle. It is taken into humans in inadequately cooked pork. As with tapeworms, the distribution of this organism is worldwide. Trichinosis is a wasting-type disease characterized by progressive weakness.

Erysipelas is caused by Beta hemolytic group *A Streptococcus.* The portal of entry is the skin or mucous membrane of the host. Again, eating or even touching an affected animal would put a human at risk.

Typhoid is caused by *Salmonella typhi,* and Paratyphoid is caused by *Salmonella paratyphi* and others. These pathogens are a potent source of disease if a population of humans or animals comes into contact with intestinal waste through contaminated food or water. Many mammals can theoretically become contaminated with these organisms, but the incidence of contact and pathogen buildup is especially high in animals with a well-developed interest in excreta such as swine (which wallow in it) and members of the dog family.

Aquatic and Marine Animals without Fins and Scales. Virtually all of the prohibited animals are scavengers or bottom feeders. All of them tend to be gathered from easily accessible (i.e., relatively shallow) estuarian waters where they lie and feed as water goes by. Centers of civilization tended to use such waters for the removal of garbage and raw sewage. Therefore, these water creatures would very likely be gathered from the dilute organic soup of human and animal waste. It is no wonder that these animals have historically been a potent source of typhoid. Incidentally, there is a modern-day hazard associated with shellfish taken from waters into which are dumped toxic industrial by-products (especially non-biodegradable products and heavy metals). Shellfish can take in sufficient quantities of these products and not die themselves, yet they transfer these products up the food chain where they accumulate because the human or animal body can't remove them quickly.

Rodents. Rodents, especially rats and mice, might seem to be a likely meat source (esthetics aside!) because they are ubiquitous and probably tender. They are, however, a natural reservoir for some of the worst diseases known to mankind. The pathogenic organisms involved can be transmitted directly by touch, by rodent bite, or by the bite from some insect or other arthropod which has bitten the rodent or is harbored by it. *Yersinia pestis* (the causative agent of bubonic plague), rabies virus, *Hymenolypsis diminuta* and other tapeworms, and *Streptobacillus moniliformis* (the causative agent of ratbite fever) are all harbored in rodent populations.

Birds of Prey. Birds of prey are noble birds, to be sure, and not really bad in and of themselves, but what constitutes the major portion of their diet? Rodents (and other small animals in the "unclean" category)!

Turtles, lizards, etc. A similar problem exists with turtles and lizards as with aquatic and marine creatures. If such animals are gathered for food from stagnant water or contaminated streams and rivers, they can't help but be a source of toxic products and microorganisms associated with waste. In fact, from time to time, *Salmonella* outbreaks are seen among children who purchase pet-shop or dime-store turtles for pets. The little plastic turtle bowls sit in sunny places while the food remnants fed to the turtle combined with egested *Salmonella* make for a wonderful broth culture.

Animals on Paws. Dogs have a propensity for excreta. They also excrete *Leptospira,* an organism which causes leptospirosis in man. Dogs in the wild are also a natural reservoir of fungal skin pathogens easily transmissible to man from either living dogs or dead carcasses. Cats are very clean animals that spend inordinate proportions of their waking hours cleaning and grooming, but what is their major source of food, especially in the wild? Rodents, again!

Agriculture

While the Mosaic writings give very specific details concerning the edibility of animals, they also contain some very important directives for plant growing and general agricultural practice,[7] directives that result in a diminished incidence of plant disease. What causes plant disease? Fungi are the main causes of plant diseases, although bacteria, viruses, and nematodes are also implicated to a lesser extent. Disease mechanisms and host-parasite relationships in plants are similar to such mechanisms and relationships in animals except that plants are generally non-motile so that pathogens have to travel from plant to plant (via wind, insects, water, animals, or contaminated farm implements). Geography and climatology are also important in plant diseases because many would-be pathogens, especially fungi, only thrive under certain environmental conditions. The presence of moisture is an especially important environmental consideration.

To infect plants, organisms must be able to survive from one season to the next. Some fungi do this by over-wintering as spores. Some survive in debris from host plants. Still others may survive in insect vectors (carriers of disease) or in some sort of alternative host. Some may survive in seed. When conditions are right, however, there have to be enough inoculum (reproductive units) of the pathogen left to cause reinfections in subsequent growing seasons.

Let's go back to an Israeli farmer living under the Mosaic law. Let's say he has a crop of some cereal grain growing in his field. *Pathogen X,* a fungus, begins to invade. Each year the disease gets worse and worse. The seventh year rolls around. Instead of planting the usual crop, the farmer elects to obey the Mosaic law, which requires him to leave his field fallow for an entire year. During the growing season, the farmer notices a few volunteer plants coming up from naturally shed or spilled seed, and the rest of the land filling in with some low weeds and wild annuals from the edge of the field. Come autumn, the weeds die when the colder weather comes, and they fall back onto the surface of the soil. The next spring comes around, and our Hebrew friend plants the accustomed crop and . . . no disease!

What events could have happened to account for this phenomenon? For one, the farmer has unwittingly practiced a primitive "crop rotation" (or at least a "plant rotation"), allowing his cereal crop to alternate with wild plants for an entire growing season. In addition, he has practiced primitive "green manuring" by plowing under the debris from volunteers and weeds.

At this point, I can't resist quoting a section from a recent and superbly written plant pathology text. The subject heading for the passage is "Crop Rotation."

In a sense, crop rotation is eradication of the chief and alternative hosts. Many plant pathogens survive for only a short time in the absence of susceptible weeds or crop plants. Some of these pathogens can survive for a time as saprophytes in decaying crop residues, but most are unable to live indefinitely in the soil. Such soil invaders are subject to eradication by starvation, which is best accomplished through crop rotation. True soil inhabitants, however, are not easily controlled by such measures.

Crop rotation is not always feasible, however, because annual cash income from a single crop may often be essential to the economic well-being of certain farmers. . . .

However, a single annual plant species, grown year after year in the same soil, is vulnerable to periodic outbreaks of devastating plant diseases particularly those caused by nematodes or those caused by root-invading fungi. . . . Such diseases may be controlled in monocultures by planting resistant varieties and, sometimes, by chemically treating the infested soil; *but when resistant varieties are not available or prove to be only mildly resistant, and when chemical treatment of the soil is not feasible, crop rotation remains the best possible control measure.*[8]

What we have before us in the writings of Moses is a dietary list and some basic agricultural principles which, if scrupulously followed, would virtually eliminate a wide spectrum of human and plant diseases, ranging from mild to deadly. That this was the very intent of those laws is quite clear from the Mosaic text: "If you will diligently listen to the voice of the Lord your God, and will do that which is right in His sight, and will give ear to His commandments, and keep His laws, I will bring none of these diseases upon you."[9]

How Did Moses Know?

Two questions may be running through your mind. "Is that all?" and "How do we explain the appearance of those laws thirty-five hundred years ago?" To the first question, the answer is, "No, that's not all. We've only just begun!" To the second question, the answer is, "Congratulations, that's a key question!" The fact is that there is indeed more, much more. In addition, the only reason we can appreciate the true significance of those laws is because of a *technological base available to us which is scarcely one hundred years old.*

How then, do we explain Moses' uncanny ability to predict sources of disease with such incredible accuracy? As I look at the problem, I see four alternatives.

1. All of these principles of disease control were known and taught in Egypt.
2. The principles were brought in from another culture or region.
3. Moses was very observant and far-sighted (i.e., he figured out the whole system himself).
4. He was informed by Jehovah, the God of the Bible, who did not need a twentieth-century technological base and could thus speak accurately and in minute detail. (Incidentally, Moses declares over and over again that this is what had happened.)

In the next section, we'll look at both of these questions. We'll examine more prescience and give careful attention to Moses as an epidemiologist and epiphytologist.

Notes

[1]1 Pet. 3:15. (This and all subsequent Scripture references in this chapter are from the New Scofield Reference Bible, copyright 1967 by the Oxford University Press. Biblical quotations may contain minor paraphrasing by the author.)

[2]S. I. McMillen, M.D., *None of These Diseases* (Old Tappan, N.J.: Revell, 1961).

[3]Robert Hooke, *Micrographia: or, Some physiological descriptions of minute bodies made by magnifying glasses, with observations and inquiries made thereupon* (1665; reprint, New York: Dover Publications, 1961).

[4]Eugene W. Nester et al., *Microbiology* (Philadelphia, Pa.: Holt, Rinehart and Winston, 1978), 48. While virtually any well-written general microbiology text contains historical notes on the development of microbiology as a science, Nester et al. do an especially good job. For some of the best available treatments of the technological chronology in microbiology and medicine, interested readers should see Robert Reid, *Microbes and Men* (New York: Saturday Review Press, 1975); and Sir McFarlane Burnet, *Natural History of Infectious Disease* (Cambridge: Cambridge University Press, 1966).

[5]Lev. 11.

[6]Ernest Jawetz et al., *Review of Medical Microbiology,* 14th ed. (Los Altos, Calif.: Lange Medical Publications, 1980), 491.

[7]Lev. 25:1–7; 26:3–5, 10, 18, 20.

[8]Daniel A. Roberts and Carl W. Boothroyd, *Fundamentals of Plant Pathology* (San Francisco: W. H. Freeman, 1972), 146.

[9]Exod. 15:26, paraphrased.

3.3

Biomedical Prescience 2
Pride & Prejudice in Science

William J. Cairney

IN THE SPRING OF 1974, I attended the annual meeting of the Aerospace Medical Association. The keynote lecture was presented by Lord Zuckerman, premier British physician and scholar, M.A., D.Sc., LL.D., M.D., Fellow of the Royal Society, Royal College of Physicians, and Royal College of Surgeons. This incredible man delivered a brilliant and insightful address entitled "Pride and Prejudice in Science."[1] In the course of his speech, he told one of the saddest stories I have ever heard. The tale, a true one, relates the experiences and contributions of a Hungarian physician named Ignaz Semmelweis. Dr. McMillen in *None of These Diseases* presents some additional points on the life of the same man.[2] Jumping back and forth from details supplied by Lord Zuckerman and Dr. McMillen, I have come up with a composite sketch of the short and tragic life of this important contributor to modern biomedical science.

Semmelweis was a young physician, who, in the 1840s, was appointed to a position in the Allegemeine Krankenhaus in Vienna, Austria. One dubious distinction of that hospital was that among expectant mothers entering the place for childbirth, the mortality rate was one in six. Zuckerman reports that women actually prayed not to be taken there. The problem was a disease called *puerperal fever* (childbirth fever) which occurred in epidemic proportions and defied control. This disease is bacterial in etiology (cause or origin). The causative agent is *Streptococcus pyogenes,* an organism capable of a variety of disease processes also including erysipelas and scarlet fever. The Vienna Hospital epidemic was apparently caused by an especially virulent strain of this pathogen.

After watching this situation for some time, Semmelweis made an important observation: the disease was not randomly distributed among the expectant mothers. It occurred with greatest frequency in patients who had been examined by physicians who had just autopsied puerperal fever victims. Semmelweis correctly assessed that "something" was being carried from these dead bodies to living patients and re-initiating the disease.

Semmelweis began a resounding outcry over this carnage. On his wards, he insisted that following autopsies all physicians would wash their hands in chlorinated lime water before examining living patients. Our current technology base allows us to predict exactly what would happen in such a scenario. The mortality rate reversed itself dramatically. Within three months, the mortality rate dropped from one in six to one in eighty-four on Semmelweis's ward. Convincing evidence, to be sure! But, rather than acknowledge that the young Semmelweis was on to something, the hospital rang out cries of protest over the requirement for constant handwashing.

The evidence became even more compelling as Semmelweis made another observation. Physicians who had carefully washed their hands after autopsy could still pass the disease from a living diseased patient to other non-diseased patients. Semmelweis thus took his procedure one step further. He laid down the law that physicians would wash their hands after contact with any body, living or dead. The mortality rate plummeted even further. Of course, his superiors and colleagues would now recognize the pattern. No! In fact, they scarcely acknowledged the reversal in morbidity and mortality. Instead, Semmelweis was ostracized and persecuted. He was eventually fired, and after several months of asking "why?" and attempting to get re-hired, he returned dejectedly to Budapest, his home town.

What of the mortality rate following Semmelweis's dismissal? Handwashing was altogether discontinued, and the mortality rate immediately reverted to one in six maternity patients. The hospital staff surely would have enough evidence now to be convinced. No! As McMillen so accurately reflects, "We mortals might as well face it—the human mind is so warped by pride and prejudice that proof can rarely penetrate it."[3]

Semmelweis? In Budapest, he joined the staff of a city hospital. Guess what disease was rampant there? Puerperal fever! Semmelweis initiated the same procedures he had instituted in Vienna. Results? Precisely the same. The mortality rate plunged. Of course, his professional colleagues in Budapest were overjoyed, and Vienna also was now convinced. No. History repeated itself. Jealousy, prejudice, ostracism, dismissal.

Fortunately Semmelweis reported his data in a book that has become a benchmark work in the history of biomedicine. After turbulent times with his critics and his difficult family situation, he died of a bacterial infection in a mental asylum at the age of thirty-one.

Health Practices in Mosaic Law

It is commonly held that Semmelweis was the vanguard for the recognition of the transmissibility of disease from dead carcasses to living people, and also from living to living, but let's reestablish our historical perspective with a question. Did the principles recognized by Semmelweis ever appear before in history? Yes, these procedures appeared in written form in a document dated from the 1400 to 1500 B.C. time period, predating Semmelweis by some thirty-four hundred years!

In the biblical books attributed to Moses, we find clear and detailed rules for a variety of health practices. In the previous chapter, for example, I discussed the dietary rules set forth in the book of Leviticus. Another Mosaic work, Numbers, states God's regulations for the Hebrews concerning touching the carcasses of dead persons and animals, especially where the entrails and excrement might have been contacted. It records that any person touching a carcass was to wash at specified intervals in running water. Also, any objects or personal effects used by that person or close to that person were to be likewise washed. Open vessels in the vicinity of a person found dead in his dwelling were to be considered unclean. They were to be smashed and never used for food again.[4]

The connection with Semmelweis here is quite clear, but what about the smashing of food vessels? Our current technology makes this practice perfectly understandable. Such uncovered vessels may have contained food remnants which would then serve as excellent culture media for certain disease-causing microorganisms which may actually have been ingested or deposited there by the deceased. They would then be present to grow nicely in new food added to the vessel. Many such organisms (sources of acute food poisoning, etc.) would be virtually impossible to get rid of in porous clay vessels unless such vessels were sterilized in pressurized steam.

At the close of the last chapter I introduced two questions: "Is that all?" and "How do we explain the appearance of those principles thirty-five years ago?" To the first question, the answer is still, "No, that's not all. We're still at the surface." As for the second question, I think it's important to note that many people have recognized the remarkable nature of the practices outlined in the Mosaic writings, but rather than give credence to the possibility of direct intervention in the affairs of humankind by a powerful personal God (with all of the implications that would bring), people have sought alternative explanations for these laws appearing where they did in time. We'll now look at the only alternatives that seem possible.

Moses Learned Disease Control Principles in Egypt

The idea that Moses learned these disease control principles in Egypt would seem to be a logical explanation were it not for the fact that ancient Egypt documented its medical practices very well. McMillen reports his readings from an Egyptian medical text dated circa 1550 B.C., contemporary with the time of Moses. The book gives remedies for a wide range of maladies from snakebite to splinters to hair loss. Drugs and prescriptions range from downright life-threatening to out-and-out hilarious. Such preparations include crushed donkey teeth, rattlesnake fat, blood of worms, magic water, fly excrement, manure from a variety of animals (even humans) applied as a paste, and on and on.[5]

The remedies on the list are essentially ridiculous. In addition, if the disease control principles in the Mosaic writings were known, why do they appear only in the Mosaic text? We have no historic evidence at all that Egypt had this knowledge. In fact, in all of my years of reading in the history of science, I have never come across evidence of advanced medical knowledge from any culture as far back in antiquity as we have record. And I've looked. This knowledge simply can't be demonstrated anywhere else.

A possible counter to my assertion is the clearly advanced state of anatomical knowledge that the Egyptians demonstrated and documented. Evidence of that shows up in the art and science of embalming. Observe, however, that the Egyptians were very advanced in macroanatomy. Their track record on things requiring microbiological knowledge was dismal. That is exactly what we would expect, because the technology which would have made microbiological knowledge possible was not available. In fact, it was thirty-two hundred years away from even the invention of the microscope, the "foundation instrument."

Disease Control Principles Came from Another Region

Well, maybe the disease control principles were brought in from another region. This is probably an even worse alternative than the first. We simply have no record of superior medical knowledge predating Moses, especially where microbiological principles would be evident. And—an interesting side-thought—if Moses had learned or intercepted these principles, why waste them on the Hebrews? Why not use them to control Egypt itself?

Moses Originated the Disease-Control System

Perhaps, then, Moses was very observant and far-sighted and figured it all out himself. This seems to be the most commonly held explanation. It has been stated quite freely in numerous sources. The author of one of my graduate school animal pathology texts, for instance, not only holds that opinion but even speculates on Moses' motivation.

The Laws of Moses, described in detail in Exodus and Leviticus, are exact and nearly complete from the sanitary point of view, and actually little has been added or retracted from these laws during the last thirty-five centuries. . . . Although the Hebrews were great hygienists and were to be admired for their food sanitation (many of our modern laws), we cannot help but notice that they accepted the theological concept as the cause of disease. . . . Did the leaders—intelligent men of the standard of Moses—recognize the cause of disease as being other than theological, but in order to hold the people, did they push the truth into the background and nourish mysticism and the theological concept of etiology?[6]

This theory seems to be a viable alternative until we consider the knowledge Moses would have needed to put his system together. To cite just a few items:

(1) Moses would have needed to know at least something about the germ theory of disease (confirmed by Robert Koch, Louis Pasteur, John Tyndall, and Joseph Lister in the latter 1800s) and the role of bacteria, fungi, protozoa, mycoplasmas, and viruses—without seeing any of them.

(2) He would have needed to be familiar with at least some of the nutritional requirements of would-be pathogenic organisms, enough to know that food particles, even in washed (but open) clay pots, would be sufficient to maintain these infectious organisms.

(3) He would have required at least some knowledge about the photolytic effect of sunlight and the effect of drying on microorganisms. The "unclean" person was directed to wash and put on clean clothes. In that day, that meant washing the clothes in running water and drying them outdoors in sunlight. (Today we know that ultraviolet wavelengths in sunlight are bacteriocidal. Desiccation [drying] alone will kill many organisms.)

(4) He would have needed to know at least something about the different types of organisms that inhabit the human body to know that some needed to be prevented from growing unchecked.

(5) He would have needed at least some information about the populations of organisms associated with a wide range of animals and which of those should be avoided by humans.

(6) He would have required a great deal of information on epidemiology and the methods of disease transmission, including the role of insects and other arthropods as vectors.

(7) He would have needed at least some knowledge about trophic structure (food chains) to know that pathogens can be carried in that manner.

(8) Finally, Moses would have needed a great deal of knowledge about the mechanisms of pathogenesis in a wide variety of host-parasite

relationships to predict disease where there is no immediate, readily observable cause and effect. (For instance, trichinosis develops slowly over weeks or months and would appear completely disconnected with the ingestion of contaminated pork on any given day.)

How reasonable, then, is the third alternative in the light of the fact that it has taken the finest minds of the nineteenth and twentieth centuries, aided by sophisticated instrumentation, money, libraries, and teams of highly skilled technicians, to come to the conclusions reflected in the Mosaic writings?

The Disease Control Principles Came from Jehovah

Just a thought or two on the remaining alternative. Moses claimed no credit for having originated any of this material. Rather, he gave complete credit to the God of the Hebrews, who, Moses claimed, had told him to write all of this down. It is also not accidental or coincidental that these laws prevented disease. They were specifically designed to do that. The evidence for that is internal to the narrative.

If you will listen to the voice of the Lord your God, and obey it (i.e., follow the rules I have set down), then I will keep you free of all of the diseases which people suffer in Egypt and the surrounding nations.[7]

Here's a statement from an almighty God who stands above space, time, and technological constraints. His promise is the simplest explanation fitting all of the known data.

"But I as an educated person just can't accept that explanation!" Is it the "explanation" or the "implications" that you can't accept? Watch those presuppositions! Sometimes they stand in the way of good science and exciting discovery. Ask the colleagues of Ignaz Semmelweis.

Notes

[1]Lord S. Zuckerman, "Pride and Prejudice in Science: William Randolph Lovelace II Memorial Lecture," *Aerospace Medicine* 45, no. 6 (1974): 641.

[2]S. I. McMillen, *None of These Diseases* (Old Tappan, N.J.: Revell, 1984), 23–28.

[3]Ibid.

[4]Num. 19:11–22; see also Levit. 6:28, 11:33; 15:12.

[5]McMillen, *None of These Diseases,* 11.

[6]Russell A. Runnells et al., *Principles of Veterinary Pathology* (Ames, Iowa: Iowa State University Press, 1965), 8–9.

[7]Exod. 15:26. (Author's paraphrase.)

3.4

Biomedical Prescience 3
How's Your Lifestyle?

William J. Cairney

IN THE LAST TWO CHAPTERS we have covered some significant ground. Specifically, we have looked at many examples of detailed biomedical prescience found in the writings of Moses. These rules of sanitation and diet stand on a foundation requiring considerable knowledge of epidemiology, microbiology, physiology, plant pathology, and animal pathology, all of which require a technological base not available until the last hundred years or so of human history. In the Mosaic text, the God of the Hebrews, speaking through Moses, promises to keep Israel free of disease if the people will follow certain commandments, which He carefully outlines. We saw this promise recorded in Exodus 15:26.

Many astute readers of this material, including numerous scientists, have recognized that these laws are accurate and complete and thus represent an anomaly in time. This anomaly is usually viewed more as a curiosity than as a problem because people generally feel that there is surely some natural explanation. We have examined the possible alternative explanations and seen that the simplest one fitting all of the available data is Moses' claim, that the God of the Hebrews had directly provided these insights. In this last chapter on prescience, we'll return to Moses for more material, then cite some additional scriptural wisdom with biomedical implications.

Circumcision

Cancer in all of its forms is one of today's greatest health concerns and the target of massive research efforts. Not too many years ago, cancer was a disease which younger people tended to link with older people. And, indeed, the incidence of many forms of cancer increases as a population grows older. Other cancers occur across a wide age range. In women between ages thirty and fifty, cancer of the cervix (neck of the uterus) is one of the most common forms. McMillen reports a battery of statistics on the distribution of cervical cancer indicating virtual freedom from the disease among women whose husbands were circumcised.[1] Jews as well as Islamic Indians were included in this nearly cervical-cancer-free population.[2]

Circumcision is the removal of excess skin over the tip of the penis in the male. The process is described in Moses' book, Genesis, where it is instituted as a practice for Abraham and his descendants:

"Your part of the contract," God told [Abraham] "is to obey its terms. You personally and all your posterity have this continual responsibility: that every male among you shall be circumcised; the foreskin of his penis shall be cut off. This will be the proof that you and they accept this covenant. Every male shall be circumcised on the eighth day after birth. This applies to every foreign-born slave as well as to everyone born in your household. This is a permanent part of this contract, and it applies to all your posterity. All must be circumcised. Your bodies will thus be marked as participants in my everlasting covenant. Anyone who refuses these terms shall be cut off from his people; for he has violated my contract."[3]

Clear enough! Currently, however, the pediatric community in the United States deemphasizes circumcision as a routine practice for all male infants. Certainly, proper hygienic care would minimize the relative benefits of circumcision as a health measure. This would be reflected (and is) in the latest disease statistics. But, consider the implications of this practice for a society with no microbiological knowledge. It just so happens that under the foreskin is an excellent incubation spot for many bacteria and certain ones in particular. For instance, *Mycobacterium smegmatis* (commonly called the *Smegma bacillus*) grows there prolifically. This organism as well as others produce carcinogenic by-products. The region under the foreskin is one that can easily be missed in washing and bathing. Scrupulous personal hygiene is necessary to insure that the area stays clean. Without knowledge of the potential problems associated with not washing under the foreskin, there would be little incentive for such hygiene. During intercourse, these multiplied organisms would be deposited on the cervix where they would easily grow, produce their by-products and cause cancer, especially in women who had any sort of genital irritation from infection, disease, or recent childbirth. *Mycobacterium smegmatis* has been linked with cancer of the penis in the male as well, if the bacteria are allowed to grow unchecked and irritation of some kind is also present.[4]

While it would have been remarkable enough for Moses to have guessed this danger, there is another dimension, the *timing* for circumcision. McMillen relays the findings of competent researchers who report that infants have an especially great tendency for bleeding between days two and five after birth. They can bleed excessively with life-threatening consequences. One of the necessary products required for blood clotting is vitamin K, which is not present until between days five and seven.[5]

Why is this so? The impression which references often give is that the body can synthesize its own vitamin K. This is not strictly true. Vitamin K is produced by the bacterial microflora in the intestine. These bacteria actually synthesize a variety of vitamins including pyridoxin, pantothenic acid, biotin, vitamin B_{12}, and vitamin K, all for their own needs. They produce a great excess of them, however, and they are absorbed through the intestinal walls where they become important in human metabolism as well.[6] If humans or animals fail to establish this intestinal microflora, they generally do not thrive and may rapidly develop signs of vitamin deficiency.[7]

Infants are not born with intestinal microflora as the amniotic fluid surrounding the fetus is sterile. The infant picks up such microorganisms in the mother's birth canal, from the mother's skin during nursing, and from miscellaneous environmental sources. It takes several days for the intestinal environment to sort and select for organisms which will naturally thrive there and for those organisms to build to population levels and establish the correct balance. If the appearance of vitamin K is an indicator of the establishment of a healthy microflora, five to seven days is the usual range for establishment. On that time scale, then, the first day for safe circumcision would be day eight, the precise day given in Genesis.

McMillen also quotes *Holt Pediatrics,* which provides an additional dimension to the timing of circumcision. Prothrombin is an inactive enzyme precursor which circulates in the blood plasma. It is a protein, which, in the presence of certain activators and calcium ions, is converted to thrombin. Thrombin, in turn, acts as an enzyme converting fibrinogen, a soluble plasma protein, into fibrin. Fibrin is an insoluble protein which forms the actual clot mesh. Thus without adequate prothrombin, an early link in the blood clotting chain, clotting would be impossible. Holt reports that on the third day of life, the available prothrombin drops to a very low level (about 30 percent of the normal adult value), but that it then begins a dramatic upswing and peaks at 110 percent of normal on the *eighth day,* thus coinciding with the microfloral vitamin K production.[8]

What would it have taken for Moses to have guessed this one? Or do we give Abraham the credit here? For us to know this, it has taken a technological base complete with microscopes, well-defined microbial culture media, methods, and instrumentation, in addition to procedures and instrumentation needed for precise measurement of plasma proteins and other critical blood components. We would need to add this to the rest of the technological base Moses was able to circumvent with his other astute guesses.

Human Factor Mishaps

There is more, much more, prescience in the Mosaic text. We'll mention a few other items in passing, but to be faithful to the title of this chapter, I do want to turn to the matter of "lifestyle." One of the hallmarks of our highly technological and competitive age is premature debilitation and death in energetic, intelligent, would-be healthy people. Terms like *executive stress* and *burnout* have become common in our vocabulary. Heart disease is an especially serious concern because it often seems to hit without warning with results that are very final.

Over the past ten years or so, the United States Air Force has made some very meaningful observations and compiled some significant data on this business of stress. One important observation is that while the overall rate of aircraft accidents is the lowest in the history of flying, the percentage of mishaps caused by so-called human factors is on the increase. In fact, these accidents attributable to human factors occupy a disproportionate share of today's accident reports. Why?

Several reasons have come to light. One is that we have designed machines that exceed human physical, psychological, and physiological limitations. Too much input, too much speed, too much accelerative force—and an accident happens all at once. We are flying incredible machines which require operators with tremendous intelligence, technical training, stamina, and reflexes. All of these factors must operate constantly and without compromise. These characteristics are especially necessary in air crews of high-performance, high-speed jet aircraft. And there is no forgiveness for aging. The leader of a squadron must maintain his physical and mental skills while taking on the management responsibilities of multimillion-dollar airplanes and the support and personnel resources necessary to make them fly and perform as advertised.

On close analysis, so-called human factor mishaps are not seen to be caused so much by single catastrophic events, but rather by a series of small compromises and stress points in certain areas that snowball and self-amplify. This is being seen clearly in military aircrews because the intensity of the operational environment causes the effects to be exaggerated. However, the same stress points are becoming evident in the corporate-industrial environment as well, and the toll is mounting. Each so-called stressor may not be overly troublesome in itself, but when combined with one or more additional stressors, synergistic effects occur which greatly amplify the problem.

There is an acrostic which has appeared in countless military and civilian aircrew publications, a device by which flight crew members can remember the common stressors and forecast problems in advance. This acrostic easily generalizes to anyone required to perform complex psychomotor skills or involved in high-level thinking or decision-making:

Drugs (caffeine in excess, antihistamines, nasal sprays, over-the-counter sleep preparations, etc.)

Exhaustion (pushing the limits on sleep)

Alcohol (reduced reaction capability, altered judgment)

Tobacco (increased heartrate, irritation of mucous membrane, reduced ciliar scrubbing in the bronchi, various allergic reactions, low-grade hypoxia due to carbon monoxide)

Hypoglycemia (low blood sugar level due to inadequate or improper diet)

The implication is clear, *death*! The combination kills, even though each stressor may seem relatively innocuous by itself. A few of these factors deserve special mention.

Alcohol Use

Alcohol abuse is covered well in the McMillen book. He goes into the statistics on actual alcoholism and its long-term implications for health. The effects of long-term immoderate use of alcohol include central nervous system damage and liver damage. The liver is responsible for detoxification of numerous substances including alcohol which may get into the blood. The liver actually detoxifies alcohol at the rate of only one-third ounce per hour (of pure ethanol). The uptake rate after ingesting alcohol is about one ounce per hour. Therefore, if a person drinks a great deal, he may have a residual blood alcohol level many hours after consuming his last drink, still enough to show a level of legal intoxication and enough to impair critical psychomotor skills. Too much alcohol for too many years causes a fat buildup in the liver as well as progressive hardening of the liver and a decrease in its ability to detoxify. Ulcers and reduced efficiency are also results of long-term abuse.

Alcohol Use in the Bible

Does the Christian Bible contain any pronouncements on alcohol use? Yes, several. While acknowledging up front that wine drinking was a cultural phenomenon throughout the entire range of history covered by the biblical text, drunkenness is uniformly condemned, and alcohol use is greatly restricted or discouraged for religious leaders and counselors and people in authority (i.e., decision-makers).[9]

From the available biblical references, it becomes apparent that whenever alcoholic beverages (notably wine, although others may be implied) are sanctioned, the standard counsel is "moderate amounts." Timothy, for instance, is told by Paul to "use a little wine for the sake of your stomach and your frequent ailments [of an undefined nature]."[10] Some research reports are now indicating that small amounts of wine (not distilled spirits, interestingly enough) have a long-term protective effect against heart disease. Some authorities claim that small amounts of ethanol from *any* source (wine, beer, or distilled) actually raise the levels of high-density lipoproteins (HDL) implicated heavily in *removing* athero-sclerotic plaque from blood vessel walls. For other experts in the field, "the jury is still out" regarding the role of alcohol-induced HDL in cardiovascular protection. They maintain that while HDL is, indeed, increased by moderate alcohol intake, that the specific HDL fraction (i.e., the particular type of HDL) increased by alcohol has not been demon-strated as protective. While it will be interesting to learn more about these mechanisms as this story unfolds, "small amounts" of wine have been identified as a longevity factor in various studies of various populations.[11]

What does the biblical instruction manual say? Long-term immoderate use of alcohol is not beneficial, especially for people in authority and decision makers. On the other hand, it has some therapeutic value when used in small quantities. Neither Moses, nor Solomon, nor Paul had the technological base to have discovered HDL and figured out its role. Nor did they know about the function and the detoxification role of alcohol dehydrogenase and pathological liver changes caused by chronic abuse. Their counsel squares exactly, however, with what biomedical science has uncovered in the last fifty years. Perhaps another good "guess"?

Heart Disease

On the overall subject of diet, another biblical precept emerges as very important, and it dovetails with the whole theme of heart disease we've just raised. In order to appreciate this precept fully, some background may again be in order. We hear so much about heart disease. It occupies its share of attention in mass media publications and is the subject of massive research efforts at major medical centers. While the search for causes and cures for cancer has been an elusive one, research into causes and cures for heart disease has yielded significant positive results. For instance, while heart disease is still the leading cause of death in the United States, the death rate due to heart disease has dropped 30 percent since 1950, with a third of the decline occurring over the last five or six years. Why? Dieting, exercise, and elimination of smoking account for much of the decline. Research has shown these to be effective, and many Americans have incorporated them into their lifestyles. The balance of the decline in deaths due to heart disease is largely a result of the greatly increased capabilites of coronary care facilities.

Two types of cardiovascular disease should probably be defined here—*arteriosclerosis* and *atherosclerosis*. Arteriosclerosis is a somewhat general term given to a hardening of the arteries and subsequent loss of elasticity believed to be caused by excessive refined sugar, cholesterol, and saturated fat intake. There are two types of arteriosclerosis. Type I, *Mönkeberg's arteriosclerosis,* is a progressive calcification of the middle layer of the arteries. This type of arteriosclerosis, while causing a loss of elasticity, does not tend to narrow the vessels nor obstruct blood flow. Type II, *atherosclerosis,* is the more serious of the two types because deposits (mainly of a low-density lipoprotein cholesterol) build up on the inner layer of the artery, causing it to become rough and thickened. This reduces blood flow, promotes clotting, and can eventually lead to complete closure of the vessel. When this process occurs in the vessels that supply the heart itself, the oxygen supply to a region of the heart muscle is cut off, and the tissue literally dies, causing chaotic activity rather than normal beating, or, in some cases, complete stoppage of normal rhythmic contraction.

Heart disease, especially heart disease with atherosclerotic origin or involvement, appears to be a product of or at least exaggerated by our fast-paced, twentieth-century life-style. We hear a lot about cholesterol and the fact that it precipitates heart attacks when we have too much of it. What is that substance? What does it do? Where does it come from?

Cholesterol is a basic "building block" molecule from which our steroid hormones are synthesized.[12] Steroid hormones are all critical and include our sex hormones, which none of us would want to be without! Cholesterol is a normal component of cell membranes.[13] Most cells can synthesize cholesterol for their own needs.[14] The cholesterol that floats through our bloodstream (i.e., plasma cholesterol) is synthesized in the body by the liver. Why does the liver do that? Bile salts are formed in the liver from cholesterol. These bile salts are transported to the gall bladder where they are concentrated by as much as a factor of ten. From there they are used as an essential material in the digestion and absorption of fats.[15] A diet which is very high in fats favors the *formation* of cholesterol (for obvious reasons). And a high level of plasma lipids (fats and oils), particularly cholesterol, is connected with the development of atherosclerosis.[16]

We will not go into the controversy over the specific mechanisms involved in the formation of atherosclerotic plaque. Several excellent articles are available on this subject, especially a *Scientific American* publication by professor of pathology Earl P. Benditt of the University of Washington School of Medicine.[17] Regardless of controversies over mechanisms, we can summarize the progression of events in chart form:

↑ **Blood Cholesterol**
⇓

Formation of Atherosclerotic Plaque
Containing deposits of cholesterol
⇓

↑ **Blood Pressure**
↓ *diameter of blood vessels, decreased flexibility, demand on heart to supply a greater number of blood vessels needed to supply more and more fatty tissue in increasingly obese person*
⇓

Heart Attack
Atherosclerotic plaque forms and promotes clotting in coronary arteries coupled with increased demands on heart from miles of extra blood vessels in overweight person

Summing up, then, it is clear that one of the greatest triggers of high levels of plasma cholesterol is high levels of dietary fat, which we tend to get in the form of saturated animal fat. It is significant that diets high in saturated fats do indeed increase plasma cholesterol levels *and* produce an overweight condition if a person's lifestyle is sedentary.

Recent studies show that many factors can increase serum cholesterol, including excessive alcohol intake, smoking, general obesity, and psychic stress (fear, anger, anxiety, etc.).[18] But the most important factor from these same studies is seen to be dietary, the steady ingestion of foods containing saturated animal fat.[19]

Cholesterol Control in Mosaic Law

Are there any references to this phenomenon or preventative measures appearing in history prior to the biomedical literature of the last fifty years? Yes! Moses again! In Moses' book of Leviticus, Moses quotes the

God of the Hebrews as prohibiting all deliberate ingestion of animal fat. The clear guidance involves trimming of all excess fat from all meat before cooking and eating.[20] Fat could be used for all sorts of things (soaps, waterproofing, etc.), but it couldn't be eaten. The Mosaic guidance eliminates a critical link in the atherosclerotic chain.

The Bible also evidences biomedical prescience in its promotion of moderation. Throughout Scripture, but especially in the New Testament, the writers stress the notion of moderation in all elements of lifestyle. Paul tells the Christians in Philippi to consciously focus their attention on good, pure, constructive things (rather than negative things, grudges, etc).[21] It so happens that chronic psychic stresses raise serum cholesterol levels, and a lifetime of negative, vengeful thought patterns correlates with increased cardiovascular disease. In another reference, Paul tells the Corinthian Christians that the body is designed to be the temple of God and that God will destroy the person who defiles that temple.[22] It is ironic that God does not even have to take an active part in that destruction (unless He chooses). Adopting an immoderate lifestyle full of self-imposed stresses causes a slow (or even rapid) destruction of that temple by its own built-in mechanisms.

It is fashionable in academic circles to affirm the "unreasonable" nature of Christian faith. This is partially due to previous exposures to negative Christian stereotypes and a degree of comfort with a secular worldview and related presuppositions. Perhaps also involved is a scarcity of Christian academicians who model and articulate genuine biblical faith as represented in Hebrews 11. In intercepting people on the street and asking them to explain or define "Christian faith," I have encountered many interesting responses. "Childlike credulity," "mental gymnastics," "closing your eyes and wishing with all your might," "belief in the impossible," and "wishing on a star" are but a few of the comebacks I've heard.

At best, these responses are an inaccurate appraisal of what *actual* Christian faith is. Actual Christian faith is an active, operational, conscious trust in a personal rational Being who has proved Himself trustworthy. This Being has provided a significant evidential base that He exists, that He stands above space and time, and that He is in control of the flow of history and individual lives. *Biblical* faith, rather than being a vague sort of positive thinking (faith in "faith"), has an object, a Person, an Intelligence who claims that He can be known personally and who has emphatically left His stamp in history, in archaeology, in science, and in the on-going affairs of humankind. The accumulated evidence provides a solid foundation for the type of "trust" He calls us to, a solid foundation in field after field that can be examined and tested.

Notes

[1]S. I. McMillen, *None of These Diseases* (Old Tappan, N.J.: Revell, 1961), 19.

[2]Ibid., 20.

[3]Gen. 17:9–14. This Scripture quotation is from The Living Bible, copyright 1971 by Tyndale House.

[4]McMillen, *None of These Diseases,* 21.

[5]Ibid., 22.

[6]George A. Wistreich and Max D. Lechtman, *Microbiology,* 4th ed. (New York: McGraw-Hill, 1964), 463.

[7]Abraham White, Philip Handler, and Emil Smith, *Principles of Biochemistry,* 3d ed. (New York: McGraw-Hill, 1964), 988.

[8]L. Emmett Holt, Jr., and Rustin McIntosh, *Holt Pediatrics,* 12th ed. (New York: Appleton-Century-Crofts, 1953), as cited in McMillen, *None of These Diseases,* 22.

[9]Num. 6:3; Judg. 13:14; Prov. 20:1; Prov. 31:4–5; Titus 1:5–7.

[10]1 Tim. 5:23. This Scripture quotation is from the New American Standard Bible, copyright 1971 by the Lockman Foundation.

[11]Edwin J. Whitney and Thomas S. Behr, *Physician Education Manual for Cardiovascular Risk Management Program* (San Antonio, Tex.: United States Air Force School of Aerospace Medicine, n.d.), 4-2.

[12]Mary Griffiths, *Introduction to Human Physiology* (New York: Macmillan, 1974), 380.

[13]Ibid., 254.

[14]Ibid., 273.

[15]Ibid., 254.

[16]Ibid., 306.

[17]Earl P. Benditt, "The Origin of Atherosclerosis," *Scientific American,* (February 1977).

[18]McMillen, *None of These Diseases,* chap. 15; Whitney and Behr, *Physician Education Manual,* 1-1.

[19]Ibid.

[20]Lev. 3:17; 7:22–25.

[21]Phil. 4:8.

[22]1 Cor. 3:17.

Part 4

Biblical Criticism and Bible Prophecy

4.1

Archaeology and the Higher Criticism of Genesis 14

John C. Studenroth

THE HIGHER CRITICISM OF GENESIS 14 is a paradigm for much that is right and much that is wrong in biblical scholarship today. In light of the accumulating evidence for the historical reliability of the patriarchal narratives in the Old Testament, a plea is made here to abandon the fruitless, outdated, unscientific, and hyperskeptical methodologies still prevailing in certain quarters of biblical studies. Freedom to follow the evidence where it leads is not only exhilarating but also can have profound and beneficial effects on one's ability to evaluate Christianity's truth claims.

W. F. Albright in 1926 noted that

the fourteenth chapter of Genesis has long been one of the most puzzling, and yet the most fascinating, sections of the Old Testament. In it we apparently have the only definite link between biblical and external history in the entire pre-royal period. If we can only identify the names and events mentioned there, we shall be able to fix the beginning of Hebrew historical tradition with an exactness otherwise quite unattainable . . . *if* the document is genuine.[1] (Italics are mine.)

Over that last statement, "*if* the document is genuine," much controversy has raged, and it continues to rage. It is probably safe to say that more scholarly attention has been devoted to Genesis 14 than almost any other chapter in the

Old Testament,[2] and the ensuing hypotheses and disagreements have been numerous. Why all the fuss? Precisely because, as Albright noted in 1926, there is no clearer link to the external setting of the ancient Near East; if we are to examine the historicity of the patriarchal narratives, Genesis 14 is of necessity the acid test! Andreasen, as recently as 1980, summarized the unchanged situation concerning the pivotal nature of this passage:

The problem centers in the Near Eastern setting of our story. In this story alone Abram is thrust into what appears to be an incident of international proportions with the tantalizing prospect of enabling us to relate the biblical story of his life to Near Eastern history in a precise way. Can Genesis 14 be said in any way to represent an identifiable historical event in the ancient Near East?[3]

Today scholars are divided into roughly two camps over the historicity of Genesis 14: (1) those who perceive a genuine historical memory from the early second millennium B.C. concerning an expedition into Palestine of four foreign kings, or at least foreign royal representatives, with an ensuing battle; and (2) those who view Genesis 14 as a late (e.g., first millennium B.C.) midrash with no discernible historical veracity.[4] Older proponents of the second view generally found the chapter to be a pure fabrication, while more recently the accumulating evidence from archaeology and paleography has compelled the critics in this camp at least to concede, if only grudgingly, the historicity of certain elements of the story, if not of the event itself.[5] An unfortunate phenomenon that will be demonstrated in this paper is the tendency in some quarters to make simplistic and credulous identifications of specific places and personages in biblical accounts with names and places discovered archaeologically and paleographically; when these rash assumptions are later shown to be false, there is new ammunition for the hyperskeptical critics to question any historical value in the biblical accounts. We will examine some specific examples of this sort of pendulum-swinging scholarship, as well as some examples of a virulent and unwarranted skepticism which in any other area of historical research would never pass muster.

It should also be noted that source critics are at a loss to assign this chapter to any of the usual sources postulated for Genesis (i.e., J, E, or P). E. A. Speiser, in the *Anchor Bible*, summarizes this quandary:

Genesis 14 stands alone among all the accounts in the Pentateuch, if not indeed in the Bible as a whole. The setting is international, the approach impersonal, and the narration notable for its unusual style and vocabulary. There is still much about this chapter that is open to wide differences of opinion. On one point, however, the critics are virtually unanimous: the familiar touches of the established sources of Genesis are absent in this instance. For all these reasons the chapter has to be ascribed to an isolated source, here marked X.[6]

The Four Kings

At this point, we would do well to refresh our memories of the narrative under consideration:

And it came about in the days of Amraphel king of Shinar, Arioch king of Ellasar, Chedorlaomer king of Elam and Tidal king of Goiim, *that* they made war with Bera king of Sodom, and with Birsha king of Gomorrah, Shinab king of Admah, and Shemeber king of Zeboiim, and the king of Bela (that is, Zoar). All these came as allies to the valley of Siddim (that is, the Salt Sea). Twelve years they had served Chedorlaomer, but the thirteenth year they rebelled. And in the fourteenth year Chedorlaomer and the kings that were with him, came and defeated the Rephaim in Ashteroth-karnaim and the Zuzim in Ham and the Emim in Shaveh-kiriathaim, and the Horites in their Mount Seir, as far as El-paran, which is by the wilderness. Then they turned back and came to En-mishpat (that is, Kadesh), and conquered all the country of the Amalekites, and also the Amorites, who lived in Hazazon-tamar. And the king of Sodom and the king of Gomorrah and the king of Admah and the king of Zeboiim and the king of Bela (that is, Zoar) came out; and they arrayed for battle against them in the valley of Siddim, against Chedorlaomer king of Elam and Tidal king of Goiim and Amraphel king of Shinar and Arioch king of Ellasar—four kings against five.[7]

Let us begin by examining the names of the four foreign kings who constituted the Mesopotamian coalition mentioned in verses 1 and 9. The process of scholarly pendulum-swinging can be seen with the various positions taken with regard to these names. At one extreme, some writers leave the impression that most if not all of the four names have been positively identified by Babylonian evidence derived from clay tablets or monuments. At the other extreme, some writers suggest that not even one has been or ever will be identified. As is so often the case, the truth lies somewhere between the two extremes of credulity and skepticism.

The first king mentioned by name is "Amraphel, king of Shinar." There is fairly good agreement that *Shinar* in Old Testament usage, and also in Egyptian usage, is simply a word for Babylonia.[8] The name *Amraphel* is more problematic. Early in this century, when the exploration of the ancient royal city of Susa uncovered the stele containing the law code of Hammurabi, it quickly became popular to identify Amraphel with Hammurabi. The well-known Hebrew lexicon by Brown, Driver, and Briggs, for example, accepts this identification.[9] This hasty conclusion has a number of serious problems[10] and has now been largely and rightly abandoned. However, there occurred an equally erroneous subsequent backswing of the pendulum from the overly credulous identification of these two names to the hyperskeptical denial of the historicity of Amraphel.[11] Given the fragmentary nature of our archaeological and paleographic data, the failure to make a precise correlation with a given name should not be deemed as sufficient warrant to deny the historicity of that personage. A much more sensible and balanced view has been proposed recently by a growing number of scholars as our knowledge of proper names in the ancient Near East increases. *Amraphel* is now generally considered to be a typical West Semitic name coming from Babylon during the twentieth to nineteenth centuries B.C., i.e., between the fall of Ur III and the rise of the Old Babylonian kingdom of Hammurabi.[12] For example, Speiser notes that "the Hebrew form accords well with several possible Amurrite (Amorite) or even Akkadian combinations; in that case, the bearer could well have been some minor prince from Lower Mesopotamia."[13]

The second king mentioned by name is "Arioch, king of Ellasar." A similar pattern of pendulum-swinging can be observed with this name. First there was an overly-ambitious attempt by earlier Assyriologists to identify Arioch with Eri-Aku (Warad-Sin), king of Larsa.[14] This required *Ellasar* to be Hebrew for *Larsa,* a problematic association. It is now generally recognized that the name *Arioch* is Hurrian in background, and is linguistically identical to the name of the fifth son of Zimri-Lim, king of Mari ca. 1750 B.C. The same name also occurs in the Nuzi documents from the fifteenth century B.C.[15] It seems unlikely that someone of the stature of Gerhard von Rad would fall into the trap of demanding a precise identification of the "Arioch" of Genesis 14 with a known personage from the extant fragmentary list of proper names from the ancient Near East, but that is apparently what he does:

The name Arioch, until recently very doubtful, has been connected with Arriwuku, a person known to us from the archive of . . . Mari. If this connection is correct, we should have to do with the son of Zimrilim, king of Mari and a contemporary of the great Hammurabi. But this identification is not at all conclusive.[16]

Far more sensible is the approach taken by R. K. Harrison: "Thus the name [*Arioch*], with slight variants, seems to have been in use somewhat frequently in the second millennium B.C, and this fact alone should preclude a definite identification of any particular individual with Arioch."[17] Furthermore, as Speiser notes, the name *Arioch* "is not attested after the middle of the second millennium. Its appearance in the present context thus presupposes an ancient and authentic tradition. No late Hebrew writer would be likely to invent such a name and to assign it correctly to a neighbor of Babylonia."[18]

The third king mentioned by name is "Chedorlaomer, king of Elam." It is clear from Genesis 14:4–5, 9, and 17 that Chedorlaomer was the leader of the coalition of Eastern kings that came against Palestine. Archaeology has not yet revealed this particular king, but much is known about his country: Elam, lying northeast of the Lower Tigris river and with its capital at Susa, was a "neighbor and traditional rival of Mesopotamian states since the dawn of history."[19] There is no doubt that the name *Chedorlaomer* is Elamitish because several Elamite kings have names which begin with what is equivalent to *Chedor*.[20] The Elamite term *Kudur/Kutir* (equivalent to Hebrew *Chedor*) means "servant" or "slave" and in personal names is usually followed by a divine name. In this case, the second component, *Laomer*, is generally recognized to be the Elamite goddess referred to in Akkadian texts of the Old Akkadian (Agade) and Old Babylonian (Mari) periods and which appears in several Elamite texts.[21] The name is therefore appropriate to the period from ca. 2000 to 1700 B.C., and would mean "servant of Laomer." Thus, although this exact name does not appear in the known king list of the Elamites, it is so transparently genuine Elamite that even a skeptic like von Rad must grudgingly admit that "there could well have been an Elamite king of this name."[22]

The last king mentioned by name is "Tidal, king of Goiim." The prevailing view is that *Tidal* represents the cuneiform *Tudhaliya;* there were at least five Hittite rulers by that name, the first one known to us being ca. 1730 B.C. Von Rad dogmatically asserts that the biblical Tidal "*cannot* be disassociated from the Hittite Tudhalia, probably Tudhalia I (ca. 1730 B.C.)."[23] But, as a matter of fact, he *can* be disassociated! Although the five Hittite rulers by this same name give much credibility to our account in Genesis 14, we are *not* "locked in" to making precise identifications with one of these five as von Rad would like us to suppose. The name itself goes back to pre-Hittite Anatolia,[24] and thus pre-existed Hittite times.[25] Speiser hits the nail squarely on the head when he observes, "Once again, this is not the kind of name that could be improvised by a late Hebrew writer."[26] The epithet "king of Goiim" is curious and problematic: literally, this would mean "king of nations." Perhaps the best suggestion so far is that Tidal was a vagabond king who was able to win various tribes and provinces into his army,[27] and *Goiim* is a Hebrew translation of the Akkadian term *Umman-*, a term

originally used to characterize various peoples (Elamites, among others) who came, usually as invaders, from beyond the pale of conventional and familiar society . . . almost the precise equivalent of what the Greeks and Romans of a later day would call the "barbarians."[28]

Sarna summarizes nicely all that we have tried to show above:

The names of the Eastern kings (in Gen. 14) . . . have about them an air of verisimilitude. While they cannot be connected with any known historic personages, three of the four can certainly be associated with the early Near Eastern onomasticon [names].[29]

And, as we have noted several times above, these are *not* the sorts of names that a late Hebrew writer could be expected to invent and correctly assign to their respective nations!

Objections to the Historicity of the Mesopotamian Coalition

With the names of these Eastern kings we have noticed a tendency among certain scholars to make hasty and credulous conjectures as to the precise identity of each royal personage, followed by a reverse tendency among other scholars to make equally simplistic assertions denying the historicity of the entire account. Credulity is followed by hyperskepticism in an almost predictable pattern. The same pendulum-swinging pattern can be discerned with numerous other features in this account, such as the route followed by the Mesopotamian coalition, the kings of Palestine who were subdued, and the other peoples cited as being subdued by the foreign invaders. We do not have time here to address all these disputed items, but two more serious objections against the historicity of the Mesopotamian coalition should be considered.

First, as part of his hyperskeptical backswing against the historicity of Chedorlaomer, king of Elam, von Rad makes the following assertions:

> The name Chedorlaomer is good Elamite ("slave of Lagamer," an Elamite divinity). There could well have been an Elamite king of this name. *Nevertheless, the difficulties here are very great,* for it seems *impossible* to imagine Elam, east of Babylon, north of the Persian Gulf, as powerful at that time, indeed, at the head of such a coalition (v. 5) and furthermore operating strategically in southern Palestine.[30]

Von Rad's "very great difficulties" seem to revolve around the power of Elam in the early second millennium B.C., and her ability to lead a Mesopotamian coalition into southern Palestine at that time. Contrast his remarks with those made by Bruce Vawter only sixteen years later:

> After the collapse of Ur III [ca. 2110–2005 B.C.] and until the rise of Babylonian dominance under Hammurabi [ca. 1750 B.C.], the Elamites were more or less the masters of the old Sumero-Akkadian empire and the determiners of Mesopotamian politics.[31]

It is my contention that the observations of Vawter, contra von Rad, can be substantiated and that therefore it would have been not only possible but indeed logical for a king of Elam to head a coalition of Mesopotamian city-states on a punitive expedition against rebel Canaanite kings in the west *precisely at this time in history!*

In substantiating the observations of Vawter, it should first be noted that Ibbi-Sin, the last king of the third dynasty of Ur, was made prisoner by the Elamites.[32] The subsequent destruction of Ur by the Elamites and

Subarians is well known to us from a lamentation text dating to the first half of the second millennium B.C., where this destruction is deplored.[33] Elam continued to share in the general round of intrigues and alliances of the Babylonian states; it was ultimately contained by the power of Hammurabi, but not until Kutir-Nahhunte, king of Elam, had raided Babylon (ca. 1725 B.C.). Indeed, during the initial phase of the expansion of the First Dynasty of Babylon under Hammurabi (ca. 1792–1750 B.C.), we find evidence of a very powerful ruler of Elam named Shirukdukh I. Walther Hinz, professor of Iranian history at the University of Göttingen, observes:

Certainly the second half of Shirukdukh's reign lay under the shadow of Hammurabi's increasing power; but the scanty sources make no more precise reference to this. Only one single tablet throws a shaft of light on Shirukdukh's foreign policy. It comes from the ancient Shusharra, near modern Rania in the Kurdish district of Iraq; it dates roughly from the period around 1790 B.C., and it states that Shirukdukh, king of Elam, had written to a certain Tabitu asking: "Why does the land of Itabalkhim not send an emissary to me?" The Elamite army was standing ready to strike, and he, Shirukdukh, was directing his attention towards the ruler of Gutium (that is the land between modern Hamadan and Lake Urmia). He also had placed twelve thousand men under the command of a certain Nabili.

This tablet, first discovered in 1957, . . . makes two things clear: first that Shirukdukh I was still ruling as "King" of Elam in about 1790, and was therefore independent of Babylonia; secondly, that he evidently pursued an aggressive foreign policy.[34]

The idea of these Elamite rulers pursuing an aggressive foreign policy also finds support in certain of the Mari letters[35] which reflect the royal correspondence of King Zimri-Lim (ca. 1782–59 B.C.). These letters may or may not refer to Shirukdukh, although it is very probable that they do. The important thing to note is that they clearly do refer to a powerful ruler of Elam at this time in history:

In one such letter it says that an emissary of the "Regent" (*sukkal*) of Elam to the prince of Qatna (near the modern Homs in Syria) had come to Mari on his way there. It is clear, however, that the prince of Qatna had first sent an emissary to Susa, which gives some idea of the powerful position Shirukdukh occupied at that time. . . . Other documents from Mari prove that a grand regent of Elam had allied himself with the king of Eshnunna (not far from Baghdad), and had gone himself to Eshnunna with his army; this grand regent might again be Shirukdukh I.[36]

During the sixty-year span from ca. 1770 to 1710 B.C., Elam's power was evidently strong enough to install her own rulers (e.g., Warad-Sin, Rim-Sin) in Larsa. Hammurabi's successors then seem to have more or less controlled Elam until their own dynasty was ended ca. 1595 B.C. The darkness that hangs over the following centuries of Babylonian history is shared by Elam.[37]

In conclusion, it seems apparent that the period from ca. 2000 to 1750 B.C. is indeed a time of significant strength for Elam, and thus for it to be able to lead a Mesopotamian coalition during this interval is highly probable; at the very least, we must reject the dogmatic skepticism of von Rad who alleges that the scenario in Genesis 14 "seems impossible."

Even less excusable than the hyperskepticism of von Rad is that exhibited by de Vaux as recently as 1978. He asserts:

If the account is regarded as authentically historical, it is necessary to accept what it says. In essence, it says that four great kings of the East, an Elamite, a western Semite, a Hurrian and a Hittite, formed a coalition headed by the king of Elam and that these four kings waged war against five towns south of the Dead Sea because these towns had been subjected to the king of Elam, but had revolted against him. There are certainly gaps in our knowledge of the history of the ANE [Ancient Near East], but we know quite enough to be able to say that it is historically impossible for these five cities south of the Dead Sea to have at any one time during the second millennium been the vassals of Elam, and that Elam never was at the head of a coalition uniting the four great Near Eastern powers of that period. This account, then, cannot be regarded as historically useful.[38]

Notice once again the dogmatic language, "historically impossible." Perhaps one problem that de Vaux has is his assumption that he has identified the "four great Near Eastern powers" that constituted the coalition led by Chedorlaomer. As we noted earlier, the name *Tidal*, derived from the cuneiform *Tudhaliya*, is *not necessarily* a Hittite name. And although *Arioch* is linguistically Hurrian in background, the identification of Arioch's kingdom of "Ellasar" is quite unknown! Both of these latter kings may have been considerably inferior to their Elamite and Babylonian counterparts, the second possibly representing a smaller city-state and the first a motley crew of "barbarians" (cf. *Umman*- discussed above). Perhaps both were thus coerced into this coalition by their larger "allies." Indeed, one or more of these coalition members may have been a constituent vassal prince in the normal Elamite system of government!

As far back into the past as the historian's gaze can penetrate the constitution of Elam appears to have been federal. Only as a federation was it possible for an empire to hold together which was made up of utterly different components. . . . From earliest times we find at the head of the Elamite confederation an overlord ruling over a body of vassal princes.[39]

At any rate, it is foolish to assume, as does de Vaux, that the coalition *must* represent the "four great Near Eastern powers of that period."

Ancient Coalitions

In addition to all the evidence presented earlier for the relative strength and capability of Elam during this period (which again refutes de Vaux's simplistic assertion that it is "historically impossible" for Elam to have had vassals in Southern Palestine), we would do well to consider the subject of coalitions in general. It is my contention that this period (ca. 2000–1750 B.C.) is *precisely* when we would most expect to see such a coalition of smaller city-states from the East; subsequent to Hammurabi's accession, "the twin kingdoms of Babylon and Assyria in due course became the *only* heartland Mesopotamian powers."[40]

In Genesis 14, rival coalitions of kings are portrayed from Mesopotamia and Transjordan. We know that petty kingdoms abounded in Canaan and Transjordan at most periods until approximately the thirteenth century B.C. and later, when larger kingdoms (e.g., Moab, Edom) swallowed up the smaller city-states in Transjordan. Thus coalitions of such city-states in Transjordan are most likely to occur anywhere from the thirteenth century B.C. or earlier. By contrast, however, we have a much narrower "window" for credible dating when it comes to coalitions of Mesopotamian and neighboring kingdoms. Between the fall of the third dynasty of Ur (ca. 2000 B.C.) and the accession of Hammurabi (ca. 1750 B.C.), "such power alliances were an outstanding feature of the politics of the day, reaching as far east as Elam, and far north-west to the borders of Anatolia."[41] The same is *not* true outside this rather narrow time period when different political patterns prevailed. For example, operating within the narrow "window" of time as defined above, alliances of ten, fifteen, and twenty kings are mentioned in a famous Mari letter from the eighteenth century B.C.[42] At least five more Mesopotamian coalitions (other than the one cited in Genesis 14) are known from the nineteenth and eighteenth centuries B.C., typically with four or five members per coalition.[43] Furthermore, there is nothing peculiar about Eastern kings making Western expeditions; such expeditions are known from at least as early as Sargon of Akkad and Naram-Sin (ca. twenty-fourth to twenty-third centuries B.C.).[44] There is the account of Yahdun-Lim of Mari (the father of Zimri-Lim, a contemporary of Hammurabi) who marched on a campaign to the Mediterranean Sea and there defeated an alliance of rebel kings;[45] likewise, there is the expedition of Shamshi-Adad I of Assyria to Lebanon in the nineteenth or eighteenth century B.C.[46]

In conclusion, it seems apparent that the period from ca. 2000 to 1750 B.C. is indeed a time of numerous coalitions, both in Canaan-Syria-Transjordan, *and* in Mesopotamia. A Western expedition by a coalition of kings from Eastern city-states with Elam as head is probable in this time frame, but not in any other time frame. At the very least, we must reject the hyperskepticism of de Vaux who alleges that the account in Genesis 14 is "historically impossible."

Arguments From Silence

We have seen the scholarly swing of the pendulum with regard to the names of the four Eastern kings mentioned in Genesis 14, and we have seen the extreme forms of skepticism that prevail in certain quarters as regards the possibility of a Western expedition by these same kings under the leadership of the king of Elam. As our knowledge of the history of the ancient Near East increases, the likelihood of such events as those described in Genesis 14 also increases. Indeed, the most likely time frame for these sorts of events (i.e., 2000–1750 B.C.) is also the one most likely to include the lifetime of "Abraham the Hebrew," as recognized by most Bible scholars. Clearly it would be premature to discard Genesis 14 as an account which "cannot be regarded as historically useful," as does de Vaux. All of this necessarily prompts the question: Why the extreme reluctance on the part of some to accept the historical evidence as it stands, and to follow where it leads? Is it possible certain presuppositions are at work which dictate the conclusions in advance? Are there unstated desires to discard the biblical accounts as "historically impossible" and not "historically useful"? Why are higher standards of evidence and certitude being demanded from the biblical accounts than historians in other fields demand of their accounts?[47]

Perhaps some useful lessons can be learned by examining the "assured results" of biblical scholarship from previous centuries. Some critics were certain that the Bible was wrong in its references to a place called *Nineveh;* they felt that this was historically impossible. All of that was forever changed when Nineveh was finally excavated.[48] Similarly we were assured that the Bible was wrong in mentioning a people called the *Hittites;* this, too, we were told, was historically impossible.[49] And yet today there are specialists who have devoted their whole lives to the field of Hittitology;[50] moreover, the Oriental Institute of the University of Chicago sponsors the "Hittite Dictionary Project"! We were even told that Moses could not possibly have written anything because, allegedly, writing was unknown in his time. More examples could be cited of similar arguments from silence that have crumbled as new discoveries have shattered the "silence."[51] There is never any end to the supposed historical problems that some men can generate in order to call the basic reliability of the biblical accounts into question. Shall we wait until *all* possible difficulties are resolved before accepting the basic historicity of the biblical accounts?

Fortunately for all of us, the same hyperskeptical mindset has not prevailed in any other field of academic study. In the natural sciences we understand the necessity and importance of moving ahead on limited evidence, temporarily making imperfect and necessarily incomplete inductions of the available data followed by deductions from the same, in a series of cycles in a total process known as *retroduction*. A very similar process is followed by those in the humanities.[52] Retroduction produces both patterns and problems: the consistent patterns are where we make progress, the problems are where we do more research. In certain quarters of biblical studies, we find those who are paralyzed in their first attempt at induction. They seem unable (or unwilling?) to relax and move in the direction where the evidence points, thus never enjoying an unfettered quest for truth. If scientists in recent centuries had been similarly inhibited in this strange fashion, we might all still be living in the "dark ages."

The great mathematician and philosopher Alfred North Whitehead has been quoted as saying that "the theory of induction is the despair of philosophy, and yet all of our activities are based upon it."[53] Of course there are still residual problems to be resolved in Genesis 14; but they are neither so numerous nor so grave as to preclude the perception of distinct patterns of credible historicity. As Speiser so aptly summarizes regarding our passage: "The narrative itself has all the ingredients of historicity."[54]

The Will Versus the Intellect

As one ponders the hyperskepticism that sometimes emerges in so-called biblical "scholarship," one wonders what level of evidence *would* persuade the skeptic. Would a personal visit from Abraham (returned from the dead, and appearing to a roomful of Bible scholars all at one time) suffice? Could even Abraham make an acceptable case for the historicity of the patriarchal narratives in Genesis? Perhaps the problems are other than intellectual. A certain involvement of the will seems apparent, which colors the so-called "scholarly" results. Aldous L. Huxley makes a surprisingly frank and revealing confession in his book *Ends and Means* that is relevant to our point: "Most ignorance is vincible ignorance. We don't know because we don't want to know. It is our will that decides how and upon what subjects we shall use our intelligence."[55] Is it possible that some Bible scholars are less willing to exercise their intelligence in dealing with their subject matter than scholars in other fields, and hence the unusual degree of skepticism that we have seen? Why? The biblical narratives ultimately force one to a personal confrontation with the God of Abraham, Isaac, and Jacob. To accept the historicity of the patriarchs moves one considerably closer to accepting the historicity (if you will) of the God whom they serve.

And what is the problem, one may ask, with accepting the "historicity" of the God of Abraham, Isaac, and Jacob? Why should a man's will interfere with his intellect in openly pursuing the evidence that may point him to the reality of that God? The answer may not be as profound as we assume. Perhaps the repulsion that we feel is our dislike for authority over us, especially the ultimate authority of a God who loves righteousness and hates lawlessness. What if there is an almost instinctive rebellion against this God which afflicts the entire human race? Can we just assume that Bible scholars are automatically exempt? Intellectual pride, the affection we feel for certain favorite sins and the pleasure we derive from those sins, peer pressure, and a host of other factors may contribute to our reticence to pursue truth wherever it may lead. And even in our more "righteous" moments, when we toy with the idea of approaching this God, we may despair as we realize that we lack the constancy of will to maintain the lifestyle that He requires. To be like Abraham, the "friend of God," would be nice; we can almost envy the patriarchs as we read the narratives of their lives. But where does one begin? Perhaps even more than any discontent, we abhor the thought of being a hypocrite.

It is at this point that the "good news" of the Gospel comes into view. The New Testament makes it abundantly plain that the detailed stories of Abraham in the first testament were intended *not* to make us despair, but to give us hope. God's kind and generous offer of pardon for sin was first established with Abraham, and has never changed.[56] To become a "friend of God" (amazing thought!) is *not* something that a person can merit, but is offered as a gift. And not only has the penalty for our rebellion been paid, but the strength to live the required lifestyle is given to us as well. Jesus could say, "Abraham saw my day and was glad";[57] i.e., the same offer is open to every person alive today. The best way to flee from God is to flee to Him! The words of Isaiah are for *every* generation:

Seek the LORD while He may be found; call upon Him while He is near. Let the wicked forsake his way, and the unrighteous man his thoughts; and let him return to the LORD, and He will have compassion on him; and to our God, for He will abundantly pardon.[58]

And what is the consequence of ignoring this generous offer? The account of the rich man in hell as told for us in Luke 16:19–31 makes it all too plain what our willfulness deserves and what we will receive if we do not repent. "And he [the rich man] cried out and said, 'Father Abraham, have mercy on me, and send Lazarus, that he may dip the tip of his finger in water and cool off my tongue; for I am in agony in this flame.'"[59]

God's justice, unmitigated by His mercy, is a fearful prospect. Only in this lifetime can we receive that mercy. After physical death it will be too late.

It seems that only a fool would suppress the evidence available to him in this lifetime which would lead him to the God of Abraham to obtain the mercy and pardon which are so freely offered. But can even a highly acclaimed scholar be such a fool? How tragic it will be on that Judgment Day if some of those who studied the text so closely prove to be among those who threw away their opportunities! This inevitably becomes very personal.

How about you? Are you free to follow the evidence where it leads? Or do you have to suppress evidence that contradicts your willful choices? The same God who paid a high price to secure your pardon has promised the strength you need to master your own will, and to live a life pleasing to Him. You can be made a friend of God! If your temporary "success" and/or "pleasure" in this fleeting lifetime mean more to you than this amazing offer, then at least give some thought to these words of Jesus:

For what shall it profit a man to gain the whole world, and forfeit his own soul? Or what shall a man give in exchange for his soul? If anyone is ashamed of me and my words in this adulterous and sinful generation, the Son of Man will be ashamed of him when He comes in His Father's glory with the holy angels.[60]

Notes

[1]William F. Albright, "The Historical Background of Genesis XIV," *Journal of the Society of Oriental Research*, 10 (1926): 231. (Italics are mine.)

[2]Cf. J. A. Emerton, "The Riddle of Genesis XIV," *Vetus Testamentum*, 21 (1971): 403. Emerton comments: "Few chapters in the Old Testament have provoked more disagreement among scholars than Genesis xiv, and its problems have often been discussed."

[3]Niels-Erik A. Andreasen, "Genesis 14 in Its Near Eastern Context," in *Scripture in Context*, ed. Carl D. Evans (Pittsburgh, Pa.: The Pickwick Press, 1980), 59.

[4]Proponents of the view that Genesis 14 is genuine history include: E. A. Speiser, (E. A. Speiser, "Genesis," in *The Anchor Bible*, ed. William F. Albright and David Noel Freedman, 3d ed. [Garden City, N.Y.: Doubleday, 1983]), who suggests an Akkadian original; and William F. Albright who, in a series of articles (1921–68; see "Further Reading"), suggests that the original source was an old Hebrew poem. For other authors who are neutral on the question of the precise nature of the original source but who agree on an early second millennium B.C. context, see the "Further Reading" list at the end of this paper. For additional proponents and references, see R. de Vaux, *The Early History of Israel* (Philadelphia, Pa.: Westminster Press, 1978), 216, note 174. Proponents of the view that Genesis 14 is *not* genuine history include: R. de Vaux, *Early History;* Michael C. Astour, "Political and Cosmic Symbolism in Genesis 14 and in Its Babylonian Sources," in *Biblical Motifs*, ed. Alexander Altmann (Cambridge: Harvard University Press, 1966); and J. A.

Emerton, "Some False Clues in the Study of Genesis XIV," *Vetus Testamentum,* 21 (October 1971). Emerton opposes Astour as well as Albright and Speiser.

[5]Cf. comments by Andreasen, "Genesis 14," 60; and by Bruce Vawter, *On Genesis: A New Reading* (Garden City, N.Y.: Doubleday, 1977), 186. Andreasen, in his footnote 10, cites W. Schatz (W. Schatz, *Genesis 14: Eine Untersuchung* [Frankfurt: Peter Lang, 1972]) as an example of the thorough-going skepticism found among the older proponents of this view, "before the recent explosion of our knowledge of the ancient Near East."

[6]Speiser, "Genesis," 105.

[7]Genesis 14:1–9. This and all subsequent Scripture references in this chapter, unless otherwise noted, are from the New American Standard Bible, copyright 1973 by The Lockman Foundation.

[8]Gerhard von Rad, *Genesis: A Commentary,* trans. John H. Marks (Philadelphia, Pa.: Westminster Press, 1961), 171.

[9]Francis Brown, S. R. Driver, and Charles A. Briggs, *A Hebrew and English Lexicon of the Old Testament* (Oxford: Clarendon Press, 1907), 57.

[10]For example, the initial *aleph* must be mistaken for *ayin,* and the final *lamedh* would have to be an error for final *yodh;* moreover, the Mari documents dictate a later date for Hammurabi than was then accepted.

[11]For example, cf. Astour, "Symbolism," 75–78. Also cf. C. A. Simpson and W. R. Bowie, *The Interpreter's Bible,* (1952), 1:592–95 (e.g., "In view of the unhistorical character of the present narrative, no light is thrown by this verse [14:1] upon the date of Abraham—or upon the chronology of the period preceding the Exodus in Israel's history").

[12]For example, cf. Andreasen, "Genesis 14," 60.

[13]Speiser, "Genesis," 107.

[14]*The International Standard Bible Encyclopedia,* 2d ed. (Grand Rapids, Mich.: Eerdman's 1982), s.v. "Arioch" by R. K. Harrison.

[15]Harrison, "Arioch," 290. Mari is an ancient north Syrian city of the upper Euphrates, about seven miles northwest of Abu-Kemal at Tell Hariri; original excavations were conducted by Andre Parrot under the auspices of the Louvre Museum (1933–39, and 1951–56). About twenty thousand cuneiform tablets were found in the palace area, which included the royal correspondence of Yasmakh-Adad and Zimri-Lim, both of whom were contemporaries of Hammurabi of Babylon. Nuzi is an ancient northeast Mesopotamian town found buried in the mound of Yorghan Tepe, about nine miles west of the modern town of Kirkut; original excavations were conducted by the American Schools of Oriental Research in conjunction with the Harvard University Museum (1925–31). "At Mari most of the tablets deal mainly with the royal family and its political activities, while at Nuzi there were found records of the life and activity of hundreds of ordinary citizens" (*The Zondervan Pictorial Encyclopedia of the Bible* [Grand Rapids, Mich.: Zondervan, 1975–76], s.v. "Nuzi" by Allan A. MacRae).

[16]von Rad, *Genesis,* 171.

[17]Harrison, "Arioch," 290.

[18]Speiser, "Genesis," 107.

[19]Ibid., 70.

[20]G. Ch. Aalders, *Genesis,* trans. William Heynen (Grand Rapids, Mich.: Zondervan Publishing House, 1981), 1:282–83.

[21]For a good summary of the evidence for the Elamite components in this name, see *The International Standard Bible Encyclopedia*, 2d ed., s.v. "Chedorlaomer" by R. K. Harrison.

[22]von Rad, *Genesis*, 171.

[23]Ibid. (Emphasis mine.)

[24]Speiser, "Genesis," 107.

[25]Vawter, *On Genesis*, 188.

[26]Speiser, "Genesis," 107.

[27]Aalders, *Genesis*, 283.

[28]Vawter, *On Genesis*, 188. Cf. also the comments by Speiser, "Genesis," 107–8.

[29]Nahum M. Sarna, *Understanding Genesis* (New York: Schocken Books, 1966), 111.

[30]von Rad, *Genesis*, 171. (Emphasis mine.)

[31]Vawter, *On Genesis*, 188. (Dates mine.)

[32]*Interpreter's Dictionary of the Bible* (New York: Abingdon Press, 1962), s.v. "Elam" by M. J. Dresden.

[33]S. N. Kramer, trans., "A Sumerian Lamentation," in *Ancient Near Eastern Texts Relating to the Old Testament*, ed. James B. Pritchard, 3d ed. with supplement (Princeton, N.J.: Princeton University Press, 1969), 455–63.

[34]Walther Hinz, "Persia c. 1800–1550 B.C.: The Dynasty of the 'Grand Regent' Rulers of Elam," in *The Cambridge Ancient History*, ed. I. E. S. Edwards et al., 3d ed. (Cambridge: Cambridge University Press, 1973), 2:263.

[35]See note 15 for a description of these Mari letters.

[36]Hinz, "Persia," 263.

[37]For more details on Elam's power, both during the period and during other periods of her history, see *Interpreter's Dictionary*, s.v. "Elam"; *International Standard Bible Encyclopedia*, s.v. "Elam" and "Elamites" by A. R. Millard; and Georges Roux, *Ancient Iraq*, 2d ed. (Middlesex: Penguin Books, 1980), passim.

[38]de Vaux, *Early History*, 219. (Emphasis mine.)

[39]Hinz, "Persia," 256–57.

[40]K. A. Kitchen, *The Bible in its World: The Bible and Archaeology Today* (Downers Grove, Ill.: Inter-Varsity Press, 1977), 72. (Emphasis mine.)

[41]Ibid.

[42]K. A. Kitchen, *Ancient Orient and Old Testament* (Downers Grove, Ill.: Inter-Varsity Press, 1966), 45; see esp. his notes 48–51.

[43]Ibid.; see his note 50 for details concerning these coalitions.

[44]Ibid., 47; see esp. his note 55.

[45]A. Leo Oppenheim, trans., "The Dedication of the Shamash Temple by Yahdun-Lim," in *Ancient Near Eastern Texts*, 556–57.

[46]Kitchen, *Ancient Orient*, 47; N.B. his note 58: "The opinion of some Old Testament scholars that Gen. 14 is merely a late midrash . . . wholly fails to account for the authentic early detail of power-alliances."

[47]Dr. Stephen M. Fuller notes that the evidence for the historicity of Genesis 14 surpasses the evidence available to L. S. Stavrianos in his classic work, *The Balkans Since 1453* (New York: Holt, Rinehart and Winston, 1958), and yet no one in his field denies the

validity of Stavrianos's work. The sorts of inferences we have been making about the basic historicity of Genesis 14 are "perfectly legitimate according to the best example of the historians' craft" (from a personal communication).

[48]There was considerable skepticism during the eighteenth century regarding not only Nineveh, but even the Assyrian empire in general during the time of the prophet Jonah. Cf. Voltaire's discussion of these matters in Francois M. A. de Voltaire, *The Philosophy of History* (1766; reprint, London: Vision Press, 1965), 45: "The imaginary empire of Assyria was not yet in existence at the time that Jonas is introduced."

[49]M. F. Unger, commenting on the biblical Horites (Hurrians) and Hittites, wrote that "until comparatively recent times these peoples, who were once prominent on the stage of Old Testament history, were known only from scattered biblical passages. Since secular history appeared silent concerning the existence of these ethnic groups, the scriptural allusions to them were customarily regarded with critical suspicion and references to them were commonly dismissed as historically unreliable" (M. F. Unger, "Archaeological Discoveries and Their Bearing on the Old Testament," *Bibliotheca Sacra* 112 [April 1955]: 137).

Similarly, Dr. A. H. Sayce, a later professor of Assyriology at Oxford, quotes an unidentified critic whom he calls "a distinguished scholar" writing in 1843 regarding the biblical reference to "the kings of the Hittites and the kings of the Egyptians" in 2 Kings 7:6. "'Its "unhistorical tone,"' [the critic] declared, 'is too manifest to allow of our easy belief in it. No Hittite kings can have compared in power with the king of Judah . . . nor is there a single mark of acquaintance with the contemporaneous history.'" Sayce then adds: "Recent discoveries have retorted the critic's objections upon himself. It is not the biblical writer but the modern author who is now proved to have been unacquainted with the contemporaneous history of the time" (A. H. Sayce, *The Hittites: the Story of a Forgotten Empire,* 4th ed. [London: The Religious Tract Society, 1925], 11–12).

[50]E.g., H. A. Hoffner, Jr., is professor of Hittitology and co-director of the Hittite Dictionary Project, The Oriental Institute of the University of Chicago.

[51]For an excellent discussion on "the inconclusive nature of negative evidence," see Kitchen, *Ancient Orient,* 30–32, 44, and esp. his note 47. Also see Kitchen, *Bible in its World,* 73. Speaking of the four kings in this Mesopotamian coalition of Gen. 14, he notes: "The individuals themselves have not yet been identified in extra-biblical documents, but this is not surprising when one considers the gaps in our knowledge of the period" (Kitchen, *Ancient Orient,* 44). Also see Edwin M. Yamauchi, *The Stones and the Scriptures* (Philadelphia, Pa.: J. B. Lippincott, 1972), 146–66.

[52]For a helpful discussion of retroduction in both science and the humanities (theology in particular), see John Warwick Montgomery, "The Theologian's Craft: A Discussion of Theory Formation and Theory Testing in Theology," in his *The Suicide of Christian Theology* (Minneapolis, Minn.: Bethany, 1970), 267–313.

[53]Cited in T. M. Little and F. J. Hills, *Statistical Methods in Agricultural Research* (Davis, Calif.: University of California, 1972), 4.

[54]Speiser, "Genesis," 109.

[55]Aldous L. Huxley, *Ends and Means,* 6th ed. (New York: Harper, 1937), 312.

[56]Cf. Gal. 3:1–29, esp. vv. 17–18, which argue this very point.

[57]John 8:56. (My paraphrase.)

[58]Isa. 55:6–7.

[59]Luke 16:24.

[60]Mark 8:36–37. (My translation.)

Further Reading

[N.B. While I cannot agree with all the views espoused by the following authors, it is safe to say that most if not all of these men are proponents of the view that Genesis 14 is genuine history. See note 4 for more details.]

Aalders, G. Ch. *Genesis*. 2 vols. Translated by William Heynen. Grand Rapids, Mich.: Zondervan, 1981.

Albright, William F. *Yahweh and the Gods of Canaan*. Garden City, N.Y.: Doubleday, 1968.

————. *From the Stone Age to Christianity*. 2d ed. Baltimore: Johns Hopkins Press, 1957.

————. "Abram the Hebrew." *Bulletin of the American Schools of Oriental Research* 163 (1961): 36–54.

————. "A Third Revision of the Early Chronology of Western Asia." *Bulletin of the American Schools of Oriental Research* 99 (1942): 28–36.

————. "The Historical Background of Genesis XIV." *Journal of the Society of Oriental Research* 10 (1926): 231–69.

Andreasen, Niels-Erik A. "Genesis 14 in its Near Eastern Context." In *Scripture in Context,* edited by Carl D. Evans. Pittsburgh, Pa.: Pickwick Press, 1980.

Bright, John. *A History of Israel*. 2d ed. Philadelphia, Pa.: Westminster Press, 1972.

Kitchen, K. A. *The Bible in its World: The Bible and Archaeology Today*. Exeter, England: Paternoster Press, 1977.

————. *Ancient Orient and Old Testament*. Downers Grove, Ill.: Inter-Varsity Press, 1966.

Roux, Georges. *Ancient Iraq*. 2d ed. Middlesex, England: Penguin Books, 1980.

Sarna, Nahum M. *Understanding Genesis*. New York: Schocken Books, 1970.

Vawter, Bruce. *On Genesis: A New Reading*. Garden City, N.Y.: Doubleday, 1977.

Yamauchi, Edwin M. *The Stones and the Scriptures*. Philadelphia, Pa.: J. B. Lippincott, 1972.

4.2

Truth Via Prophecy

John A. Bloom

HOW DO YOU *KNOW* THAT YOU'RE RIGHT? A good scientist focuses his entire research program on this question. He seeks objective experimental data and justifies his theoretical assumptions in the effort to prove that his model best explains the data available. Emotions, however, cannot substitute for objective data in a scientific endeavor. Many a scientist has *felt* absolutely convinced that his theory and experimental data were true, only to find that someone else's results blew his beautiful theory out of the water.

Is such a "hard-nosed" approach to truth unrealistic? Surely it is obvious that in most areas of life one must act on the basis of facts and not trust in our emotions. When driving a car, we stop at intersections if the light is red, not because we feel like it, but because if we don't the odds are that we will eventually be hit by another car or be stopped by another red light, this time accompanied by a siren.

The more important the decision, the more important it is to look for facts upon which to base that decision. A doctor does not judge the drugs he prescribes on the basis of their color and flavor, but on their effectiveness. When people set out to buy a house, they tend to ask if it has termites, if the roof leaks, whether the basement floods every spring, and how attractive the neighborhood is. However, all realtors know that some people will select a particular house merely because they like its color. Thus in the real world, one of the wisest things we can do is ask ourselves, How good is the *evidence* that this is right? By doing so we can prevent being tricked by our emotions into doing something we will later regret.

What is true of other matters is also true in religion: we need to make decisions based on facts or evidence. Assuming that by *religion* we mean any philosophy or system of belief that purports to tell us what will happen to us after we die, it is important to ask this question of the various religions. After all, our condition after we die may depend upon decisions which we make while we are alive. Unfortunately, religion seems to be one area where this question, How do you know you're right? is never asked; or if it is, the answer is: Because I just know it's true! or, I prayed and asked God to show me if it was true, and I felt this burning in my heart that it was! To the thinking person, such subjective criteria only beg the question.

Another problem with religion is that it comes in so many brands that differ and even conflict in telling what you must do in order to survive death happily. For example, Mormons say that you must be baptized in one of *their* special ceremonies in order to "make it," while evangelical Christians argue that you can only gain salvation by trusting in Christ's death on the cross (and His resurrection from the dead) to be the total and sole payment for your sins—baptism and the like are symbols, but not essentials. Who is right? In science, when people develop differing theories, they make an immediate appeal to the physical, reproducible, experimental data in order to verify their claims. However, most religions appeal to emotional ("spiritual") experiences in order to "verify" theirs. For example, in the flyleaf of the Book of Mormon, we find written:

And when ye shall receive these things, I would exhort you that ye would ask God . . . if these things are not true; and if ye shall ask with a sincere heart, with real intent, having faith in Christ, he will manifest the truth of it unto you, by the power of the Holy Ghost.[1]

In practice this alleged manifestation, "by the power of the Holy Ghost," is a subjective inner experience. In essence Mormons are promising that if you are sincere enough you can have the same emotional experience they have had. Of course, every scientist knows that if you set up your experiment in exactly the same way as an earlier researcher, you can usually duplicate the previous results. *Duplication proves consistency, but not truth.*

While feelings may be plausible criteria to use in deciding what clothes to put on after getting up in the morning, emotions certainly should have little place in our search for truth in religion. The questions that should be asked are: How do they come to think that they are right? Is their basis something testable, or am I asked to park my brains at the door and accept what they say on "blind faith"? Worse, am I told to trust in some slippery emotional experience that could have come from any number of sources? Is a gushy feeling ("inner witness") the only assurance they can offer to *prove* that if I believe and do what they say, then I will survive death successfully? Is it safe for me to *assume* that if a given religion makes me feel good now, it will make me feel good after I die?

Obviously, the best way to test a religion would be to believe it, die, and come back to life again if we were unhappy with our state in the afterlife. That way we could try some other religion in our new life. Unfortunately, we do not have any objective proof that the average person can come back to life again once he is really dead, so we need to use some other test. Given that we have a limited amount of time in this life to study religions, we can dispense with those that offer us a second chance in the afterlife or which will reincarnate us if we make a mistake in this life, or which promise us that all will be well eventually no matter how we live now. Prudence dictates that we first ought to consider the claims of those religions which say that everything depends upon the decisions made and lived by in this one life.

Of these, let's begin by investigating the religion which describes the most severe consequences for those who do not believe it when they die: biblical Christianity, which teaches there is an eternal hell (in contrast to the purgatory of Catholicism and the "no hell" view of liberal forms of Protestantism). How are we to know that the claims of the Bible, as contrasted with those of religious books from other cultures, are to be taken as true? Does the Bible only offer us "proof" in the form of emotional experiences like others? Consider the following:

"Present your case," says the LORD. "Set forth your arguments," says Jacob's King. "Bring in your idols to tell us what is going to happen. Tell us what the former things were, so that we may consider them and know their final outcome. Or *declare to us the things to come, tell us what the future holds, so that we may know that you are gods.* Do something whether good or bad, so that we will be dismayed and filled with fear."

Who then is like me? Let him proclaim it. Let him declare and lay out before me what has happened since I established my ancient people, and what is yet to come—yes, *let him foretell what will come.* Do not tremble, do not be afraid. Did I not proclaim this and foretell it long ago? You are my witnesses. Is there any God besides me? No, there is no other Rock; I know not one.[2]

The God of the Bible is calling for a rigorous test which involves the objective prediction of *future* events in human history. The God of the

Bible does not ask us to trust Him on the basis of a "leap in the dark" kind of faith or a mere emotional experience. Logically, we can reverse this challenge to other "gods" and ask if the God of the Bible can predict the future Himself. If He can, and if no other religion can substantiate a similar claim, then we have an objective, historically testable verification that the God of the Bible alone exists.

Criteria of Fulfillment and Assorted Hoaxes

Before proceeding, we must define what we mean by "predicting the future." In general, four criteria should be satisfied:

Clarity

The prediction must be clear enough to be recognized when it has occurred. By this we mean that it cannot be vague or have double-talk in it so that no matter what happens, it would be "fulfilled." The Oracle of Delphi, an ancient Greek shrine to the god Apollo, was well-known for this type of ambiguous "prophecy."[3] One of the more tragic cases concerns Croesus, King of Lydia, who sent to the Oracle of Delphi to inquire about his planned attack on Cyrus, King of Persia. The "prophetess" there informed him, "If Croesus should make war on the Persians, he would destroy a mighty empire." Not catching the ambiguity, Croesus was greatly encouraged and went out to attack Cyrus, and indeed a mighty empire was destroyed—his own![4]

Prior Announcement

The prediction must be known to have been made before it is fulfilled. Otherwise, how could it be called a prediction? On the flyleaf of the Book of Mormon we find such a dubious claim of fulfilled prophecy. Under the heading, "A Few Interesting Book of Mormon References," we read:

America's history foretold 2500 years ago.–1st Nephi, Chap. 13, page 22.
 A–Columbus—Verse 12
 B–Fate of the Indians—Verse 14
 C–The Puritans—Verse 16
 D–The Revolutionary War—Verses 17–19
 E–The Bible—Verses 23–29[5]

These would truly be incredible prophecies but for one problem: The earliest date for any known tangible manuscript of the Book of Mormon is 1827,[6] long after the above events were fulfilled. Thus the claim to be twenty-five hundred years old is only that—a claim, with no objective evidence to back it up.

Independence

A fulfillment should not be influenced by the prophet himself, or by his zealous band of followers. Brigham Young, one of the founders of Mormonism, is also recognized as one of its "prophets."[7] However, upon studying his teachings and predictions one finds that very few of them are considered "canonical" or authoritative. One is his vision that the Great Salt Lake valley would be the place where the Mormons would settle.[8] The fulfillment of Young's vision by the establishment and growth of Salt Lake City can hardly be considered a significant prophecy as its fulfillment required the effort of his followers.[9]

Likelihood

A prediction must be more than a good guess. Either the fulfillment should be sufficiently remote so that it could not be a good guess (i.e., predicting the next president versus predicting who will be president a hundred years from now); or sufficiently detailed so that it could not have been guessed (predicting the next president being a Republican versus his winning by 2,300,541 votes).

To clarify our terminology, we will call any prediction that meets all of the above requirements a *prophecy*. Obviously, genuine prophecies are extremely difficult to make: ask television weathermen. It seems that, more often than not, one hears an announcer predicting a fine sunny afternoon while it is actually raining outside. Sports announcers are also quite unreliable when they try to guess which team will win. Nevertheless, there are people today who sometimes make accurate prophecies. Perhaps the most famous is Jeanne Dixon, who predicted President Kennedy's assassination. However, when one studies the various predictions which she has made over the years, one finds that in fact many have not come true at all.[10] Does this mean that Jeanne is a 40 percent prophet, or that we can trust what she says 40 percent of the time? On this point, the God of the Bible makes an important comment:

But a prophet who presumes to speak in my name anything I have not commanded him to say, or a prophet who speaks in the name of other gods, must be put to death. You may say to yourselves, "How can we know when a message has not been spoken by the LORD?" If what a prophet proclaims in the name of the LORD does not take place or come true, that is a message the LORD has not spoken. That prophet has spoken presumptuously. Do not be afraid of him.[11]

Thus the God of the Bible asserts that complete predictive accuracy will characterize those who are actually His prophets: if anyone who claimed to be a prophet of the Lord ever made a mistake in even one prediction, he was to be executed. Certainly this additional test quickly narrows the field of contestants. We need not be afraid of, nor should we trust in, any prophet who has made even one obvious mistake.

Faced with such stringent criteria, very few religions offer objective prophecy to support their truth claims. The Koran is one of many religious books which does not even try:

They say, "Why have signs not been sent down upon him [Mohammed] by his Lord?" Say: "The signs are only with God, and I am only a plain warner." What, is it not sufficient for them that We have sent down to thee the Book that is recited to them?[12]

Despite his ambivalence regarding the presentation of evidence, Mohammed does go on to give ample predictions and warnings about the Last Judgment. However, by the time one can verify those prophecies, it may be far too late to change sides.

Thus, few "gods" will permit their authority to be challenged by any tangible evidence which we can test today. Now that we have a well-defined test with which to work, we can investigate the biblical prophecies themselves.

Prophecies from the Bible

From reading the Old Testament, we find that its writers were regarded as inspired, usually because they were recognized as true prophets. Of course, we cannot check the predictions which proved this claim to their ancient audiences, because we have no proof today that their short-range predictions were actually made before the events took place. However, we can ask if they made any long-range predictions, ones which were obviously fulfilled well after the prophecy was given. For our purposes, this is any time near or after the time of Christ, as by then the Old Testament was at least two hundred years old and was widely distributed throughout the Roman Empire both in Hebrew and Greek translations, making it difficult to insert changes, "corrections," or adjustments.

After finding that prophecies in the Koran and Book of Mormon are notably weak or non-existent, it might seem strange to note that there are so many long-range prophecies in the Bible. In fact, if all the long-range prophecies of the Scriptures were simply compiled in this brief essay, it would turn into a book.[13] Consequently, we will only be able to consider a few examples in this discussion. For those who wish to investigate further, I have mentioned several books for additional study in the notes.[14]

When conducting an experiment, a scientist usually tries to have a "control"; that is, he attempts to verify his results by comparing them to a standard or to a parallel experiment in which some critical elements are changed. Thus when a chemist studies a new reaction he may set aside a portion of his reagents to compare the unreacted originals with the product of the reaction. In this way he can be sure that the reaction itself, and not some process that would have happened anyhow without doing anything special, is responsible for the new product he observes. Is it possible to have such things as controls or standards when studying prophecy? Ideally we could institute controls by repeating history over again, the first time without making the prophecy and the second time with the prophecy in effect, to compare what happens. Since history does not repeat itself in such a manner, we need to look for a more realistic standard.

In biology and psychology, two scientific fields where this same difficulty of repeating experiments on live subjects exists, the problem of controls is largely overcome by the use of identical twins or littermates. Close genetic similarity suffices as a control when experiments cannot be repeated on the same individual. Such a twin-type standard is an approach we can use in studying prophecy, because the God of the Bible has made predictions about ancient "twin cities": cities within the same nation or geographical region which were of the same size and relative importance at the time the prophecies were made. The only significant difference between them is that the God of the Bible predicted that one city would have a substantially different future than the other. Because as simple a mistake on the part of the prophet as confusing the city names would jeopardize the prophecy, such city pairs provide an excellent control of the predictive accuracy of biblical prophets.

Memphis and Thebes

Memphis. The great capital city of Egypt for most of her ancient history, Memphis was also the northern center for Egypt's many religious groups.[15] Thus we are not surprised when the God of the Bible declares through Ezekiel: "I will destroy the idols and put an end to the images in Memphis."[16] Was this prediction fulfilled? At around the time of Christ, several hundred years after this prediction was spoken and about one hundred years after it was disseminated throughout the Roman world in both Hebrew and Greek versions, it was not fulfilled: Strabo (the Greek historian) found the city "large and populous, next to Alexandria in size" and gave a description of the many gods, temples, and statues which occupied this religious center.[17] Scholars have noted that zealous Christians during the third century defaced and destroyed some of the idols in Memphis.[18] While this is noble, it is not what one would call a fulfillment of prophecy by an independent party.

In the seventh century, however, the scene changed: The followers of Mohammed swept through the Middle East, conquering city after city and converting people from idolatry to Islam by the threat of the sword. Following the conquest of Egypt, the caliph Omar restricted the army from making Alexandria the Moslem capital because water (the Nile) would come between the caliph and the army. With his further restriction that they could not own property or take root in Egypt, the army chose to settle at the encampment from which they had besieged the fortress protecting Memphis. This army headquarters, called *Fustat*, grew over the centuries into the city of Cairo.[19] As this new city grew, the population of Memphis drifted to Cairo, and the stone work of Memphis became a convenient "quarry" for expanding the new capital city because it happened to be only ten miles away.

By the late 1800s, this quarrying was so complete that the only significant relic of Memphis above ground was a single colossal statue of Ramses II.[20] From 1908 to 1913, the famous archaeologist Flinders Petrie excavated the site with great difficulty as the "ground was nearly all cultivated, and the search must be always below water level."[21] It is striking that any remains which Petrie left exposed soon disappeared due to weathering and the continued quarrying efforts of nearby villagers. Today the statue of Ramses II is once again the only significant monument at Memphis visible above ground and even it has been moved to a display near the site.[22]

Thus the idols and images of Memphis have been destroyed and used to build the city of Cairo. Notice how exactly this prophecy came true: it certainly is not the sort of thing that would have happened anyway. True, all ancient cities have been attacked and ravaged at least once by now, and many sites have been abandoned, but rarely have their ruins been quarried to the point that nothing visible is left of them today. In contrast, let us consider the prophecy concerning another Egyptian religious center.

Thebes. As the largest city in southern Egypt, Thebes was another famous center for Egyptian religions. In the same context as the above prophecy concerning Memphis, the God of the Bible says: "I will . . . inflict punishment on Thebes. I will . . . cut off the hordes of Thebes. . . . Thebes will be taken by storm."[23] From history we find that God clearly did execute judgment on Thebes. While Nebuchadnezzar and Cambyses both captured and burned Thebes, the city recovered a good measure of its former strength. In 92 B.C. Thebes withstood a three-year siege before Ptolemy Lathyrus (the grandfather of Cleopatra) sacked and burned the city in anger. Although Thebes recovered again, it was finally destroyed by Cornelius Gallus during the reign of Augustus for having joined in an insurrection against the tax-gatherers. Thus it was not until about two hundred years after the latest liberal date for this prophecy that the "hordes of Thebes" were reduced to only a small collection of villages.[24]

Thebes has never regained its stature as a city, and today about nine small villages dot the area. Certainly the hordes of Thebes have been "cut off" (a Hebrew colloquialism for "killed"), yet the area is still sparsely populated (in contrast with prophecies against other cities like Petra, of which it was predicted that no one would live in them any more).

Moreover, the ruins of Thebes still stand: Griffith notes, "Thebes still offers the greatest assemblage of monumental ruins in the world."[25] Most of the temples and statues (aside from the pyramids) which we associate with ancient Egyptian culture are located at this religious center.[26] The contrast between people and idols is striking in these two prophecies and fulfillments: The idols are gone from Memphis; they still stand in Thebes. Memphis was never attacked and ravaged as severely as Thebes. The people of Memphis were not wiped out; they simply moved to Cairo.

We have seen two cases of predictions made centuries before the fulfillments occurred. The predictions were concise, rather than so vague that they could be applied to any ancient city. No zealous band of followers assisted the fulfillment of these prophecies. (Moslems are not that fond of the Jewish Scriptures.) Note how the prediction concerning one city is in effect a control for the other: If Ezekiel had merely reversed the city names in his prophecies, both would have been wrong. It appears then that these are genuine prophecies which were given by the God of the Bible to substantiate His claim that He can be trusted.

Tyre and Sidon
Tyre. To this Phoenician city, the prophet Ezekiel warns:

This is what the Sovereign LORD says: I am against you, O Tyre, and *I will bring many nations against you,* like the sea casting up its waves. *They will destroy the walls of Tyre and pull down her towers, I will scrape away her rubble and make her a bare rock. Out in the sea she will become a place to spread fishnets,* for I have spoken, declares the Sovereign LORD. She will become plunder for the nations, and her settlements on the mainland will be ravaged by the sword. Then they will know that I am the LORD.

For this is what the Sovereign LORD says: From the north I am going to bring against Tyre Nebuchadnezzar king of Babylon, king of kings, with horses and chariots, with horsemen and a great army. He will ravage your settlements on the mainland with the sword; he will set up siege works against you, build a ramp up to your walls and raise his shields against you. He will direct the blows of his battering rams against your walls and demolish your towers with his weapons. His horses will be so many that they will cover you with dust. Your walls will tremble at the noise of the war horses, wagons and chariots when he enters your gates as men enter a city whose walls have been broken through. The hoofs of his horses will trample all your streets; he will kill your people with the sword, and your strong pillars will fall to the ground. They [note the change from "he"] will plunder your wealth and loot your merchandise; *they will break down your walls and demolish your fine houses and throw your stones, timber and rubble into the sea.* I will put an end to your noisy songs, and the music of your harps will be heard no more. *I will make you a bare rock, and you will become a place to spread fishnets. You will never be rebuilt,* for I the LORD have spoken, declares the Sovereign LORD.[27]

This prophecy concerning the destruction and fate of Tyre is one of the more startling of all biblical predictions against ancient cities. In the time of Ezekiel, Tyre was the greatest maritime city on the Mediterranean. It was situated on the coast, with an excellent natural harbor protected by an island about a half-mile offshore.[28] As predicted, Nebuchadnezzar took the mainland city in 573 B.C. after a thirteen-year siege.[29] However, by then most of the people had moved their wealth out to the island, and since Nebuchadnezzar did not have a navy, he had to abandon any further assault on Tyre.

In 332 B.C. Alexander the Great attacked Tyre on his way to Egypt. Since Nebuchadnezzar's time, Tyre had remained on the island, not rebuilding appreciably on the mainland.[30] Having no navy to aid him, Alexander attempted to use brute force to build a land bridge two hundred feet wide through the sea out to the island. This was no easy task; it required the combined slave labor from many nations that he had already conquered. For building material, Alexander used the walls and buildings of the old mainland city; so much material was needed to build the land bridge that the workers had to scrape the ground bare. Although enemy fire stopped construction of the land bridge within one hundred yards of the island city, Alexander was then able to muster a navy by granting amnesty to anyone with a ship who would help him. Thus Alexander, with the help of many nations, finally succeeded in capturing the island refuge.[31] However, the city on the island quickly recovered. At the time of Christ, Tyre was once again a major port.

During the Crusades, the island city was fought over heavily. In 1291 it was recaptured by the Moslems, who then completely destroyed it to prevent its use as a beach-head for future incursions.[32] The site remained desolate for hundreds of years, and in the late 1700s a small fishing village began on the island.[33] Today this village has a population of about twelve thousand, but it does not occupy the ancient mainland site of Tyre as it is situated on the northern end of the island. These fishermen use the surrounding large flat, bare areas as a place for spreading their nets out to dry.[34]

Even if it were true that parts of this prophecy were "predicted" after both Nebuchadnezzar and Alexander's attack on Tyre (as alleged by some liberal Christians who would like to date the book of Ezekiel as late as 200 B.C.[35]), the long-range aspects that the metropolis was never rebuilt after its devastation in 1291 and that fishermen today use the site as a place to dry their nets show that much of the prediction was certainly not guesswork.

Sidon. As many ancient cities have become ruins, we should look at the fate of another Lebanese coastal city as a scientific control for Tyre. Sidon, today a modern port twenty miles further up the coast, is a particularly good control because in ancient times it was considered to be a twin city with Tyre; in fact, the evidence seems fairly clear that Sidon founded Tyre.[36] When we look in the Bible for any prophecies regarding Sidon, we find:

This is what the Sovereign LORD says: I am against you, O Sidon, and I will gain glory within you. They will know that I am the LORD, when I inflict punishment on her and show myself holy within her. I will send a plague upon her and make blood flow in her streets. The slain will fall within her, with the sword against her on every side. Then they will know that I am the LORD.[37]

Other than noting that war and plagues will ravage the streets of Sidon, little more is said. Note there are no comments regarding Sidon's total destruction, or that she will be abandoned or never rebuilt.

When we look over the history of Sidon, we find that this prediction is a good summary of the past: Sidon has been attacked and fought over repeatedly, but after every ravaging it was quickly rebuilt and refortified. Although it is not as important a coastal city as it once was (being eclipsed by Beirut to the north), it is a significant modern Lebanese port.[38] We see again that if the names of these two cities, only twenty miles apart, were reversed in the prophecies, we would have to admit they had failed. This shows that there is no double-talk or vagueness in these biblical prophecies: What was predicted has simply happened.

Ekron and Ashkelon

The city pair which we will consider next involves two cities within Israel itself:

Gaza will be abandoned and Ashkelon [a coastal city] left in ruins. At midday Ashdod will be emptied and Ekron [an inland city] uprooted. . . . The land by the sea, where the Kerethites dwell [i.e., around Ashkelon], will be a place for shepherds and sheep pens. It will belong to the remnant of the house of Judah; there they will find pasture. In the evening they will lie down in the houses of Ashkelon.[39]

Ashkelon, a major ancient port on the Mediterranean, was an enemy city of Israel in biblical times because it was held by the Philistines (referred to as "Kerethites" in the above prophecy). In later history it continued to thrive under the influence of whatever foreign power dominated the important coastal trade routes until it was destroyed by Sultan Bibars in 1270 A.D.[40] To prevent further use of the natural harbor, they filled it with stones.[41] The surrounding lands were then largely abandoned and became a sheep-herding area, as predicted.[42] However, after the Israelites returned in 1948 (the "remnant of the house of Judah"), they constructed a modern harbor city at the site, as was also predicted.[43]

Ekron, another Philistine city located several miles inland, was also occupied into the Crusader period. In contrast to Ashkelon, the site of this ancient city has not been positively identified in modern times. Khirbat al-Muqanna' (Tell Miqne), the most probable site, is not settled and has been tilled in recent times.[44]

Note that neither of these predictions about the abandonment of these cities was fulfilled until the Middle Ages, approximately one thousand years after the prophecies were recorded. Further, Ashkelon has been reinhabited in modern times, and that by the "remnant of Judah."

Babylon and Nineveh

Babylon and Nineveh were the capital cities of two great Mesopotamian empires which dominated the Ancient Near East during the era of the prophets in Israel. Whenever Israel's loyalty to her God waned, she found herself under the threat of Assyrian or Babylonian conquest. No other foreign cities are discussed and condemned in such detail in the Bible; probably this is a reflection of God's anger because of their pride, power, and ruthless military practices.[45] It is interesting to compare the fates which the God of the Bible decrees for this city pair.

Babylon. The prophets Isaiah and Jeremiah say the following:

Babylon, the jewel of kingdoms, the glory of the Babylonians' pride, will be overthrown by God like Sodom and Gomorrah. She will never be inhabited or lived in through all generations; no Arab will pitch his tent there, no shepherd will rest his flocks there. But desert creatures will lie there, jackals will fill her houses; there the owls will dwell, and there the wild goats will leap about. Hyenas will howl in her strongholds, jackals in her luxurious palaces.[46]

"No rock will be taken from you for a cornerstone, nor any stone for a foundation, for you will be desolate forever," declares the LORD.[47]

Here again we find prophecies that have come true to the letter. At the time these prophecies were made (750–550 B.C.), Babylon was the largest city in the ancient East.[48] When Alexander the Great conquered Babylon in 332 B.C., he was so impressed by it that he planned to make it the capital city of his empire. However, the long series of political struggles and battles for control of the empire after Alexander's death sapped the city's strength, so the Seleucids decided around 275 B.C. that it would be easier to build a new city than to restore Babylon. From this time Babylon's population began to decline greatly, although archaeological remains show that a group of priests occupied the site until about 100 A.D.[49] About the time of Christ, Strabo visited the city, which had been the cultural and political center of the world for two thousand years,[50] and found Babylon so deserted that he remarked jokingly, "The great city is a great desert."[51]

Today the site of Babylon is one of complete desolation.[52] The meanderings of the Euphrates River, which used to flow through the heart of the city, have eroded away the ruins which may have been on its western bank, leaving a flat swampy area in their place.[53] The ruins to the east of the river are merely low mounds of bare rubble. The nearest civilization is found in Al Hillah, six miles away. For superstitious reasons, Arabs do not live in the ruins, which have become the home of desert animals.[54] The soil among the ruins is so poor that it does not provide enough grass for sheep.[55] Most amazingly, natives who vandalize the site for building materials only take bricks; they burn the stones they find for lime.[56] Even non-Christian archaeologists who visit the site are amazed that Isaiah's picture of the ruins of Babylon is so accurate.[57]

Note that the doom of Babylon was not evident until the Seleucid period, several hundred years after the time of the exile and of the prophets Isaiah and Jeremiah. Certainly, after two thousand years of being abandoned, the prediction that it will be "desolate forever" seems like a reasonable summary.

Nineveh. Although Nahum describes the conquest of Nineveh, the only passage in the Bible which portrays the final desolation of this Assyrian city is found in Zephaniah 2:13–15:

He will stretch out his hand against the north and destroy Assyria, leaving Nineveh utterly desolate and dry as the desert. Flocks and herds will lie down there, creatures of every kind. The desert owl and the screech owl will roost on her columns. Their calls will echo through the windows, rubble will be in the doorways, the beams of cedar will be exposed. This is the carefree city that lived in safety. She said to herself, "I am, and there is none besides me." What a ruin she has become, a lair for wild beasts! All who pass by her scoff and shake their fists.

The demise of Nineveh came with the collapse of the Assyrian empire about 610 B.C. The site was desolate when Xenophon and his troops fled past the ruins in 401 B.C.[58] When Layard worked the site around 1850, a small village shared the mound with wild animals.[59] Today the area is gradually being incorporated within the suburbs of Mosul, Iraq. Strikingly, the largest mound of the site bears the old Arabic name *Kuyunjiq,* which means "many sheep."[60] Irrigation and rainfall are plentiful enough that the plains around the mound are cultivated,[61] and the ruins in this area can be grazed during the rainy season.[62]

Nineveh was destroyed too close to the time of Zephaniah for us to know today that the prediction was made before the event took place or appeared imminent. However, we *can* see today that the prophet's description of its desolation has remained true for over two thousand years, and that this is a surprising destiny for the capital city of a former world power.

Note the contrast between the prophecies made against these two world capitals: One would be desolate forever, unoccupied and not even used for sheep grazing. The other will be desolate for a time (no duration limit is given) but will be used for sheep and cattle grazing. Some might argue that a prediction of desolation is a trivial matter, but this is not so: many major ancient cities are still occupied today (Sidon, Aleppo, Damascus, Jerusalem, etc.). Moreover, guesses about the length of desolation and of future land usage are hardly simple.

From a brief investigation of the biblical prophecies regarding some ancient cities, we have found evidence strikingly different from that in the Koran or the Book of Mormon. We have word-pictures and descriptions of the ruins which agree with what we see today, and further, most of these cities met their destruction very close to or after the time of Christ, at a time when the Old Testament books were fixed and distributed throughout the Roman empire. Cities which were predicted to be destroyed and never rebuilt, have been destroyed and never rebuilt; cities which were not predicted to be desolate, still flourish, all in just the manner specified by the God of the Bible. Perhaps there is a good reason why Isaiah said:

O LORD, you are my God; I will exalt you and praise your name, for in perfect faithfulness you have done marvelous things, things planned long ago. You have made the city a heap of rubble, the fortified town a ruin, the stronghold of the foreigners to be a city no more.[63]

Conclusions

Of course, the Bible contains much more than predictions regarding the future fates of a few dozen ancient cities, but such was the limited scope of this discussion. Again, our purpose was to establish objective, verifiable grounds for testing the truth claims of any religion. We found that the God of the Bible calls for a test in challenging all other religions to be able to predict the future as accurately as He does. We found that the Bible contains genuine prophecy that can withstand rational scrutiny, even to the point of having controls—that is, we analyzed "twin cities" where one received a different condemnation than the other, and where if the names of the cities had merely been switched, it would be obvious that the predictions had failed. We surveyed some other major religions and found nothing as verifiable.

What is so important about prophecy? Isn't any religion that makes one feel good about oneself and other people sufficient? No. The prime importance of a religion is to tell you about God, what will happen to you after you die, and to prepare you to enjoy your afterlife to the fullest extent. Note that this in itself is a prophecy—a prediction that involves you personally. Obviously, you would want to choose a religion that gives you verifiable prophecies before you bet your life, lifestyle, and afterlife on its prediction of what is going to happen to you after you die. Thus it is quite fair to ask: What evidence does an atheist have to prove his prediction that when he and you die, you both will simply cease to exist and "go out like a candle"? To what predictions can a Moslem turn to verify his prediction of what his and your future state will be like in his religious system? Can one trust in the future state which Mormons promise us when the flyleaf of their holy book enumerates only unverifiable "predictions"?

Who or what are you going to trust, ultimately? Your feelings? By what basis can you use your present psychological contentment to predict how you will feel after you die? How well can you trust the arguments of the atheist/agnostic, who argues, like Hume, that miracles did not occur in human history because no one could convince *him* of them even if they had actually happened? How comfortable can you be with simple logic that says, "Because evil exists, God cannot exist," when there is objective evidence like fulfilled prophecy to the contrary? Remember that experimental data have overthrown many a cozy theoretical model, and that a brilliant argument in a classroom might seem foolish when used directly with God. In other words: How can you know what is right?

From what we have seen, it seems that the God of the Bible is giving verifiable, objective evidence and demonstrating, even to us in the twentieth century, that He alone can and should be believed among the hordes of religions. Could it be that He wants us to have a more sound basis for trust than the usual "religious" experiences? Consider the testimony of one of the New Testament writers:

We did not follow cleverly invented stories when we told you about the power and coming of our Lord Jesus Christ, but we were eyewitnesses of his majesty. For he received honor and glory from God the Father when the voice came to him from the Majestic Glory, saying, "This is my Son, whom I love; with him I am well pleased." We ourselves heard this voice that came from heaven when we were with him on the sacred mountain. *And we have the word of the prophets made more certain, and you will do well to pay attention to it, as to a light shining in a dark place.*[64]

Peter does not claim that after he had this *objective* religious experience, he just knew in his heart that Christianity was true; what clinches it for him is that the things which Jesus did, and what people did to Him, were all prophesied hundreds of years before He came. Further, for us who were not eyewitnesses, Peter recommends that we heed not our own emotional experiences, or even trust his personal report about the things he has seen: no, Peter calls us to heed the data that can be tested and retested—the prophecies.

What is the advantage of prophecy over eyewitness experience? Prophetic data are objective and written. If we worry that we misinterpreted something, we can go back and check it again. The evidence of prophecy and history does not change with our mood; we can trust this type of data as much as we can trust that the sun rose this morning.

Some people may respond that the data presented here just aren't enough to be convincing, especially when the existence of a supernatural being other than themselves is at stake. Unfortunately, one cannot condense all of the biblical prophecies and all of the history of the Near East into one short article.[65]

Others may be made so uncomfortable by the "threat" of Christianity that they cease to be objective, saying, "I wouldn't believe in Jesus unless someone came back from the dead and stood right here in front of me, and warned me about hell!" While it's possible for God to do this, it's dangerous to try to get God to dance to our tune by setting hypothetical limits which must be exceeded before we will be convinced. The core question in any objective investigation is not, Do we have all of the data that we want? for this condition could never be met by any realistic scientific endeavor. Rather, we must ask, Do we have enough reliable data to make a reasonable decision? In the physical sciences no one ever gets all of the data he desires, for more questions and new areas of research are continually opening up while one's funding and time are running out. Yet, by cleverly designing his experimental approaches, enough data can usually be gathered to enable the researcher to make an intelligent decision as to which of several models is most accurate. We must be careful not to demand more data from God than we commonly use in other important decisions.

In Luke 16:29–31 Jesus tells us the evidence contained in Moses and the Prophets is sufficient. Maybe it is not as exciting and glamorous as *we* want, but then glamor is as bad a guide to truth as emotion. Is there a reasonable basis to conclude that the God of the Bible exists and that He should be heeded? Certainly in comparison to the rest of the gods of this world, that answer is simply "Yes."

Notes

[1]Moroni 10:4, from the flyleaf of The Book of Mormon (Salt Lake City, Utah: The Church of Jesus Christ of Latter-day Saints, 1976).

[2]Isa. 41:21–23 and 44:7–8, respectively. (Emphasis mine.) These and all subsequent Scripture references in this essay are from the New International Version, copyright 1978, by the New York International Bible Society.

[3]*Encyclopaedia Britannica*, 15th ed., s.v. "Oracle."

[4]Herodotus 1.53. To add to the humor, when Croesus complains to the oracle after his defeat, the "prophets" respond with excuses and convince Croesus that it was his fault for not asking which empire would fall (Herodotus 1.91).

[5]"A Few Interesting Book of Mormon References," in The Book of Mormon (Salt Lake City, Utah: The Church of Jesus Christ of Latter-day Saints, 1920).

[6]"Brief Analysis of the Book of Mormon," a subsection of the introduction to the edition of the Book of Mormon cited above.

[7]See Doctrines and Covenants of the Church of Jesus Christ of Latter-Day Saints, sec. 136, where Young, as president of the church, relates a revelation he received from the god of the Mormons.

[8]B. H. Roberts, *A Comprehensive History of the Church of Jesus Christ of Latter-Day Saints: Century One,* 6 vols. (Provo, Utah: Brigham Young University Press, 1965), 3:279.

[9]For more information and other examples of Mormon inconsistencies, contact the Utah Lighthouse Ministry, Box 1884, Salt Lake City, Utah 84110. Good books on Mormonism include: James Bjornstad, *Counterfeits at Your Door* (Glendale, Calif.: Gospel Light Publications, 1979); Marvin W. Cowan, *Mormon Claims Answered* (Marvin W. Cowan, P.O. Box 21052, Salt Lake City, Utah, 1975).

[10]"Seer in Washington," *Time Magazine,* 13 August 1965, 59–60; Ruth Montgomery, *A Gift of Prophecy* (New York: William Morrow, 1965), 114, 176–77; John Warwick Montgomery, *Principalities and Powers: The World of the Occult* (Minneapolis, Minn.: Bethany, 1973; enlarged ed., 1975).

[11]Deut. 18:20–22.

[12]Sura 29: 49–50, *The Koran Interpreted,* trans. Arthur J. Arberry, 2 vols. (New York: Macmillan, 1955).

[13]J. Barton Payne, *Encyclopedia of Biblical Prophecy* (New York: Harper & Row, 1973).

[14]Numerous books are mentioned in the body of this article. However, a good place to begin studying in this field is by reading the three books mentioned here. These works provide a good overview of the field: Josh McDowell, *Evidence that Demands a Verdict* (San Bernadino, Calif.: Here's Life Publishers, 1972); and Urquhart, *The Wonders of Prophecy* (Harrisburg, Pa.: Christian Publications, n.d.). Urquhart is particularly interesting when he treats the prophecies regarding the return of the Jews to Palestine from the perspective of the 1800s, before the Zionist movement became popular. For a good discussion of the role of archaeology in biblical study, see Edwin M. Yamauchi, *The Stones and the Scriptures* (New York: J. B. Lippincott, 1972).

[15]Ancient references to at least nineteen temples are cited in W. M. Flinders Petrie, Ernest Mackay, and Gerald A. Wainwright, *Memphis I* (London: School of Archaeology in Egypt, 1909), 2.

[16]Ezek. 30:13.

[17]Strabo, *Geography*, 17.1.31–32.

[18]*Encyclopaedia Britannica*, 15th ed., s.v. "Memphis" by Barbara G. Mertz. Her statement, "Zealots of that faith defaced and destroyed the remaining pagan temples" should not be taken too strongly. Flinders Petrie and other investigators have recovered some intact idols from several of the major temples of Memphis (Petrie, *Memphis I*, 5); cf. Petrie's other reports cited below, and Rudolf Anthes, *Mit Rahineh 1955* (Philadelphia: University of Pennsylvania, 1959), 4. However, the total amount of surviving remains from Memphis is surprisingly small given the original size of the ancient city. Petrie notes regarding the Temple of Ptah area: "The site has been so much exhausted for building stone in the Arab ages, that it is not likely that a complete turning over of the whole ground would repay the work" (W. M. Flinders Petrie, Ernest Mackay, and Gerald A. Wainwright, *Meydum and Memphis III* [London: School of Archaeology in Egypt, 1910], 39).

[19]Stanley Lane-Poole, *The Story of Cairo* (London: J. M. Dent, 1902), 39–42; *Encyclopaedia Britannica*, 15th ed., s.v. "History of Egypt" by Donald P. Little.

[20]Amelia B. Edwards, *A Thousand Miles up the Nile*, (1891; reprint, Los Angeles: J. P. Thacher, 1983), 65–67.

[21]W. M. Flinders Petrie, *Seventy Years in Archaeology* (New York: Henry Holt, 1932), 224.

[22]Mertz, "Memphis." We should also note that any significant statuary recovered by Petrie was removed to museums, in effect clearing the site. See W. M. Flinders Petrie, Gerald A. Wainwright, and A. H. Gardiner, *Tarkhan III and Memphis V* (London: School of Archaeology in Egypt, 1913), 32; and Petrie, Mackay, and Wainwright, *Memphis III*, 38–40.

[23]Ezek. 30:14–16.

[24]*Encyclopaedia Britannica*, 11th ed., s.v., "Thebes" by Francis Llewellyn Griffith.

[25]Ibid.

[26]For excellent illustrations of the ruins at Thebes, see Charles F. Nims, *Thebes of the Pharaoh: A Pattern for Every City* (New York: Stein and Day, 1965).

[27]Ezek. 26:3–14. (Emphasis mine.) Notice that the shift in subject from "he" to "they" corresponds to the shift from Nebuchadnezzar's to Alexander's activity in fulfilling the prophecy.

[28]The question of the existence of an ancient mainland city of Tyre is disputed by some scholars, perhaps to weaken the power of this prophecy. For a discussion of this issue see Wallace D. Fleming, *The History of Tyre* (New York: Columbia University Press, 1915), 3, note 5. That a strong city named Tyre existed on the mainland during the time of Nebuchadnezzar seems obvious since Ezekiel in his contemporary prophecy describes an attack against it using only land forces. That the majority of Tyre was originally on the mainland seems evident from the Greek name for the city which grew up there after Alexander: "Palaetyrus" or "Old Tyre" (cf. Fleming, *History of Tyre*, 4). That little archaeological evidence of the old mainland Tyre remains is due to the efforts of Alexander's forces in building the mole out to the island.

[29]Herodotus, 2.161.

[30]Fleming, *History of Tyre*, 46.

[31]The classical reference to Alexander's siege of Tyre is Arrian, *The Campaigns of Alexander* (London: Chaucer Press, 1971), 129ff. See also A. B. Bosworth, *Commentary on Arrian's History of Alexander* (Oxford: Clarendon Press, 1980), 235ff.

[32]Fleming, *History of Tyre*, 122.

[33]Ibid., 123–32.

[34]Nina Nelson, *Your Guide to Lebanon* (London: Alvin Redman, 1965), 220.

[35]As does C. C. Torrey, in *Pseudo-Ezekiel and the Original Prophecy*, cited in *The Interpreter's Dictionary of the Bible* (New York: Abingdon Press, 1962), s.v. "Ezekiel" by C. G. Howie.

[36]Homer mentions Sidon several times but not Tyre, cf. *Iliad*, 6.288–90; Isaiah calls Tyre a "daughter of Sidon" in Isa. 23:12.

[37]Ezek. 28:22–23.

[38]Nina Jidejian, *Sidon through the Ages* (Beirut: Dar El-Machreq, 1971), esp. 108–9; cf. *Encyclopaedia Britannica*, 15th ed., s.v. "Sidon."

[39]Zeph. 2:4, 6–7.

[40]Convenient summaries of Ashkelon's history can be found in *The Encyclopedia of Archaeological Excavations in the Holy Land* (Englewood Cliffs, N.J.: Prentice-Hall, 1975–8), s.v. "Ashkelon" by M. Avi-Yonah and Y. Eph'al; *The Zondervan Pictorial Encyclopedia of the Bible* (Grand Rapids, Mich.: Zondervan, 1975–76), s.v. "Ashkelon" by W. White, Jr.; *Encyclopaedia Britannica*, 15th ed., s.v. "Ashqelon."

[41]*Encyclopaedia Britannica*, 11th ed., s.v. "Ascalon" by Robert A. S. Macalister.

[42]C. F. Volney, *Travels through Syria and Egypt*, (London: G. G. J. and J. Robinson, 1787), 2:335–36. Unlike many early travelers to the Holy Land, Volney was not a Christian in any meaningful sense of the term. See Alexander Keith, *Evidence of the Truth of the Christian Religion*, 38th ed. (London: T. Nelson and Sons, 1861), 370, note 2.

[43]*Encyclopaedia Britannica*, 15th ed., s.v. "Ashqelon"; *Encyclopaedia Judaica* (Jerusalem: Encyclopaedia Judaica; New York: Macmillan, 1971), s.v. "Ashkelon" by Natan Efrati and Efraim Orni.

[44]*Encyclopaedia Judaica*, s.v. "Ekron" by M. Avi-Yonah; J. Naveh, "Khirbat al-Muqanna'—Ekron: An Archaeological Survey," Israel Exploration Journal 8 (1958): 91, note 7.

[45]Nineveh is the principal topic of the prophetic books Jonah and Nahum, and is mentioned in Zephaniah. Babylon is repeatedly condemned in Isaiah, Jeremiah, and elsewhere.

[46]Isa. 13:19–22.

[47]Jer. 51:26.

[48]Robert Koldewey, *The Excavation of Babylon*, trans. Agnes S. Johns (London: Macmillan, 1914), 5.

[49]Joan Oates, *Babylon* (London: Thames and Hudson, 1979), 140–43.

[50]Ibid., 142.

[51]Strabo, *Geography*, 16.1.5.

[52]The government of Iraq is in the process of restoring some of the ruins of Babylon in order to build an outdoor museum as a tourist attraction. Although President Saddam Hussein has stepped up the pace of this project for propaganda purposes (portraying himself as a successor to the Neobabylonian king Nebuchadnezzar), and this fact has

been sensationalized by Charles Dyer's *The Rise of Babylon: Sign of the End Times* (Wheaton, Ill.: Tyndale House, 1991), the scale of the project even at this time hardly amounts to any significant rebuilding or reinhabiting of the ruins—any more than some future effort to rebuild Coney Island would qualify as a reestablishment of the financial and commercial empire of New York City.

[53] Austen Henry Layard, *Discoveries in the Ruins of Nineveh and Babylon* (London: John Murray, 1853), 484, 493.

[54] Claudius James Rich, *Memoir on the Ruins of Babylon* (London: Richard and Arthur Taylor, 1815), 27; Richard Mignan, *Travels in Chaldea* (London: Henry Colburn and Richard Bentley, 1829), 201; Layard, *Discoveries*, 484. A note to those who may be skeptical of sources over a century old: As with any science, archaeology is a field which builds upon the information learned by earlier investigators. The earliest European visitors to Babylon could not take photographs of the ruins so they gave precise verbal descriptions of their findings. More recent works on Babylon convey its desolation with photographs or by referring to these earlier, and still accurate, descriptions.

[55] Koldewey, *Excavation of Babylon*, 108; Mignan, *Travels*, 234–35. Note that there are shepherds in the plains surrounding the ruins (Layard, *Discoveries*, 484).

[56] Observations of Mr. Rassam, quoted without reference in Urquhart, *Wonders of Prophecy*, 144. Unfortunately, we cannot tell which of the Rassam brothers, Christian or Hormuzd, is being cited. However, both were involved with Layard in his archaeological campaigns in Mesopotamia and were credible observers.

[57] Koldewey, *Excavation of Babylon*, 314; Andre Parrot, *Babylon and the Old Testament* (New York: Philosophical Library, 1958), 148–49; H. M. F. Saggs, "Babylon," in *Archaeology and Old Testament Study*, ed. D. Winton Thomas (London: Oxford University Press, 1967), 41.

[58] Xenophon, *Anabasis*, 3.4.7–12. See also: Nora Benjamin Kubie, *Road to Nineveh* (Garden City, N.Y.: Doubleday, 1964), 54; Layard, *Discoveries*, 61.

[59] The village of Nebi Yunus has been on the site for some centuries. For the reference to animals, see Layard, *Discoveries*, 661–62.

[60] *Zondervan Pictorial Encyclopedia*, s.v. "Nineveh" by D. J. Wiseman. Compare Layard, *Discoveries*, 76; Layard translates it as "little sheep" after an abandoned village on the mound.

[61] Layard, *Discoveries*, 77.

[62] Austen Henry Layard, *Nineveh and its Remains* (New York: George P. Putnam, 1849), 1:28–29.

[63] Isa. 25:1–2.

[64] 2 Pet. 1:16–19. (Emphasis mine.)

[65] See note 13.

4.3

Israel's History
Written in Advance
A Neglected Evidence for the God of the Bible

Robert C. Newman

ACCORDING TO AN OLD STORY, Frederick the Great had a chaplain who was a Bible-believer, though Frederick himself was a rationalist. One day, Frederick challenged his chaplain, "In a word, give me a good argument for the God of the Bible." His chaplain, a knowledgeable man, responded, "The Jew, your majesty!" To unpack the chaplain's concise remark is the purpose of this chapter.

The history of the Jews is a demonstration of God at work, sometimes miraculously, sometimes providentially, in the affairs of men and nations. The particular significance of the Jews—in contrast to other nations—lies in their being declared God's special people by means of His covenants with them through Abraham, Moses, and David. In addition, the Old Testament part of the Bible preserves substantial information telling us in advance what God planned to do with His people. Let us look at three rather wide-ranging prophecies about the nation Israel and see how they have come to pass. These involve the covenant curses; an acted parable of the marital relations between God and Israel; and a prediction of Israel's return to her own land.

Israel's Covenant Curses: Threats of This-World Punishment

When the Israelites were rescued from slavery in Egypt about the middle of the second millennium B.C., a contract or covenant was drawn up by God to define their relationship to Him as His own special people. This covenant reminded them of what God had already done for them and what He promised to do in the future, that He had saved them from slavery, brought them safely through the desert, was about to bring them into possession of the land of Canaan, and would protect them from all disasters if they would be faithful to Him. To provide a standard of faithfulness, God gave them an elaborate set of laws—some moral, some civil, some ceremonial—which also functioned to demonstrate to the nations around them the existence of the God of the Bible through the lifestyle that He had designed for Israel and its prosperity. As Moses explained it:

See, I have taught you decrees and laws as the LORD my God commanded me, so that you may follow them in the land you are entering to take possession of it. Observe them carefully, for this will show your wisdom and understanding to the nations, who will hear about these decrees and say, "Surely this great nation is a wise and understanding people." What other nation is so great as to have their gods near them the way the LORD our God is near us whenever we pray to him? And what other nation is so great as to have such righteous decrees and laws as this body of laws I am setting before you today?[1]

In the twenty-eighth chapter of Deuteronomy and the twenty-sixth chapter of Leviticus, the sanctions of the covenant are set out in the form of blessings and curses—blessings if Israel would obey God's commands and curses if they disobeyed. By means of these sanctions, Israel would be reminded of how they were doing in obeying God, and their neighbors would see an objective demonstration of God's judgment in history.

To summarize nearly a hundred verses, the disobedience of the Israelites will bring wasted effort in various labors; natural disasters such as drought, blight, and locusts to their crops; and disease and death to their animals and themselves. The Israelites will be invaded and oppressed by foreigners, who will rob them of their crops, animals, fields, and houses; rape their wives; and enslave their children. Their enemies will defeat them in battle and beseige their cities, resulting in plague, famine, cannibalism, and starvation. They will destroy their cities, ruin their land, and scatter the Israelites to foreign countries. There some will die; others will live in constant fear of both real and imagined disasters; still others will turn to other gods. They will be sold as slaves, creating a glut on the slave market. Their numbers will decline greatly, as they suffer from fearful plagues, prolonged disasters, and lingering illnesses. This is a fearful list of disasters!

Not only is the severity of these curses remarkable, so is the relative space assigned to them. In Deuteronomy, fourteen verses are occupied with the blessings and fifty-four with the curses. In Leviticus, eleven verses are blessings and thirty-two are curses. Altogether, over 75 percent of the verses concern curses for disobedience. This clearly suggests that the disasters will predominate.

This proportion in itself is highly unusual. Other religious people might concede that their own history has been three-fourths disaster, but who would admit it had been three-fourths disobedience? And this proportion is borne out not only by the history of Israel recorded in the Bible, where one might claim the biblical history writers either molded the narrative to match the prophecy or adjusted the prophecy to match the history. It is also demonstrated in the long history of disaster experienced by the Jews after Bible times, since their exile by the Romans in A.D. 70.[2]

No other national group has experienced such disaster as the Jews. Part of this, no doubt, is because most nations so treated have not survived long enough to experience so much disaster! Yet Israel has experienced disaster at every point sketched in the long lists of Leviticus and Deuteronomy. They have, unfortunately, been persecuted again and again for over two thousand years. For most of that time they were without a national homeland, having been driven out of Palestine. They have faced decimation and sometimes genocide from nearly every group they have lived among: Greeks, Romans, Christians, Muslims, Nazis, and Communists. Even now the recently re-established nation of Israel faces continual harassment and threats of annihilation from hostile forces on their borders.[3]

In the midst of these curses, however, comes a promise that Israel will not be totally destroyed. "Yet in spite of this, when they are in the land of their enemies, I will not reject them or abhor them so as to destroy them completely, breaking my covenant with them. I am the LORD their God."[4]

And indeed the Jews still exist as a people today, just as predicted. "Of course!" you say. "If Israel had been destroyed, we would never have heard of them." Not true—unless they had been destroyed before the coming of Jesus. For with the rise of Christianity, the books of the Old Testament have been preserved by non-Jews and would have been whether the Jews survived or not. Moreover, many of the most serious threats which the Jews have faced have come in these past two thousand years. Yet Israel, unlike most oppressed nations of antiquity, has survived as a distinct people.

Thus the evidence from Israel's predicted covenant curses points to God's activity in history, keeping His words of both judgment and promise.

Hosea's Marriage: A Parable of Israel's History

In another predictive passage, the Bible uses an acted parable to draw a sociological sketch of the nation of Israel, neatly describing its status for some two thousand years. According to the Old Testament book of Hosea, that prophet was divinely directed to live out a powerful parable depicting God's relationship with Israel.

In chapter 1, Hosea is instructed to marry a harlot, Gomer, and have children by her. He obeys, thereby picturing God's choice of the nation Israel for a personal relationship with Him, even though Abraham was an idolater when God called him out of Chaldea and the Israelites were idolaters when they were called out of slavery in Egypt.

Later on, in chapter 2, Gomer runs off with her lovers. Just so, Israel abandoned God for the more sexually exciting worship of the Canaanite Baals, even though God had brought the people safely into the promised land. Finally Gomer winds up in slavery, just as Israel would later be taken captive to Assyria and Babylon.

At this point, in chapter 3, Hosea is directed to go and buy her back. But now she is to be given a different status for a while, as she is to have no relations with Hosea[5] even though she is also kept from relations with her lovers. This last event in Hosea's living parable is a prediction of the status of Israel for a long time to come:

For the sons of Israel will remain for many days without king or prince, without sacrifice or *sacred* pillar, and without ephod or household idols. Afterward the sons of Israel will return and seek the LORD their God and David their king; and they will come trembling to the LORD and to His goodness in the last days.[6]

Here we see predicted that Israel for "many days" will lack a king, even though God had established the royal house of David, and promised that Israel would never lack a descendant to sit on the throne if the nation proved obedient to God.

In fact, the prediction states that Israel will lack even a prince. In Hebrew, the word translated prince, *sar*, is basically a government official rather than a son of the king. Apparently Israel is not only to have no king, but not even its own government.

The other four items mentioned as lacking (sacrifice, pillar, ephod, household idols) involve religion. Two are associated with the sacrificial system and two with idolatry. Sacrifice was an integral part of Israel's covenant and worship, and was established by God at Sinai. The ephod, a sort of vest, was one of the most important of the ceremonial garments worn by Israel's high priest. Although some pillars had orthodox uses, the most common reference is to those used in Canaanite worship of Baal and his consort Ashtoreth. Apparently the nation Israel is to lack both Sinai religion and the false religion which had been such a problem since it entered Canaan, an interpretation which matches the marriage imagery of the acted parable very nicely.

This is exactly what has happened! Since the death of Herod Agrippa I in A.D. 44, Israel has had no native king to this day. For 1,878 years, from the fall of Jerusalem in A.D. 70 to the formation of the modern nation in 1948, Israel had no government of its own either. Thus the predictions regarding Israel's governmental status were fulfilled in detail.

As regards the religious items, these too have been fulfilled. With the fall of Jerusalem came the destruction of the temple and the end of the sacrificial system, which has not been reinstituted even yet. The priestly garments were lost in the destruction of the city. Though descendants of the high priests doubtless survived, none were able to serve after that time and have not to this day.

In general, the continual Israelite temptation to pagan idolatry seems to have been cured some centuries earlier by the Babylonian captivity; in any case, idolatry has not been a significant problem since the time of the Maccabees (second century B.C.). Thus all these years the Jews have neither sacrificed (though the Torah commands it) nor have they had any problem with image-worship. Thus from A.D. 70 to 1948, the "sons of Israel" have lacked all six of these items predicted in Hosea 3:4. Now they have a government, but still lack five of the items today. Hosea 3:4 has been literally fulfilled.

Now it even appears that the next verse (Hos. 3:5) may now be in the process of fulfillment. Many Jews have physically returned to Palestine in this century. If their seeking of "God and David their king" is understood as a turning to Jesus of Nazareth as the true Messiah, we can point to the growing Messianic Jewish movement which has begun to flourish greatly in the past decade. We are still too close to these events to be sure.

Israel's Return to Its Land

Whether or not Hosea 3:5 refers to Israel's return to the promised land, a number of other Old Testament passages do. Let us consider one such passage, Isaiah 11:11-16. Verse 11 reads:

Then it will happen on that day that the LORD will again recover the second time with His hand the remnant of His people, who will remain, from Assyria, Egypt, Pathros, Cush, Elam, Shinar, Hamath, and from the islands of the sea.[7]

Sometime after Isaiah wrote these words, Israel was to be regathered to its homeland. The reference to a "second time" as well as the places from which they would return suggests that this is not the return from

Babylonian exile. The context (vv. 1–10) refers to the coming of the Messiah and the golden age which He is to inaugurate, suggesting that this return is at or near the end of the age.

According to the whole passage, several significant features will characterize this return. First, Israel will no longer be two nations as it was after Solomon's time, but a single unified country (v. 13). Second, Israel will fight the surrounding nations (the Philistines, the Edomites, the Moabites, the Ammonites, and the Egyptians) as a part of this return (vv. 14–15). Third, something spectacular will happen to dry up the "tongue of the sea of Egypt" and the "River," presumably the Euphrates (v. 15). Fourth, the places from which the return will take place are explicitly named, except for the general phrase "islands [or 'coastlands'] of the sea" (v. 11).

Of these four items, three have already occurred in the return of Jews to Israel that is occurring in our own generation; only the third has not yet taken place.

The return of Jews to Palestine and the formation of a state of their own is amazing in itself, given that just a century ago the territory was controlled by the Muslim Turks who had no interest in providing the Jews with a homeland. Yet a world Zionist movement was formed; the land came under the control of Britain at the end of World War I; Britain owed a favor to Jewish chemist Chaim Weitzmann, and he asked Britain to allow the Jews to have a homeland; the Nazi holocaust drove Jews to Palestine who otherwise would have stayed in Europe; the United Nations agreed to partition Palestine into an Arab and a Jewish state; and the Jews were able to defeat a coalition of Arab states bent on their destruction.

The Jewish state formed in 1948 in Palestine included persons descended from both the northern and southern tribes. The enmity of the divided kingdoms that existed at Isaiah's time has, in fact, been healed.

Israel has already fought with all the surrounding nations, in 1948, 1956, 1967, and 1973. Though the Philistines, Edomites, and such are no longer identifiable as separate peoples, the Arab nations occupying their lands (and most likely including some of their descendants) are Egypt, Palestine, Jordan, and Syria. These were the very nations Israel fought with and dispossessed to regain its territory.

The *Encyclopaedia Judaica* gives population figures for Jews living in various lands in 1947 and in 1967.[8] Converting the ancient names of verse 11 into the corresponding modern countries, Assyria becomes Syria and Iraq; Egypt, Pathros, and Cush correspond to modern Egypt; Elam and Shinar to Iran and Iraq; and Hamath is now in Syria. The departure of Jews from these places is described in Table 4.3. Notice, that, except for Iran, nearly all the Jews left these other countries in the twenty years following the formation of the state of Israel.

Jewish Population In Middle Eastern Countries

Country	1947	1967
Egypt	66,000	2,500
Iran	95,000	60,000
Iraq	150,000	2,500
Syria	15,000	3,000

Table 4.3

When I gave a seminar course in fulfilled prophecy some years ago, one of our students researched this topic and gathered these figures. At the time it appeared that we were in the middle of the fulfillment of this prophecy. Since then, this has been further borne out by the Islamic revolution in Iran, as a result of which most Jews have left Iran. The population of Jews in Iran is now down to about twenty-seven thousand.[9] It appears, indeed, that history is in the process of fulfilling Isaiah 11:11–16!

Conclusions

After examining three significant passages relating to the history of Israel as predicted in the Bible, we have shown that numerous prophecies from the Old Testament regarding Israel have been fulfilled. We have made the following observations:

1. The Jews would face fierce and repeated persecution and disaster. This, as anyone familiar with Jewish history knows, has been characteristic of the nation for two thousand years.
2. In spite of such disaster, the Jews would continue to exist as a recognizable people group. This has been true to date, in spite of treatment which has destroyed other such people groups.
3. Israel would be without a king for a long period of time. Israel is presently without a king and has been for nearly two thousand years, despite the fact that the Davidic royal dynasty was an important part of the Old Testament revelation.
4. Israel would lack government officials for a long time. The Jews now have them, but lacked them for almost 1,850 years.
5. Israel would lack sacrifice and ephod, both associated with God's commands at Mt. Sinai. This has been true for nearly two thousand years and is quite surprising in view of the place which sacrifice and priesthood occupy in the Jewish Scriptures.

6. Israel would lack pillar and idols. This is a commonplace to us today, who think of the Jews as staunch proponents of monotheism, but the situation was rather different when Hosea made the prediction about 800 B.C.
7. Israel will return to its land as a single united nation. A century ago, such an event would have seemed almost impossible. Palestine was controlled by a Muslim government which had no interest in providing a homeland, much less an independent state, for the Jews. Yet it has come to pass!
8. The countries explicitly named in Isaiah 11 have been nearly depopulated of Jews in this return to Palestine.
9. The Jews have fought successfully with the surrounding nations in establishing and maintaining their presence in the new state of Israel.

Are these trivial predictions? Did they just happen by chance? Or is the God of the Bible indeed the One who controls history and who announces the end from the beginning? Here is the evidence. The decision is yours to make.[10]

Notes

[1]Deut. 4:5–8. This and subsequent Scripture quotations in this chapter, unless otherwise noted, are from the New International Version of the Bible, copyright 1978 by the New York International Bible Society.

[2]See, for example, Samuel H. Kellogg, *The Jews: or, Prediction and Fulfillment,* 2d ed. (New York: Anson Randolph, 1887), esp. chap. 4, where this is discussed in detail. The data, though not the discussion, may be found in standard Jewish histories, e.g., Heinrich Graetz, *History of the Jews,* 6 vols. (Philadelphia, Pa.: Jewish Publication Society, 1926); W. D. Davies and L. Finkelstein, eds. *The Cambridge History of Judaism,* 4 vols. (Cambridge: Cambridge University Press, 1984); more concisely, Max Margolis and Alexander Marx, *History of the Jewish People* (New York: Meridian, 1960). Sadly, some elements of the Christian church have ignored or participated in the persecution of God's special covenantal people, the Jews. Yet chapters 9 through 11 of the book of Romans reveal that Christians should never rejoice in the misfortunes of the Jews. To do so brings shame to the church and to our Lord.

[3]God's activities in the disasters of history seem fierce to us, for at least two reasons: (1) we regularly ignore the biblical teaching that there is a life beyond this one, and that in the last judgment with its rewards and punishments everything will be made right and no one will get less than he or she deserves; and (2) we regularly minimize our own sin at least ("I'm OK, you're OK"), blaming our actions on circumstances and environment. Whatever may be the faults of our parents, teachers, society, etc., God will apportion to them (and us!) exactly what we deserve—unless we accept the offer of God's forgiveness through believing on Christ as our personal Savior.

[4]Lev. 26:44.

[5]Hos. 3:1–3.

[6]Hos. 3:4–5. This quotation is from the New American Standard Bible, copyright 1973 by the Lockman Foundation.

[7]Isa. 11:11 (NASB).

[8]*Encyclopaedia Judaica* (Jerusalem: Encyclopaedia Judaica; New York: Macmillan, 1971–2), 5:1502; 8:1439, 1441, 1449; 13:896; 15:646.

[9]Personal correspondence, 12 December 1983, from Oded Ben-Haim, Consulate General of Israel, Philadelphia, Pennsylvania.

[10]Further and more detailed discussion of these topics may be found in Samuel H. Kellogg, "The Dispersion and Oppression of the Jews," John A. Bloom, "Hosea's Prophetic History of the Jews," and Eugenie Johnston, "The Return of the Jews," all in *The Evidence of Prophecy,* ed. Robert C. Newman (Hatfield, Pa.: Interdisciplinary Biblical Research Institute, 1988). The powerful fulfillment of this material in the history of the Jewish people argues against a common tendency to allegorize Old Testament prophecies and apply them to the church.

4.4

The Testimony of Messianic Prophecy

Robert C. Newman

AMONG THE PREDICTIONS found in the Old Testament, those concerning Israel's promised Messiah are especially important. The Messiah, according to the Bible, will one day come and rescue His people from their oppressors. He will bring in a golden age. Israel will become the chief nation and Jerusalem, the world's capital. Mankind will be ruled with justice, and oppression will cease. All will live in safety on their own property and enjoy the fruits of their own labors.

In spite of the appealing nature of these prophecies, reactions to them have been mixed. According to Christians, the Messiah has already come, though He will not inaugurate this golden age until He returns; He is Jesus of Nazareth. According to orthodox Jews, the Messiah has not yet come, but he will; he is certainly not Jesus. According to more secular persons—whether irreligious or religiously liberal—the Messiah was merely a vain hope of the ancient Bible writers; no such figure will ever appear, though we may occasionally expect great world leaders.

Who is right? Does the evidence of biblical text and human history have anything to say about this question? We suggest that it does; that the evidence is substantial; and that it supports two propositions: (1) If the

Messiah has come, He is Jesus of Nazareth; and (2) the Messiah has come. Let's see.

If the Messiah Has Come, He Is Jesus

There are a number of features predicted about the Messiah that fit very nicely with what we know about Jesus of Nazareth as He is pictured in the New Testament. He is to be a light to the Gentiles, born yet pre-existent, humble yet exalted, suffering yet reigning, and king yet priest.

A Light to the Gentiles

Let us begin with a line of evidence so obvious that many overlook it. I refer to two predictive passages in Isaiah, namely 42:6–7 and 49:5–6. In the former, God says to His servant the Messiah: "I will appoint you as a covenant to the people [Israel], as a *light to the nations,* to open blind eyes, to bring out prisoners from the dungeon, and those who dwell in darkness from the prison."[1]

We see here that not only will the promised Messiah have a ministry to His people Israel, but that He will also enlighten the nations, delivering them from blindness and bondage.

In the second passage, we see that this servant is not a personification of the nation Israel, as some have suggested, but is distinguished from Israel as being instrumental in bringing Israel itself back to God:

And now says the LORD, who formed Me from the womb to be His Servant, to bring Jacob back to Him, in order that Israel might be gathered to Him . . . He says, "It is too small a thing that You should be my Servant to raise up the tribes of Jacob, and to restore the preserved ones of Israel; I will also make You a *light of the nations,* so that My salvation may reach to the end of the earth."[2]

This is just what Jesus of Nazareth has done! No other person ever claiming to be the Jewish Messiah has come anywhere near matching His achievement. Before the first century A.D., only the Jews and a few Greek philosophers were believers in one God. Only a small percentage of the world's population had ever read the Bible. Most worshiped a whole committee of gods, who set rather poor examples for their followers; the resulting level of morality was understandably quite low. But today those who believe in one God include not only the Jews (14.2 million in 1980), but also the predominantly Gentile Christians (1.4 billion). We could also include the Muslims (723 million), as the rise of Islam was at least an indirect result of Christianity (Muhammad considered himself in the line of prophets including Jesus). Thus about one-half the world's population now claims allegiance to the God of Abraham, most of these as a result of the work of Jesus.[3]

Even neglecting Islam and most Jews, about one-third of the earth's people accept Jesus as Messiah. These are found on every continent and in nearly every country: both in the more developed nations (790 million) and less developed (643 million); in the Western nations (547 million), the Third World (632 million), and even in Communist countries (254 million).[4] Truly Jesus of Nazareth has become a light to the Gentiles, as news of Him has spread throughout the world and brought spiritual enlightenment and deliverance from the bondage of sin to multiplied millions throughout the past two thousand years!

Jesus is the only Messianic claimant so far to have established a world religion. He is also the only one whose claims solve a number of puzzling paradoxes in the Old Testament Messianic prophecies.

Born Yet Pre-Existent

According to the prophet Micah, the Messiah will count Bethlehem as His hometown even though He has existed for ages: "But you, Bethlehem Ephrathah, though you are small among the clans of Judah, out of you will come for me one who will be ruler over Israel, whose origins are from of old, from ancient times."[5]

The term translated "origins" here is literally "goings out," which may also be translated "activities"; it is often used to picture the warfare of kings. The phrase "from ancient times" can be used either of a finite or infinite span of time.[6]

A similar picture is given by the prophet Isaiah, who says:

For to us a child is born, to us a son is given, and the government will be on his shoulders. And he will be called Wonderful Counselor, Mighty God, Everlasting Father, Prince of Peace. Of the increase of his government and peace there will be no end. He will reign on David's throne and over his kingdom, establishing and upholding it with justice and righteousness from that time on and forever. The zeal of the LORD Almighty will accomplish this.[7]

That this one is the Messiah is obvious from the reference to His worldwide eternal rule. That He is born is explicitly stated, yet He is given the titles "Everlasting Father" and "Mighty God," which point to His pre-existence and deity. Both religious liberals and (non-Messianic) Jews attempt to minimize these titles in order to avoid this conclusion.[8] Yet the textual evidence favors this paradox, and it is neatly explained in the New Testament picture of Jesus: One who is eternal God and who yet became a human being in order to pay for the sins of those who will trust in Him.

Humble Yet Exalted

The manner of Messiah's coming had been a puzzle to interpreters of the Old Testament even before the time of Jesus. In the prophecy of Daniel He is pictured as coming in great glory:

In my vision at night I looked, and there before me was one like a son of man, coming with the clouds of heaven. He approached the Ancient of Days and was led into his presence. He was given authority, glory and sovereign power; all peoples, nations and men of every language worshiped him. His dominion is an everlasting dominion that will not pass away, and his kingdom is one that will never be destroyed.[9]

Notice again, as in Isaiah 9:6–7, above, that this One is to rule over an eternal, universal kingdom. In addition He is to come with the clouds of heaven.

By contrast, the coming of the Messiah is quite modest as pictured by the prophet Zechariah: "Rejoice greatly, O Daughter of Zion! Shout, Daughter of Jerusalem! See, your king comes to you, righteous and having salvation, gentle and riding on a donkey, on a colt, the foal of a donkey."[10]

The passage goes on to explain how He will bring peace to Israel and the nations and how He will rule from "sea to sea, and from the River to the ends of the earth." Yet this One comes riding a donkey, a very humble form of transportation.

Jewish explanations have tried to make the Zechariah coming more spectacular (by invoking a miraculous donkey!),[11] or they have claimed that the Daniel and Zechariah comings are merely alternative possibilities.[12] Neither of these has any warrant in the biblical text. By contrast, the New Testament view, where Jesus comes first in humility and then returns in exaltation, fits both nicely. It even explains how the Messiah could come both as a child and as an adult, as seems to be implied in the passages we have already looked at.

Suffering Yet Reigning

A number of Old Testament passages picture One who is to suffer, and whose suffering and deliverance by God becomes worldwide news.[13] Some Jewish interpreters in the early Christian centuries sought to explain these passages by means of a second Messiah figure, the so-called Messiah ben-Joseph.[14] This figure was postulated to be a general; he would gather the forces of Israel, fight the wicked Gentile armies of Gog and Magog in the end-time battle, but be killed by them before the coming of the king-Messiah, called Messiah ben-David.

Yet this suffering figure pictured in the Old Testament is apparently pierced by Israel rather than by the Gentiles.[15] The lowly coming of

Zechariah 9:9 would most reasonably be assigned to Him, yet the figure there is explicitly called *king*. And the primary suffering passage in the Old Testament, Isaiah 52:13–53:12, is the climax of the so-called Servant passages, two of which we looked at earlier (Isa. 42:6; 49:6). These picture One who is to be a "light to the Gentiles"—not exactly an appropriate figure for One whose major activity toward the Gentiles is fighting them!

Indeed, Isaiah 52:13–53:12 beautifully fits the New Testament picture of Jesus: "despised and rejected" at His crucifixion by both Jew and Gentile alike (53:3), to such an extent that many considered Him under the wrath of God (53:4). He was strangely silent at His trial and execution (53:7). Though scheduled to be thrown in a common grave with criminals, He was actually buried in a rich man's tomb (53:9). Yet His death was God's way of providing payment for our sins (53:4–6, 8), a fulfillment of the Old Testament picture of sin offering (53:10). After His death for sin, He was to "prolong his days," "see His offspring," and "justify many" (53:10–11, NIV). In fact, using Levitical cleansing terminology, He shall "sprinkle many nations" (52:15, NIV). Kings will shut their mouths when they hear about Him, and He will be highly exalted (52:13, 15).

King Yet Priest

The offices of king and priest were kept strictly separate in the Old Testament. The priests were to be sons of Aaron from the tribe of Levi; the kings were to be sons of David from the tribe of Judah. When King Uzziah sought to take upon himself the priestly prerogative of offering incense in the temple, the high priest Azariah with eighty associates tried to stop him. Probably their efforts would have been unsuccessful had not God Himself intervened and struck Uzziah with leprosy.[16]

Thus it is not surprising that when priestly features appear in Messianic prophecy, some of the ancient Jewish interpreters postulated two Messiahs, one a priest and another a king.[17] Yet a crucial Old Testament passage makes this priest and king a single individual. In Psalm 110, which speaks of the Messiah sitting at God's right hand until God subdues His enemies, the psalmist pictures the Messiah as king with the words,[18] "The LORD will extend your mighty scepter from Zion: you will rule in the midst of your enemies. Your troops will be willing on your day of battle."

Yet in the next sentence, obviously speaking to the same individual, he says,[19] "The LORD has sworn and will not change his mind: 'You are a priest forever, in the order of Melchizedek.'"

Thus one person will be both priest and king, "judging the nations" and "crushing the rulers of the whole earth."[20] In fact, because the priesthood and kingship of Israel have been kept so strictly separate, the psalmist must go back to Melchizedek,[21] a Gentile king in the book of Genesis, to find any example of a righteous priest-king as a basis for comparison with Messiah.

Yet the New Testament picture of Jesus fits this scenario easily. He not only acted as priest, He also served as sacrifice in making atonement for the sins of His people.[22] Yet at His return, He will come as king to rule forever.[23]

Thus Jesus of Nazareth has admittedly started a world religion which has at least introduced the Gentiles to the light of monotheism, the God of Abraham, and the ethics of the Bible. He has also made claims which solve and fit certain Old Testament paradoxes concerning the Messiah: how He would be born yet pre-existent, humble yet exalted, suffering yet reigning, and king yet priest. If the Messiah has come, He is certainly Jesus of Nazareth!

The Messiah Has Come

But maybe the Messiah hasn't come yet. Both Jews and theological liberals regularly reject the Messiahship of Jesus on the grounds that He has not yet come in any glorious way, nor physically put down all opposition to God and brought in a golden age of peace and righteousness. Therefore He has not yet accomplished the most obvious work which the Bible assigns to the Messiah. And if He has not yet returned, how do we know He will?

This is a good question. If Jesus is not the Messiah, we don't want to go on believing in Him, giving our lives to a delusion, and waiting in vain for a coming that will never occur. On the other hand, if Jesus is the Messiah, we cannot afford to wait until His second coming to do something about it, if for no other reasons than that we may not live that long and that He claims to be the only remedy for sin. How can we decide?

We suggest that the Messiah has come because certain time-oriented prophecies concerning Him have run out, and these have expired in such a way as to point to Jesus as the Messiah.

The Messiah Was to Come While Judah Had Its Own Rulers

As the patriarch Jacob was about to die, he gave his twelve sons an oral poetic testament, predicting something of the future for the tribes which subsequently descended from them. Concerning Judah, he said: "The scepter will not depart from Judah, nor the ruler's staff from between his feet, until he comes to whom it belongs and the obedience of the nations is his."[24]

Thus the World-Ruler, to whom the scepter belongs, is to come before the scepter departs from Judah. It was not until some one thousand years after the death of Jacob that the kingship of the Jews first passed to the tribe of Judah in the person of David, having previously been held by Saul of the tribe of Benjamin. Thereafter, the kingship remained in David's family (though the northern tribes rebelled and formed their own nation) until the fall of the southern kingdom in 587 B.C. Thus the scepter remained in the tribe of Judah for some five hundred years until the Babylonian captivity. At that point, in one sense, the scepter departed from Judah, and has never returned. If one follows this line of interpretation, one might say the Messiah had to come before 587 B.C., but that He didn't, and, therefore, we should all become Buddhists or atheists.

Yet, in another sense, the scepter did not depart then, because at a later time kings of the Jews again ruled over Judah. There is an ambiguity here, just as the English phrase "to leave school" is ambiguous—in one sense one may leave school every day, yet in another sense not leave school until graduation. So here. First there were the Hasmoneans, more popularly known as the Maccabees, who ruled with the title "king of the Jews" from 103 B.C. to 63 B.C. Then came Herod the Great, an Edomite said by his biographer to be part Jewish, who ruled as "king of the Jews" from 40 B.C. to 4 B.C. Finally there was his grandson Herod Agrippa I, a descendant of both the Hasmoneans and Herods, who ruled with the same title from A.D. 41 to 44. Thereafter, no one has ruled as king of the Jews to this day.

In this second sense, the scepter did not depart from Judah until Jesus came. But no one coming after A.D. 44 can make this claim. If Genesis 49:10 is understood in this sense, the Messiah must have come before A.D. 44.

The Messiah Was to Come While the Second Temple Stood

At the rebuilding of the Jerusalem temple about 515 B.C., the prophet Haggai sought to encourage the people, their governor Zerubbabel, and the high priest Joshua. Remarking on the fact that the new building was obviously not much in comparison to Solomon's temple, Haggai says:

"Who of you is left who saw this house in its former glory? How does it look to you now? Does it not seem to you like nothing? But now, be strong, O Zerubbabel," . . . declares the LORD, "and work. For I am with you," declares the LORD Almighty. "This is what I covenanted with you when you came out of Egypt. And my Spirit remains among you. Do not fear." This is what the LORD Almighty says: "In a little while . . . I will shake all nations, and the desired of all nations will come, and I will fill this house with glory," says the LORD Almighty.

"The silver is mine and the gold is mine," declares the LORD Almighty. "The glory of this present house will be greater than the glory of the former house," says the LORD Almighty. "And in this place I will grant peace," declares the LORD Almighty.[25]

Clearly Haggai predicts that the glory of the second temple will surpass that of the first, or Solomonic, temple. In this prophecy two terms are ambiguous, *desired* and *glory*. The former can be used to refer to persons[26] or to wealth.[27] The latter can mean God's presence[28] or wealth.[29] All of these make sense in the context. Solomon's temple was filled with wealth, and the glory of God's presence fell upon it at its dedication. With the restoration to the promised land, the Jews would doubtless be looking forward to the coming of the Messiah, who, as a light to the Gentiles, would be one "desired by all nations." Haggai's colleague Zechariah, in fact, makes a number of Messianic predictions at this time.[30]

We do not know just how much wealth Solomon's temple had, in order to compare it with the second temple, but it was certainly considerable. Of the second temple we know that Herod the Great enlarged and greatly enriched it in the years following 20 B.C. until it became one of the architectural marvels of the ancient world. Certainly, the physical glory of the second temple finally became very great, as wealth came in to it from all over the ancient world during the century before its destruction in A.D. 70.

But for the Jews, the principal glory of Solomon's temple, as with the tabernacle before it, was the presence of God manifested in the glory cloud and in the ark of the covenant. The ark was apparently lost at the destruction of Jerusalem by the Babylonians in 587 B.C. Whether it was taken to Babylon, destroyed by fire when the temple burned, or hidden away, is not known. In any case, there was no ark in the second temple. The glory cloud which came upon the tabernacle[31] and the first temple[32] when they were dedicated was also lacking for the second temple, unless it came in the person of Jesus, who, according to the New Testament, was God Himself dwelling with men.[33] Jesus Himself, in fact, made some allusion to this early in His public ministry when, standing in the temple, He said, "Destroy this temple, and I will raise it again in three days."[34] His opponents still remembered this claim three years later at His trial,[35] but they did not realize that He was speaking cryptically of Himself. In this most important sense, then, the glory of the second temple did not exceed that of the first except in the Christian view that Jesus the Messiah visited it before its destruction in A.D. 70.

The Messiah Was to Come After the Sixty-ninth Sabbath Cycle

In the ninth chapter of the book of Daniel, the prophet has just learned from his study of Scripture that the Babylonian captivity is to last seventy years. Realizing that this timespan is almost completed, Daniel prays to God, confessing his sins and those of his people. While he is praying the angel Gabriel appears to him and informs him that seventy sabbath cycles yet remain to complete God's program for Israel. Part of this prophecy gives a time sequence leading up to the coming of the Messiah:

Know and understand this: From the issuing of the decree to restore and rebuild Jerusalem until the Anointed One [Messiah], the ruler, comes, there will be seven "sevens" [sabbatical cycles] and sixty-two "sevens." It will be rebuilt with streets and a trench, but in times of trouble. After the sixty-two "sevens," the Anointed One will be cut off and will have nothing.[36]

The context of Daniel 9, regarding the length of the Babylonian captivity, sends us to Jeremiah, where the seventy-year length is specified.[37] The covenant curses given by God to Israel in Leviticus give the general principle that lies behind this specific number:

I will scatter you among the nations and will draw out my sword and pursue you. Your land will be laid waste, and your cities will lie in ruins. Then the land will enjoy its sabbath years all the time that it lies desolate and you are in the country of your enemies; then the land will rest and enjoy its sabbaths. All the time that it lies desolate, the land will have the rest it did not have during the sabbaths you lived in it.[38]

According to Leviticus,[39] the Jews were commanded to let the land enjoy a rest one year out of every seven by not planting it, something like our crop rotation except that all the land rested on the same year. Apparently, the Jews had not observed this required seventh year of rest for the land on some seventy occasions during their occupation of the promised land. Now God sends them into captivity, and the land gets its seventy missed sabbaticals all in a row. Thus when Gabriel comes with his message about seventy "sevens" still to come, the "seven" is naturally to be read as referring to this seven-year land use cycle. The Messiah is to come and be cut off after sixty-nine (seven then sixty-two) such cycles.

Where does the calculation of this timespan begin? According to the prophecy, "from the issuing of the decree to restore and rebuild Jerusalem." The most likely such decree is that issued by the Persian king Artaxerxes I, in the twentieth year of his reign,[40] allowing Nehemiah his Jewish cupbearer to return to Jerusalem as governor with a commission to rebuild it. According to the best available information,[41] this would be 445 B.C.

The calculation itself is to be carried out in units of sabbatical cycles rather than years. Recent archaeological work has enabled us to locate the beginning and end of the sabbatical cycles in antiquity.[42] We find that our starting point, 445 B.C., falls in the sabbatical cycle from 449 to 442 B.C.

By the usual Jewish inclusive counting method, this would be the first sabbatical cycle. The sixty-ninth cycle then turns out to be from A.D. 28 to 35, and "after" this cycle means after it begins.[43]

Thus the Messiah is to come and be cut off in the period A.D. 28 to 35, which exactly spans the public ministry of Jesus of Nazareth!

Conclusion

As we suggested in the first section above, the biblical prophecies about the Messiah indicate strongly that if the Messiah has come, He must be Jesus of Nazareth. The material just discussed indicates first that the Messiah was to have come while Judah still had its own rulers, a situation which ended in A.D. 44. The prophecy about the greater glory of the second temple at least suggests, second, that the Messiah was to have come while the second temple still stood. That temple was destroyed by the Romans in A.D. 70. Third and finally, the so-called seventy weeks prophecy of Daniel indicates that the Messiah should come and be cut off in the sabbatical cycle from A.D. 28 to 35. All of these strictures fit Jesus of Nazareth and no one else.

It is interesting that most of the Old Testament passages cited here have been recognized as Messianic by ancient rabbis.[44] Also many of these fulfillments involved public knowledge about Jesus and cannot have been fabricated by the New Testament writers.

Of course, one may object that the Bible is just the guesswork of ancient man and only accidentally happens to fit Jesus in these points. I suggest that the historical information we have about Jesus indicates that He Himself is no accident, that the evidence of His miraculous work and resurrection from the dead is strong,[45] and that one would be a fool to keep appealing to accident when the evidence suggests one's worldview is faulty.

Of all the Messianic claimants that Judaism has ever had, the only one ever considered an outstanding historical figure and ethical teacher (even by atheists) is Jesus of Nazareth. And He "just happened" to conduct His short public ministry and be "cut off" (killed) in the period A.D. 28–35!

Notes

[1]Isa. 42:6–7 (NASB, emphasis mine). Scripture quotations in this paper, unless stated otherwise, are from the New American Standard Bible (NASB), copyright 1971 by The Lockman Foundation or from the New International Version (NIV), copyright 1978 by the New York International Bible Society.

[2]Isa. 49:5–6 (NASB, emphasis mine).

[3]Statistics from David B. Barrett, *World Christian Encyclopedia* (New York: Oxford University Press, 1982), 4, 6.

[4]Ibid.

[5]Micah 5:2 (NIV).

[6]See, e.g., Francis Brown, S. R. Driver, and Charles A. Briggs, *A Hebrew and English Lexicon of the Old Testament* (Oxford: Clarendon Press, 1907), 761–62; R. Laird Harris, Gleason L. Archer, Jr., and Bruce K. Waltke, *Theological Wordbook of the Old Testament* (Chicago: Moody Press, 1980), 672–73.

[7]Isa. 9:6–7 (NIV).

[8]The *Holy Scriptures According to the Masoretic Text* (1945; Philadelphia, Pa.: The Jewish Publication Society, 1971) transliterates the titles in the text as a gigantic proper name, relegating the translation to a footnote where it is handled as a sentence referring to God rather than the Messiah. The New English Bible (1970) translates the second title as "in battle God-like," though elsewhere it always renders the phrase as "God Almighty."

[9]Dan. 7:13–14 (NIV).

[10]Zech. 9:9 (NIV).

[11]Babylonian Talmud, Sanh 98a.

[12]Ibid.

[13]See, e.g., Psalm 22, vv. 1–21 for the suffering, vv. 27–31 for the worldwide news.

[14]See the *Jewish Encyclopedia* (1907), 8:511–512; *Encyclopaedia Judaica* (Jerusalem: Encyclopaedia Judaica; New York: Macmillan, 1971–2), 11:1411.

[15]Zech. 12:10.

[16]2 Chron. 26:16–21.

[17]Manual of Discipline 9.10; Testament of Levi 18:16; Testament of Judah 24:9.

[18]Ps. 110:2–3 (NIV).

[19]Ps. 110:4 (NIV).

[20]Ps. 110:6 (NIV).

[21]Gen. 14:18–20.

[22]Heb. 4:14–5:10; 7:1–10:18.

[23]Heb. 1:8; Rev. 19:11–16.

[24]Gen. 49:10 (NIV).

[25]Hag. 2:3–9 (NIV).

[26]1 Sam. 9:20; Dan. 9:23; 11:37.

[27]2 Chron. 20:25; 32:27.

[28]Exod. 40:34–35; 1 Kings 8:10–11.

[29]Ps. 49:16–20.

[30]See, e.g., Zech. 6:12; 9:9; 12:10.

[31]Exod. 40:34.

[32]1 Kings 8:10.

[33]John 1:14, 17–18.

[34]John 2:19 (NIV).

[35]Matt. 26:61.

[36]Dan. 9:25–26 (NIV). Bracketed material supplied by author.

[37]Jer. 25:11–12; 29:10.

[38]Lev. 26:33–35 (NIV).

[39]Lev. 25:1–7.

[40]Neh. 2:1–9.

[41]Jack Finegan, *Handbook of Biblical Chronology* (Princeton: Princeton University Press, 1964), sec. 336.

[42]Ben Zion Wacholder, "The Calendar of Sabbatical Cycles During the Second Temple and the Early Rabbinic Period," *Hebrew Union College Annual*, 44 (1973): 153–96.

[43]The Jewish inclusive counting method counts as the first time unit, the unit containing the starting point. The phrase "after *n* units" means after the *nth* unit has begun. Note this usage in the Gospels, where "on the third day" and "after three days" are equivalent.

[44]Alfred Edersheim, "List of Old Testament Passages Messianically Applied in Ancient Rabbinic Writings," in his *The Life and Times of Jesus the Messiah* (Grand Rapids, Mich.: Eerdmans, 1967).

[45]On the evidence for the resurrection of Jesus, see Frank Morison, *Who Moved the Stone?* (London: Faber & Faber, 1944); John Warwick Montgomery, *History and Christianity* (Minneapolis, Minn.: Bethany, 1985); John Wenham, *The Easter Enigma* (Grand Rapids, Mich.: Zondervan, 1984); Josh McDowell, *More Than a Carpenter* (Wheaton, Ill.: Tyndale House, 1977); Gary R. Habermas and Antony Flew, *Did Jesus Rise from the Dead? The Resurrection Debate* (San Francisco: Harper and Row, 1987).

4.5

The Canon of Scripture
Can We Be Sure Which Books Are Inspired of God?

Allan A. MacRae

ONE OF THE CARDINAL PRINCIPLES of the Reformation was the right and duty of all believers to interpret the Scriptures for themselves up to the limit of their knowledge. Our doctrine is not determined according to human ideas and philosophies. It is not the result of human speculation, or of human aesthetic feeling. Our convictions about God and His will must be determined by careful objective study of His Word.

This right and duty of private judgment on the interpretation of Scripture has always been claimed by evangelical Protestants. Inevitably, however, another question arises: How do we know what is the Word of God? If we have been born again through the Holy Spirit, we know that Jesus Christ is our Savior and Lord, and we are anxious to accept those books which He approves. Yet this does not immediately determine the question as to selection of the individual books. After all, the Bible was not written by one man, nor at one time. Its books were written by many different men over a period of many centuries. These men varied greatly in their characteristics. Some were kings upon the throne, while others were shepherds caring for the sheep. Some were prophets and some were priests. They discussed a great variety of subjects, and used many types of literary styles. These various books are now combined together into one volume which we call the Bible, but until our present book form came into general use, at some time between the second and fourth centuries A.D., such a unified volume was not known. Before that time the various books existed as separate scrolls. How are we to know whether the men who combined these books into our present Bible were correct in the books they chose to include?

Roman Catholics assert that the Bible is the production of their church and that its hierarchy has the right to determine which books should be accepted as being inspired of God. Protestants have reacted strongly against this position. They assert that there is no evidence in Scripture or elsewhere that the Lord Jesus Christ established a continuing group of officials with authority to determine religious matters for Christian believers. Protestants insist that each individual Christian must determine his own attitude on religious matters by study of the Word of God. Having taken this position, however, we are immediately faced with this question, How is the individual to know which books are to be accepted as part of God's inspired Word? Must the individual believer study the evidence regarding the genuineness of each book for himself and make a decision as to every book which claims to be divine Scripture? Or is there some way in which he can have more certainty on this point?

Apostolicity and Canonicity

Sometimes it is said that "apostolicity determines canonicity." According to the view that this phrase summarizes, each believer must determine for himself which books of the New Testament were written by apostles or under apostolic direction and which books in the Old Testament were written by prophets. Moreover, he must accept these books, and only these books, as the inspired books that God desires His people to accept as complete and accurate presentations of His truth. This view of the canon would require that each believer make personal judgments as to which books he will consider inspired and that he base these judgments on precise evidence regarding the authorship of the books.

Unfortunately, however, such evidence is not always available. There is great difficulty in determining with certainty the authorship of some of the books. Even when the authorship is known, it is sometimes extremely difficult to find evidence on which to determine whether the author was actually a prophet or an apostle.

What, for instance, should be the attitude of the Christian toward such a book as the Epistle to the Hebrews? Nobody knows who wrote this book. There have been many opinions about the matter. All sorts of guesses have been made. Probably the guess that has been made more frequently than any other is that it was written by the Apostle Paul, but there is no sufficient evidence to prove this position. Great numbers of outstanding Christian leaders have agreed with the conclusion of Martin Luther and John Calvin, that there is more evidence against the Pauline authorship of Hebrews than in its favor. What then is the Christian to do? If he does not know who wrote the book of Hebrews, he can surely have no certainty that it was written by an apostle, or even under apostolic direction. He cannot even find a claim in the book itself that the unknown author was writing under the direction of one of the Apostles. If the person assumes that the Apostle Paul wrote it, then he must recognize that he is taking a position upon which great numbers of scholars and consecrated Christians differ with him.

Surely it would be very foolish to build a doctrine, or to preach a sermon, upon a text drawn from a book of which we cannot be sure. If our decision as to whether a book is divine Scripture depends upon our ability to prove that it was written by an apostle, or under apostolic direction, it would then be hazardous to preach a sermon based upon a text from the book of Hebrews.

Even when the authorship of a book is quite certain, we sometimes find ourselves in an equally difficult position. James and Jude, the brothers of the Lord, are not included in the list of the Twelve Apostles. They make no claim in their books that they were writing under the direction of one of the Twelve Apostles. If apostolicity determines canonicity, what right have we to include their books among those on which we can safely base determination of the facts about our eternal destiny?

The situation is, in fact, even worse than this. The Gospels tell us the names of the Apostles and reveal that Jesus appointed them. There is no mention in the Gospels of Paul being appointed as an apostle. Nor is there any statement in the book of Acts that the Apostles decided to add Paul to their number. Except for two cases in Acts 14,[1] every use of the term *apostle* in the book of Acts refers to the group selected by Christ during His earthly ministry, and not one of those occurrences can be shown to include Paul. In all the chapters devoted to Paul's missionary journeys, the word *apostle* is never applied to Paul or his associates with the sole exception of the two instances in chapter 14. In these two cases, it would seem to be used in a general sense, for it is used in the plural, so as to include Barnabas, and in fact, where the names are given, that of Barnabas is mentioned first! It has never been claimed that Barnabas was an apostle, and no portion of the Christian church accepts the so-called Epistle of Barnabas as inspired Scripture. It is only in the letters written by Paul himself that we find any evidence that he was an apostle. He begins nine of his epistles with the assertion that he is an apostle by divine appointment.

Approximately half of the books of the New Testament, therefore, come from a man who is not mentioned among the Twelve Apostles, and for whom our only evidence that he was an apostle rests upon the statements that he makes in his own writings. Do we believe that these books are inspired because Paul was an apostle and then prove his apostleship by the statements which the books contain? Or can we rest our belief that they are inspired books upon some other basis, and therefore have a solid foundation for belief in Paul's apostleship?

If we have some other basis on which to believe that these books are the inspired Word of God, then we are safe in drawing from them the teaching that Paul was an apostle. But if we accept them on the ground that he was an apostle, and then find our belief that he was an apostle to be based only upon statements contained in the books, we come dangerously close to arguing in a circle. Our faith must have a stronger basis than this!

Of the Twelve Apostles actually appointed by the Lord Jesus while He was here on earth,[2] only three left books that are contained in the New Testament. If apostolicity determined canonicity, it would be very strange that we should have nothing from any of the remaining Apostles. It would also be strange that we have no explicit statement from the apostolic group, or from individual apostles, setting the seal of their approval upon those books that were not written by one of their number.

Even when we consider the Gospels and the book of Acts we find ourselves in difficulty. If we are to base our faith upon these books as infallibly inspired of God and entirely free from error, we must be absolutely sure that we are right. We must run no risk of being wrong. We cannot gamble on the issues of eternal life and eternal death. If the individual believer must make a decision for himself as to whether or not these books are apostolic, he must insist on solid certainty. What does he find?

Of these five books only two have even been considered to be actually written by apostles. The other three, Mark, Luke, and Acts, were written by men who were not apostles, either by the original appointment of Christ, or by any subsequent appointment of the Holy Spirit, as far as any evidence goes. There is no claim in any one of these three books that the book was written under apostolic supervision, or with the specific approval of an apostle. There is a tradition that Mark was an associate of Peter; the book of Acts tells us that Luke was closely associated with Paul; and Luke is generally considered to be the author of both Luke and Acts. This, however, is very far from actual proof that these books were written under the supervision of apostles or received specific approval of apostles.

Roman Catholics claim to base their doctrine upon Holy Scripture plus tradition. Protestants reject tradition as a source of religious knowledge and insist that God's Word be recognized as our *only* rule of faith and practice. This being the case, they can hardly regard mere tradition as a safe basis for determining whether a book is apostolic and therefore inspired. Without real proof that Peter supervised Mark, no one who believes that apostolicity determines canonicity can safely accept the Gospel of Mark.

If each individual believer is required to base his belief that specific books are inspired upon an ability to prove that they come from apostles or were written under apostolic direction, he is in a very difficult situation indeed. There are very few books of the New Testament which he would be safe in quoting as the infallible Word of God. The area of individual interpretation would have been extended to the point where Christian life and conduct would become extremely difficult.

Prophetic Inspiration of the Old Testament

When the Old Testament is considered, we find an even more difficult situation. It has been the belief of the Christian church that the five books of the Pentateuch were written by Moses, and this belief is still held by most evangelical Christians, despite the efforts of the higher critics to demolish it. When we come to the books of Joshua, Judges, Samuel, and Kings, however, we have no way of knowing who wrote them. It is thought likely they were written by prophets, but there is no proof. We have no certainty as to who wrote the books of Chronicles, or any way of making even a good guess as to who might have written the book of Ruth. Is it then impossible for us to know whether they are inspired or not?

We do not know who wrote Esther. If we assume, as has been traditionally believed, that Nehemiah and Ezra wrote the books that bear their names, it would be very difficult to find proof that either of these men was a prophet. There is no evidence that they gave the traditional signs of a prophet or performed the activities which normally were characteristic of a prophet.

It has been traditionally believed that Proverbs, Ecclesiastes, and the Song of Solomon were written by Solomon, and conservatives do not accept the higher critical arguments that these were written far later than the time of Solomon. Nevertheless, we must ask the question, Was Solomon a prophet of God? What evidence do we have of his ever acting in a way similar to Moses, or to Isaiah or Jeremiah? It is true that God gave him great wisdom and that in the early part of his life he showed remarkable insight in dealing with legal problems. He also seems to have had unusual scientific understanding. Later on, however, we are told that his heart drifted away from God, and he did much that was contrary to God's will, even going after false gods.[3] Deuteronomy 13:1–3 lays down explicit commands for such a case. It describes the possibility that a prophet, after seeming to prove himself by performing miracles or making correct predictions of the future, might go on to say, "Let us go after other gods."[4] Moses' command for such a situation is absolutely clear, as given in verse 3: "Thou shalt not hearken unto the words of that prophet." Here is a man of whom we are told that he actually did go after other gods.[5] Should we hearken unto his words, even including them in our sacred canon?

Is it the duty of each of us to decide whether Solomon was a prophet in such a sense that his writings, if we can prove that they were definitely his, deserve a place among those we consider to be inspired of God and free from error? If we conclude that Solomon was a true prophet in his early life but that later he did what God had so precisely forbidden in Deuteronomy, does it then become our duty not to hearken to anything he said or wrote in his later years? Does the individual believer have the responsibility of personally seeking evidence on which to determine whether Proverbs, Ecclesiastes, and the Song of Solomon were written in Solomon's early days or in his later years, and of thus deciding whether they are books that can safely be used as a guide in spiritual matters, or whether they are books to which the words of Deuteronomy apply: "Thou shalt not hearken unto the words of that prophet."[6]

Is it an individual question for each of us to determine for himself, which of the Old Testament books were written by true prophets, and which of the New Testament books were written by apostles or under apostolic supervision? If it is, we must be very careful indeed. We dare not quote the word of fallible man as if it were the Word of the infallible God. Yet in the case of certain Old Testament books the evidence is simply not available for us to determine today whether it was written by a true prophet. In the case of certain New Testament books we have no way of proving with certainty that they were written by an apostle, or under apostolic supervision. Must each believer decide which books he dares to take as God's Word? If so he must beware of sermons or doctrines drawn from other books. He will soon find himself of necessity in an almost impossible situation, with large sections of the Bible lost to him.

Evidence for the Canon

It is the author's conviction, however, that this is not the real situation. I believe thoroughly in the right and duty of the individual believer to determine objectively the meaning of the Scripture for himself. Further, I believe that God has given us a means of knowing exactly what books the Bible should include, without the necessity of trying to make an individual judgment on the basis of evidence which is no longer available. This can be shown by examining certain definite propositions:

(1) *As a first step toward finding the answer to this problem we should note that for the Christian the supreme authority is the Lord Jesus Christ.*

A Christian is one who has accepted Jesus Christ as Savior and Lord, who is grateful to Him for having died on the cross for his salvation, and who is anxious to follow where his Master leads. If one is a true Christian he is ready to declare that whatever Jesus believed is normative for him. If we can find what Jesus thought about the Old Testament, this should settle the matter for all true Christians.

(2) *Jesus considered the Old Testament God's Word, free from error and dependable in all things.*

Even considering the New Testament books simply as sources giving us evidence about the views of people in the first century A.D. and leaving out of consideration for the present any question of their inspiration or inerrancy, one cannot avoid reaching the conclusion that these books witness clearly to the fact that Jesus Christ considered the Old Testament as the Word of God, free from error, and authoritative. He often appealed to it in such a way as to show that there was no doubt about the matter. He strongly criticized the people of His day for "making the word of God of none effect through your tradition."[7] He sharply distinguished between anything added to the Word of God and what is actually contained in it. He criticized the religious leaders of His day for many things, but He never made the slightest suggestion that they might be in error as to which books belong in the category of inspired Scripture.

(3) *Christ and the Apostles considered the Old Testament as a definite unit, the extent of which is clearly fixed.*

The Old Testament was never published as one book in Christ's day. Ordinarily it was on twenty-two separate scrolls. These scrolls were not even numbered in any fixed order. Yet the Lord Jesus Christ referred to them by terms which lump them all together into one book, generally calling the entire group of books "the law and the prophets"[8] or simply "the Scriptures."[9] From the way the terms are used it is quite clear He expected that those to whom He spoke would understand exactly what He meant. The way in which He spoke of the Old Testament leaves no doubt that He considered it as a fixed unit.

The same is true of the Apostles. Peter speaks of the Word of God as a definite unit. Paul describes it as "the holy scriptures, which are able to make thee wise unto salvation,"[10] indicating that by the term *holy scriptures* he means the books that Timothy has known from his youth. Paul says that each of these books is "given by inspiration of God, and is profitable for doctrine, for reproof, for correction, for instruction in righteousness."[11]

(4) *The Jews of Christ's day were unanimous in their agreement as to which books were inspired.*

The words used by Christ and the Apostles in reference to the Old Testament would be strange indeed if it could be shown that the Jews of that day were actually in doubt as to what books belonged in the Old Testament. The evidence is clear that there was no such doubt. It is made absolute when we read the words of Josephus in a book written to defend his people against anti-Semitic attacks and therefore intended to be widely distributed. Josephus had carefully investigated many different groups of Jews in his early days. Yet he speaks positively of the fact that these specific books were accepted by all Jews as commands of God, and that no Jew would willingly add anything to them or take anything from them.[12]

There is abundant evidence that the Jews in the first century hotly disputed many questions. The Talmud gives evidence of some discussion as to whether certain books of the Old Testament were inspired. Yet examination of the evidence for these disputes shows that actually what they amount to was a discussion of the ways to defend these books from attack. There is no evidence of any Jewish suggestion in the first century that a book which is not now contained in our Old Testament might really belong there. The way in which the discussions were carried on clearly presupposes a definite and fixed canon. The evidence fits with the statement of Josephus that there was a definite unanimity among the Jews as to which were the inspired books.

(5) *This unanimity of the Jews as to which books belong in the Old Testament came about because the Holy Spirit providentially led the people of God.*

It is an interesting question just how the Jews came to have such unanimity about the books of the Old Testament. There is no difficulty in seeing how it would have been reached regarding the first five books, since we are definitely told that Moses, who was the great leader of the people, received revelations from God which he passed on to them as God's will for them. God commanded him to write down the law and to place it in the Holy of Holies in order that it might be treasured and observed (Deut. 31:9–11, 24–26). It is not at all strange that the Jews from that time on accepted these five books as part of God's Word. We are in quite a different situation, however, as regards most of the prophetic books of the Old Testament.

Many of the prophets did not speak as recognized leaders of the nation. When we read their strong criticism of many of the leaders of the people, and even of the nation as a whole, we find it hard to imagine how any nation would accept such books as part of its national treasure. It is a phenomenon that can hardly be paralleled in any other nation.

Nor was there any lack of attempts to dispute the authority of the prophets during their lifetime. Jeremiah tells us that there were other prophets, both in Palestine and in Mesopotamia, who denied his claim to be a prophet. Some of them gave alleged revelations from God that were directly contrary to what he was saying. While some of these men were hypocrites and liars, others probably believed that what they said was true. Doubtless many of the people accepted the books of these other prophets. The natural result would be that some groups of people would accept the books of Jeremiah as inspired, while others would accept those of one or more of his opponents. Some might accept both, while some might deny the claims of both. Thus many shades of opinion as to which books were inspired might be expected to develop.

The fact that there is no disagreement among the Muslims as to what belongs in the Koran is no objection to this expectation, since the entire Koran was composed by one man, and he was the recognized leader of the entire Islamic movement. The case of the Old Testament is entirely different, for the books were written by more than a score of different writers, and included men from many different social classes, with very diverse backgrounds. It would not have been at all strange if the Jews at the time of Christ had been divided into several groups, each of which considered a different selection of books to be inspired.

This, however, did not occur. Within a very few centuries after the last book in our Old Testament was written, the entire Jewish nation was unanimous in accepting every one of its books as canonical and in rejecting as false the claims of any other book to similar recognition.

That such unanimity should thus have been reached is little short of a miracle. There is absolutely no evidence that this result was due to the influence of a particular leader or that it resulted from the decision of any council. Neither is there any reason to believe that God gave a direct revelation on the matter, precisely specifying the correct books. Nevertheless it would seem that acceptance of certain books gradually spread to larger and larger groups, along with a gradually spreading rejection of other books. This pattern continued until within a few centuries after the writing of the last book of the Old Testament the entire nation accepted all the correct books and rejected all the false ones. The achievement of unanimity on such a matter in such a way would be difficult to parallel anywhere else. It would be hard to believe that it was purely a result of chance, and yet one would hesitate to say that the Holy Spirit had providentially led the people of God to this result if there were no further divine attestation. Fortunately, such attestation was very clearly given by the Lord Jesus Christ. He set the seal of His approval on the books that the Jews accepted and affirmed that these books are indeed the very Word of God. Clearly, then, the Holy Spirit guided His people to select and approve the correct books.

(6) *Since it is on the authority of Christ that we believe that the result of this process is correct, His authority authenticates not only the result, but also the process.*

Apart from the authority of Christ we could not be at all sure that any particular group of Jews, or all Jews together, were correct in their decision as to which books had been inspired of God. The Lord Jesus Christ indicated that He believed in the correctness of the conclusion to which the people of God had unanimously come within a very few centuries after the writing of the last book of the Old Testament. Consequently, we also must believe that God providentially guided the process by which these books became known to and accepted by wider and wider circles of Jews, until the entire nation had accepted the correct books and had discarded those books which were not really inspired.

(7) *The Lord Jesus Christ gave us reason to expect that a New Testament would also be written.*

Jesus said: "I have yet many things to say unto you, but ye cannot bear them now. Howbeit when he, the Spirit of truth, is come, he will guide you into all truth."[13] Thus Jesus made it clear that the disciples were to expect further dependable revelations from God. He also said: "But the Comforter, which is the Holy Ghost, whom the Father will send in my name, he shall teach you all things, and bring all things to your remembrance, whatsoever I have said unto you."[14] These verses show, not only that further truth would be revealed to the disciples after Jesus' death, but also that what He had already told them would be made available to them in a form that would be free from error.

It is easy to see how necessary this was. The Gospels tell us that on several occasions Jesus predicted His death and resurrection.[15] Yet when the actual events took place, the disciples were completely surprised.[16] Until the events actually took place, much of His teaching was incomprehensible to them, and hence easily forgotten. The only way we today can know exactly what Jesus taught or can know the additional revelations that God gave after Christ's departure, is through the books of the New Testament. These books are free from error because they were written under the inspiration of the Holy Spirit. The verses quoted above show that Jesus, who authenticated the Old Testament as an inerrant presentation of God's earlier revelation, authenticated in advance a similar inerrant New Testament.

(8) *Since Jesus did not give any method by which these books could be infallibly recognized, there is an inevitable suggestion that a process similar to that which occurred in the case of the Old Testament might be used.*

Jesus promised that the Holy Spirit would lead the disciples to further truth and would bring to their remembrance the precise words that He Himself had spoken. He did not say how they would be able to distinguish the particular books that would be kept from error from other good books that were not inerrant.

It can be assumed that when a book was written under the inspiration of the Holy Spirit, the human author gave it to the people of God as the Word of God and they accepted it as such. Yet the Christians did not continue to be in one place. Persecution soon scattered them in various directions, and they went everywhere preaching the gospel. Little groups of Christians sprang up here and there. Each of these groups would tend to be particularly interested in whatever they might hear from those who had first brought them the gospel and not quite so ready to accept teaching from other sources. We know from the Corinthian epistles that many disagreements arose in some of these bodies.

The writing of the books of the New Testament extended over many years. A few of them were written by men who were listed among the Twelve Apostles Jesus had named, but most of the books were written by men who were not included in this list. Many of them were letters addressed either to one church or to an individual. These books were written at various places, and their spread from one church to another must have taken quite a long time.

In addition to the inspired books other good books were written by Christian leaders and were widely read, yet they were not considered to be inerrant and authoritative like the books the Holy Spirit inspired. Since Jesus did not state any way in which the books that were free from error could be distinguished from the others, it would be natural to expect that soon there would be great disagreement about this question. Those churches that knew the author of a particular book or group of books would be strongly inclined to accept his books, while other churches where he was less known might question whether his writings were inspired. It would be natural to expect there would be different views in different places and even considerable differences of opinion within certain groups as to which were the books God wanted accepted as part of His infallible Word. The attitude of Christ toward the Old Testament would naturally raise the suggestion that perhaps a similar unanimity might be reached in the case of the New Testament, but humanly speaking it would be quite unnatural to expect such a result. Since Jesus did not state any way in which the books that were free from error could be distinguished from others, it is hard to see how such a result would be attained, unless the Holy Spirit should providentially lead in a way similar to what had occurred in the case of the Old Testament.

(9) *Contrary to what would normally be expected, the same unanimity was ultimately attained in the case of the New Testament as in the case of the Old Testament.*

The evidence is quite definite that the Christian church did not decide on its canon because of the attitude of any one influential human leader. Nor was a decision made by any Christian council to include a certain book in the New Testament or to drop out any book that some had considered to belong to it. Yet within a few centuries after the last New Testament book was written there was a unanimous attitude on the part of all portions of the professing Christian church, accepting exactly those books which are in our present New Testament. When we find Christian councils making statements as to the books that are to be accepted as part of God's Word, they are so expressed as to show that a new decision is not being stated, but that the council is merely affirming its adherence to what was already universally believed.

In the case of the New Testament we have more knowledge about the process by which this unanimity was attained than in that of the Old Testament, though even here our evidence is scanty. Within two centuries after the last book was written all groups of Christians agreed as to about twenty of the New Testament books. Many of the Christians in the Eastern portion of the Roman Empire accepted three or four additional books which some Western Christians thought of as rather questionable. Similarly many Christians in the Western portion of the empire accepted three or four books which some Eastern Christians regarded as questionable. There was by this time no way in which any objective investigation of the authorship of these books could be made, nor is there any evidence that such an investigation was even attempted, but soon all groups of orthodox Christians came to a complete agreement, accepting the twenty-seven books that are contained in our present New Testament and no others. The attainment of such a unanimity, within a few centuries after the writing of the last book, among people so widely scattered as the early Christians, is almost miraculous, particularly when we consider the great arguments and strong divisions of opinion that were found among them on various doctrinal questions. That the unanimous conclusion reached in such a way should be correct could hardly be assumed aside from the providential activity of the Holy Spirit.

(10) *The authority of Christ, which is our major basis for being sure that we have the correct books in the Old Testament, authenticates the same process in the case of the New Testament, since it also occurred there.*

We have seen that we can be sure that we have the correct books in our Old Testament, because Jesus Christ set the seal of His approval upon it. A marvelous process took place. There was unanimity among the people of God within a few centuries after the last book was written. Jesus approved the conclusion and thereby gave recognition to the fact that this unanimity had been produced by the providential leading of the Holy Spirit. Exactly the same process took place as regards the New Testament. Jesus authenticated the New Testament in advance. He thereby authenticated the same process if one should occur, as it did. The only conclusion possible is that Jesus authenticated this process, and that we can rest secure that its results are correct.

The fact that the Roman Catholic Church, since the sixteenth century, considers the Old Testament to contain seven additional books which Protestants reject, does not affect this conclusion. The people of God to whom the Old Testament was given were Jews. At the time of Christ all groups of Jews agreed on the contents of the Old Testament. The New Testament was given to the Christians, who took over the Old Testament from the Jews. Among the Christians unanimity regarding the books of the New Testament came into being within a few centuries, and has continued ever since.

(11) *As a result of this authentication by the Lord Jesus Christ, we can be sure that our Bible contains those books, and only those books, that God intended it to contain.*

All Christians have the right and duty of private interpretation as to the meaning of Scripture. Its great outstanding teachings are very clear. On lesser points we must study up to the limit of our knowledge and abilities, see what is clearly taught in the Scripture, and stand upon it. This is God's will for all Christians.

Christians do not have a similar right when it comes to deciding which books to accept as inspired. This is not a matter on which the organized Church has a right to speak, other than to affirm the unanimity which the Christian Church has had for many centuries. Individual Christians have no basis, either subjective or objective, on which they could now make a correct decision for themselves, regarding whether a particular book belongs in the Bible. We must accept the authority of Jesus with respect to the Old Testament books. Jesus' approval of that process authenticated in advance a similar process if it should occur in the case of the New Testament, as it did. Our whole Christian faith is based on the authority of Christ, and on this authority we can be sure which books are inspired of God.

Notes

[1] Acts 14:4, 14.

[2] Luke 6:13–16. (Cf. Matt. 10:2–4; Mark 3:13–19.)

[3] 1 Kings 11:4–10.

[4] Deut. 13:2. This and all subsequent Scripture quotations in this chapter are from the King James (Authorized) version of the Bible.

[5] 1 Kings 11: 4–5, 7, 10.

[6] Deut. 13:3.

[7] Mark 7:13.

[8] E.g., Matt. 7:12; Luke 16:16.

[9] E.g., Matt. 21:42; Mark 12:24; John 5:39.

[10] 2 Tim. 3:15.

[11] 2 Tim. 3:16.

[12] Flavius Josephus *Against Apion*, 1.8.

[13] John 16:12–13a.

[14] John 14:26.

[15] E.g., Matt. 16:21.

[16] See Luke 24:19–26.

Part 5

God's Existence and Christ's Claims

5.1

The Problem of Evil

John E. Hare

I AM GOING TO EXAMINE the most powerful and most commonly used disproof for the existence of God.[1] It is the disproof that goes like this: God is supposed to be first omnipotent (He can do anything), second omniscient (He knows everything), and third omnibenevolent (He wills all good for His creatures). Yet, fourth, the world is full of evil—of moral evil that humans choose and of natural evil, like the pain and suffering that they do not choose. It cannot be the case, so the disproof goes, that these four propositions are true together. Since the objector is more convinced of the existence of evil than he is of the existence of God, he takes the inconsistency he thinks he has shown as a disproof of the existence of an omnipotent, omniscient, and omnibenevolent God.

Consistency can easily be regained by dropping one of the four propositions. Suppose God is omniscient and omnibenevolent but not omnipotent. This is the solution in the recent popular book *When Bad Things Happen to Good People*.[2] Here God wills all good for His creatures and knows the evil that is happening to them but cannot prevent it. Or God might be omnipotent and omnibenevolent, but not omniscient. He would prevent the evil if He knew about it, but it is hidden from Him. Or God might be omnipotent and omniscient, but not omnibenevolent. He knows about the evil and could prevent it if He wanted to, but He does not want to. This was perhaps the answer of Epicurus, who first formulated the problem in the form I have just stated.[3] We might imagine the gods enjoying the spectacle of our miseries as we now enjoy soap operas on the television. Finally, evil might be an illusion. I do not mean by this that evil might be the absence of good, or parasitic upon good. For these positions still maintain the reality of the absence of good and have to reconcile this with the omnipresence of God. There are Eastern philosophies which do hold that evil is an illusion, but they tend to hold that good is also an illusion, so that the tension I am interested in disappears.

I am going to be talking about systems that try to incorporate all four of the propositions I started with and in particular about the Judaeo-Christian tradition. It has been a central part of the philosophy of religion within this tradition to discuss whether these four propositions can be asserted together consistently. Most recently, the discussion has centered around the work of Alvin Plantinga.[4] I will start by describing his approach to the problem.

The Negative Project

I think Plantinga is largely successful in what I shall call the *negative project*. This is the project of showing that there is no demonstrative or conclusive proof from the existence of evil to the non-existence of God. This leaves, however, the more important *positive project* untouched. Plantinga is himself completely pessimistic about the success of any positive project. The positive project is to explain why God should allow the evils He does. This can be differentiated into two different tasks. One of them is the pastoral task of giving comfort to those who are themselves suffering. It is unlikely that philosophy as such is going to have much to say here, although Boethius (480–524) would not have agreed. He wrote the *Consolation of Philosophy* on the verge of his execution, and there is a long tradition of Stoic and Epicurean thought which aspired to help individuals through their sufferings. Perhaps what we can say is that the philosopher, unlike the pastor, is not primarily concerned with comforting his audience. He is aiming primarily to understand.

The second task is to show why God should allow the various types of evil to exist. This is the project of justifying the ways of God to men, sometimes called *theodicy*. I will describe some attempts at theodicy, none of which seem to me successful. The trouble is that such attempts always end up sounding glib, as though the writer had not understood the full awfulness of suffering. There is something cheap about trying to prove all is well when one has not suffered deeply oneself. It is like the chirpy visitor at the hospital who insists on trying to keep up the patient's spirits. She may even have had some lesser suffering which she claims she triumphantly surmounted, but the comfort is hollow, though well meant. I am going to say something at the end about the positive project, because I think something needs to be said. But I think it is also necessary to be tentative here. I will start from Job, because I think this is the fullest treatment of the problem in the Scriptures.

The Free Will Defense and Moral Evil

First, though, Alvin Plantinga. Much of what he says is a restatement of a traditional account of the subject, but he adds to the discussion great sophistication in the contemporary theory of necessity. I am going to present his argument informally, without numbered propositions or logical notation. The traditional account is that God allows evil because He wants to allow free human worship of Him, and He cannot allow humans this freedom unless He allows them the choice to do evil. The kind of evil that this free will defense is most clearly relevant to is the kind of evil that humans choose, namely, moral evil. It extends from Eve's eating the fruit in the Garden to the concentration camps of World War II, and beyond. The other kind of evil, that humans do not choose but happens anyway, needs a different treatment. Most human and animal pain from disease falls into this category. I will discuss later how natural evil fits into the free will defense.

The free will defense starts with what is, I think, its most important point. This is that the existence of evil would only prove the non-existence of God if we could add the premise that God could have no reason for allowing evil to exist. The reason we would need this premise is that otherwise a good God might quite consistently allow the evil because it was necessary for some greater good. If God's omnibenevolence consists in His willing all available good for His creatures, and if some evil is necessary for the production of some greater good, then God not only might but should allow that evil in accordance with His omni-benevolence. It may seem strange that an omnipotent God should be constrained in this way, that there should be some good that He would be *unable* to produce without allowing some evil. It is the function of the free will defense to produce an example of such a pair, a good that even God could not produce without allowing an evil. But my point here is that an example is not strictly necessary in order to cast doubt on the disproof of God's existence. All that has to be done is to show that there *might* be such a pair, that this is possible. For as long as it is possible, God might have a reason for allowing the existence of evil, and the disproof fails.

I said this was the most important part of the defense, even though nothing is yet said about free will, because we could stop here if we wanted. How could it be shown that God could not have a reason for allowing some evil in the world? The skeptic is trying to show that the four propositions I started with cannot be asserted together consistently. One of the four is the proposition that God is omniscient. The skeptic does not claim to be omniscient, and he is unlikely to be able to prove that an omniscient God could not have a reason of the specified sort.

Other possible examples of reasons of this sort are available that do not involve freedom at all. It is possible that some pain-receptor mechanism is the best way to prevent some greater pains or harms in the animal world. This might be true even if most animals do not have free will. It is possible that this might be a reason God has for allowing some animal pain. In any case, I will not pursue this here, but go on to the free will defense. It might be that giving humans beings free will requires God to allow them to do evil. Note that all the defender is doing is giving a *possible* example. It is not necessary for his purposes to claim that the example is true, or even plausible. As long as it is possible, the disproof fails.

Difficulties with the Free Will Defense

Now, I want to discuss two difficulties with the free will defense. The first arises from the question, "Why could not God have created people who always freely choose to worship Him?" The second difficulty is with the notion of freedom that the free will defense presupposes. The question is whether this defense presupposes that the external causation of an action is incompatible with the freedom of that action.

Freedom of Choice. First, then, could God have created people who always freely choose to worship Him? If He could, then presumably He should. I am using here a very broad notion of worshiping God which includes obedience to His will. Assuming a logical connection (unanalyzed) between what is right and what is in conformity with God's will, we can put the same question another way: Could God have created people who always freely choose to do right? If He could and did, there would be no moral evil, but there would be free worship of God.

It certainly seems possible that every person should always freely choose to do right. By *possible* here I mean "logically possible." Those who believe in total depravity as a result of the Fall believe that there is a tendency not to do right which is somehow built into human beings. According to this doctrine it is *not* now possible for human beings always freely to choose to do right, at least not without special divine assistance. But unless the Fall was itself logically necessary, it should be logically possible for humans to have continued indefinitely in the state of grace. So, to repeat, it seems logically possible that every person should always freely choose to do right. Now God's omnipotence should mean that He can bring about every logically possible state of affairs. I am not here arguing about whether God can also bring about logically impossible states of affairs. Some people think that God is above or beyond the laws of logic, so that His omnipotence is not constrained by them. I do not myself see what this would mean. In any case I am assuming that God can bring about all—and only—those states of affairs that are logically possible for Him to bring about.

Putting it this way makes another thing clear. Some things are in themselves logically possible which are not logically possible for God to bring about. For example, take some state of affairs that God did not bring about. Call it S. God's not having brought about S is a logically possible state of affairs. But this is not a state of affairs that God can bring about. For as soon as He has brought it about, it is no longer a state of affairs that He has not brought about. I think what is true of S here is also true of the state of affairs: "All persons always freely choose to do what is right." The reason is that as soon as God *brings about* this state of affairs, the people are no longer choosing to do what is right *freely*. If "bringing about" is a causal notion, and if God is causing them to choose what is right, then they are not doing so of their own free will. So it is not the case that God could bring it about that people always freely choose to do right.

There are, however, other complications here. First, there might be some alternative way for God to bring about some action than by directly causing someone to choose it. Let us call the state of affairs we are interested in $S1$. God might be able to cause directly some other state of affairs $S2$, which then all by itself brings about $S1$. One example of this would be where God creates free persons, who then freely choose to do right. Now suppose that God has what is sometimes called *middle knowledge*.[5] Middle knowledge is knowledge of so-called *conditionals of freedom*. A conditional of freedom has the following form: If x were to be created, he would freely choose y. If God did have middle knowledge, He could consult it to find out which—of the many people He could create—would be the ones who would always freely choose to do right. It would then be the case that He should only create those ones. The free will defense would then have failed to provide an example of an evil that God would have had to allow in order to bring about a greater good.

One of the complexities here is about whether middle knowledge is possible. This was much debated in the seventeenth century, and both sides to the dispute have contemporary adherents. Fortunately the soundness of the free will defense is independent of this issue. The reason for this is that we can show that God might have a reason for allowing evil whether middle knowledge is possible or not. First, let's take the case in which middle knowledge is possible. This means that God can know what the various people He might create would freely choose to do. It is logically possible that every person He might create would choose to do some wrong. Note, again, that this does not have to be likely to be true or even plausible. For the free will defense to work, the example has merely to be logically possible. It seems logically possible that depravity should, so to speak, be extended to all the people God could create. I said before that it was logically possible that all existing persons might always freely choose to do right. Here we have the opposite possibility. It is logically possible that all possibly existing persons (all those God could create) might choose to do some wrong. If this possibility were actual, God would not be able to create people who freely, all on their own, always choose to do right, even if He could know how all the people He would create would freely choose.

Take, secondly, the case where middle knowledge is not possible. If God cannot know what free creatures will freely choose, He cannot be held responsible, at least directly, if they go wrong. Suppose, though, that what God can know is how the people He might create would *probably* choose. Here again it is possible that He creates someone, say Adam, who will probably always choose to do right, but who actually chooses to do wrong. It is possible that this is so for anyone God might create. So, again, it is possible that He could not create people who always freely choose to do right.

My argument has been that this conclusion follows whether we admit middle knowledge or not. If I am right, then we are left with a reason that God might have for allowing some evil to exist, and therefore we have defeated the disproof of the existence of God from the existence of evil.

The Nature of Freedom. The second difficulty with the free will defense which I said I would discuss is the difficulty about the nature of freedom which the free will defense presupposes.[6] The general question is whether freedom of the will is compatible with determinism of any kind. Philosophers who think it is are often called *compatibilists*. They say that freedom involves not the absence of antecedent cause, but a limitation on what kinds of cause can be operative. For example, if I choose to strike the face of the person next to me, this choice may be caused by the antecedent conditions of my brain. There may even be a determinate causal chain from the state of the world two months before I made the choice. The choice is still free, according to the compatibilist, as long as the causal chain goes through my will. If, on the other hand, someone takes my arm and with it strikes the face of the person next to me, I have not chosen to do this. Here the causal chain has by-passed my will.

It might be argued that on the compatibilist notion of freedom God *could* bring it about that people always freely chose to do right. The free will defense presupposes that causal interference, by God or anything else, is sufficient to render a choice unfree. But on the compatibilist notion of freedom, this presupposition is false.

What I want to suggest is that God's causing a person to behave in a certain way is the kind of cause that should be ruled out even by the compatibilist. The idea is roughly this, that causes which would be compatible with freedom, for a compatibilist, if they came from many different sources, should not be considered compatible if they come from a single personal agent. A relevant example here is the hypnotist. Suppose a hypnotist puts the idea into your mind that whenever you smell pizza, you will rise up and sing the national anthem. Suppose you then smell pizza and choose to stand up and sing the national anthem. I want to say that this choice might go "through the will" in the way the compatibilist wants, but it is still not free. The reason is that the idea and the causal mechanism which makes the idea effective comes from the hypnotist. We would naturally talk about the hypnotist's control over you, whereas it is less natural to talk this way if the association between pizza and the desire to sing the national anthem is one that comes to you with overwhelming force from the distant past with no known personal source.

My motivation in making this point is that I want it to be possible for a compatibilist to use the free will defense. If I am wrong in the argument I have been making, what will follow is that a choice has to be made between the compatibilist view of freedom and this particular response to the problem of evil.

The Free Will Defense and Natural Evil

So far, I have been dealing only with moral evil. I said I would talk later about the connection of the free will defense and the problem of natural evil. This connection can be made in two ways. Remember again that what the free will defender needs is a logical possibility. Now suppose it is the case that natural evil is the work of a free, moral, but non-human agent. According to some theological systems, this is the truth about Satan, the Prince of this World. But we do not here need to believe it to be true, only to believe it to be possible. If this is possible, we can use the same argument to deal with natural evil as we previously used to deal with moral evil, for natural evil will be the result of a moral agent's choice to do wrong. God, in creating the angels, gave them freedom of choice, because their free worship of Him was so great a good. But in creating them, He could not create them such that they always freely chose to do right.

238 EVIDENCE FOR FAITH

Alternatively, we can suppose that the whole of creation somehow fell with Adam. It is hard to see how this would deal with animal pain, if there were such, before the existence of human beings. It is slightly easier to see how it might be possible that no person suffered from disease, tornadoes, droughts, etc., until Adam's fall.[7]

In my experience of discussing the free will defense with people, these two attempts to deal with natural evil have a lower initial plausibility than the rest of the defense. The method of the defense, however, is to show possibility, not plausibility. Until the skeptic can show that God could not have such a reason, the skeptical disproof from natural evil fails.

The Amount of Evil

There is an important part, however, of the negative project still to come. I think that most people who have trouble believing in the existence of a good God because of evil are troubled by the argument in a different form than the one given so far. The skeptic will say that the most convincing disproof of God's existence is not from the mere existence of evil, but from the existence of the *amount* of evil we in fact experience in the world. This argument needs to be divided again. It might be construed as a demonstrative disproof of the existence of God from the existence of the amount of evil in the world. Then it would be just like the last argument and can be answered in much the same way. The skeptic has to show that God *could* not have a reason for allowing as much evil as we in fact experience, that there *could* not be a sufficient good for which this much evil was necessary. But how would the skeptic show such a thing?

The second way to construe the argument is that the amount of evil we experience makes the existence of an omnipotent, omniscient, and omnibenevolent God *unlikely*. The difficulty in discussing this argument is that discussion requires use of the theory of probability, which is very complicated. There is a theorem, called *Bayes's Theorem,* which gives an account of the probability of a hypothesis, given some piece or pieces of evidence. This is what we are interested in here, the probability of the hypothesis that an omnipotent, omniscient, and omnibenevolent God exists, given the evidence of the amount of evil there is. Bayes's Theorem introduces one other element in the calculus, which is the background information we have relevant to the hypothesis and the evidence. According to the theorem the probability of the hypothesis, given the evidence and the background information, is dependent on two things: the prior probability of the hypothesis independent of this evidence and the explanatory power of the hypothesis over this evidence.[8]

This sounds very complicated, but I think it will seem more straightforward if we look at the example we are presently interested in.

We are interested in how probable it is that God exists, given that there is a certain amount of evil. This depends, first, on how probable it is that God exists anyway. This is the so-called *prior probability* of the hypothesis. It also depends on whether this much evil is more likely to exist if God exists or if He does not. This is very roughly the *explanatory power* of the hypothesis.

Appealing to Bayes's Theorem here makes something clear. This is that estimating the probability of the hypothesis, given the evidence, depends on one's judgment about these two factors. The difficulty in discussing the question is that the believer and the skeptic are likely to make different judgments about them. Given these different judgments about prior probability and explanatory power, the believer and the skeptic will *quite properly* come to different conclusions about the probability of the hypothesis, given the evidence. We can put this same point comparatively. Does the amount of evil in the world make theism or atheism more likely? This depends on the comparative prior probabilities of theism and atheism and on how much more likely the evil would be if God existed than if He did not. But the theist and the atheist are not going to agree about these two things.

The theist's assessment of the prior probability of God's existence is likely to be high. Before considering the existence of evil at all, he will say that it is more likely that God exists than that He does not. The atheist's assessment is likely to be that the prior probability of God's existence is 50 percent or less. As for the explanatory power of the hypothesis that God exists, the theist and the atheist will differ about this too. It will depend upon judgments about how much evil there is. This is notoriously hard to say. I have sometimes had the experience of living through two days which were very similar in external circumstance, but finding one of those days full of joy and goodness and the other one full of heaviness and frustration. A believer will perhaps say that on the first day I was living closer to God, for joy is one of the fruits of the Spirit.[9] This is not to say that the believer is supposed to be blind to the evils that exist, but that he should tend to see a different ratio of good and evil.

This will not be the end of the disagreement between the theist and the atheist. They may disagree about whether or not there is an afterlife. This will affect strongly the judgment about the explanatory power of the hypothesis that God exists, for it may be that there are evils which the theist thinks are compensated for in the afterlife but not in this life. The theist may believe in fallen angels, like Satan, and he may attribute some natural evils to the working of these angelic beings. I am not trying to give an exhaustive list here, but one more consideration should be mentioned. The Christian theist will put a very high value upon salvation, upon a restored relation to God; he may see that some evils make sense because they encourage people to turn to God. The atheist is not going to agree. He may disagree that there is any such thing as salvation, or he may disagree about the value of it.

This does not mean, however, that there is no point in the theist and the atheist talking about the problem of evil. I will give an example of how the discussion might go, drawing from the work of Robert M. Adams, to illustrate the *structure* of the argument.[10] Suppose the atheist thinks that the prior probabilities of theism and atheism are about the same. This means that for him the question turns on the existence of evil, which he thinks makes the non-existence of God far more probable than His existence. The theist, on the other hand, thinks that the prior probability of God's existence is far higher than the prior probability of His non-existence. The key question is what the theist thinks about evil. The atheist can show that the theist has an untenable position if the theist agrees that evil makes God's existence less likely, and this lessening in the probability is more than the higher prior probability he assigns to God's existence. It is a question, in other words, of the balance between what the theist thinks about evil and what he thinks about God independent of evil. Theists, in my experience, usually agree with atheists that the amount of evil in the world makes it harder to believe in a good God. But they have to be careful. For if theists agree that it is *much* harder, and they do not think that God's existence is, independent of evil, *much* more likely, they may be in an untenable position.

One word of caution here. I am not saying that the believer has to be able to assign numbers to these probabilities. Nor am I saying that the believer has to be able to explain why, given the existence of God, the amount of the evil in the world is not extremely unlikely. The believer may say something like the following: "God has some reason for allowing it all, but the reason is probably far too complex for me to understand. After all, God is omniscient, and I am not." The structure of this reply could be that the probability of the existence of so much evil, given the existence of God, cannot be estimated at all. Or it could be that the prior probability of God's existence is not only higher than that of God's non-existence, but higher than any assignable probability of the existence of this much evil, given either God's existence or His non-existence.[11] In other words the believer is more confident of the existence of God than of any estimate of how likely God's existence makes the existence of this much evil.

One other thing is clear, I think, as a result of using Bayes's Theorem. This is that the negative project shades into the positive project. The negative project was to show that there is no disproof of God's existence from the existence of evil. The positive project was to try to show God's reasons for allowing evil in the world. When one gets to the question of whether the existence of so much evil in the world makes the existence of a good God unlikely, these projects tend to merge. This is because any plausible reason one gives for why God might allow some evil makes it more probable that this evil would exist, given the existence of God. In turn, this increases the probability of the hypothesis that God exists, given the existence of the evil in the world.

The Positive Project

What I am going to do next is to turn to the positive project. I think it will be considerably easier to follow than the discussion of the negative project. On the other hand, the results of the discussion will be less definitive. I will consider three attempts to provide a theodicy, an explanation of why God allows the evils He does. These will be the attempts of John Hick, Richard Swinburne, and Eleanore Stump.[12] I will outline the kinds of objections I think there are to each one.

John Hick

First, John Hick. Hick's view is that God allows evil, including natural evil, in this world as part of His work of soul-making. We humans could not, he thinks, develop moral character to the full in a world that was a paradise; there must be problems to be solved, challenges to be met, and difficulties to be overcome. In his solution to the problem of evil, Hick explicitly disavows what he calls the *Augustinian approach,* which relies on the Fall, original sin, and the possibility of eternal damnation. For Hick, there was no original state of goodness from which men fell, and there is universal salvation. This means that he cannot explain the existence of evil by appealing to the work of Satan or by emphasizing human responsibility. In his view all will be exalted to a state of grace whatever their previous choices have been.[13]

Hick faces the question of whether all the evil we experience is really necessary for soul-making. His answer is to claim that the highest kinds of human moral excellence are only called forth by unmerited suffering.

It seems, then, that in a world that is to be the scene of compassionate love and self-giving for others, suffering must fall upon mankind with something of the haphazardness and inequity that we now experience. It must be apparently unmerited, pointless, and incapable of being morally rationalized.[14]

His point here is that if we could find a good reason for suffering, in particular that it was a just reward or that it benefited the sufferer, then our highest moral sympathies would not be engaged.

But there are some difficulties with this account. The first is that he has not shown that the highest human moral excellencies require for their acquisition so much unmerited suffering. Stanley Kane says, "It is hard to see why a man or a woman cannot develop just as much patience, fortitude and strength of character in helping his or her spouse complete a doctoral dissertation as in caring for a sick child through a long and serious illness."[15] Even if we grant that unmerited suffering is necessary, it does not follow that we now have an explanation for the amount or the degree of suffering. Hick might claim that the greater the unmerited suffering, the greater the opportunity for the use of the highest human virtues. But what he has not shown is that there would not be more than *enough* opportunity with a good deal less suffering in the world than we presently experience.

The second difficulty is that great suffering does not by itself, or even usually, produce improved moral character. Bishop Neill says this:

The first effect of severe suffering is a kind of paralysis. It produces such a concentration of the mind upon itself that the sufferer becomes almost unaware of anything outside himself. The mere effort demanded by endurance of the suffering is so exacting that no energy is left over for anything else. The mental faculties become dulled and lucid thought becomes difficult. The long continuance of suffering results in a terrible burden of weariness which always seems to have reached the limit of what can be endured, and yet always opens out afresh into deeper depths of weariness. It is not surprising that suffering quickly reveals the real character of the sufferer, and brings to light all the weaknesses that in days of health may have been concealed."[16]

Sometimes, it is true, God can redeem suffering, so that those who suffer come to realize their dependence on God. On the other hand, sometimes suffering just wears people out. I suppose that this would not matter so much if one thought, like Hick, that God will in the end restore all people to fellowship with Himself. I do not mean to imply here that Hick is treating suffering lightly. But still it is true, on his view of things, that everyone will be able to say with Paul that the sufferings of this life are as nothing compared with the joys of heaven. This has the effect of making theodicy easier in this respect than what he calls the *Augustinian picture,* which allows the possibility that someone might curse God and die and never be reconciled to Him.

Richard Swinburne

I could say more about Hick's theodicy, but I want to go on to Richard Swinburne. Swinburne uses a variant of the free will defense to explain why God should allow the possibility of moral evil. He goes on to say that once there is the possibility of such evil there is a high probability of its occurrence; though without bringing in some version of human depravity to the argument, I do not see how he is justified in this. The originality in Swinburne's theodicy is in his detailed attempt to explain natural evil as necessary in order to give humans the right kind of knowledge so that they can make significant moral decisions. His general point is that reliable knowledge comes from experience; if humans are to be able to know how to cause or prevent harm, they must have experience of this harm, and this experience would be natural evil.

I will consider two objections to this account.[17] The first is that the knowledge Swinburne is talking about can be acquired without natural evil. It would be possible, for example, for God simply to tell humans what the results of their choices would be. This is what He is reported to have done for David, for example, at Keilah, where David was told that if he stayed, the inhabitants would hand him over to Saul.[18] This information was helpful to David, but it did not force him to leave, except in a weak sense of *force*. The first objection to Swinburne is that we could make free moral choices without having experienced natural evil if God would give us this sort of information about the consequences of our choices.

I think Swinburne has a reply to this objection. He can point out that according to the biblical stories God gives this sort of information to very unusual individuals for special purposes. It would be a very different situation if He were to give this sort of information to all humans all the time. Swinburne points out that this would interfere considerably with human freedom of choice. For one thing, people would know immediately that there was a God who was in control of all their surroundings, and who would reveal their private choices to the rest of the world. Everyone would presumably believe in the existence of God in these circumstances.

The second objection, however, is more serious. It is that we could have *enough* experience to give us the knowledge required for significant moral choice with far less natural evil than we in fact experience. We might take the concentration camps of World War II as an example. It might be said that the knowledge that gas can kill people did not require any experience of this kind of death; all it required was the hypothesis that gas would kill people, backed by evidence of how it behaves in other contexts, and knowledge of human physiology. But suppose we grant Swinburne the necessity for some experience of people dying from gas. It was not necessary to have experience of mass killings in order to know that mass killings would be possible. From a little experience can come enough knowledge for enormous moral wrong. Why should God want to give us the opportunity to perform the moral wrongs, if there are any, which *do* require massive experience of natural evil to give us the requisite knowledge to perform them?

Eleanore Stump

I will mention one more contemporary attempt to provide a theodicy, that of Eleanore Stump. One great merit of her account is that it makes theodicy relate explicitly to a wider theological context. She is attempting to reach an explanation on the basis of Christian doctrine taken as a unit, not from bare theism, from the bare doctrine that there exists an omnipotent, omniscient, and omnibenevolent God. In particular, she makes use of three doctrines: that Adam fell; that natural evil entered the world as a result of Adam's fall; and that after death, depending on their state at the time of their death, human beings either go to heaven or go to hell. I say that it is a merit in her account to bring in these doctrines, not because I think the doctrines do the job she wants them to do, but because I think it is implausible that bare theism has the resources to provide a satisfactory theodicy all by itself.[19]

Stump's key notion is that because of the results of the Fall, humans need evil in order to come freely to will that God should work on them. There is here a complex interplay between human and divine responsibility. If God restored us to fellowship with Himself without our freely willing it, this would be to treat us as His puppets. On the other hand, Stump says, self-repair is not possible for a person with post-Fall free will. So there has to be a kind of co-operation; humans willing that God change their will. But evil is necessary, on this account, to make humans sufficiently unhappy with their situations for them to will this to happen. Moral evil makes them see their true nature, and the grosser moral evils make this more vivid. Natural evil makes them see their frailty, "turning their affections towards other-worldly things." We can see, she says, from the growing-up of children, how useful moral and natural evil is in their education.

There is a principle which Stump uses in her account which is the focus of my disagreement with her. The principle is a restriction on how a perfectly good entity, who is also omniscient and omnipotent, could permit the distribution of the evil resulting from the human misuse of significant freedom. Namely, the evil must be distributed so that the sufferings of any particular person are outweighed by the good which the suffering produces *for that person*. I have two objections to this. The first is that it is very hard to see how the amount of natural evil there is could be justified on this principle. I am thinking of two kinds of cases here. The first is the suffering that happens to godly people, who are doing their very best to live in God's will, and who are willing that God change their wills in just the way Stump describes. It seems to be the case that these sorts of people suffer just as much natural evil as anyone else. Perhaps all these people who are suffering have some hidden defect which can only be remedied by the suffering; if so, they would all be benefited. But this is, to my mind, highly implausible. The second kind of case I have in mind is those people who are not interested in God and whose lack of interest is attributable to their experience with evil. Again, it might be that there is some hidden fault in all these people that explains their lack of interest—not their experience with evil at all. But again, this does not seem plausible.

The other objection I have to Stump's principle is that it seems incompatible with the very body of doctrine she is trying to make use of. It seems to me that vicarious suffering is at the heart of the gospel. Vicarious suffering is suffering that is justified not by the benefit it procures for the sufferer, but by the benefit it procures for someone else. My understanding of the tradition is that when Scripture speaks of us sharing in the sufferings of Christ, it is vicarious suffering that it has in mind.[20]

The Disjunctive Theodicy

I think these three contemporary attempts at theodicy all share a common failing. They are all attempts to provide a unitary or at least a dominant explanation of why God allows so much evil in the world.[21] The truth is rather, I think, that if there is an explanation available to us at all, it is what I will call a *disjunctive explanation*. It will have the form: Either God is purposing this, or that, or some other thing. I will not claim that I know of any overriding purpose which holds all these subsidiary purposes together. It is no doubt possible to give a name to such an overriding purpose; no doubt God allows all the evil He does out of *love* for His creation. But, as Aristotle said about happiness, it is not necessarily an advance to have a single name for the object of one's enquiry; the important thing is to have a single account, and I am pessimistic about the chances of providing one.

Job

I am going to start by looking at the book of Job, because I think it is the most worked-out treatment of the topic in the Bible. Perhaps *worked-out* is the wrong term. The book gives nothing like a theodicy, nothing that resembles what Hick or Swinburne or Stump give us. Indeed Elihu, who is the fourth friend who comes to talk to Job, and is, I think, more to be trusted than the first three, asks Job why he strives against God: "For He giveth not account of any of His matters."[22] This failure to give a theodicy has caused scandal to some and comfort to others. What in fact happens in the book is that Job, after being afflicted by Satan with every conceivable calamity, after initially cursing the day of his birth, and after listening and replying for thirty-four chapters to his so-called friends, is then confronted by God by a series of unanswerable questions which demonstrate God's power over His creation. As a result, Job confesses that he did not know what he was talking about, he repents, and he is blessed by God with even greater prosperity than he started off with.

I think that one way to understand this story is to look back at Bayes's Theorem. The probability of the hypothesis that God exists, given the existence of evil, is related by the theorem to two further things, the prior probability of the hypothesis and the explanatory power of the hypothesis over the evidence that evil exists. I introduced this theorem in discussing the claim that the amount of evil in the world makes it unlikely that God exists, i.e., a God who is supposed to be omnipotent, omniscient, and omnibenevolent. I said that the theist is in an untenable position if he agrees with the atheist that God's existence makes the amount of evil in the world less likely *and* if he thinks that the existence of God does not have much greater prior probability than His non-existence, independent of the problem of evil.

The effect of Job's encounter with God is to raise for him the prior probability of God's existence. This is partly because direct personal experience of something or someone strongly confirms that thing's or that person's existence. It is also because in His questions God demonstrates His character. His power is shown by the list of things Job cannot do, for the implication is always that God can do these things. His knowledge is similarly shown by the list of things Job does not know. Finally His love for the creation is shown in the affection with which He describes it, like the ostrich who, "when she lifteth up herself on high, she scorneth the horse and his rider."[23] This is the affection of an artist for his own work when he is pleased with it.

In preparing this paper, I talked to a Jewish survivor of the Holocaust. She reminded me of Job. She said that her experience was that those like her who started with a strong faith in God had their faith strengthened. But she did not claim to have an answer to the question of why God should have allowed six million Jews to be killed in this way.

The Prior Probability of God's Existence

I think it is true to much experience of suffering that the believer becomes more assured of what I have been calling the *prior probability* of God's existence. The sufferer may start by asking the "why" questions: "Why me?" and "Why was I born?" But in the heart of the suffering there is energy only to hold on to God's goodness, not because there is some reasoning which justifies this, but because this is all there is to hold onto.

I think this is the most important thing I am saying in this chapter. I am saying that in the heart of their suffering people can in fact continue to find strength in God when they do not find strength any more anywhere else. I think this is part of what they mean when they say that God is with them in their suffering; they feel, if they are Christians, that God suffers with them in the person of Jesus Christ. The prophecy of Isaiah about the Messiah was that in all His people's afflictions He would be afflicted.[24]

Sometimes, God does give a reason for His allowing some suffering; but the reason seems to be given to the individual sufferer, not, so to speak, to the philosopher. In this respect, the reasons He gives are rather like the confirmations of His presence which He gives. Quite often God gives some special sign that it is indeed He who is present. A vivid example is Gideon's fleece. As a special sign, and at Gideon's request, the fleece was wet one morning when the surrounding ground was dry, and dry the next morning when the surrounding ground was wet. Gideon needed such a sign before he could believe he should go out and fight the Midianites.[25] There is no indication that this sort of confirmation is repeatable, yet a similar kind of thing happens sometimes with suffering. Sometimes God enables an individual to know why he has been allowed to suffer. For example, when Jesus healed the blind man, His disciples asked Him whose sin was responsible for the blindness, the man's own or his parents. Jesus answered, "Neither hath this man sinned, nor his parents, but that the works of God should be made manifest in him."[26] The man who was healed of his blindness subsequently became a follower of Jesus.

I read recently two contemporary books, written by people who have suffered severely but who think that God has given them reasons for why He allowed that suffering. The first is *A Severe Mercy* by Sheldon Vanauken, in which the author tells the story of his love for his wife, their brief marriage, and her death.[27] The other is *A Step Further* by Joni Eareckson Tada, in which she continues the story of her life after a swimming accident that left her a quadriplegic.[28] The experience of those who have suffered greatly should have considerable authority in the context of our topic.

I am not claiming, however, that those who suffer are always given reasons like this, or that if they are given reasons, these can be generalized so as to give an overall theodicy. I started with Job partly because he is not given such a reason. The closest he comes, I think, is when he says about God: "But he knoweth the way that I take; when he hath tried me, I shall come forth as gold."[29] What God does give him is the encounter described earlier. The importance of this for our present purposes is that it shows that even without a theodicy that makes sense of suffering, the believer's conviction that he is in the hands of a good God may be strengthened by the experience of God's presence. In terms of Bayes's Theorem, this is one good way to solidify one's belief in the existence of a good God, even given the existence of so much evil.

A Disjunctive Theodicy

Finally, then, what kind of theodicy can be given? I said earlier that I was going to give a "disjunctive explanation." By its nature this is rather a messy project. It amounts to saying that God might have this reason or that reason or the other reason, or perhaps none of the above. It may be that *explanation* is too dignified a title for what emerges from this project; but it is the best I can do. I will give nine kinds of considerations that can enter into a disjunctive explanation of this type. The list is not supposed to be exhaustive. The considerations are all supposed to be additional to the point about free will discussed earlier. Some of the nine considerations merge with others to some extent, and I am not claiming there are firm boundaries between them. Finally, I shall be very brief in going through the list. A full treatment would take a book.

First, there is the kind of testing Job mentioned. He said that when God had tested him, he would come forth as gold. Here he is seeing his suffering as like a fire refining out the impurities in precious metal. Another biblical story with the same sort of moral is the story of God's testing of Abraham by demanding the sacrifice of his only son, Isaac.[30] Abraham did not actually have to kill his son, and a ram was provided for the sacrifice at the last minute. What was God achieving, then, in putting Abraham through such torture? One possibility is that Abraham had to learn that he could trust God to that degree because of the amount of trusting he was going to have to do later. There is something rather Kantian about this kind of testing. Kant would say that the moral agent has to learn to act solely from duty, independently of any natural inclination. In the same sort of way, the "knight of faith" like Abraham has to learn to trust God independently of any apparent benefit to be achieved. I hope it is true that this kind of testing is reserved for God's extraordinary servants.

Second, there is the explanation Jesus gave for the blindness of the man He healed, "that the works of God should be made manifest in him." This is a hard one to understand. It is, after all characteristic of a bully to inflict misery so that he can reveal his power when he lets up. C. S. Lewis says of this case that Jesus was giving the final, not the efficient cause of the blindness. That is to say, we are not given an explanation of what produced the blindness; we are not told that God inflicted it. We are given an explanation of the good that was achieved by it. It is true, also, that the healing became widely known, and that the man himself became a follower of Jesus. Still, I am not confident that I have understood the story.

Third, there is vicarious suffering. Human beings can bear each other's burdens. Sometimes I think this is not known, or only dimly known, to the sufferer. In a family, for example, one person's suffering can make possible another person's freedom to flourish. Vanauken describes how he took his wife's fear of death in the hospital. Because he took the fear, she was freed from it. I do not know how this sort of thing works, but I have no doubt that it does.

Fourth, there is the soul-making explanation that I discussed in relation to John Hick's theodicy. I do not think that suffering is in itself ennobling, for reasons I have given. There are cases, however, where "tribulation worketh patience; and patience, experience; and experience, hope."[31] The quotation is from the letter to the Romans, and the "hope" here has a theological dimension. A distinction should no doubt be made between the explanation that suffering makes people better morally, and the explanation that it leads them to God. I will deal with the second of these at the end. In terms of moral virtue, it is surely true that suffering can sometimes produce fortitude and clarity of purpose in the sufferer, and compassion and generosity in others. The trouble is that it can also produce the opposites of all four of these positive characteristics.

Fifth, there is the possibility of retributive justice. Suffering, that is to say, may be deserved. Many philosophers deny that there is a moral justification for retributive punishment. I do not want to get very far into this issue. It is true that God is recorded in Scripture as saying things like "Vengeance is mine."[32] The main point in these sayings, I think, is that vengeance is not *our* proper concern. One way to understand the teaching about retributive justice is that humans have been created in such a way that when they turn to God, they receive certain characteristic blessings; when they turn away from God, they do not receive them. Some of the blessings in question are the "fruits of the Spirit," such as joy and peace. It is a bit like heliotropic plants, which flourish when they turn towards the sun. If this is how things are, then the absence of these blessings would be suffering that was the indirect result of free choice, and this suffering would in some cases have physical results. Perhaps hell is best understood as the continually chosen absence of fellowship with God.[33]

Sixth, there is biologically useful pain. The child, and some of the higher animals, can learn not to touch fire by suffering once or twice the pain of a burn. This mechanism cannot be effective unless it is fairly reliable. It will not work unless the child can predict that touching the fire will hurt. But if the mechanism is to be reliable, then those who persevere in ignoring the milder stimulus will sometimes experience quite severe pain. I am not sure how far this can be taken. Suppose nicotine, if taken above certain amounts, is harmful to the body, and suppose someone perseveres through the danger signals until he develops severe emphysema. It would seem that while the disease itself is not biologically useful (it is fatal), it is the result of ignoring a set of signals which are useful. The existence of the signals, therefore, is part of a complex state of affairs which probably requires that people will contract the disease if the signals are ignored.

Seventh, there is Swinburne's point about human knowledge. This is close to what I have just said about biologically useful pain. If moral action consists in the causing of benefits and harms, and these benefits and harms are to be roughly predictable (so that we can hold agents responsible for their moral actions), then humans must have some experience of natural evil in order to acquire this power of prediction. As Swinburne says, unless someone died accidentally of cyanide poisoning, we would not have the significant choice of trying to prevent cyanide poisoning. There is, however, a limit to how much natural evil this account can explain.

Eighth, there is the doctrine Plantinga refers to about the activity of Satan and his angels. Jesus himself says, about a crippled woman He cured: "Ought not this woman, being a daughter of Abraham, whom Satan hath bound, lo, these eighteen years, be loosed from this bond on the sabbath day?"[34] It is possible to explain that there is a literally demonic character to some evil. Many people claim to have experienced this. If there is, this means, as Plantinga says, that God allows the evil indirectly, by allowing the free choices of demons.

Ninth, and last, there is the point about salvation which Stump uses. Some suffering may be intelligible because it is what C. S. Lewis calls *God's megaphone*. To understand this point, it is necessary to understand that in the Christian view all men and women are sinners. The doctrine of salvation is that this sin causes a separation between us and God, and that we cannot by our own wills remove this separation; Christ's death on the cross provided a way for us because He Himself bore this penalty for our sin. The doctrine has two important consequences for the understanding of evil. The first is that our salvation must be of the utmost value if it caused God to send His Son to the cross. Getting through to us, the "megaphone," may sometimes require allowing us to suffer the results of our sin. But, if this suffering gets our attention, and we come to realize our true condition, that is the first step toward repentance and turning to God for help. If suffering is a necessary part of this process, it is justified by what is, on the Christian view, our highest possible good. The second important consequence of the doctrine of salvation is that we are following a Lord who has Himself suffered; He knows by experience, not only by omniscience, what it is for a human to suffer, because He became a man and suffered. On the Christian view, this explains why the sufferer can find God sharing the suffering with him.

Notes

[1] For one classic statement, see Hume, *Dialogues Concerning Natural Religion* (1779), part 10. See also John Hick, *Evil and the God of Love* (New York: Macmillan, 1966), and M. B. Ahern, *The Problem of Evil* (London: Routledge & Kegan Paul, 1971).

[2] Harold Kushner, *When Bad Things Happen to Good People* (New York: Schocken Books, 1981). See also John Stuart Mill, *Three Essays on Religion* (London: 1874); E. S. Brightman, *The Problem of God* (Nashville, Tenn.: Abingdon Press, 1930); and Charles Hartshorne, *Omnipotence and Other Theological Mistakes* (Albany, N.Y.: State University of New York Press, 1984).

[3] The view of Epicurus was that the gods dwell in the *intermundia*, not thinking of human affairs. It is not clear how much knowledge they had of the human world. See Lucretius, *De Rerum Natura* 3:18–22.

[4] Alvin Plantinga, *The Nature of Necessity* (Oxford: Oxford University Press, 1974), chap. 9; idem, *God, Freedom and Evil* (New York: Harper Torchbook, 1974); idem, "The Probabilistic Argument from Evil," *Philosophical Studies* 35 (1979): 1–53. There has been a large literature on this topic since the present chapter was originally drafted; see Kelly Clark, "Evil and Christian Belief," *International Philosophical Quarterly* 29, 2 (June 1989): 175–89.

[5] The belief that he has was defended by Luis de Molia in *Liberi arbitrii cum gratiae donis, divina praescientia, praedestinatione et reprobatione concordia*, ed. John Rabeneck (Ona and Madrid: 1953). See Robert M. Adams, "Middle Knowledge and the Problem of Evil," *American Philosophical Quarterly*, 14 (1977): 109–17.

[6] For one recent (hostile) discussion of compatibilism see Peter Van Inwagen, *An Essay on Free Will* (Oxford: Clarendon Press, 1983). One thing I have not discussed is the relationship between the free will defense and the doctrine of predestination.

[7] Eleanore Stump, "The Problem of Evil," in *Faith and Philosophy*, vol. 2, no. 4. (October 1985), 392–423, esp. 405.

[8] These are the terms used by Richard Swinburne, *The Existence of God* (Oxford: Clarendon Press, 1979), esp. 64–69. The explanatory power of the hypothesis over the evidence can be expressed as the probability of the evidence if the hypothesis is true divided by the prior probability of the evidence (independent of the hypothesis), assuming that the background information stays constant. Bayes's Theorem is that

$$P\,(h/e\;\&\;k) = \frac{P\,(e/h\;\&\;k)}{P\,(e/k)} \times P\,(h/k)$$

Here P stands for the probability, h for the hypothesis, e for the evidence, and k for the background information.

[9] Gal. 5:22.

[10] Robert M. Adams, "The Problem of Evil," in *Alvin Plantinga*, ed. James E. Tomberlin and Peter Van Inwagen (Dordrecht: Reidel, 1985), 225–56.

[11] This might be easier to understand in symbols. Here H stands for the proposition that God exists, E is a proposition asserting the existence of exactly those evils that actually exist, and k is the background information.

$$\frac{P\,(H/k)}{P\,(Not\;H/k)} > \frac{P\,(E/Not\;H\;\&\;k)}{(E/H\;\&\;k)}$$

[12]For Hick, in addition to the work cited, see *God and the Universe of Faiths* (London: Macmillan, 1973), esp. chap. 4–5, where he responds to some criticisms. For Swinburne and Stump, see the works cited.

[13]For Hick's progressively divergent treatment of the tradition see *The Myth of God Incarnate*, ed. John Hick (Philadelphia, Pa.: Westminster Press, 1977).

[14]Hick, *Evil and the God of Love*, 370–71.

[15]G. Stanley Kane, "The Failure of Soul-Making Theodicy," *International Journal for the Philosophy of Religion*, 6 (1975): 1–22. Cited in Stump, "The Problem of Evil."

[16]Stephen Neill, *Christian Faith To-day* (London: Penguin, 1955), 111.

[17]Stump, "The Problem of Evil," considers these two objections. I disagree with her on the first and state the second rather differently.

[18]Stump mentions, in addition to 1 Samuel 23:9–11, 1 Samuel 30:7–8, Jeremiah 42:1–16, and Daniel 8–10. These sorts of cases all require some analysis of what appears to be middle knowledge.

[19]I do not think Adam's fall can explain animal pain before the creation of humans, and I do not think Stump's account is as easily squared with the theory of evolution as she suggests.

[20]1 Cor. 12:26–7; 2 Cor. 1:4–5.

[21]Stump allows that there may be other accounts of evil that can supplement hers.

[22]Job 33:13b. Throughout this article I have quoted from the King James Version of the Bible.

[23]Job 39:18.

[24]Isa. 53.

[25]Judg. 6.

[26]John 9:3.

[27]Sheldon Vanauken, *A Severe Mercy* (San Francisco: Harper & Row, 1977).

[28]Joni Eareckson Tada and Steve Estes, *A Step Further* (Grand Rapids, Mich.: Zondervan, 1978).

[29]Job 23:10.

[30]Gen. 22. See Søren Kierkegaard, *Fear and Trembling*, trans. W. Lowrie (Princeton, N.J.: Princeton University Press, 1941).

[31]Rom. 5:3–4.

[32]See Rom. 12:19; Deut. 32:35. For one statement of the philosophical objection to retributive punishment, see Jonathan Glover, *Responsibility* (Atlantic Highlands, N.J.: Humanities Press, 1970), 150–60.

[33]Stump attributes something like this view to Dante in her "The Problem of Evil," 400–401, and in a forthcoming paper, "Dante's Hell, Aquinas's Theory of Morality, and the Love of God." It does not seem right to say, as some do, that hell is the experienced absence of God, for God is omnipresent in the tradition, and the demons know this. What is absent in hell is the comfort of God's presence to those who believe in Him.

[34]Luke 13:16.

5.2

The Argument from Experience

John E. Hare

GOD EXISTS, I HAVE MET HIM[1] is the title of an influential recent autobiography of a French journalist who had the following experience. He was traveling with a friend. When his friend went into a church and stayed longer than expected, the author went in to find him. Prior to this, the journalist had not been much impressed with any religion. But in that church he was overwhelmed with a sense of the presence of God, and he later wrote the book to describe his conversion.

This is not the usual claim of religious experience. That is to say, religious experience is not usually used as the basis for a move like the one the French journalist made from unbelief to belief. The people who have these sorts of experiences are usually theists of some kind—they already believe that God exists, and His existence is not itself a question for them.[2] It is more likely that they will say, as a result of their experience: "It was God who directed me," or "God forgave me this sin," or "God strengthened me through this trial," or "God's presence comforted me in this distress." The topic of this chapter is the connection between the personal experience that lies behind claims such as these and the claims themselves. In the first two sections I will argue that the believer is typically not making two kinds of mistakes in claiming to experience God directly: the first mistake is to confuse what one wants to be the case with what is the case; the second is to confuse psychological certainty with truth. In the last two sections I will try to show that the believer can sometimes claim to have confirmation of direct encounter, and that this is desirable. I will not be dealing with the claim to justify the initial belief in the existence of God from religious experience.

I will be talking about claims to direct encounter with God. These are different from claims to what I will call *indirect encounter.* This is analogous to the difference between meeting my wife and seeing a flower arrangement I know she has done. In the case of God, the distinction is certainly much harder to draw, but there is still a difference. On the one hand, one can experience a sense of comfort in some painful time and thank God for providing the comfort, and on the other hand one can get comfort from God's presence itself. Only the second would count as a direct encounter with God. This chapter is about this latter kind of claim.

In the first two parts, I will be defending the believer's entitlement to the claim of direct encounter. This is not to say that believers are always right when they make these claims; but it is to say that there is nothing wrong with the kind of claim the believer is making. It is sometimes held, in contrast, that the believer is not entitled to the claim to have had direct encounter with God on the basis of religious experience. C. B. Martin, for example, in his article "A Religious Way of Knowing," says, "The only thing that I can establish beyond correction on the basis of having certain feelings and sensations is that I have these feelings and sensations."[3] This objection can be construed this way: that I am never entitled to make a claim on the basis of experience if my claim can possibly be corrected by later information, or experience, or in fact from any source whatever. Thus interpreted the objection is far too strong. If I am an ornithologist, I am surely entitled to claim that I have seen a goldfinch in a tree, even though it is possible that I will turn out to have been mistaken. To deny this, at any rate, is to embrace a skepticism that goes a long way beyond common sense, and I am going to suppose that we want to avoid this. We need, then, a weaker statement of the objection—one which provides a serious objection to claims to encounter God directly in experience, but not an objection to the ornithologist's claim to encounter the goldfinch.

One way to put the objection is that the religious believer's interpretation of his experience as a direct encounter with God cannot be tested or checked in ways the human community regards as authoritative. The key contrast is with perceptual claims. Suppose I look into my cup and see coffee.[4] I can check the belief that there is coffee in the cup by smelling it or tasting the contents; I can get other observers to look at it, smell it, or taste it; I can run chemical tests on it and get other people to do so. With claims to have encountered God directly none of this seems available.

The believer might respond, "Why should there be a demand for checks and tests? After all, God is Spirit, and we should not expect His activity to be detectable by our normal measuring instruments. Moreover, He selects the persons whom He is going to meet, and we should not expect to be able to submit these occasions to controlled public scrutiny."

There are, however, at least five reasons why the absence of tests and checks is a weakness in the believer's position.[5] First, these purported direct encounters are far from universally distributed in the population. Second, even for the people who have them, they are infrequent, fleeting, indistinct, and obscure. Third, they frequently yield mutually contradictory claims about what God is like, and what He wants of us. Fourth, there are often alternative explanations of a naturalistic kind for these experiences. Why should we believe a hermit who fasts and then sees the Virgin Mary any more than we would believe a man who drinks whiskey and then sees a purple elephant? The point is that religious believers, especially mystics, tend to put themselves through disciplines that might be expected all by themselves to produce bizarre mental states. Fifth, it is unclear what the human receptor mechanism could be for receiving an encounter with God.

I cannot deal with all these points here. I am going to proceed in the first two sections by examining two arguments of Norman Melchert in a paper titled, "Mystical Experience and Ontological Claims."[6] Melchert is interested primarily in mystical experience, but his arguments can be broadened to encompass religious experience more generally. Both of the arguments are for disbelieving that religious experience is direct experience of God. The first is what he calls a *psychological explanation;* the second a *logical explanation.*[7] In both cases the "explanation" has the effect of explaining away, or defeating, the claim to direct encounter. In the third section I will try to show that there are in fact some types of confirmation available for the claim to direct encounter. The confirmation of the direct encounter will often be by way of indirect encounter. In the fourth section I will urge that the believer should welcome, and indeed search for such confirmation; but I will stress that the type of confirmation available is limited by the nature of the direct encounter itself.

Melchert's Psychological Explanation

The psychological explanation is that the religious experience is interpreted by the believer as direct encounter because of the believer's strong antecedent desire to meet with God. Melchert shows that in the mystical literature, the mystic is often acutely aware of his or her lack of worth. It is not just that he has done some things of which he is ashamed. Rather, as Melchert says: "He suffers from his very existence." In the mystical experience his ego seems to disappear into God or the Absolute or the All. The mystic is thus strongly motivated to believe that the experience reveals the truth—that the unsatisfactory limited self he deals with every day is not the true self, which is what is revealed in the mystical union as unlimitedly great.

The structure of this explanation is that the mystic wants so desperately to be different from his ordinary self that he leaps to an interpretation of his experience that makes this happen. The kind of mystical experience here is typically associated with Eastern mysticism; but Melchert gives examples from Christian sources as well. His objection can be brought against the more ordinary kinds of religious experience I have mentioned. The objection is not to the experiences themselves (Melchert thinks them quite valuable) but to the interpretation of them as direct encounters with God. The objection is that this interpretation is wish-fulfillment.

When is the presence of a person's antecedent desire for some situation to occur reason not to believe that person's claim that the situation has occurred? It is necessary to distinguish three questions here. When is it a reason for the person himself, when is it a reason for a third party who shares the person's background beliefs, and when is it a reason for a third party who does not share those beliefs? I will start by talking about the first of these questions, and then say something at the end of this section about the other two.

Defeaters

It will be helpful here to make use of the notion of a *defeater.*[8] The notion depends on the claim that justification-conferring conditions are prima facie justifiers—that they are sufficient to justify providing that there are not "defeaters" present. Normally, to use Austin's example, my thinking I see a goldfinch in the tree suffices to justify my saying, "I see a goldfinch in the tree."[9] But if I have taken a hallucinogen, or I know the tree has been the locus for a set of advanced holographic experiments, the claim can justifiably be overridden.

Now the question is: "When does a person's wanting a particular situation to occur count as a defeater against the justification of the person's claim that this situation has occurred?" To put the question this way, when we are talking about religious experience, may seem to prejudge one important issue. It may seem to assume that a claim to have encountered God directly is prima facie justified. All I am saying, however, is that this assumption belongs to the structure of the psychological explanation for religious experience. The psychological explanation is that the believer's claim would be warranted if it were not for the presence of the strong antecedent desire. This is to say that the desire constitutes a defeater, and this *implies* an otherwise warranted claim that is being defeated.

Background Beliefs

Two parts of the psychological explanation have to be conceded. First, the religious believer does characteristically have very intense desires of the sort indicated. Second, the presence of such desires can, though it does not always, defeat the prima facie justification of a claim to direct encounter. Care is needed to discriminate those cases where desire has corrupted belief from those cases where it has not. Here is an example where there has been no such corruption. Suppose a child wants above all a tricycle for her birthday, and she has told her parents this. A large package arrives at the door, large enough to house a tricycle inside. The child is sure it is a tricycle. Does her antecedent desire constitute a defeater? Not if she has a set of background beliefs which include the warranted belief that her parents always give her what she most wants for her birthday. In this case, the desire is not a defeater, but actually evidence for the belief. What constitutes a defeater or legitimate evidence is relative to the set of background beliefs.

In the case of the religious believer, suppose he has an experience of peace in the middle of a period of stress and claims that it is the presence of God that has comforted his distress. In this case, his background beliefs are likely to include the belief that if he sincerely asks for the comfort of God's presence, God will grant it. Assuming that he has warrant for this, and that he believes he has sincerely asked, is he not warranted in believing he has experienced God's presence? Indeed, is not his antecedent desire for this presence in fact evidence that he has received it?

An objection arises immediately. What is in question is whether a believer can have warrant for believing he has had direct encounter with God. It begs the question to *assume* that he has *warrant* for believing that God grants experience of His presence to those who sincerely ask. In the case of the child, she could open the parcels she had received in the past, and her subsequent experience is what warranted the belief that her parents always give her what she most wants for her birthday. In order to assume that in the religious case the believer's background belief that God grants experience of His presence to those who sincerely ask is *warranted,* it seems that we have to assume that his antecedent desires have not in the past been defeaters. But that is what we are trying to show.

We might try modifying the situation to avoid the circularity. Suppose the believer's background belief is not that God's presence can be experienced but rather that it can be *if* what is said about God in authoritative sources is true. The believer may not yet have experienced God's presence himself, so that his belief that God's presence can be experienced is not yet warranted by his own experience. This would be like the scientific explorer who believes that if Bigfoot exists, then, given what is said of him in local legend, one will find him if one looks hard enough in the forests of the Northwest. The scientist may have a tentative belief in this legend. Now suppose that he has a very strong antecedent wish that the Bigfoot should exist. He may have invested thousands of dollars in the expedition to find out. Would this by itself constitute a defeater, for the explorer himself or for a third party, if the explorer subsequently claims that the expedition saw Bigfoot disappearing through the trees? Surely not, for most scientists have strong antecedent wishes that their research should succeed. Perhaps the believer who claims to have experienced God's presence is in the same case; then his antecedent desire for the experience would not count against his claim.

Unfortunately, however, the position is more complicated. The doctrine that the believer is likely to have as part of his background beliefs is that God by His presence relieves the distress of those who ask sincerely *and* believe in Him.[10] To go back to the scientific explorer, it would be as though Bigfoot was only visible to those who already believed that he existed (like the fairies in some fairy tales). Something like this happens on the frontiers of science, as when William Herschel saw Uranus, though other astronomers did not see it for another fifty years. Would the explorer's antecedent desire, coupled with this strange fairy-tale feature, defeat the prima facie justification of his claim to have seen Bigfoot?

The Justification of Experience

Here it is necessary to distinguish again the three questions I mentioned before. First, will the sighting be a sufficient basis for the explorer himself? I do not see good reason to deny this. We are supposing that he already has a (tentative) belief in the existence of Bigfoot, which was not and could not have been based on any sighting, since any sighting (we are supposing) presupposes belief. Nevertheless, after the sighting the scientist can surely say that what he saw confirmed his antecedent belief. (I will be saying more about this kind of confirmation in the third section of this chapter.) It is possible to have a belief based on one set of considerations, or even based on no considerations at all, and then arrive at the same belief as a result of a different set of considerations.[11] Similarly with the religious believer. He may have adopted the belief that

God's presence can be experienced on grounds independent of personal religious experience. Perhaps he was convinced by the mere authority of the traditional sources.[12] The believer can then come to base his belief (that God's presence can be experienced) on confirmations by experiences that he would not have had without the antecedent belief already in place.

A different question is whether the scientist's report gives evidence to third parties that Bigfoot has been sighted. Suppose there are no photographs, and it is only the scientist himself who had the sighting. The answer is difficult. It is usually best to take the question of what counts as evidence as dependent on the historical situations of particular persons with particular sets of background beliefs.[13] We can ask, then, whether the background beliefs of the third parties in question include the belief that this particular scientist is generally reliable in this sort of context—that he is unlikely to falsify the evidence. If this is one of the background beliefs, then the scientist's report should constitute evidence even if the sighting *did* require the scientist's previous belief in Bigfoot's existence. On the other hand, the outside observer may have, as one of his background beliefs, the belief that the scientist tends to let his imagination run away with him. This would constitute a defeater. In the same way the question is whether some religious believer's experience is vitiated as evidence because of his previous desire for confirmation of his belief. We need to know whether he is generally reliable in this sort of context, or whether he is in the habit of distorting his experience. This information will go into the background beliefs against which his claim to have evidence has to be measured. There is the additional difficulty in this case of determining what counts as the same sort of context.

I distinguished earlier the question of whether the justification is supposed to work for a third party who shares the believer's background beliefs, or a third party who does not. If an outside observer does not have belief in God, it is most unlikely that a believer's account of personal religious experience will be sufficient to change the unbeliever's mind. This is because the background beliefs of this observer give such a low probability to the existence of God, let alone direct experience of Him. It will not matter much how reliable the believer is on other questions. Similarly, the generally reliable Buddhist is unlikely to have his religious experience given much credence by the Christian. But I have qualified the judgment here. I have not said there will be no credence at all. Even if we do not share the religious views of persons we otherwise trust, we may give their reports of their religious experiences careful attention. Their reports may raise significantly our estimate of the probability that their claims are true, without raising this estimate sufficiently high for us to believe the claims.

Melchert's Logical Explanation

The second kind of explanation Melchert offers as to why the mystic might be misled into making ontological claims on the basis of experience is *logical*. It can be analyzed as a mistake about the nature of knowledge. It is generally held that if a person knows some proposition, it follows that the proposition is true. It might also be thought (mistakenly) that knowledge can be characterized subjectively, that there is a kind of experiential or phenomenological mark of knowledge. This would be to say that genuine knowledge *feels* different to the knower than mere opinion. If one assumed that these experiential marks of knowledge could themselves be known (or even reliably discerned), then one could move legitimately from having this sort of feeling to claiming guaranteed truth. Both in the case of mystical or "unitive" experience and in the case of the more ordinary religious experience we have been discussing, it can seem plausible that some mistake like this is being made.

The mystic claims that the gap between the subject and the object of knowledge disappears in the mystical experience. Normally the knower and the known are distinct, and there is thus the possibility of error. But if they are not distinct, it might seem there could not be a mistake. This is why Plato thought philosophers infallible in as much as their minds become one with the forms they see. The mystic, then, experiences a certain state of mind, and concludes that this guarantees the truth of the interpretation he or she puts on his or her experience.

In the case of more ordinary religious experience, the argument is simpler. People who have religious experiences of the kind I have been referring to are characteristically quite sure it is God they have experienced. It might be objected that they are mistaking psychological certainty for knowledge. If they think that there is a felt quality to the experience which all by itself guarantees the truth of their interpretation, they are mistaken.

It is true, then, that psychological certainty does not guarantee truth. But is the religious believer correctly understood as making this mistake? In the case of perception, following the line stated earlier, we can say that we are within our epistemic rights, or warranted in believing certain propositions about our sensory environment under certain conditions. We are not infallible, and the warrant for belief can be overridden by defeaters. But in the absence of defeaters, seeing what seems to me a goldfinch in full daylight, etc. (and it is admittedly very hard, perhaps impossible, to specify what these conditions are), I am warranted in asserting that I see a goldfinch.[14]

Why, then, should we deny that the believer's experience gives him warrant for his belief that it was God he experienced? The "logical" explanation is that the believer is confusing subjective certainty with truth. But the believer is not usually arguing, I think, that it must be God because he, the believer, is psychologically certain. Rather, he is arguing that it is God because the conditions are right for his experience to warrant the claim, and there are none of the potential defeaters present that he would recognize as overriding the claim.

What sorts of defeaters are there? Teresa of Avila, to take one example, has an interesting discussion of diabolical visions. She says:

> That which purports to come from God is to be received only insofar as it corresponds with the sacred writings; but if it varies therefrom ever so little, I am incomparably more convinced that it comes from Satan than I am now convinced that it comes from God, however deep that conviction may be.[15]

She always went straight to her confessors to test out her visions. She records on one occasion, after a vision that did not involve a sensory image at all, that her confessor asked her how she knew it was Christ. She replied that she did not know how she knew it, but she checked with Friar Peter of Alcantara, and he said "that this vision was of the highest order, and one with which Satan can least interfere."[16]

John of the Cross says that there is a great difference in the effects of diabolical and divine visions. He says that the first produce spiritual dryness in one's communication with God and an inclination to self-esteem, to admitting them and to considering them important. Diabolical visions do not cause the mildness of humility and love of God, and they are not impressed with a delicate clarity upon the soul, as are the others. He says the same about the memory of these visions.[17]

The presumption that these are encounters with God can thus be overridden by numerous considerations. Most important, they may be judged diabolical, or hysterical self-delusions, if they are inconsistent with Scripture or the doctrine of the church. The same sort of judgment may be made on the basis of the effects of these visions. They may produce the inclination to self-esteem or an arid spiritual life. A pattern of such experiences may lead a person away from a life of obedience to the principles laid down in Scripture. The point is that there are potential defeaters here, and tests for them. The believer takes it that in the absence of such defeaters, he has good reason for his claim that he has experienced God. Why should this be denied?

Confirmation and Religious Experience

I think the central objection of the skeptic is that the believer's claim to direct encounter is arbitrary. There are, after all, many people who think deeply about the nature of what there is beyond the human world and experience an overwhelming sense of its emptiness or impersonality. Why should the believer's experience of the presence of God be preferred to the skeptic's experience of the absence of God? If a doctor and a layman both look down my ear, and the doctor sees incipient inflammation but the layman does not, I am justified in believing the doctor. He is the expert. But if the believer and the skeptic have both devoted themselves equally to the search, and one finds God in his experience and the other does not, it seems arbitrary to prefer the believer's conclusion to the skeptic's. The skeptic's conclusion is about the believer's experience, too, and the believer's conclusion is about the skeptic's experience. The skeptic is likely to think the believer is gullible; the believer will think the skeptic has not repented, or is blocked by sin. There is no reason to believe in expertise here in the way doctors have expertise. The objection, then, is that it is arbitrary to prefer the believer's account to the skeptic's. Another way to put this is that the believer's experience does not confirm in the right way his hypothesis that it is God whom he encounters.

Four Criteria for Confirmation

In scientific cases we have criteria and tests that we can apply. I will state four conditions which, if present, we usually take to indicate that an experience *confirms* a hypothesis.[18] First, the hypothesis must raise the probability that the experience will be forthcoming under certain conditions. For example, consider the hypothesis that bean plants will absorb radioactive isotopes in the soil fastest where there is least growth in the plant. The prediction generated is that we will get certain readings from the geiger counter at some points on the plant and lower readings at other points. It is immensely difficult to say what predictions a theory will yield, and what constitutes the appropriate conditions, but I think the idea is still plausible. With this example we can say that the more accurately and precisely the experience is predicted, the stronger the confirmation.

Second, the experience must not be antecedently probable. The probability of our having the experience must not vary independently of the probability of the hypothesis being true. In particular, if the hypothesis were false, we should not expect to have the experience. Suppose my hypothesis is that if I keep on breathing, the sun will rise tomorrow. A prediction is generated, and experience bears it out. I do see the sun rise tomorrow. But the sun would have risen whether I kept on breathing or not.

Third, if the experience is not forthcoming under the appropriate conditions, there is less reason to accept the hypothesis. If I do not get the right readings from the geiger counter, I will be given pause about the hypothesis. Again, it is very difficult to say in general terms how *much* pause I will be given. It is too strong to say that I will abandon the hypothesis if the predicted experience is not forthcoming.

Finally, the hypothesis must be more ambitious than what we already know of the confirmatory hypothesis. One good sign of this is where the hypothesis is constructed before the experiences are available—in other words if it predicts experiences which we can check after the construction of the hypothesis. But this is not necessary. The reason for this condition is that the experience cannot give any independent confirmation of the hypothesis if the hypothesis is just a restatement of the experience.

Application of Criteria to Biblical Experience

Now we can take some examples of religious experience and see if they meet these tests. What I will be arguing in this section of the paper differs from the section on Melchert's psychological explanation in the following way. In the former section I was arguing that the presence of antecedent desire does not constitute a defeater against the prima facie justification of the claim by the believer to have an experience of God. What I am arguing now is that confirmation is sometimes available to the believer that it is indeed God whom he experiences. I am not trying to show that this sort of confirmation is necessary, or that it is always available.

First, from the Old Testament, there are the examples of Gideon and Moses.[19] Gideon was threshing wheat when the angel of the Lord appeared to him and said, among other things, "I will be with you, and will strike down the Midianites as if they were but one man." Gideon replied, "If now I have found favor in your eyes, give me a sign that it is really you talking to me." He then asked the angel to wait while he went to get a sacrifice. When he returned, the angel touched the meat and the unleavened bread with his staff. Fire flared from the rock, consuming the meat and the bread, and the angel disappeared. Gideon, knowing now that it was the angel of the Lord, exclaimed, "Ah, Sovereign LORD! I have seen the angel of the LORD face to face."

The angel of the Lord appeared to Moses in flames of fire from within a bush, saying, "I will be with you. And this will be the sign to you that it is I who have sent you: When you have brought the people out of Egypt, you will worship God on this mountain." There seems to be a pattern here, evident also in the encounters of God with Abraham, Isaac, and Jacob.[20] The pattern is that God provides some kind of sign to confirm His presence, and it is God who is in control of the confirmation process. With Gideon, fire flamed from the rock. With Moses, the sign was a prophecy. In Isaiah there is the claim made three times that fulfilled prophecy is the primary test in critical cases.[21] In Jeremiah there is a similar example.[22] An interesting variation is the later experience of

Gideon, who feels the need to test whether God will really carry out His promise to save Israel by Gideon's hand. Gideon puts a fleece on the threshing floor and says that he will know it is God if the next morning the fleece is wet with dew and the surrounding ground is dry. This is just what happens. And on the next morning, again by Gideon's request, the opposite occurs—the ground is wet and the fleece is dry. This is not the standard case, because it is the believer and not God who is dictating what the confirmation will be.

In the New Testament the same sort of pattern emerges in the way Jesus reveals Himself to be God. This is particularly true, I think, in the Gospel of John. Jesus starts His ministry at the wedding in Cana. He turns water into wine, and the episode ends, "This, the first of his miraculous signs, Jesus performed in Cana of Galilee. He thus revealed his glory and his disciples put their faith in him."[23] There was nothing esoteric about seeing the miracle. For those who believed, it was a confirmation. It is not, surely, John's meaning, that the disciples did not put their faith in Jesus *until* Cana. Andrew has already told his brother Simon, "We have found the Messiah."[24] The sign is, then, a confirmation; but it does not force belief. Jesus tells a parable elsewhere about the rich man and Lazarus. The rich man, after he has died, begs Abraham to send Lazarus, who has also died, back to the rich man's household to warn his brothers. Abraham replies, "If they do not listen to Moses and the prophets, they will not be convinced even if someone rises from the dead."[25] This is the sort of text Kierkegaard is relying on when he says, "The wonder is not immediately but is only for faith, inasmuch as the person who does not believe does not see the wonder."[26]

We can examine these claimed confirmations of direct encounter and see whether they fit the model. Suppose the hypothesis in each case is, "It is God who has spoken to me." The relevant experience here is not the encounter itself, but the experience of the "sign" that is attached to it. The question is whether it confirms the hypothesis. Take the experience of the fleece as the most vivid (though atypical, as I said). First, the hypothesis yields a prediction: the fleece will be wet when the ground is dry and dry when the ground is wet. Second, the double observation is not antecedently probable—that is the "wonder" of the sign. Third, if the observation is not forthcoming, the hypothesis is falsified. Finally, the hypothesis is formulated independently of the experience; it is formulated before Gideon knows what the outcome of the test will be.

The same four points can be made about Moses' experience. He is told that he will know it is God speaking to him because he will worship on this mountain with the people whom he has successfully led out of Egypt. He is also told that the elders of Israel will listen to him, that the Egyptians will be struck with the wonders God will perform among them, and that the Pharaoh will finally let the people go. Again the hypothesis that it is God speaking will be confirmed by all these experiences. The same can be said, though more remotely, about Abraham, Isaac, and Jacob.[27]

Application of Criteria to Contemporary Experience

Perhaps it may be worthwhile if I add a personal experience which, though much more modest, has the merit of being contemporary. When I was at graduate school, I belonged to a group of friends who met together regularly. One night just as I was getting into my pajamas, I had the strong conviction that God was telling me to get back into my clothes and go to the room of one of these friends because he needed me. It was very late at night. I did what I thought I had been told, feeling embarrassed about it, and discovered that my friend had just broken up with his fiancée and was acutely miserable. Suppose the hypothesis was, "It was God who told me to do that." If I had gone up to my friend's room, and found him asleep, I would, I think, have concluded that I had been mistaken in the hypothesis. As it was, the hypothesis yielded a prediction that was not antecedently probable (that my friend badly needed someone to talk to in the middle of the night)—the first and second criteria. My experience was not itself the origin of the hypothesis—the fourth criterion. At least on the four criteria proposed so far, I was within my rights to say that my hypothesis was confirmed. My guess is, though it would take a lot of work to show it, that Christian experience is often like this, and follows the Old Testament pattern we have observed. God provides with the experience the tests by which the experience is to be judged as a genuine meeting with Him.[28]

We should ask again who is being given confirmation; is it the person who makes the initial claim to direct encounter, is it the third party who shares the same background beliefs about God, or is it the skeptic? The skeptic will no doubt respond to my story that if the believer does this kind of thing often enough (e.g., "hearing" and obeying voices in the night), then statistically some such hypotheses will be confirmed and some will not; and believers characteristically focus on the cases of confirmation and forget the rest. The believer may reply that, in as far as he can tell, the closer he walks with God, the more this kind of confirmation occurs.

The Fifth Criterion

The skeptic, however, may argue that we have not yet got the right set of criteria. He may try to supplement them, focusing on the criteria for what experiences can properly enter into the confirmation process. In particular, he may say that they have to be of the following kind: the experiences have to be of the specific kind that virtually any one of sound mind would have in circumstances that are the same in the relevant respects. It is important to note that the criterion is not that the direct encounter has to be repeatable, but that the tests which confirm that it is direct encounter have to be repeatable.[29]

The confirmation of direct encounter with God seems to fail the fifth criterion. When God specifies a test whereby Moses can know that it is God speaking to him, this test is meant for Moses. There is no indication that it is repeatable for anyone else. The test is subject to God's will, and God gives His signs to particular people on particular occasions. God's redemptive activity is often particular in this way. On the other hand, with Teresa of Avila we have something like repeatability. She was worried that her visions might have been diabolical. The confirmation that it was Christ who came to her seems to have three sources: first, from the consistency with Scripture and the doctrine of the church; second, from the spiritual effects of the vision; third, from checking with her confessor and Friar Peter of Alcantara to be sure that the vision was of the right type. She seems to be saying that anyone who has visions of this type could test them in these same ways.

It is also true, however, that the sorts of tests John of the Cross and Teresa of Avila are talking about are rather soft on the first four criteria. They do not predict with much accuracy or precision. One test, for example, is that diabolical visions do not cause the mildness of humility and love of God and do cause an inclination to self-esteem. But it is hard to specify accurately what degree or kind of humility or love would count here. Moreover the proposed confirmation fails the second and third criteria. The humility and the love of God and, one might add, the fruit of the spirit such as joy and peace, are antecedently probable, in the sense that Teresa would quite likely have experienced them anyway, even without the vision. The absence of such fruit would not have falsified the claim that it was an experience of God, given the number of other possible causes for their absence.

These sorts of tests do not give strong confirmation on the first four criteria. They are not like the fleece being wet when the ground is dry. It seems as though there is a pattern here. Where the test does meet the first four criteria, it does not meet the fifth. Where it meets the fifth, it does not meet the first four.

The Appropriateness of the Quest for Confirmation

In the previous section I argued that confirmation, often by way of indirect encounter, is available for the claim to have had direct encounter.

I now want to argue that this kind of confirmation is desirable. It is useful to distinguish three positions on the question of whether confirmation is appropriate to Christian faith. I will give the positions the following names, the no-confirmation view, the ready-confirmation view, and the cautious-confirmation view. Let me repeat first, however, that I am not talking here about the more contentious issue of whether the initial belief in God, the initial gift of faith, needs or can receive confirmation. I am talking about whether a person who already has faith can or should look for confirmation that he or she has had direct encounter with God. The three positions can be distinguished in terms of an analogy George Mavrodes makes with three positions on the question of whether a particular body of water is drinkable.[30] One might take the position that the water is hopelessly and irremediably polluted, or the position that it is completely clean, or the position that it is partly polluted but drinkable if boiled.

Three Views of Confirmation

The no-confirmation view thinks of confirmation as hopeless and the quest dangerous. For God will impress Himself on the believer's consciousness, and anything other than that direct impress which the believer might use as confirmation will have less authority than the initial experience. The danger arises because the attempt to secure the more authoritative on the basis of the less authoritative will tend to weaken the initial sense of the authority of the original experience.

The ready-confirmation view is that our experience is readily available for the purpose of confirming direct encounter. This view might point out that God has the general supervision of a believer's life, and is likely to provide all sorts of occasions for reinforcement of the believer's faith. Direct encounter may be one such occasion, but we should expect that the influence of this encounter will be sustained by the rest of a believer's experience, which is in the hands of the same God. It is sometimes said, for example, that health and wealth can be taken as good indications of a personal relationship with Jesus Christ.

The cautious-confirmation view is that confirmation is sometimes available, and desirable, but that even where it is available it needs to be treated with great caution. This is because of the effects of sin, which make the believer's experience unreliable in different ways. Despite the caution, however, this confirmation should be looked for; this is partly because sin also affects spiritual experience, so that the believer does not have an infallible sense of when he or she has a direct encounter and when he or she does not.[31]

I myself want to support the cautious-confirmation view; but first it is important to point out one thing that this view does not say. It does not say that every Christian is obliged to back up his or her claim to direct encounter by argument and inference. Charles Hodge writes: "It is very possible that the mind may see a thing to be true without being able to prove its truth, or to make any satisfactory exhibition of the grounds of its belief."[32] We can here use David Burrell's distinction between the meaning of the term *foundations* for the builder and for the archaeologist.[33] The builder constructs and the archaeologist reconstructs. Beliefs can have confirmation of which most holders of the beliefs are unaware. In the adoption, or the discovery, or the initial "construction" of the beliefs, evidence may not be necessary. But in the "reconstruction" or analysis of the beliefs at a later point such confirmation can be very useful.

What will the cautious-confirmationist say, then, about the apparent failure of religious experience in the form of direct encounter to be confirmable by all five of our criteria? He will say that what we are trying to confirm is unlike the case of the hypothesis about the bean plants and radioactivity in two ways. First, we are trying to confirm a hypothesis about a personal relationship, about an encounter between one party in that relationship and the other. Second, we are trying to confirm a hypothesis for which our competence to evaluate the evidence is severely limited by the nature of the hypothesis itself. I will give examples of both these differences in a moment. The general point, however, is that the kind of hypothesis we are trying to confirm puts limits on what kind of confirmation will be available. This should give rise to caution, but not despair. Aristotle says we should not "look for the same degree of exactness in all areas, but the degree that fits the subject-matter in each area and is proper to the investigation."[34] What we should do is to think about the inherent limits in the kind of confirmation that could be available and not be disappointed when we do not find confirmation beyond those limits.

Limits to Confirmation

First, consider experiences that involve personal relationships. Suppose I am trying to tell whether it was my wife who did the flower arrangement on the table. The best thing to do would be to ask her, but suppose I cannot do that. The next best thing is to look for marks of her style. Perhaps I know that she likes crisp-edged flowers like daffodils and does not like soft-edged flowers like petunias, that she tends to make full arrangements so that there are few gaps between flowers, and that she is careful to choose flowers that last well when picked. The arrangement on the table is ten long-stemmed roses. Is this her style? The point is that when dealing with claims about people, and their choices, we do not apply the same standards for confirmation as we do for bean plants and radioactive isotopes. Suppose it suddenly occurs to me that this is our tenth wedding anniversary, which I had quite forgotten. I remember that I gave her flowers on our last anniversary, which she had forgotten, and we joked about how absent-minded we were getting. All this is an understanding that arises out of a shared history of relationship between two people. I do not have, in this case, a hypothesis that yields an exact prediction of experience or one that can be confirmed by repeatable evidence. In these sorts of ways, the confirmation is weakened when we are dealing with hypotheses about people and their actions. But I am nonetheless quite legitimately sure that this arrangement is by my wife.

Second, consider cases where the subject's competence to evaluate an hypothesis is severely restricted. Suppose I am not a very good pianist, perhaps with two years of lessons in my youth, and I am trying to evaluate the claim that Peter Serkin is as good a pianist as his father. This is very difficult because it involves aesthetic judgment. It is also difficult because I would have to know a great deal about music and piano playing in particular to know what experiences to look for in order to confirm the claim. I am at an almost insuperable disadvantage. But I can still make the attempt, by listening to their recordings and reading music reviews. My point again is that we quite properly use the experience we have available together with our background beliefs in order to give us the best confirmation available to us.

The cautious-confirmer will use these kinds of example to show that requirements and expectations for confirmation vary with the *object* about which the claim is being made and with the *relative* status of the subject doing the confirming. If the claim is that it is God who spoke to me, my attempts at confirmation will be a little like the attempt to confirm that it is my wife who did the flower arrangement and a little like the attempt to tell whether Peter Serkin is as good a pianist as his father. They will be like the first because God is a person, and the actions of persons are not usually (at least not by us) predictable with precision; nor are they repeatable in the same way as experiments on bean plants. They are like the second, because our capacities are so limited. Bean plants and geiger counters and tables stay put, and are in the right size-range for our sensory capacities. God is not proportioned to our present cognitive capacities in the same way. We do not have a very complete idea about what actions we should expect God to perform. These weaknesses of ours belong under the general heading of our sinfulness, which is what gives the cautious-confirmer his general awareness of the need for caution. But even though confirmation is weakened in these two ways, both kinds of weakness are familiar from our everyday experience.

The position of the cautious-confirmer is thus that sin affects both the kind of confirmation available for direct encounter, and the desirability of such confirmation. It affects the desirability because of the effects of sin even (or perhaps especially) on our spiritual life. Our claims to direct encounter are not infallible. There is a traditional Christian doctrine which Calvin expressed as follows:

> There is within the human mind, and indeed by natural instinct, an awareness of divinity. . . . God himself has implanted in all men a certain understanding of his divine majesty. . . . Men one and all perceive that there is a God and that He is their maker.[35]

This teaching is consistent with the phenomenon observed by anthropologists that most peoples do worship a god or gods. Members of Wycliffe Bible Translators, whose translations of the Bible are often the first written works in tribal languages, report that there is always a term for "God" that they have been able to use for translation purposes. Calvin also stressed, however, that this natural apprehension of God has been clouded by sin. Everything we do that is against God's will takes us farther away from seeing Him clearly. In the New Testament, the connection is drawn repeatedly (especially in John's Gospel) between obedience and seeing God.

Conclusion

My conclusion is that there is the sort of confirmation we should expect, given the relationship between God and human beings presented in Scripture. God does give us signs of His presence, and believers are warranted in taking their experiences to yield a perception of these kinds of signs. To be sure, believers should retain a proper modest sense that they might be mistaken, as Teresa of Avila did despite the number and vividness of her religious experiences. But this does not mean that believers should labor under the fear that the experiential warrant for their beliefs is in a quite different, less privileged category than the experiential warrant other people have for most of their beliefs. Repeatability and accurate predictability are very rare, especially for beliefs about persons and their actions.

I have argued in two ways. The first way involved the claim that the believer's experience can be presumed to give warrant in the absence of "defeaters" of various kinds. I made the analogy with the experience of seeing a goldfinch. I argued in the first two sections that the presence of an antecedent desire for such experience does not constitute a defeater, and that the believer is not confusing psychological certainty with truth.

The second way, argued in the third and fourth sections, involved the claim that God does give significant confirmation of His presence, and that believers should look for this. My point was that although God is in control of this confirmation, it is of a type analogous to what we accept as confirmation in non-religious contexts. God is, so to say, speaking our language here, and He has created us as beings who can respond to Him in this way. Because we are also sinners, we should try to check our claims to direct encounter with Him by the methods He has given us.[36]

Notes

[1]André Froissard, *Dieu existe, je l'ai rencontré* (Paris: A. Fayard, 1975).

[2]The case of the conversion of Paul on the road to Damascus is one of direct encounter with Christ occurring to a theist, though not yet a Christian. The case of Simone Weil is perhaps a case of direct encounter occurring to someone who is not even a theist.

[3]C. B. Martin, "A Religious Way of Knowing," in *Readings in the Philosophy of Religion: An Analytic Approach,* ed. Baruch A. Brody (Englewood Cliffs, N.J.: Prentice-Hall, 1974), 516–29. This article is responded to by George Mavrodes in "Rationality and Religious Belief—A Perverse Question," in *Rationality and Religious Belief,* ed. C. F. Delaney (Notre Dame: Notre Dame Press, 1979), 28–41.

[4]The example and the analysis of it are taken from William P. Alston, "Christian Experience and Christian Belief," in *Faith and Rationality: Reason and Belief in God,* ed. Alvin Plantinga and Nicholas Wolterstorff (Notre Dame: Notre Dame Press, 1983), 103–34, esp. 121.

[5]I have taken the first four of these from William P. Alston, "The Place of Experience in the Grounds of Religious Belief" (Unpublished manuscript), 21.

[6]Norman P. Melchert, "Mystical Experience and Ontological Claims," *Philosophy and Phenomenological Research* (June 1977): 445–63.

[7]The actual structure of Melchert's paper is a phenomenological account of mystical experience, then a general argument based on an analogy with Kant's "paralogisms of pure reason," and then three explanations, of which I am discussing the first two.

[8]The word appears in the writing of Keith Lehrer and John Pollock. The idea is articulated for the context of religious claims by Alvin Plantinga, "Reason and Belief in God," in Plantinga and Wolterstorff, *Faith and Rationality,* 84f. His account is similar to that of Thomas Reid, that we have a credulity disposition, a disposition to believe what we apprehend people are telling us. We then find occasions when this disposition should be resisted, and we develop adequate reasons to believe the deliverances of the disposition to be in certain kinds of circumstance unreliable. See Nicholas Wolterstorff, "Can Belief in God Be Rational If It Has No Foundations," in Plantinga and Wolterstorff, *Faith and Rationality,* 163.

[9]J. L. Austin, "Others Minds," in *Philosophical Papers* (Oxford: Clarendon Press, 1961), 77.

[10]See Heb. 11:6.

[11]Aristotle would ask whether you are on the road to or the road from the starting points (*Nicomachean Ethics,* 1095a30f). Or we might talk about "prospective" and "retrospec-

tive" justification. See David B. Burrell, "Religious Belief and Rationality," in Delaney, *Rationality and Religious Belief*, 84–115, esp. 107.

[12]See Plantinga and Wolterstorff, *Faith and Rationality*, 55ff.

[13]See Mavrodes, *Rationality and Religious Belief*, 38.

[14]There are muddles in terminology in the literature on this topic. It is possible to hold that justification is properly a matter of inference; and since there are many propositions which we are within our epistemic rights in believing, but which we do not infer from other propositions, we should say that we are warranted in believing non-justified propositions. Alternatively we can say that these propositions do have justification, and "ground," but not "evidence."

[15]Teresa of Avila, *Life,* trans. David Lewis (Newman Press, 1962), chap. 25, par. 17. I am indebted for this and the following three examples to Dan Crawford.

[16]Ibid., chap. 27, par. 3–5.

[17]John of the Cross, *Ascent of Mount Carmel,* bk. 11, chap. 24, sec. 7. But the author himself went on to deny that mystic apprehension is a legitimate source of propositional knowledge. For a discussion, see Nelson Pike, "John of the Cross on the Epistemic Value of Mystic Visions," in *Rationality, Religious Belief, and Moral Commitment,* ed. Robert Audi and William J. Wainwright (Ithaca, N.Y.: Cornell University Press, 1986), 15–37.

[18]For a similar list of criteria, see Kelly J. Clark, *Return to Reason,* (Grand Rapids, Mich.: Eerdmans, 1990), 37. I have not included here the prior probability of the hypothesis, which is included in Bayes's Theorem for determining the probability of the hypothesis, given the evidence. In the cases I am going to consider, the people who have the religious experiences are already believers, so that they would regard the prior probability of God's existence as high. They will also be predisposed to believe that it is God they are meeting in the experience.

[19]The stories are in Judges 6 and Exodus 3 and 4. This and all subsequent quotations from Scripture in this chapter are from the New International Version of the Bible, copyright 1978 by the New York International Bible Society.

[20]E.g., Gen. 12:1–7.

[21]Isa. 41:21–24, 26; 43:9–11; 46:8–13; see Ezek. 14:9–11.

[22]Jer. 32:6–8 in the context of the whole episode.

[23]John 2:11.

[24]John 1:41.

[25]Luke 16:31.

[26]Søren Kierkegaard, *Philosophical Fragments* (Princeton: Princeton University Press, 1985), 93.

[27]To Abram, God identified Himself as the Lord who brought him out of Ur of the Chaldees to give him Canaan to take possession of it. To Jacob: "I am the LORD, the God of your father Abraham and the God of Isaac. I will give you and your descendants the land on which you are lying. . . . I am with you and will watch over you wherever you go, and I will bring you back to this land" (Gen. 28:13–15).

[28]It is always possible to provide alternative explanations for these sorts of stories. Perhaps I saw a premonition in my friend's eyes that night at dinner. But many people have these kinds of experiences. If the skeptic insists on an alternative explanation every time, he is liable to the charge that his own background beliefs are not open to revision.

I am suggesting, contrary to John Wisdom for example, that religious experience is still open to some kinds of empirical testing. What makes it different from, say, perceptual experience is not primarily the absence of testing, but the absence of repeatable testing. I will say more about this later.

[29]Much will depend on how *repeatability* is defined. There can be a pattern of repeated confirmation for a particular family over a particular period, so that they come to rely on God utterly, for example, for their financial needs. It will take more work to see if this would count as repeatability if we bear in mind, also, the points about the kind of confirmation to be expected.

[30]George Mavrodes, "Jerusalem and Athens Revisited," in Plantinga and Wolterstorff, *Faith and Rationality,* 192–93.

[31]This point is made persuasively in Stephen J. Wykstra, "Toward a Sensible Evidentialism: On the Notion of 'Needing Evidence,'" in *Philosophy of Religion,* ed. William Rowe and William J. Wainwright (New York: Harcourt Brace Jovanovich, 1972), 426–37.

[32]Charles Hodge, "The Ground of Faith in the Scriptures," in *Essays and Reviews* (New York, 1879), 191.

[33]Burrell, "Religious Belief and Rationality," 105.

[34]Aristotle, *Nicomachean Ethics,* 1098a26.

[35]John Calvin, *Institutes of the Christian Religion,* trans. Ford Lewis Battles (Philadelphia, Pa.: Westminster Press, 1960), bk. 1, chap. 3, 43–44.

[36]I want to thank my colleagues at Calvin College for much helpful discussion of the subject of this chapter.

5.3

Miracles and the Historicity of the Easter Week Narratives

Robert C. Newman

CENTRAL TO THE MESSAGE OF THE NEW TESTAMENT are the events of Easter week, particularly the death and resurrection of Jesus of Nazareth. If these events did not happen, then there is little to be said in favor of *biblical* Christianity, whatever one may think of modernized religions labeled Christianity by such theologians as Schleiermacher, Tillich, or Bultmann.

Let us consider the question, Are the biblical accounts of Easter week trustworthy? I am personally convinced that they are. In fact, I gave up a career in astrophysics to go into theology because I believed these accounts were reliable. My personal convictions and decisions, however, are no guarantee of truth. Many have even given up their lives for mistaken causes. But here we are not concerned about belief as a blind leap in the dark. The reliability of the Gospel narratives is based on excellent evidence, and this evidence includes the events surrounding the death and resurrection of Jesus of Nazareth. There is more solid evidence for the reliability of these accounts than for any historical accounts that come to us from the ancient world.

Of course, there are some in academic circles who seem to have difficulty seeing the Gospel accounts as reliable. The problem, as they see it, is the presence of miracles in these accounts. In the events of Easter week, the one miracle primarily involved is the resurrection of Jesus. Ever since the eighteenth century, many people have almost a priori discounted any narrative describing supernatural events. Since the Gospels report many such miracles, it is only natural that those who reject the miraculous should find the Gospels untrustworthy. I agree with them! If it can be said authoritatively that miracles do not happen, then they have not happened, and the Gospel accounts are not trustworthy. If miracles are ruled out, then the resurrection of Jesus did not occur. Indeed, it would be foolish to call the narratives of Easter week "trustworthy" if the one central event they narrate is a myth, a legend, a delusion, a fraud, or a lie.

Why do so many people today reject the reality of miracles? Certainly the rise of anti-Christian philosophy among modern scientists has had an influence. Sir Isaac Newton, whose laws of motion and gravity brought order to a vast array of phenomena that once seemed mysterious, seemed to some to make acknowledgement of the Creator unnecessary. Yet Newton himself understood these laws better than anyone else of his time, and he saw no reason to reject miracles just because he had learned something of the system by which God providentially controls the physical world. Rather it was the science popularizers of his day—the French encyclopedists and English deists—who extrapolated the concept of natural law to the extreme that God became unnecessary, or at least unable to intervene in His universe.

Arguments Against the Miraculous

Probably the classic argument against miracles—judging by the frequency with which it is cited—is that of the philosopher David Hume,[1] first published in 1748. Essentially, his argument is the following:

Experience is our only guide in all our decisions regarding matters of fact. Because we cannot see connections between events, all our inferences about cause and effect are based merely on our observation that certain events consistently occur together.

Likewise our belief in the reliability of human testimony is derived from the usual agreement between facts and the reports of witnesses. But if someone reports an extraordinary or marvelous event, we tend to discount the value of his testimony in proportion to the extent to which the reported event is unusual.

Now a miracle, by definition, is a violation of the laws of nature. Yet these laws of nature are themselves established by firm and unalterable experience, so a miracle goes against the very evidence by which we determine matters of fact. Thus we conclude that no human testimony is sufficient to establish the occurrence of a miracle unless the testimony is of such a kind that its being false would be more miraculous than the fact which it seeks to establish.

For Hume, this argument led to the following methodology:

When anyone tells me that he saw a dead man restored to life, I immediately consider with myself whether it be more probable that this person should either deceive or be deceived, or that the fact which he relates should really have happened. I weigh the one miracle against the other, and according to the superiority which I discover, I pronounce my decision and always reject the greater miracle.[2]

Apparently Hume never encountered a witness or a number of witnesses so reliable that he judged resurrection to be the lesser miracle.

There are three serious problems with Hume's argument: one of definition, another of epistemology, and a third of methodology. First, Hume's definition of miracle as a violation of natural law is at least questionable. In orthodox Christianity, Judaism, and (presumably) Islam, a miracle is an action produced by a spiritual intelligence (God, Satan, angel, or demon) intervening in the natural world to produce a result which would not otherwise happen. In principle, then, a miracle need no more violate natural law than I (a physical intelligence) do when I intervene in the natural world to pick up a pen, causing it to rise from the desk—an event which certainly would not have happened without my intervention. Human volition thus provides a simple analogy for a whole class of miracles which do not violate natural law. If God or other non-material personal beings exist, there is no obvious reason why they might not intervene in such a way as well.

Epistemologically, Hume claims that natural law is established by "firm and unalterable experience." Clearly, something we call *natural law* exists. There are many real advantages to discovering and using such laws, as our modern technology attests. But in saying these laws are established by "unalterable experience," Hume extrapolates far beyond anything our limited observations can establish. At most, we can only list all events which we have actually observed, not those which have happened but were not observed, nor those which could happen but so far have not. Thus our natural laws are not based on a complete induction, but only upon a subset of observations which are quite limited both in space and time. Within the subset of events known to mankind there are many reports of miraculous events. So even if we define miracle as a violation of natural law, we only know that natural law is established by "firm" experience if in fact all these reports of miracles are actually false. This we do not know, as no one has investigated each of these reports and found them to be false. Hume thus begs the question by importing his conclusion into his premises.

In fact, Hume's argument is really a methodology in disguise. In analyzing reports of events, Hume tells us to adopt any other explanation rather than the miraculous. But wait a moment! Do me the favor, if you please, of suspending your disbelief in miracles for a few seconds. Consider the consequences of Hume's procedure if miracles do in fact occur. Using Hume's methodology, we will never admit the reality of a miracle even if it has occurred. We will always assume it more likely that the testimony of any number of witnesses, indeed our own senses, is false, since witnesses can lie and our senses can be deceived. Hume's procedure will thus explain away a miracle even if it does occur. Therefore Hume has neither an argument against, nor even a real test for, the occurrence of the genuinely miraculous.

Of course, one may object that Hume's method is merely a special case of Occam's Razor, the principle that says explanations of phenomena should not be complicated beyond necessity. Wouldn't it undermine science itself to throw away Occam's Razor? I agree. We should be careful not to undermine this process of gathering and organizing knowledge, which has shown considerable ability to help us understand reality. Yet we must also be aware of two problems that face us here.

First, Occam's Razor suggests that theories should not be more complicated than necessary *to fit the data*. Hume's position, however, is to *discard* or explain away the data necessary to substantiate miracles. His method, therefore, is not really a proper application of Occam's Razor.

Second, Occam's Razor is a procedural rule; it has us start with simpler theories and move to more complicated ones as each simpler theory is eliminated by the data. Now it is not even obvious that non-miraculous universes are simpler than miraculous ones. But even if it *is* simpler to deny miracles than to accept them, what guarantee do we have that the universe is simple? What guarantee is there that it doesn't matter whether we reach certain truths before we die? Christianity claims to be a revelation from God, who says it does matter, and that we have only one life in which to find and embrace the truth. Perhaps, like any other razor, we should be careful how we use Occam's. We don't want to cut our own throats!

There are other arguments against the miraculous. Let us look briefly at three more. The theologian Rudolf Bultmann claims that science and history see the universe as a closed system of cause and effect which cannot be "perforated by supernatural powers."[3] Indeed many people think the universe is like this, but they may be wrong. Many more admit that the miraculous may occur, but define *science* and *history* as methods which do not consider the miraculous. I think such definitions only add to the confusion. Most people use the word *science* to mean the attempt to find out what the universe is really like, and they use *history* for the study of what really happened. If we confuse these two types of definitions—explanation forced into agreement with a no-miracle axiom, and attempting to learn what really happens—we beg the question of the miraculous without bothering to investigate.

Is the universe (or history) actually "a closed system of cause and effect"? Certainly we have evidence for the existence of cause and effect in the universe. Likewise we have reason to believe the universe is a system, in the sense that the same physical laws which operate on earth seem to be operating in distant stars and galaxies. But is this system closed in the sense that there are no external influences? This assumption is not only unproved, but two lines of evidence suggest it may even be unlikely.

First, discoveries in this century regarding the atom, its nucleus, and subatomic particles show us that there are physical limitations on our ability to investigate small-scale phenomena. As smaller volumes are probed by scientists, larger energies are needed for the investigation. Yet the point has already been reached that these larger energies severely disrupt the integrity of smaller phenomena. Think how we would disrupt the structure of a china shop if we were to investigate it in the dark by throwing baseballs! In a similar way things are happening behind this epistemological barrier which the universe poses for us. Think, for instance, how radioactive nuclei decay by spitting out electrons, neutrons, protons, and alpha particles. These events are regular in a statistical sense, yet individually, they appear to us to be random. Are they actually random? Are they due to some deeper regularity? Are they influenced by spiritual forces? Competent scientists can be found advocating each of these views.[4]

Second, turning to the large-scale end of scientific investigation, we find in cosmology, also, that the closedness of the universe is an open question. There is a substantial consensus today that some form of the big bang cosmology best fits the known data. Yet there appears to be no way, directly or indirectly, of investigating what may have preceded the big bang "creation" event. Many would like to view this event as merely a "bounce" from a previously collapsing universe, but they must postulate very specialized unknown laws to stop the collapse and start the present expansion.[5] Robert Jastrow, director of the Goddard Institute for Space Studies and professor at both Dartmouth and Columbia, suggests that even such a force would not solve this problem, but that an actual creation at the time of the big bang gives a better fit with the data.[6] Thus the claim that the universe (or history) is a closed system of cause and effect is a presupposition which may not be true. If we allow this assumption to control our investigation, it may very well keep us from reaching the correct answer.

Church historian Adolf Harnack has argued that miracles were accepted in ancient times because people then were scientifically ignorant, but today we know better than to believe such things. Harnack says:

In those days, the strict conception which we now attach to the word "miracle" was as yet unknown; it came in only with a knowledge of the laws of nature and their general validity. Before that, no sound insight existed into what was possible and what was impossible, what was rule and what was exception.[7]

With all due respect to Professor Harnack, this argument is incredible! Though many ancients thought lightning, meteors, and comets supernatural, they still had a good conception of what was natural and what supernatural, just as most of us have today.

Harnack's argument is especially weak with respect to biblical miracles. Have scientists been able to show how Jesus' miracles described in the Gospels may be produced naturally? Do we find the Gospel crowds gaping at what are obviously natural phenomena or tricks in the repertoire of contemporary stage magicians? No! Even most liberal theologians have scorned the absurd attempts of some to see Jesus' walking on the water as really walking on a sandbar, His feeding the five thousand as getting them to share their own lunches, and His ascension as walking up a hillside into the clouds! We certainly have our share of twentieth-century chauvinism if we imagine the ancients were such fools as that.

In a somewhat similar vein, Harnack argues that miracles were thought to be common in antiquity, whereas today we know they don't occur. He says: "The Gospels come from a time in which the marvelous may be said to have been something of almost daily occurrence. People felt and saw that they were surrounded by wonders."[8]

Here again Harnack overstates his case. Certainly it is fair to say that the rejection of the miraculous has a stronger hold on our society than it did in ancient times, though at present the trend seems to be away from naturalism rather than toward it. Yet antiquity had its Skeptics and Epicureans who rejected miracle accounts, and we have our spiritists and charismatics who expect a miracle every day.

The biblical picture of miracles is that of rare but real events, whose frequency is under the control of God and may vary considerably from age to age. According to mainstream Judaism of the first century, "big-time" miracles had ceased long ago, probably when the prophets ceased from Israel about 400 B.C.[9] The New Testament likewise pictures Jesus' miracles as no commonplace events. We don't see the crowds or the disciples treating Jesus' activities casually. Instead they flock to Him in such numbers that He must withdraw from the population centers to get any rest. In fact, Jesus' predecessor, John the Baptist, was recognized as a great prophet even though he worked no miracles,[10] hardly likely if miracles were considered almost daily events. There is a false dichotomy made, then, in driving a wedge between antiquity and our own times, in order to dismiss the ancients as credulous people unable to distinguish between natural and supernatural, or between charlatans and real miracle-workers.

Other arguments have been raised against miracles; we have tried to deal here in a limited space with the most important ones. Such arguments are by no means as strong as they at first appear to be. Typically, they tend to beg the question or overstate the case so as to invalidate the argument. This being so, we should not go into an examination of the New Testament accounts with a presumption against the miraculous. Yet if we set aside such a presumption, we shall find that these accounts look very reliable indeed.[11]

The Character of the New Testament Materials

The biblical accounts of Easter week are found mainly in the canonical Gospels—Matthew (chapters 21–28), Mark (11–16), Luke (19–24) and John (12–20)—our primary documentary sources on Jesus of Nazareth. Incidental notices also occur in the letters of Paul to various early churches, principally 1 Corinthians, with a little material in Romans, 1 and 2 Thessalonians, and 1 Timothy.

In considering the character of these New Testament materials, it is important that we compare these with the major historical writings of antiquity rather than with modern histories written in a time of more sophisticated technology. If God chose to send His Son to an age without printing presses, television, telephones, aircraft, and computers, we should not be surprised that He did not choose to have the Gospel writers use techniques now required in doctoral dissertations.

Here we shall examine not only histories from the same period but also earlier Greek histories. (A summary table is found in Appendix 5.3a.) From roughly the same period as the New Testament come the writings of the Jewish historian Flavius Josephus. His major works are his *Antiquities of the Jews*, narrating events from creation to the outbreak of the Jewish revolt against Rome in A.D. 66, and his *Jewish War,* describing the revolt itself and two centuries of background leading up to it. A contemporary Greek historian is Plutarch, author of some forty-six *Parallel Lives* of famous Greeks and Romans. Among Roman historians, the most important are Tacitus, whose *Annals* narrate the history of Rome from Tiberius to Nero, and Suetonius, whose *Lives of the Twelve Caesars* include the careers of the emperors from Julius Caesar to Domitian.

The major earlier Greek histories are: (1) the *History* of Herodotus, describing the rise of the Persian empire and its wars with Greece; (2) the

History of the Peloponnesian War by Thucydides, narrating the epic struggle between Athens and Sparta; (3) the *Anabasis* of Xenophon, relating the retreat of ten thousand Greek mercenaries across Asia Minor after their leaders were assassinated deep in Persian territory; and (4) the *History* of Polybius, describing the rise of Rome from the Second Punic War to the conquest of Greece.[12]

The Text

The first question we need to consider is the reliability of the text of the biblical accounts. In contrast to our modern publishing technology, by which an author can check his work in page proofs and then have thousands of identical copies run off on a printing press, the ancient author was faced with the problem that each copy was made individually. For manuscripts of any substantial length, new errors were bound to arise in each copy. In addition, the passage of nearly two thousand years and the intervention of the Dark Ages have resulted in the loss of the vast majority of the copies actually made for any ancient published work. How, then, does the New Testament compare in textual purity with other ancient works? Is there an objective means of determining reliability?

The earliest complete manuscripts of the Gospels and Pauline letters date back to the middle of the fourth century, about three hundred years after the original works were written.[13] This date corresponds to the end of official persecution of Christianity and to the general adoption of more durable parchment in place of fragile papyrus as writing material. Fragmentary papyrus manuscripts have survived, however, from an earlier period. Among these manuscripts are: (1) parts of ten manuscripts of Matthew, the earliest two from about A.D. 200; (2) fragments of a manuscript of Mark from about 225 (possibly another from the first century);[14] (3) parts of four manuscripts of Luke, the earliest from about 200; (4) parts of nine manuscripts of John, including a tiny fragment from about 130 and two substantial portions from about 200; and (5) parts of two manuscripts of 1 Corinthians, the earliest from about 200. The total manuscript evidence for the New Testament up to the age of printing consists of more than five thousand Greek copies, over eight thousand Latin copies, and several thousand copies in other languages, all in addition to thousands of quotations found in early Christian writers.

By contrast, the earliest substantial manuscripts for the text of our other ancient historians come from the ninth century A.D., when a new style of Greek handwriting was introduced to the book trade to lower production costs. The best case is that of Suetonius, for which the first good surviving copy comes from more than seven hundred years after the book left its author's hands. The worst case among these is Xenophon's *Anabasis;* its earliest surviving manuscript is from the fourteenth century, over seventeen hundred years after the book was written. Three of these historians were not even preserved in their entirety. The first few chapters of Suetonius on Julius Caesar were lost between the sixth and ninth centuries. Only ten of Tacitus's sixteen books survive complete, and two others in part. For Polybius we have only five complete books out of forty, though condensations of others have survived. The entire manuscript evidence for these ten ancient historians totals about two hundred manuscripts.

Thus, compared with the New Testament, the best attested of these secular histories is known by a manuscript more than twice as far removed from its author. The total documentary evidence for the worst attested history is thousands of times smaller than for the New Testament, and for all these put together it is fifty times smaller. In fact, the New Testament survives in more manuscripts than any other work of classical antiquity. The runner-up is Homer's *Iliad*, which survives in about 650 manuscripts, still less than one-twentieth as many.[15]

How sure can we be that the texts we reconstruct from surviving manuscripts are close to what the author originally wrote? Without the actual manuscripts written or proofed by the author, there will always be a possibility of error. But exactly the same may be said for any modern author. However, the procedure called *textual criticism* was especially developed to deal with this problem in works written before the advent of printing. What may be said, then, about this?

Perhaps you have heard that there are 150,000 to 200,000 variant readings in the New Testament, so how can anyone trust anything it says? This is true but misleading, as the phrase *variant reading* is a technical term. Each time a manuscript of an ancient work is discovered, its text is compared with some standard printed edition. At each place it differs from the standard, a "variant reading" is recorded. If ten manuscripts differ in the same way at the same place from the standard, ten variant readings are recorded. Thus, *the more manuscripts which survive for a particular work, the more variant readings it will usually have.* Thus our only real concern then is what *fraction* of the text is debatable.

Professor F. J. A. Hort of Cambridge, in his classic work on the New Testament text, notes that seven-eighths of the text is accepted by all as preserved just as penned by its original authors. The remaining one-eighth consists largely of matters of spelling and word order, both relatively trivial in ancient Greek. If scholars are correct in their consensus that the Alexandrian family of manuscripts preserves the best text, this area of doubt is reduced to about one-sixtieth of the text, from which Hort estimates that substantial variants make up only about one-one thousandth of the text.[16] Other estimates have been made; for instance, Professor Abbot of Harvard suggests that only one-four hundredth of the text is doubtful.[17]

Detailed statistics on the classical texts are hard to come by. Remember that three of our ten secular histories have not even been preserved over substantial portions of their text. For Homer's *Iliad*, 750 to 1000 lines are in dispute out of a total of 15,600.[18] This makes for about 6 percent disputed material. By contrast, Hort's estimate of "substantial variation" for the New Testament is one-tenth of 1 percent; Abbot's estimate is one-fourth of 1 percent; and even Hort's figure including trivial variation is less than 2 percent. Sir Frederic Kenyon well summarizes the situation:

> The number of manuscripts of the New Testament . . . is so large that it is practically certain that the true reading of every doubtful passage is preserved in some one or other of these ancient authorities. This can be said of no other ancient book in the world.
>
> Scholars are satisfied that they possess substantially the true text of the principal Greek and Roman writers whose works have come down to us, of Sophocles, of Thucydides, of Cicero, of Virgil; yet our knowledge depends on a mere handful of manuscripts, whereas the manuscripts of the New Testament are counted by hundreds and even thousands.[19]

Authorship

Of course, one may admit that the text of the New Testament is good—that it is substantially what its original authors wrote—and still claim that it is historically unreliable. This is commonly done in theologically liberal circles, where a rejection of the miraculous means that the Gospels *must* be inaccurate. Persons with such beliefs thus make strenuous attempts to deny that the Gospels were written by the traditional authors or depend on eyewitness testimony. Yet the methodology employed for such denials is sufficient to explain away many of the ancient historians as well.

The Gospel narratives are anonymous in their texts, in that none of them says, "I, Matthew, wrote this," or something of the sort. The reason for this anonymity is unknown. Perhaps it was done to emphasize their subject, Jesus of Nazareth, by deemphasizing their authors. Even so, the authors were probably known to their original audiences. The prologue of Luke[20] suggests the author is known to its recipient and patron Theophilus. Likewise, the author of John's Gospel is known to some group which vouches for him.[21] Thus two of the Gospels were apparently not anonymous to their first recipients.

In this light, it is significant that early Christian tradition is *unanimous* in assigning the canonical Gospels to Matthew, Mark, Luke, and John; and that the earliest surviving papyri have titles also, all of which give the traditional authors only. This is most naturally explained if indeed these men were the authors and it was common knowledge in the early church.

Otherwise, one must explain the complete loss of the correct names and their complete replacement by a *single* set of spurious names—a set, moreover, in which three of the names are relatively obscure. One would have thought that, for invented names, any apostle would be more likely than Mark or Luke, and any of the major apostles—Peter, Paul, James, Andrew, Philip, or Thomas—more likely than Matthew.

There is considerable historical evidence external to the Gospels for the traditional authors. Papias, bishop of the church at Hierapolis in Asia Minor and an old man by A.D. 130, names Matthew and Mark as Gospel writers, indicating that Matthew wrote in Hebrew or Aramaic and describing Mark as one who recorded Peter's reminiscences. Papias was himself a student of the Apostle John.[22]

Justin Martyr, after studying many of the contemporary Greek philosophies, converted to Christianity sometime before A.D. 130. He speaks of the Gospels as "memoirs of the apostles."[23] He says they were written "by apostles and those who followed them,"[24] which matches the traditional ascription to two apostles (Matthew and John) and two followers (Mark of Peter, Luke of Paul). He quotes from or mentions matters found in each of the four Gospels, and apparently alludes to Mark's Gospel as Peter's memoirs.[25] Justin wrote in the sixth decade of the second century, but apparently his *Dialogue with Trypho*, in which most of his testimony occurs, actually took place in the fourth decade.[26]

The anonymous *Muratorian Canon*, written in Italy late in the second century, is damaged at its beginning but lists Luke as author of the third Gospel and John as author of the fourth.[27]

Irenaeus, bishop of Lyons in southern France about A.D. 180, was raised in Asia Minor and studied under Polycarp, a student of the Apostle John. He names each of the four Gospel authors and gives relative dates for the writing of three of these.[28]

Clement and Origen, Christian teachers in Alexandria around A.D. 200, mention all four Gospels and give the traditional authors.[29] None of these men gives any indication that they are guessing, innovating, or borrowing from one another. All this suggests that the information was common knowledge from the previous generation.

Internal evidence in the Gospels supports these identifications to a greater or lesser extent. Matthew was obviously written especially for those of Jewish background, for it emphasizes Jesus as the Messiah fulfilling Old Testament prophecy, and it presents Jewish customs without explanation. Mark's Gospel fits the vividness and brusqueness of Peter's personality. The incident it reports of a young man who loses his clothing to the mob arresting Jesus[30] makes good sense if it is a little touch from Mark's personal history, but it is quite puzzling otherwise. Paul tells us that Luke is a Gentile physician;[31] his Gospel shows special interest in the Gentiles and abounds with technical medical terminology.[32] John is the only Gospel that calls John the Baptist merely "John"; the other Gospels use the term "Baptist" to distinguish him from John the Apostle, who is never named in the Gospel of John. According to John 21:20, 24, the author of this Gospel is "the disciple whom Jesus loved," who raced Peter to the empty tomb on Easter morning, and who saw and heard the resurrected Jesus on several occasions. Of course, one may claim that the original authors faked these details, that the early Christians were taken in by this deception, and that they unanimously agreed in guessing who wrote each one. Such procedures, however, will explain away any historical data whatever.

That the Apostle Paul wrote 1 Corinthians is as certain as that he existed. Not even the radical criticism of F. C. Baur denied Paul this letter, and external evidence shows why this is so. Not only does the letter claim to have been written by Paul, but the earliest extrabiblical Christian writing still in existence affirms it. Clement's letter to the Corinthians, written about A.D. 95, quotes from it, names it, describes it, and assigns it to the Apostle Paul.[33] All this occurs within thirty years of Paul's death in a writing by the leader of the church at Rome where Paul had labored and given his life for the faith.

To the best of my knowledge, none of the ten classical histories we have been examining has such external attestation as does 1 Corinthians or even the Gospels. Of course, none of these histories is anonymous, as the Gospels are. On the other hand, I have not been able to find any descriptions by ancient writers of the circumstances of their composition, as we have for the Gospels. Admittedly, I have not spent my lifetime in the study of secular classical literature, but the very fact that such things are not discussed in the *Oxford Classical Dictionary, Harper's Dictionary of Classical Literature and Antiquities*, or the relevant volumes of the Loeb Classical Library shows how little modern historians studying the classical period share the skepticism so endemic to liberal New Testament studies.

Would the early church have accepted writings which were anonymous or for which they could not check authorship claims, as liberal theologians believe? Not according to the evidence preserved in the New Testament and early Christian writers. The New Testament regularly rebukes lying, and it warns of the dangers of heresy, especially from false teachers and false prophets.[34] Though Paul had his letters written out by scribes (in accord with the usual practice of that time), he always wrote the final greetings in his own hand to guard against forgery.[35] Such safeguards were a common practice in antiquity.[36] That this concern extended to "orthodox" forgeries is seen from the fact that a church in

Asia Minor deposed one of its elders for writing the Acts of Paul and Thecla, even though he claimed to have written out of love for Paul.[37]

The early church was also concerned to have multiple attestation for the narration of its history and teachings. Paul tells Timothy: "The things you have heard me say in the presence of *many witnesses*, entrust to reliable men who will also be qualified to teach others."[38]

It seems that the burden of proof is on those who deny the traditional authorship of the New Testament books to come forth with some real evidence to support their speculations.

Thus we take Matthew, Mark, Luke, John, and Paul as authors of the works ascribed to them and ask, "How do they compare with other history writers of antiquity?" We would very much like the historian to be an eyewitness of the events he narrates, but this is rarely possible for all the events involved. It is certainly important that he have access to eyewitness testimony.

We would like the writer to be unbiased, but he must also be sufficiently interested to write on the subject at an early time when eyewitnesses are still living. In fact we would have little history writing, ancient or modern, if we had to depend on totally unbiased writers. It is more important that the writer be concerned to report the truth even if it is not always favorable to his side.

In addition, it is most helpful to be able to test the historian's statements by corroboration from other sources. But for antiquity especially, it is too much to expect corroboration for all points of a narrative, especially when the narrative being tested is the most detailed or only detailed account of the events in question. Room must be allowed for a source to *add* to our knowledge of history.

Let us consider the matter of eyewitness testimony first. On the basis of biblical information, John and Matthew were Jesus' disciples, the former from the very beginning of His public career, the latter throughout His Galilean ministry. Mark probably had much less direct contact with Jesus, as he appears to have been young and living in Jerusalem at this time. Paul was probably older than Mark, but he says little about pre-conversion contact with Jesus. Probably he had seen Jesus only once or twice in Jerusalem. Unlike the others, Luke is a Gentile, probably a native of Antioch, perhaps converted during the work of Paul and Barnabas there in the 40s. He would have had the least direct contact with eyewitnesses, as the others were in Judea for five or more years immediately following Jesus' ministry. Yet Luke had considerable contact with Paul and Silas, stayed several days with Philip, and apparently spent two years in Palestine (ca. 58–60) while Paul was imprisoned in Caesarea. All five writers, then, had considerable opportunity to make use of eyewitness testimony.

Comparing the biblical writers with the classical historians, the status of John and Matthew, as participants in many of the events they record, is parallel to that of Pliny the Younger, Xenophon, Polybius, and Thucydides. Paul's situation, having been on both sides of the controversy, is parallel to that of Josephus during the Jewish revolt, with the notable difference that Josephus switched to the side with wealth and political power in order to save his life, while Paul endangered his life by changing to the side without these attractions. Luke and Mark are in positions comparable to those of Tacitus, Suetonius, and Herodotus in those cases where the latter report on events before their time but recent enough to have living eyewitnesses. None of these five biblical writers is in the position of Plutarch for most of his material, or of Josephus, Suetonius, and Herodotus for their earlier material, where eyewitnesses were no longer living. Thus the New Testament situation here is comparable to the best cases among ancient historians. In fact, if students of ancient history had to depend on eyewitness testimony alone, we would know little of antiquity.

What about bias? It is true that the biblical writers are all Christians, and they see events from that perspective. This does not rule out the possibility that they were sincere and that they only reported events for which they had good evidence. For example, note the sketch that Luke gives of his methodology:

Many have undertaken to draw up an account of the things that have been fulfilled among us, just as they were handed down to us by those who from the first were eyewitnesses and servants of the word. Therefore, since I myself have carefully investigated everything from the beginning, it seemed good also to me to write an orderly account for you, most excellent Theophilus, so that you may know the certainty of the things you have been taught.[39]

It is also significant that each author reports events which reflect unfavorably on himself (except Luke, who was not present in the events narrated), the apostles, and early Christians in general. Only Jesus receives no unfavorable notice, in agreement with the biblical picture that He is God incarnate and therefore sinless. No attempt is made, however, to remove seemingly harsh statements made by Jesus or charges against Him by His opponents. Nor do the biblical writers seek to hide the fact they are Christians by pretending to give an impartial account, as we see in the (Jewish) Letter of Aristeas and the apocryphal (Christian) Acts of Pilate. It is also significant that two of the five writers—Luke and Paul—were not on Jesus' side during His ministry. Paul, in fact, was a violent and high-ranking member of the opposition. Surely Paul knew whatever could be said against Jesus and His followers!

By comparison, we find that our classical historians had their biases, too. Josephus was very favorable to the Roman emperors and the Pharisees but highly antagonistic to the Zealots who led the revolt against Rome.[40] Tacitus, on the other hand, was against the imperial system and longed for a return to the republic.[41] Suetonius found it hard to pass up a good scandal, no matter how unlikely the story.[42] Pliny, shocked by Roman vices, preferred to emphasize more pleasant matters.[43] Plutarch wrote his biographies to teach virtue and warn against vice. One writer characterizes him as "tantalizing and treacherous to the historian."[44] Herodotus is highly regarded for his careful work and reserve, yet he too is charged with "strong religious feeling, bordering on superstition."[45] Xenophon wrote the first part of his *Anabasis* under a pseudonym; the latter part is tense and aggressive as he answers his critics. He was notably sympathetic to Sparta and other authoritarian regimes.[46] Polybius blasts previous historians in book 12 and was prejudiced against the regions of Aetolia and Boeotia, yet he is still regarded as having high standards of honesty.[47]

In spite of these evidences of bias, each of these secular historians is important for our understanding of the events of antiquity; each reports many events for which we have no other evidence. And these are the best ancient historians we have. As a result, A. N. Sherwin-White, classical historian at Oxford, remarks:

It is astonishing that while Graeco-Roman historians have been growing in confidence, the twentieth-century study of the Gospel narratives, starting from no less promising material, has taken so gloomy a turn in the development of form-criticism that the more advanced exponents of it apparently maintain—so far as an amateur can understand the matter—that the historical Christ is unknowable and the history of His mission cannot be written. This seems very curious.[48]

Indeed, such a development has more to do with ideology than with history.

The Events of Easter Week and Their Corroboration

Let us now turn to the four Gospels and see what events are reported as occurring during Easter week. We will here briefly summarize all events reported in two or more Gospels and a few of those found only in one. For brevity, we will indicate the attestation by using the symbols *4* (all four Gospels); *M* (Matthew); *m* (Mark); *[m]* (disputed passage in Mark); *L* (Luke); *J* (John); *A* (Acts).

Five days before Passover (*J*), Jesus approaches Jerusalem with the crowds of pilgrims (*4*). He rides into Jerusalem on a young donkey (*4*), recalling Zechariah 9:9 as the crowds greet Him with shouts of

"Hosanna" (*MmJ;* Hebrew for "deliver us"), "Blessed is he who comes in the name of the Lord" (*4*), and acclamation as king of Israel (*4*). After looking around the temple, Jesus returns to Bethany where He is staying for the festival (*Mm*).

The next day He returns to Jerusalem, cursing a barren fig tree on the way (*Mm*). He then casts the merchants and their animals out of the temple courts (*MmL*). The following day, Jesus again returns to the temple, where His authority is challenged by the temple officials (*MmL*). The Pharisees and Herodians seek to trap Him with a question on Roman taxes (*MmL*). Jesus turns each attack back on His opponents (*MmL*) and then discusses God's greatest commandments with a lawyer (*Mm*). Jesus ends the debate by asking the Pharisees how the Messiah can be merely David's son when He is also his lord (*MmL*). This is followed by Jesus' scathing rebuke to the Pharisees for their hypocrisy (*MmL*). Jesus observes and approves a widow's sacrificial gift to the temple (*mL*), and then He leaves the temple for the last time (*MmL*). On the way back to Bethany, Jesus gathers His disciples on the Mount of Olives and gives them a detailed description of the coming destruction of the temple and His own return in glory (*MmL*).

Sometime during this period, Judas secretly makes arrangements with the chief priests to betray Jesus to them (*4*).

The next day or the following, Jesus sends some of His disciples to make preparations for their passover meal in an upper room in Jerusalem (*MmL*). He and the other disciples arrive (*4*), and He washes their feet as a lesson in humility (*J*). Judas is shown by a signal that his betrayal has been detected, but Jesus lets him go (*4*). Jesus then warns the remaining disciples of the dangers ahead in which they will fall away, Peter especially being singled out (*4*). The Lord's Supper is instituted, symbolizing His coming death (*MmL*), and Jesus speaks at length with His disciples (*J*). Finally they leave the room and cross the Kidron Valley to pray in a garden on the Mount of Olives (*4*). There Judas and the temple soldiers find them and arrest Jesus as the disciples flee (*4*).

Jesus is taken to the Jewish leaders (*4*), tried by the Sanhedrin (the Jewish supreme court), and early the next morning formally condemned for blasphemy (*4*). Then He is taken before the Roman governor Pontius Pilate, who is reluctant to ratify their decision (*4*). After some stalling (*4*), the leaders apply mob pressure (*MmL*) and threaten to report him to Caesar (*J*). As a result, Pilate permits Jesus' condemnation for claiming kingship (*4*).

Jesus is crucified at a place called Golgotha (*4*) between two bandits (*4*) and dies that afternoon (*4*) after several hours of unusual darkness (*MmL*). His body is claimed by a wealthy Jew named Joseph of Arimathea, who buries Him in his personal tomb (*4*), while women in

Jesus' party look on (*MmL*). The next day a guard is set at the tomb on the insistence of the Jewish leaders, who recall predictions of Jesus' resurrection and fear the disciples will try to steal the body (*M*).

On the third day of Jesus' burial and the first day of the week (Sunday), a group of women come at dawn to anoint Jesus' body, but they find the tomb empty (*4*). The soldiers have fled the scene but take a bribe to spread the story that Jesus' body was stolen by his disciples (*M*). Angels announce Jesus' resurrection to the women, and tell them to notify the disciples (*MmL*). On their way to do so, Jesus appears to some of them (*M*). Meanwhile, Mary Magdalene has notified Peter and John, who run to the tomb and find it empty (*J*). She follows them back to the tomb and there sees Jesus (*J*). Later in the day, Jesus appears to Peter (*L[m]*), then to two disciples on the way to a nearby village (*L[m]*). Returning quickly to Jerusalem, these disciples have just reported to the others when Jesus appears to the whole group (*LJ*).

Easter week ends at this point, but the Gospels and Acts recount several other appearances of Jesus after His resurrection. The first is a week later in Jerusalem to the disciples including Thomas (*J*). Later He appears to seven disciples by the Sea of Galilee as He had specified in advance (*M*). Finally there are two appearances in Jerusalem before His ascension (*LA*). Several years later Jesus appears to Stephen and to Paul (*A*).

Corroboration by Paul

Because the Apostle Paul does not give us a detailed account of the life of Jesus, some have erroneously assumed he had no interest in the subject. Instead, it is important to note that Paul's writings are all letters addressed to established churches. When Paul does mention certain details of Christ's life in his letters, his purpose is not biographical but doctrinal. He draws from Christ's life and teachings to clear up confusion in the churches.

Thus when the Thessalonian church is disturbed over claims that the end of the age has come, Paul repeats the substance of Jesus' teaching regarding His return. This material, according to the Gospels, Jesus gave on the Mount of Olives after leaving the temple for the last time. There are at least twenty-four detailed points of parallelism between Paul's comments in 1 and 2 Thessalonians and Jesus' Olivet Discourse as recorded in Matthew 24–25, Mark 13, and Luke 21.[49]

When, for example, the Corinthians are abusing the Lord's Supper, Paul describes its institution for them in some detail,[50] simply mentioning in passing that this occurred on the night Jesus was betrayed.

Paul speaks frequently of Jesus' death and its significance. Once he mentions that it was "the rulers of this age" who "crucified the Lord of glory."[51] Elsewhere he identifies these rulers as including Pontius Pilate[52] and the Jews.[53]

The post-resurrection appearances of Jesus are given by Paul to answer opponents in Corinth who denied bodily resurrection.[54] Paul's list of six appearances matches no other list in the Gospels but overlaps them all and is helpful in fitting them together.

Lastly, Paul speaks of Jesus' ascension in Romans 8:34 and 1 Timothy 3:16. Clearly, then, numerous details of Easter week through the ascension are corroborated in Paul's epistles.

Corroboration by Pagan Sources

References to Jesus are rare in surviving pagan literature from before about A.D. 150. Yet there are more references to Jesus than to Josephus or Pontius Pilate, two notable actors in first-century Palestine. We have two brief notices in Suetonius, one of which is uncertain;[55] one reference in Tacitus;[56] and another in Pliny the Younger.[57] In addition, a letter from a Syrian Stoic philosopher Mara to his son Serapion makes reference to Jesus.[58] These passages are given in full in Appendix 5.3b.

From these sources we learn the following information about Jesus, information more or less relevant to Easter week. According to Tacitus, Jesus lived in Judea when Tiberius was emperor and Pilate was governor of Judea (A.D. 26–36). He was a controversial teacher, as the Roman authors label His teaching "superstition" while Mara considers Him "wise." A claim to be Messiah was ascribed to Him: Roman historians know Him only by His title, "Christ," which they take to be His name; Mara calls Him a king. According to Tacitus, He was put to death by Pilate; Mara blames the Jews. According to Pliny, who was conducting trials of Christians in Asia Minor before A.D. 115, Jesus' followers worshiped Him as God, though they would not worship the gods of Rome. True Christians, according to Pliny, will die rather than curse Christ or offer incense to Caesar.

Corroboration by Jewish Sources

Among early Jewish sources, there are two references to Jesus in the Greek manuscripts of Josephus.[59] One of these has been questioned because it seems too Christian for Josephus (affirming Jesus' messiahship). Recently an epitome of this controversial passage was found in a tenth-century manuscript of an Arabic church history,[60] which provides an apparently less Christian version. The Babylonian Talmud, a compilation of the traditions of the rabbis, contains a number of cryptic references to Jesus and one definite one.[61] The definite reference, to which we confine our remarks, is known to pre-date A.D. 200. These passages are given in Appendix 5.3c.

According to Josephus, Jesus lived in Judea while Pontius Pilate was governor. The Talmud is consistent with this, but not very definite, merely locating Him in the Tannatic period (100 B.C.–A.D. 200). Jesus' character was controversial; He is viewed rather favorably by Josephus and negatively by the rabbis. Both Josephus and the Talmud report that He worked miracles, though the latter explains them as sorcery. According to both, He gathered followers, and Josephus notes these considered Him to be the Messiah. Both the Greek and Arabic Josephus say Jesus was crucified by Pilate. The Greek Josephus also involves the Jewish leaders in His condemnation. The Talmud sees the whole proceeding as Jewish, even giving the traditional form of execution (stoning and hanging) instead of the pagan crucifixion (which, however, the rabbis also called "hanging"). The Talmud dates the execution on Passover eve, in agreement with the Gospel of John. The Talmudic charge against Jesus is "sorcery" and "enticing Israel to apostasy." Josephus notes that Jesus' disciples reported His resurrection on the third day.

Discussion of Corroborations

These corroborations are significant in judging the trustworthiness of the Gospel accounts of Easter week. The Gospels themselves give hundreds of details, many of which are reported by two, three, or all four of the Gospels. Yet the number of divergences among the Gospel accounts—which opponents of their trustworthiness regularly recount— do not suggest that the writers tried to harmonize their accounts. In addition, the Apostle Paul, though attempting no narrative himself, corroborates dozens of both major and incidental details found in the Gospel accounts.

The pagan and Jewish sources agree with the Gospels and Paul on the date of Jesus' activities, their controversial nature, His miracles, His Messianic claim, and His death at the hands of both Roman and Jewish authorities. This is especially important in view of the fact that many today seek to deny that Jesus worked miracles, made a Messianic claim, or was put to death by Roman-Jewish cooperation. The historical sources which touch on the subject are all against them.

At first sight, the Talmud's charges against Jesus seem to differ from those of the Gospel accounts. Yet the Gospels mention an attempt at Jesus' trial to convict Him of offering to rebuild the temple in three days, which could easily be understood as sorcery. According to the Gospels, Jesus was actually condemned for blasphemy, because He claimed to be the Messiah, the Son of God. This may indeed be the "apostasy" to which Jesus "enticed Israel," according to the Talmud. In Jewish usage, a phrase like "Son of God" would be a claim to deity, a blasphemous apostasy in the eyes of most Jews. Pliny's note that Jesus' followers worshiped Him as God, though written by a polytheist, is in line with this suggestion.

There is no non-Christian corroboration for Jesus' resurrection having actually occurred, but this is hardly surprising, as any believer in Jesus' resurrection would be considered a Christian. Of course, any source could report the disciples' belief in Jesus' resurrection, and Josephus does. For a Roman, such a belief would merely be another Christian "superstition" (Tacitus, Suetonius, Pliny). A Stoic like Mara would also reject bodily resurrection, and the Talmud has chosen to ignore it. In any case, we know from Justin's debate with Trypho (in the 130s),[62] from the anti-Christian polemic of Celsus (ca. 180)[63] and from the Talmud[64] that the Jews were aware of the Christian Gospels, and from Matthew and Justin[65] that they sought to explain away the Resurrection as a case of body-snatching by the disciples.

The one significant divergence of the non-Christian materials from the Gospels involves the manner of Jesus' death. The Talmud says Jesus was "hanged" and "stoned and hanged." The Gospels speak of crucifixion, along with Paul and all Christian literature. This is supported by Josephus (both versions) and less directly by Tacitus, who has Jesus put to death by the Roman Pontius Pilate, presumably by a Roman method. Since the term "hanged" is used by the rabbis for crucifixion as well as for the traditional hanging up of the body after stoning to death,[66] it is not unreasonable to suppose the Talmud gives a somewhat garbled account, perhaps based on the facts that Jesus had a religious trial and was "hanged," but supplying other details from traditional practices.

Conclusions

We have looked at the four Gospel accounts of Easter week. We have noted the large amount of detail they have in common regarding the events of this period. The divergences they contain suggest they were not contrived to fit one another. To use the divergences to cast doubt on the historicity of events on which they obviously agree is a strange sort of historical methodology. These accounts find some detailed corroboration in the writings of Paul, a persecutor of Christians who himself became a Christian. In fact, significant corroboration occurs in several pagan and Jewish sources as well. This is more than can be said for most events reported from antiquity.

We have also examined traditional beliefs concerning the authorship of the four Gospels, i.e., that they were written by two apostles and by two apostolic disciples, all with substantial access to eyewitness testimony. The unanimity of substantial evidence for this tradition is impressive. This is more evidence than we have for the authorship of most ancient histories.

We have also examined the transmission of these narratives from their original writing to the advent of printing. It appears that they were copied with a care at least equal to that afforded the secular historians, and with a frequency so far exceeding those that a vast quantity of material exists for reconstructing their original readings. If there is any reason for confidence in having substantially the original texts for other ancient historians, we have more for the Gospels.

Of course, we can, if we wish, reject as untrustworthy any narratives containing miracles, but that is really to beg the question at the very places where the existence of miracles may be solved affirmatively. It is also possible to set our criteria for accepting the miraculous so high that no evidence from antiquity could ever satisfy us. This is surely unwise if our concern is to find out what really happened rather than to avoid a certain class of explanations because they are distasteful.

It is also possible to reject the Gospel materials as untrustworthy because of the controversial nature of the events they narrate. Remember, however, that the Gospels themselves make it clear that Jesus' words and actions were most controversial from the very beginning. If history is an attempt to find out what really did happen, we must investigate controversial events as well as mundane ones. We will often find that some of the most important events are also the most controversial, and that one side of a controversy, sincere or not, may be dead wrong.

We may also claim that the real picture of Jesus would be very different if we had more materials preserved from the opposition. The various forms of opposition had over three hundred years to make their cases, long before those who claim the name of Christian ever had the political power to oppose them. This damaging evidence could have been buried in jars or taken out of the Roman Empire for safekeeping. Where is it? It is more likely that the opposition had no real case better than "Tell the people his disciples stole the body while you were sleeping," so they chose to ignore Christianity when possible, and ridicule or persecute it when not.

Indeed, it is possible to claim that Christianity is a lie or delusion, but only by the more drastic handling of the historical data. If the first disciples were credulous, they certainly were clever enough to make themselves look pretty skeptical in the Gospel accounts. If they were liars, they must have put together the most impressive plot in history, and (as a by-product) accidentally created in Jesus one of the most unforgettable characters in fact or fiction.

Are the Gospel narratives of Easter week trustworthy? On the basis of such historical tests as do not beg the question of the miraculous, they stand up as well as any accounts from antiquity.

Appendix 5.3a: A Comparison of Some Ancient Historical Writings[67]

Author and Work	Author's Lifespan	Date of Events	Date of Writing*	Earliest Extant Manuscript**	Lapse of Event to Writing	Lapse of Event to Manuscript
Matthew, *Gospel*	ca. A.D. 0–70?	4 B.C.–A.D. 30	50–65/75	ca. 200	<50	<200
Mark, *Gospel*	ca. A.D. 15–90?	A.D. 27–30	65/70	ca. 225	<50	<200
Luke, *Gospel*	ca. A.D. 10–80?	5 B.C.–A.D. 30	60/75	ca. 200	<50	<200
John, *Gospel*	ca. A.D. 10–100	A.D. 27–30	90/110	ca. 130	<80	<100
Paul, *Letters*	ca. A.D. 0–65	A.D. 30	50–65	ca. 200	20–35	<200
Josephus, *War*	ca. A.D. 37–100	200 B.C.–A.D. 70	ca. 80	ca. 950	10–300	900–1200
Josephus, *Antiquities*	ca. A.D. 37–100	200 B.C.–A.D. 65	ca. 95	ca. 1050	30–300	1000–1300
Tacitus, *Annals*	ca. A.D. 56–120	A.D. 14–68	100–120	ca. 850	30–100	800–850
Suetonius, *Lives*	ca. A.D. 69–130	50 B.C.–A.D. 95	ca. 120	ca. 850	25–170	750–900
Pliny, *Letters*	ca. A.D. 60–115	A.D. 97–112	100–112	ca. 850	0–3	725–750
Plutarch, *Lives*	ca. A.D. 50–120	500 B.C.–A.D. 70	ca. 100	ca. 950	30–600	850–1500
Herodotus, *History*	ca. 485–425 B.C.	546–478 B.C.	430–425 B.C.	ca. 900	50–125	1400–1450
Thucydides, *History*	ca. 460–400 B.C.	431–411 B.C.	410–400 B.C.	ca. 900	0–30	1300–1350
Xenophon, *Anabasis*	ca. 430–355 B.C.	401–399 B.C.	385–375 B.C.	ca. 1350	15–25	1750
Polybius, *History*	ca. 200–120 B.C.	220–168 B.C.	ca. 150 B.C.	ca. 950	20–70	1100–1150

*Where slash occurs, first date is conservative, second is liberal.

**New Testament manuscripts are fragmentary. (Earliest complete manuscript is from ca. 350; lapse of event to complete manuscript is about 325 years.)

Appendix 5.3b: Pagan Sources on Jesus

Gaius Suetonius, *Lives of the Twelve Caesars:*

He expelled the Jews from Rome, on account of riots in which they were constantly indulging, at the instigation of Chrestus. (*Claudius* 25.4)

Punishment was inflicted on the Christians, a body of people addicted to a novel and mischievous superstition. (*Nero* 16.2)

Cornelius Tacitus, *Annals:*

But neither the aid of men, nor the emperor's bounty, nor propitiatory offerings to the gods, could remove the grim suspicion that the fire had been started by Nero's order. To put an end to this rumor, he shifted the charge on to others, and inflicted the most cruel tortures upon a group of people detested for their abominations, and popularly known as "Christians." Their name came from one Christus, who was put to death in the principate of Tiberius by the Procurator Pontius Pilate. Though checked for a time, the destructive superstition broke out again, not in Judaea only, where its mischief began, but even in Rome, where every abominable and shameful iniquity, from all the world, pours in and finds a welcome. (15.44)

Mara bar Serapion, *Letter to His Son Serapion:*

What advantage did the Athenians gain from putting Socrates to death? Famine and plague came upon them as a judgment for their crime. What advantage did the men of Samos gain from burning Pythagoras? In a moment their land was covered with sand. What advantage did the Jews gain from executing their wise king? It was just after that that their kingdom was abolished. God justly avenged these three wise men: the Athenians died of hunger; the Samians were overwhelmed by the sea; the Jews, ruined and driven from their land, live in complete dispersion. But Socrates did not die for good; he lived on in the teaching of Plato. Pythagoras did not die for good; he lived on in the statue of Hera. Nor did the wise king die for good; he lived on in the teaching which he had given.

Pliny the Younger, *Letters*

To Trajan:

It is my rule, Sire, to refer to you in matters where I am uncertain. For who can better direct my hesitation or instruct my ignorance? I was never present at any trial of Christians; therefore I do not know what are the customary penalties or investigations, and what limits are observed. I have hesitated a great deal on the question whether there should be any distinction of ages; whether the weak should have the same treatment as the most robust; whether those who recant should be pardoned, or whether a man who has ever been a Christian should gain nothing by ceasing to be such; whether the name itself, even if innocent of crime, should be punished, or only the crimes attaching to that name. Meanwhile, this is the course that I have adopted in the case of those brought before me as Christians. I ask them if they are Christians. If they admit it I repeat the question a second and a third time, threatening capital punishment; if they persist I sentence them to death. . . . All who denied that they were or had been Christians I considered should be discharged, because they called upon the gods at my dictation and did reverence, with incense and wine, to your image . . . and especially because they cursed Christ, a thing which, it is said, genuine Christians cannot be induced to do. Others named by the informer first said they were Christians and then denied it, declaring that they had been but were no longer, some having recanted three years or more before and one or two as long ago as twenty years. They all worshiped your image and the statues of the gods and cursed Christ. But they declared that the sum of their guilt or error had amounted only to this, that on an appointed day they had been accustomed to meet before daybreak, and to recite a hymn antiphonally to Christ, as to a god, and to bind themselves by an oath, not for the commission of any crime but to abstain from theft, robbery, adultery and breach of faith and not to deny a deposit when it was claimed. After the conclusion of this ceremony it was their custom to depart and meet again to take food; but it was ordinary and harmless food, and they had ceased this practice after my edict in which, in accordance with your orders, I had forbidden secret societies. I thought it the more necessary, therefore, to find out what truth there was in this by applying torture to two maidservants, who were called deaconesses. But I found nothing but a depraved and extravagant superstition, and I therefore postponed my examination and had recourse to you for consultation. (10.96)

Trajan's Reply:

The method you have pursued, my dear Pliny, in sifting the cases of those denounced to you as Christians is extremely proper. It is not possible to lay down any general rule which can be applied as the fixed standard in all cases of this nature. No search should be made for these people; when they are denounced and found guilty they must be punished; with the restriction, however, that when the party denies himself to be a Christian, and shall give proof that he is not, that is by adoring our gods, he shall be pardoned on the ground of repentance, even though he may have formerly incurred suspicion. Informations without the accuser's name subscribed must not be admitted in evidence against anyone, as it is introducing a very dangerous precedent, and by no means agreeable to the spirit of the age. (10.97)

Appendix 5.3c: Jewish Sources on Jesus

Flavius Josephus, *Antiquities:*

He [Annas the Younger] convened a judicial session of the Sanhedrin and brought before it the brother of Jesus the so-called Christ—James by name—and some others, whom he charged with breaking the law and handed over to be stoned to death. (20.200 or 20.9.1)

Now, there was about this time Jesus, a wise man, if it be lawful to call him a man, for he was a doer of wonderful works, a teacher of such men as receive the truth with pleasure. He drew over to him both many of the Jews and many of the Gentiles. He was the Christ. And when Pilate, at the suggestion of the principal men amongst us, had condemned him to the cross, those who loved him at the first did not forsake him, for he appeared to them alive again at the third day, as the divine prophets had foretold these and 10,000 other wonderful things concerning him. And the tribe of Christians, so named from him, are not extinct at this day. (18.63–64 or 18.3.3)

Agapius, *Universal History:*

At this time there was a wise man who was called Jesus. And his conduct was good and he was known to be virtuous. And many people from among the Jews and other nations became his disciples. Pilate condemned him to be crucified and to die. And those who had become his disciples did not abandon his discipleship. They reported that he had appeared to them three days after his crucifixion and that he was alive. Accordingly he was perhaps the Messiah concerning whom the prophets have recounted wonders. (Arabic version of above passage)

Babylonian Talmud:

On the eve of Passover Yeshua was hanged. For forty days before the execution a herald went forth and cried, "He is going to be stoned because he has practiced sorcery and enticed Israel to apostasy. Anyone who can say anything in his favor, let him come forward and plead on his behalf." But since nothing was brought forward in his favor he was hanged on the eve of Passover. (Sanhedrin 43a)

Notes

[1]David Hume, *An Enquiry Concerning Human Understanding* (1748), sec. 10.

[2]Ibid.

[3]Rudolf Bultmann, *Jesus Christ and Mythology* (New York: Scribners, 1958), 15.

[4]See, e.g., Paul Davies and J. Brown, eds., *The Ghost in the Atom* (New York: Cambridge University Press, 1986), 31–39; Nick Herbert, *Quantum Reality* (New York: Doubleday, 1985), 16–29, 41–53.

[5]For further discussion of this point, see my papers "A Critical Examination of Modern Cosmological Theories," *IBRI Research Reports* 15 (1982); and "A Critique of Carl Sagan's TV Series and Book *Cosmos*," *IBRI Research Reports* 19 (1984).

[6]Robert Jastrow, *Until the Sun Dies* (New York: Norton, 1977), chaps. 1–4.

[7]Adolf Harnack, *What Is Christianity?* (New York: Harper and Row, 1957), 25.

[8]Ibid., 24.

[9]Flavius Josephus *Against Apion* 1.8; 1 Macc. 4:46; 9:27; 14:41.

[10]John 10:41.

[11]Besides our discussion to follow, the following works provide helpful material on the reliability of the Gospel narratives: John Warwick Montgomery, *Where is History Going?* (Minneapolis, Minn.: Bethany, 1969); idem, *History and Christianity* (Minneapolis, Minn.: Bethany, 1985); F. F. Bruce, *The New Testament Documents: Are they Reliable?* (Grand Rapids, Mich.: Eerdmans, 1960); Gary R. Habermas, *The Verdict of History* (1984; reprint, Nashville, Tenn.: Thomas Nelson, 1988); R. T. France, *The Evidence for Jesus* (Downers Grove, Ill.: InterVarsity, 1986); Craig Blomberg, *The Historical Reliability of the Gospels* (Downers Grove, Ill.: InterVarsity, 1987).

[12]Most of the material on these works comes from *The Oxford Classical Dictionary*, 2d ed. (Oxford: Clarendon Press, 1970); *Harper's Dictionary of Classical Literature and Antiquities*, 2d ed. (New York: Cooper-Square, 1965); or the relevant editions of each work in the Loeb Classical Library.

[13]Bruce M. Metzger, *The Text of the New Testament* (New York: Oxford, 1968), chap. 2; for details on the papyri, see 246–56; Kurt Aland and Barbara Aland, *The Text of the New Testament* (Grand Rapids, Mich.: Eerdmans; Leiden: E. J. Brill, 1987), chap. 3.

[14]Jose O'Callaghan, "Papiros neotestamentarios en las cueva 7 de Qumran?" *Biblica* 53 (1972): 91–100. See discussion and bibliography on this in *The New International Dictionary of Biblical Archaeology* (1983), s.v. "Qumran New Testament Fragments."

[15]Bruce M. Metzger, *Chapters in the History of New Testament Textual Criticism* (Leiden: Brill, 1963), 145.

[16]B. F. Westcott and F. J. A. Hort, eds., *The New Testament in the Original Greek* (New York: Harper and Brothers, 1882), 2:2.

[17]Ezra Abbot, *The Authorship of the Fourth Gospel, With Other Critical Essays* (Boston: Ellis, 1888).

[18]Metzger, *Chapters*, 148–50.

[19]Frederic G. Kenyon, *Our Bible and the Ancient Manuscripts* (New York: Harper and Brothers, 1941), 23.

[20]Luke 1:1–4. All quotations from Scripture in this chapter are from the New International Version of the Bible, copyright 1978 by the New York International Bible Society.

[21] John 21:24.

[22] Recorded in Eusebius *Church History* 3.39.15–16.

[23] Justin *Apology* 1.33, 66, 67; idem, *Dialogue with Trypho* 100–104, 105, 106, 107.

[24] Justin *Dialogue* 103.7.

[25] Ibid., 106.3.

[26] Johannes Quasten, *Patrology* (Westminster, Md.: Newman Press, 1950), 1:202–3; F. L. Cross, ed., *Oxford Dictionary of the Christian Church* (1957), s.v. "Justin Martyr, St."

[27] Text in Henry Bettenson, ed., *Documents of the Christian Church* (London: Oxford, 1963), 40–41; J. Stevenson, ed., *A New Eusebius* (London: SPCK, 1963), 144–47.

[28] Irenaeus *Against Heresies* 3.1.2.

[29] Clement *Outlines,* cited in Eusebius *Church History* 6.14.5; Origen *Commentary on Matthew 1,* cited in Eusebius 6.25.3ff.

[30] Mark 14:51–52.

[31] Col. 4:14.

[32] William K. Hobart, *The Medical Language of St. Luke* (Grand Rapids, Mich.: Baker Book House, 1954).

[33] Clement 47, 34.

[34] Matt. 7:15; Mark 13:22; Gal. 1:8; 1 Thess. 5:21; 2 Pet. 2:1; 1 John 4:1.

[35] 2 Thess. 2:2, 15; 3:17.

[36] R. N. Longenecker, "Ancient Amanuenses and the Pauline Epistles," in *New Dimensions in New Testament Study,* ed. R. N. Longenecker and Merrill C. Tenney (Grand Rapids, Mich.: Zondervan, 1974).

[37] Tertullian *On Baptism* 17.

[38] 2 Tim. 2:2. (Emphasis mine.)

[39] Luke 1:1–4.

[40] F. J. Foakes-Jackson, *Josephus and the Jews* (Grand Rapids, Mich.: Baker Book House, 1977), xi, xv.

[41] *Oxford Classical Dictionary,* 1034.

[42] Ibid., 1021.

[43] Ibid., 846.

[44] Ibid., 849.

[45] Ibid., 508–9; *Harper's Dictionary,* 806.

[46] *Oxford Classical Dictionary,* 1142–42.

[47] Ibid., 853–54.

[48] A. N. Sherwin-White, *Roman Society and Roman Law in the New Testament* (Oxford: Clarendon Press, 1963), 187.

[49] G. Henry Waterman, "The Sources of Paul's Teaching on the 2nd Coming of Christ in 1 and 2 Thessalonians," *Journal of the Evangelical Theological Society* 18 (1975): 105–13.

[50] 1 Cor. 11:23–26.

[51] 1 Cor. 2:8.

[52] 1 Tim. 6:13.

[53]1 Thess. 2:14–15.

[54]1 Cor. 15:1–11.

[55]*Nero* 16.2 and *Claudius* 25.4 in Suetonius *Lives of the Twelve Caesars.*

[56]Tacitus *Annals* 15.44.

[57]Pliny the Younger *Letters* 10.96.

[58]The text of Mara may be found in F. F. Bruce, *Jesus and Christian Origins Outside the New Testament* (Grand Rapids, Mich.: Eerdmans, 1974), 31.

[59]Flavius Josephus *Antiquities* 20.200; 18.63–64.

[60]Shlomo Pines, *An Arabic Version of the Testimonium Flavianum and Its Implications* (Jerusalem: Israel Academy of Science and Humanities, 1971), 9–10.

[61]Babylonian Talmud, Sanh 43a; more cryptic passages are discussed in Bruce, *Jesus and Christian Origins,* chap. 4; R. T. Herford, *Christianity in the Talmud and Midrash* (Clifton, N.J.: Reference Book Publishers, 1966); and Joseph Klausner, *Jesus of Nazareth* (New York: Macmillan, 1925).

[62]Justin *Dialogue* 10.

[63]Origen *Against Celsus* 2.27, 49, 74.

[64]Babylonian Talmud, Shab 116a.

[65]Matt. 28:13; Justin *Dialogue,* 108.

[66]*Tosefta,* Sanh 9.7.

[67]For biblical data, see the standard New Testament introductions, e.g., Donald Guthrie, *New Testament Introduction* (Downers Grove, Ill.: InterVarsity, 1971); W. G. Kuemmel, *Introduction to the New Testament* (London: SCM, 1966). For the classical data, see *The Oxford Classical Dictionary; Harper's Dictionary of Classical Literature and Antiquities;* and the relevant editions of each author in the Loeb Classical Library.

Part 6

A Time for Decision

6.1

Why Isn't the Evidence Clearer?

John A. Bloom

WHY ISN'T THE EVIDENCE CLEAR ENOUGH to prove beyond any doubt that the God of the Bible exists and that the Christian message is true? In keeping with the satire of Carl Sagan in his recent book, *Contact*,[1] why isn't there a glowing cross in the sky at night to serve as irrefutable proof of Jesus' resurrection? Perhaps one could continue this further and ask why God doesn't have His own television channel and toll-free "hotline" telephone number?

Unfortunately, the quality of the evidence that validates the biblical Christian position is not enhanced by the subjective appeals made by many believers. While I would heartily agree that "Jesus lives in my heart and has radically changed my life," such testimony carries little weight when applied to another person. Such "Try it, you'll like it" appeals come across as circular arguments unless they can be backed with evidence which is external to the individual.

Despite Sagan's ridicule, I think he does have a legitimate point which we need to consider. Why must we read a two-thousand-year-old book and study ancient history for proof of the existence of God? Why isn't the evidence for the existence of the God of the Bible painted across the sky in a form that is obvious to everyone, no matter how rebellious or sin-blinded he is? This question should be addressed seriously, and, as we do so in this brief discussion, I think we will find that the answer is more profound than many realize. Of course, I will only attempt to answer this question for the God of the Bible and evangelical Christianity, and let other religions (liberal "Christianity," Buddhism, etc.) speak for themselves.

My approach may shock some liberal scholars because I will work with the hypothesis that the biblical accounts are basically historical. However, a moment's reflection shows that this assumption is a necessary corollary to the question at hand, because what we are really asking here is, Are there any reasons for the evidence to appear obscure other than the possibility that the God of the Bible does not exist? While the purpose of the different arguments in this book is to justify the hypothesis that the God of the Bible does exist, for purposes of this discussion, let us temporarily take the agnostic position. Therefore, if the God of the Bible really exists, and if the Bible is basically accurate in matters of history (as the God of the Bible says it is), then why hasn't He made the evidence for His existence clearer? Are there any reasons for the evidence to appear obscure other than the possibility that the God of the Bible does not exist?

It would be a mistake to deduce from the above comments that the evidence for the truth of the Bible is marginal, meager, or non-existent, or that a person should not think critically when evaluating the nature of the biblical evidence. For example, the following are what I would consider to be reasonable demands for any set of evidence: First, the evidence should be clear enough to be intellectually sound at the certainty level at which one operates when making other important decisions. Nothing can be proven 100 percent, yet this residual uncertainty or doubt does not hinder the average person from performing normal day-to-day tasks. For example, one tries not to step in front of cars when crossing the street. Although a person can never have absolute proof that no cars are approaching, most people—even existential philosophers—learn to trust their senses enough to risk their lives on the basis of reasonable evidence that they can cross safely. Second, the evidence must be clear enough to select Christianity over the truth/proof claims of other religions. If the evidence for the truth of Christianity is no greater than that for any other religion, we cannot reasonably claim it to be more trustworthy.

Some might be tempted to apply the rule, "the more critical the decision, the more clear the evidence must be," to the religious arena. Consequently, they would demand that the evidence for Christianity must be extraordinarily and especially clear in order for it to win their allegiance, not merely that it be "the most trustworthy." The fault with this "more critical/more clear" logic is that it assumes a neutral observer—one who would not be affected personally by the decision at hand. In a court of law, it is reasonable for the jury (neutral observers) to demand clearer evidence when a death sentence is at stake rather than a jail term.

However, in biblical Christianity, no one is a neutral observer, for withholding acceptance is *de facto* rejection. In cases where agnosticism has consequences, an observer cannot demand extraordinary evidence, but merely sufficient evidence. For example, a paranoid person who is fearful of being poisoned by his enemies does not have the leisure to apply this "more critical/more clear" rule, for if he waits for clear evidence that his food is not poisoned, he may starve to death anyhow. Consequently he must eat what he has determined to be the most trustworthy food, for he could very well die if he held out for exhaustive analysis or extraordinary evidence.

Therefore, when considering biblical Christianity, the more appropriate rule to apply is: "The more severe the consequences, the less we should take risks." Even if biblical Christianity has less than a one-in-ten-million chance of being true, we should believe it and live in the light of it because the possibility of an eternal hell is such a great torment.[2] If the available evidence shows that biblical Christianity is "the most trustworthy" of all religions, then we are on even firmer ground.

The basic question, however, still stands: "Why isn't the evidence for the existence of the God of the Bible clearer and more obvious?" I would like to consider this question from several perspectives.

The Scientific Perspective

The chief task of the scientist is to comb through "raw" data in order to extract usable information from it. From this information he constructs a hypothesis which he tests against the original data and against new data derived from experiments which his hypothesis predicts should be helpful. While it is all too often the case that a rigorous conclusion cannot be reached because the available data are inadequate or ambiguous, it is a very poor methodology to abandon research in a particular area because "ideal data"[3] are not available. Indeed, the natural order rarely produces such ideal data, nor does it provide simple and obvious answers for such basic questions as the nature of light, the behavior of electrons in conductors, or the structure of subatomic particles. Such complexity in the physical universe should make us wonder if we can expect the God who claims to be its Creator to be less simple.

A scientist should be a healthy skeptic, and he or she should desire controls in experimentation, carefully double-checking all results. However, the extremely skeptical position of demanding "a glowing cross in the sky" cannot be considered scientific. It is like requiring that a person go into space and bring a galaxy back to earth for study in a lab before one can be really sure of its existence. After all, aren't galaxies only visible at night to a few esoteric individuals who themselves must use special, expensive, and rare instruments in order to see them? Further, how could one demonstrate to such a skeptic that the heavier elements are synthesized in the cores of exploding stars?

It is unfortunate that many people consider someone to be a brilliant scholar if he doubts the authority of the Ten Commandments because they are not written on the surface of the moon; but someone who doubts the authority of the periodic table because it is not written on the surface of the moon they would regard as an idiot. Since the degree of skepticism exercised by each person is the same, why are these skeptics judged differently? Because in science one must place practical limits on his skepticism and recognize that clarity is relative, not absolute. It is not scientific to abandon an area of research because the data do not satisfy some arbitrarily-chosen or absolute level of clarity.

The clarity and conclusiveness of experimental data must be judged relative to two factors: competition and random events. By *competition* I refer to alternate mechanisms which can account for the observed phenomena just as well as the favored hypothesis. Stated more simply, competition occurs when the data are not clear enough to choose between any of several explanations for the observation. In our case, the clarity of the evidence for the truth of biblical Christianity would be obscured by competition from other religions if any of them had comparable evidence to support their truth claims. By *random events,* I refer to noise, "flukes," or variable results which can render experimental data statistically insignificant. This is the explanation which atheists propose for biblical miracles: They are unusual events which are misinterpreted in the Bible but are in reality nothing more than random events. To summarize, no serious scientist would ask, "Why aren't the data clearer?" What he would demand is that the evidence be clear enough to be significant in the light of all possible competing mechanisms, including random events.

If a scientist could design his own data, doubtless he would pick the ideal, irrefutable sort. However, scientists have found long ago that they can learn more about the universe by studying the evidence which *is* available than by abandoning a topic until the data are perfect and the conclusions drawn from them are philosophically irrefutable.

The Historical Perspective

Arguments based on a "Why isn't it clearer?" foundation can appear stronger than they are because of the distortions inherent in recording history. For example, a casual reading of the Bible might lead one to the conclusion that miracles were a daily occurrence in ancient Israel. Thus their absence in modern times could lead one to conclude that "God is dead" or that modern man is more sophisticated and does not perceive certain events at which the ancients would have marveled (lightning, the seasons of the year, etc.) as miraculous. However, a little study shows that the impression we have of "daily miracles" in biblical times is an artifact due to the compression of the historical portions of the biblical record. Miracles were rare in Israel's history and were mainly clustered around four specific points: Moses and the Exodus, the time of Elijah and Elisha, the lives of Jesus and the Apostles, and the coming Return of Christ. Between these clusters are centuries-long gaps of "normal living": the slavery in Egypt, most of the period of the Judges, the inter-testament period, and our present age. In the text we see indications that miracles or divine interventions were quite rare.[4] In fact, rituals like the Passover Seder were often established to preserve the remembrance of miraculous historical events.[5]

Thus the miracles recorded in the Bible did not occur every day, but only around specific times in ancient history and then usually in conjunction with the disclosure of additional divine revelation that was written down to be preserved. For us to expect miracles today or to feel neglected by God because we are not inundated with them is only the artificial result of the compression of ancient historical accounts. In order to have manageably-sized records that could be transmitted by hand-copying, the mundane material had to be omitted.

Another historical observation is that most biblical miracles did not occur in the more sophisticated population centers (Palestine, when compared to the great Mesopotamian and Egyptian cultures, was a "rural" area). On the other hand, we do have recorded the miraculous events surrounding Moses before Pharaoh in Egypt and Daniel with the kings of the powerful Neo-Babylonian empire. Moreover, there is grudging extrabiblical evidence from the "enemy" side about some of these miracles, as we find with Sennacherib's attack on Jerusalem.[6] Although many miracles did not take place in major urban centers, they were not hidden from view, either. As far as we can tell, all biblical miracles were open to investigation and confirmation in their own age and territory. That Paul can testify before local Roman authorities that the miraculous events surrounding the life of Jesus were not "done in a corner"[7] implies that the leaders were well aware of them. Thus the evidence was publicly and adequately substantiated, but only rarely did a miracle occur in a center of civilization.

What is important to learn from this historical perspective is that we should not expect God to work spectacular miracles in New York City today, if Jesus did not do them before Caesar in Rome. Only at rare moments in history did the God of the Bible act so as to catch the immediate attention of millions of people. Why this is so will be apparent from our next vantage point.

God's Perspective

God's perspective is probably the most important viewpoint to consider because it looks at the situation from other than the human perspective. In posing a "Why isn't the evidence clearer?" question, the skeptic is assuming that a god, if he existed, would try as hard as possible to make his existence obvious to us. This assumption appears reasonable because somehow we see no reason why an all-powerful god should not try desperately to make himself known to us, especially if the consequences of ignoring him are very severe. However, this assumption ignores the possibility that an all-powerful god may temporarily make himself relatively "invisible" in order to achieve a goal which is more important to him than merely convincing every last human being that he exists.

That the God of the Bible may be more sophisticated in this area than we think He is becomes evident when we look at His expressed reasons for His relative silence. Repeatedly we find the God of the Bible stating that He is in no way dependent upon mankind.[8] Such independence is quite contrary to most ancient thought, which claimed that the gods made man because they were in need of servants. It also runs counter to much modern thought which argues that God made man because He was lonely or did not have anyone around to appreciate or love Him. However, the God of the Bible does not reveal Himself to us for egotistical reasons or to satisfy any inner need for fame or worship. That He reveals Himself at all is only for our benefit, not for His.[9]

But even if He reveals Himself only to benefit us, why isn't He more forthright about it? The answer is this: If He made His presence too obvious, it would interfere with His demonstration, which is intended to draw out or reveal the true inner character of mankind. That the God of the Bible has this purpose for maintaining a relative silence is clear from several passages: "Was I not silent even for a long time so you do not fear Me?"[10] "These things you have done, and I kept silence; you thought that I was just like you; I will reprove you, and state the case in order before your eyes."[11] "Because the sentence against an evil deed is not executed quickly, therefore the hearts of the sons of men among them are given fully to evil."[12]

From these statements we get the picture, not that God is struggling desperately but vainly to get man's attention, but rather that He is restraining Himself in order to demonstrate to us something about *our* inner character. We might call this "the Sheriff in the tavern" principle:

People tend to be good when they think they are being watched by an authority. If a Sheriff wants to find out who the troublemakers are in a tavern (or if he wants to make them evident to others), he must either hide or appear to be an ineffective wimp, otherwise the bad guys will behave as well as everyone else. Any mother with young children is familiar with this principle, since she is well aware that they behave better when they think she is around.

This restraint strategy of the God of the Bible makes better sense in light of the coming Day of Judgment: if God is going to accuse men of being evil, His case will be greatly strengthened if men have been allowed to carry out their evil deeds and to display publicly their evil intentions. However, if God were to put a big cross in the sky or if He were to strike blasphemers dead with lightning bolts, He would merely frighten people into acting good. While this would greatly improve living conditions on earth (virtually putting an end to crime and false religions), it would not satisfy God's stated intent—to allow man to exhibit the contrast between good and evil, clearly and concretely.[13]

Like the Sheriff, who allows a fight to break out in the tavern in order to have the best possible evidence against the troublemakers, God has decided to either hide Himself from, or appear as an ineffective wimp to, evil men so that they will do evil acts. Of course we should not push this analogy too far: God does not need to see men's evil actions in order to accurately judge them. Moreover, He has not stated His full reasons for allowing men to demonstrate their evil intent through their actions. The point here is to find models so that we as humans can appreciate to some degree why God has chosen to run the world the way He has.

So why isn't the evidence clearer? To use another analogy, it is because God is a good scientist who does not want to perturb His experiment by intruding into it. The problem of perturbing an experiment while measuring it is the bane of the experimental sciences. While it is painfully obvious at the level of quantum mechanics, it applies to all systems in that any and every measurement changes and thus distorts to some degree the system it measures. That God should choose to work within similar constraints as these in His dealings with mankind is not logically impossible. Of course, we should not push this analogy too far either: God is running a public demonstration, not a physical experiment. The uncertainty principle is hardly applicable to God's dealings with mankind.

The Human Perspective

The final viewpoint which we need to consider in the clarity problem is the human factor that is involved whenever a person tries to judge the quality of the evidence. One does not have to live very long to realize that people often distort facts in order to make them appear to work in their favor. The method can be statistical, or involve "selective forgetfulness," but human ingenuity finds a way to bend the truth—whether it be selling used cars, padding calculations of corporate profit, or cheating on one's income tax.

In order to verify His existence, God has given human beings sufficient evidence that He exists. However, we should not be surprised when we find that many people often distort the evidence that God has already given them (yet keep demanding more). This happens because whenever evidence points toward an authority other than themselves, those who wish to deny that anything could be more intelligent or authoritative than the protoplasm within their skulls will attempt to dismiss it.

Given this tendency on the part of man, how clear does the evidence have to be before people would universally recognize the existence of the God of the Bible? Would a cross in the sky actually be sufficient? Would a personal appearance of Jesus on *The Tonight Show* suffice? Would the performance of an undeniable miracle in a scoffer's presence be enough? However impressive such feats would be, the records of history show that most people choose to ignore whatever evidence they have, no matter how clear it may be.

We find that during the wilderness wanderings, the Israelites, who had personally observed the miracles in Egypt and who were being fed and guided daily by miraculous means (manna and the pillar of fire), repeatedly rebelled against the God-directed leadership of Moses.[14] We find that the miracles performed by Elijah and Elisha were not sufficient to convert the Northern Kingdom of Israel to unperverted forms of biblical worship.[15] Even in New Testament times, we find arguments in the crowds surrounding Jesus as to whether God the Father spoke to Him from heaven or if the noise everyone heard was merely some un-seasonable thunder.[16] After Jesus healed a blind man[17] and raised Lazarus from the dead,[18] the Jewish leaders wanted to kill Him although they could not dispute the genuineness of His miracles.[19]

In His account of an unnamed rich man and a poor man named Lazarus, Jesus Himself makes our point clear: The rich man, now in hell, pleads with Abraham to send Lazarus back from the dead to warn his brothers so they will not face the same torment that he is experiencing. Abraham replies, "If they do not listen to Moses and the Prophets, they will not be convinced even if someone rises from the dead."[20]

Looking from this human perspective, why isn't the evidence clearer? Because God knows, and has already demonstrated in history, that no matter how clear He makes the evidence, it will never be sufficient for some. More evidence by itself will not convince people whose minds are already emotionally attached to an opposing view, because people are not always rational. The mind is all too much the servant of the desired fantasy.

Is God frustrated and defeated by this state of affairs: that man is so sinful that he will not pay attention to God no matter how big the flag is that God waves in front of him? Only if we assume that God's purpose in giving evidence is to convert everyone. To understand this idea better, we need to approach it from a different direction. Let's first review where we have been.

Results

We have analyzed from several viewpoints the question of "Why isn't the evidence that would prove the existence of the God of the Bible clearer?"

Scientifically, we noted that this question reflects a poor methodology and may even beg the question by demanding ideal data in order to avoid heeding the data which are available. We saw that a proper scientific approach recognizes that clarity is a relative, not an absolute feature and would ask instead, "Is the available evidence clear enough with respect to alternative explanations or random causes that any firm conclusions can be drawn from it?"

Historically, we saw that we should not be embarrassed by God's relative silence in modern times because this silence is consistent with most of the past.

We then saw that the God of the Bible is not seeking to make His presence compellingly obvious because this would curb men's desire to do evil publicly. While a dramatic show of His presence might improve living conditions on earth now, God would then have to base His future judgment of evil people on less explicit grounds.

Finally, we saw that because men may distort data to their own seeming advantage, they will tend to obscure any evidence which hints that there is an authority or power greater than themselves, especially one which they cannot control and to which they should be subject.

Given this state of affairs, that the God of the Bible does not intend to make His presence so obvious that it curbs the actions of evil men, and that most men will ignore whatever evidence they receive anyway, why does God bother to give any evidence at all? Why doesn't He hide Himself even better? From the Bible we deduce that God gives the level of evidence He does for two reasons:

Grace
Some people will repent upon seeing evidence, although people have different levels of "what it takes to get them to believe" in the God of the

Bible. With some people this level is very low, with others it is high,[21] but in any case it is known to God.[22] God, being in sovereign control of things, will see that those people He wants to repent will get a sufficient level of evidence no matter what their "belief threshold" is. He can withhold evidence from gullible people (by teaching in parables)[23] and strike professional scoffers miraculously (as with Paul on the road to Damascus)[24] so that the individuals He has sovereignly chosen will repent. We also see that some people will get more evidence than would have been needed to convert others, yet they still will not repent.[25] To use biblical terminology, evidence is one means which God uses to call His elect to repentance effectively.

Accountability

Despite the varying levels of evidence to which people are exposed throughout various times and cultures, God states that He has given each person enough so that they know better than to continue doing evil.[26] Given the willful rejection of the evidence which they *do* receive, God is not obligated to provide more. It would be as if someone needing a free car turns down the offer of a good used vehicle; would anyone then feel *obligated* to offer him a chauffeured limousine?

What is this basic evidence which is given to all people? At the very least it includes God's glory as seen in nature,[27] evidence which we obscure in our day and age by ascribing it to less personally demanding causes like "chance" or the "laws of nature."

However we might feel about it, God says that the evidence He provides to each and every human being is clear enough that he or she is morally responsible to respond to it. As we noted above, this is why God is not frustrated that everyone does not respond to His evidence: His goal is not to give everyone overwhelming evidence, but to give sufficient evidence that every human being is responsible to respond to it. And if the biblical message is correct, He will be the one to whom we will have to answer for ignoring it. That will be a very difficult position to be in, somewhat like arguing with a judge over a speeding ticket: How can we say we did not see the sign when the judge himself posted it? How much more foolish would we be if we tried to argue that we saw it but thought it was too small and quaint to take seriously?

This brings us to one main purpose for miracles and for all other biblical evidence: a miracle is a warning sign to get us to pay attention to the associated message. Before we brush off a miracle as inconsequential, we must look at the message being conveyed in it and ask ourselves how great the risk is of ignoring that message. Are we dealing with merely an advisory speed limit for negotiating a sharp curve (which is usually an underestimate), or is it a warning that the bridge is out ahead? Wouldn't we consider ourselves careless if we accelerated while passing a "Bridge Out" sign because we thought the sign seemed a little too small?

Yet the warning God conveys through these miracles is far worse than a bridge being out. There is an eternal torment facing those who brush aside the commands to humble ourselves properly before the God of the Bible and become His willing subjects, especially in view of the forgiveness which He offers for all our evil deeds. Just how clear does the evidence have to be before we will stop risking our eternal destiny in the face of such a fate? How blind and vain are we to brush aside continually the evidence that there is Someone out there who is wiser and more powerful than we are—especially as He has our best interests at heart and will richly forgive us if we will but humble ourselves and acknowledge His righteous lordship over us?

Certainly we do not want to con ourselves into thinking there is a God out there to be reckoned with when we could better spend our time eating, drinking, and being merry. But what we finally must ask ourselves is this: Is the evidence so ambiguous and ill-defined that we can safely ignore the warning message that comes with it?

To this question there are two responses: The first is like that which we see in the Pharisees when they challenged Jesus in Matthew 12:38–39.[28] From Jesus' response, we deduce that some people are like the Pharisees, who brush aside the evidence they do receive and who wish to challenge God by demanding that He perform a miracle impressive enough to force them to believe His warnings. Such people may remain disappointed— and eternally damned—because God does not feel obligated to cater to the egos of those who are so committed to a morally and sexually corrupt lifestyle that they will bend whatever evidence they receive to suit their own ends, no matter how much they may claim to be "honest lovers of truth." While this answer sounds harsh, with a moment's reflection we can see its truth: to demand that God perform miracles according to our specifications is expressing sovereignty over God and is quite the opposite of repentance. Should we expect God to jump through any hoop we set up in order to please us? Is God so insecure and psychologically unstable that He needs our approval? Are we dealing with the Creator of the universe as if He were a dog? Yet despite this attitude, God *does* provide such self-centered people with sufficient evidence, evidence enough that they cannot blame Him for their choice to remain in their unbelief.[29]

On the other hand, someone who wishes to know if the biblical data, when compared to that offered by other religions or atheists, is clear enough to show that the God of the Bible really exists and that His warnings should be heeded, will find that the evidence is indeed sufficient. Such a person would be like John the Baptist, who had second thoughts about Jesus being the Messiah because his expectations about the Messiah probably reflected the popular view that He would be a great military deliverer. However, Jesus handled his doubts by reminding him that the Messiah would be a teacher and healer.[30] In a similar way, we may feel that the evidence available is not as dramatic or flashy as we might desire, but it is objective enough to make sense and sufficient enough to give us the confidence to trust Christ. If we do, He will give us the confidence to live this life and to face the reality of death knowing that He has not created a fantasy.

Notes

[1]Carl Sagan, *Contact* (New York: Simon and Schuster, 1985), 170.

[2]This rule is called "Pascal's wager," after Blaise Pascal, the seventeenth-century French philosopher and mathematician.

[3]By *ideal data* I mean those results which are obvious to a casual, untrained observer and which will convince the most ardent skeptic that you deserve the Nobel prize. Perhaps one should also require that they be capable of being presented at a conference within a five-minute time limit using only one slide. Joking aside, such data are obtained in the physical sciences, but only in extremely rare cases. The bulk of scientific knowledge rests upon a less "ideal" base, yet it is employed daily. Thus it is hypocritical for a scientist to demand "ideal data" in the religious sphere.

[4]See the episode between Samuel and Eli, 1 Sam. 3:1ff.

[5]Exod. 12:23–27; 13:8–10, 14–16.

[6]James B. Pritchard, ed., *Ancient Near Eastern Texts Relating to the Old Testament,* 3d ed. with supplement (Princeton, N.J.: Princeton University Press, 1969), 287–88.

[7]Acts 26:26. This and all subsequent quotations from Scripture in this chapter, unless otherwise noted, are from the New American Standard Bible, copyright 1973 by The Lockman Foundation.

[8]Ps. 50:9–12; Acts 17:24–25.

[9]Job 22:2–3. Although many Christian doctrinal statements truly assert that God created mankind to glorify Him, this verse and those above imply that God does not *need* men to do this. The theological concept here is called the self-sufficiency of God.

[10]Isa. 57:11.

[11]Ps. 50:21–22.

[12]Eccles. 8:11.

[13]See sources listed under footnotes 10 through 12.

[14]1 Cor. 10:1–11.

[15]For example, see 1 Kings 18:20–19:14.

[16]John 12:28–30.

[17]John 9.

[18]John 11:1–45.

[19]John 11:46–57.

[20]Luke 16:31 in the context of Luke 16:19–31. This quotation from Scripture is from the New International Version of the Bible, copyright 1978 by the New York International Bible Society.

[21]Luke 16:19–31.

[22]Matt. 11:20–24.

[23]Matt. 13:11–15.

[24]Acts 9:1–17.

[25]Matt. 11:21.

[26]Rom. 1:18–21; John 1:9–12; John 3:14–21.

[27]Rom. 1:19–21.

[28]The Pharisees' challenge is especially striking in the larger context of Matt. 12:22–45. Note that Jesus was doing miracles in their presence whose authenticity they could verify (Matt. 12:9–14 and 12:22), but they were rejecting His claims anyhow (Matt. 12:14, 24). Jesus' response to their challenge implies that He feels the evidence they have already received is adequate, and the true problem is not the quality or quantity of the evidence, but their resistance to His accompanying message.

[29]Matt. 12:39–42. Note how the testimony of others will be used to prove that it should have been sufficient.

[30]Matt. 11:2–5.

6.2

The Jury Returns
A Juridical Defense of Christianity

John Warwick Montgomery

EXISTENTIAL, BLIND "LEAPS OF FAITH" can be and often are suicide jumps, with no criteria of truth available before the leap is made. But suppose the truth of a religious claim did not depend upon an unverifiable, subjectivistic leap of faith? What if a revelational truth-claim did not turn on questions of theology and religious philosophy—on any kind of esoteric, fideistic method available only to those who are already "true believers"—but on the very reasoning employed in the law to determine questions of fact?

The historic Christian claim differs qualitatively from the claims of all other world religions at the epistemological point: on the issue of testability. Eastern faiths and Islam, to take familiar examples, ask the uncommitted seeker to discover their truth experientially: the faith-experience will be self-validating. Unhappily, as analytical philosopher Kai Nielsen and others have rigorously shown, a subjective faith-experience is logically incapable of "validating God-talk"—including the alleged absolutes about which the god in question does the talking.[1] Christianity, on the other hand, declares that the truth of its absolute claims rests squarely on certain historical facts, open to ordinary investigation. These facts relate essentially to the man Jesus, His presentation of Himself as God in human flesh, and His resurrection from the dead as proof of His deity.

319

Thus the rabbinic lawyer, Christian convert, and apostle—Paul of
Tarsus—offered this gospel to Stoic philosophers at Athens as the
historically verifiable fulfillment of natural religion and the natural law
tradition, with their vague and insufficiently defined content.

Certain Epicurean and Stoic philosophers encountered [Paul at Athens]. And
some said, What will this babbler say? Others said, He seems to be setting forth
strange gods—for he had been preaching Jesus and the resurrection to them. And
they took him to the Areopagus, saying, May we know what this new doctrine is
of which you are speaking? . . .
   Then Paul stood at the center of the Areopagus and said, You men of Athens, I
note that in all things you are too superstitious. For as I passed by and beheld
your devotions, I found an altar with this inscription: TO THE UNKNOWN
GOD. Whom therefore you ignorantly worship I declare to you. . . . The times of
this ignorance God winked at, but now commands all men everywhere to repent,
for he has appointed a day when he will judge the world in righteousness by the
Man whom he has ordained, and he has given assurance of it to all in that he has
raised him from the dead.[2]

At one point in his speech, Paul asserted that human life is the product
of divine creation, "as certain also of your own [Stoic] poets have said,"
thereby making clear that classical natural law thinking was correct as far
as it went, though it did not by any means go far enough.[3] Its completion
could be found in Jesus, the Man whom God ordained, and His divine
character was verifiable through His resurrection from the dead.
   Elsewhere I have argued this case by employing standard, accepted
techniques of historical analysis.[4] Here we shall use legal reasoning and the
law of evidence. The advantage of a jurisprudential approach lies in the
difficulty of jettisoning it: legal standards of evidence develop as essential
means of resolving the most intractable disputes in society (dispute settlement
by self-help—the only alternative to adjudication—will tear any society apart).
Thus one cannot very well throw out legal reasoning merely because its
application to Christianity results in a verdict for the Christian faith.[5]
   Significantly, both in philosophy and in theology, there are moves to
introduce juridical styles of reasoning. Stephen Toulmin, professor of
philosophy at Leeds and one of the foremost analytical philosophers of
our time, presents a veritable call to arms:

To break the power of old models and analogies, we can provide ourselves with a
new one. Logic is concerned with the soundness of the claims we make—with
the solidity of the grounds we produce to support them, the firmness of the
backing we provide for them—or, to change the metaphor, with the sort of *case*
we present in defence of our claims. The legal analogy implied in this last way of
putting the point can for once be a real help. So let us forget about psychology,
sociology, technology and mathematics, ignore the echoes of structural engineering and *collage* in the words 'grounds' and 'backing,' and take as our model the

discipline of jurisprudence. Logic (we may say) is generalized jurisprudence. Arguments can be compared with law-suits, and the claims we make and argue for in extra-legal contexts with claims made in the courts, while the cases we present in making good each kind of claim can be compared with each other.[6]

Mortimer Adler, at the end of his careful discussion of the question of God's existence, employs, not the traditional philosophical ideal of Cartesian absolute certainty, but the legal standards of proof by preponderance of evidence and proof beyond reasonable doubt:

If I am able to say no more than that a preponderance of reasons favor believing that God exists, I can still say I have advanced reasonable grounds for that belief. . . .
I am persuaded that God exists, either beyond a reasonable doubt or by a preponderance of reasons in favor of that conclusion over reasons against it. I am, therefore, willing to terminate this inquiry with the statement that I have reasonable grounds for affirming God's existence.[7]

And from the jurisprudential side, Jerome Hall recognizes the potential for arbitrating central issues of religion and ethics by the sophisticated instrument of legal reasoning.

Legal rules of evidence are reflections of "natural reason," and they could enter into dialogues in several ways, for example, to test the validity of theological arguments for the existence of God and to distinguish secular beliefs, even those held without any reasonable doubt, from faith that is so firm (Job's) that it excludes the slightest shadow of doubt and persists even in the face of evidence that on rational grounds is plainly contradictory. In these and other ways the rationality of the law of evidence in the trial of an issue of fact joins philosophical rationalism in raising pertinent questions about faith.[8]

In terms of our discussion, what are the "pertinent questions about faith"? Four overarching questions need to be answered: (1) Are the historical records of Jesus solid enough to rely upon? (2) Is the testimony in these records concerning His life and ministry sufficiently reliable to know what He claimed about Himself? (3) Do the accounts of His resurrection from the dead, offered as proof of His divine claims, in fact establish those claims? (4) If Jesus' deity is established in the foregoing manner, does He place a divine stamp of approval on the Bible so as to render its pronouncements apodictically certain? Let us see how legal reasoning helps to answer each of these key questions.

Basic to any determination of the soundness of Christian claims is the question of the reliability of the pertinent historical documents. The documents at issue are not (pace the man on the Clapham omnibus) Josephus, Tacitus, Pliny the Younger, or other pagan references to Jesus, though these do of course exist. Such references are secondary at best, since none of these writers had firsthand contact with Jesus or with His disciples.

The documents on which the case for Christianity depends are the New Testament writings, for they claim to have been written by eyewitnesses or by close associates of eyewitnesses (indeed, their origin in apostolic circles was the essential criterion for including them in the New Testament).

How good are these New Testament records? They handsomely fulfill the historian's requirements of *transmissional reliability* (their texts have been transmitted accurately from the time of writing to our own day), *internal reliability* (they claim to be primary-source documents and ring true as such), and *external reliability* (their authorships and dates are backed up by such solid extrinsic testimony as that of the early second-century writer Papias, a student of John the Evangelist, who was told by him that the first three Gospels were indeed written by their traditional authors).[9] Harvard's Simon Greenleaf, the greatest nineteenth-century authority on the law of evidence in the common-law world, applied to these records the "ancient documents" rule: ancient documents will be received as competent evidence if they are "fair on their face" (i.e., offer no internal evidence of tampering) and have been maintained in "reasonable custody" (i.e., their preservation has been consistent with their content). He concluded that the competence of the New Testament documents would be established in any court of law.[10]

The speculation that the Gospel records were "faked" some three hundred years after the events described in them (a viewpoint gratuitously proffered by Professor Trevor-Roper) is dismissed by Lord Chancellor Hailsham, England's highest ranking legal luminary, with an apt lawyer's illustration.

[What] renders the argument invalid is a fact about fakes of all kinds which I learned myself in the course of a case I did in which there was in question the authenticity of a painting purporting to be by, and to be signed by, Modigliani. This painting, as the result of my Advice on Evidence, was shown to be a fake by X-ray evidence. But in the course of my researches I was supplied by my instructing solicitor with a considerable bibliography concerning the nature of fakes of all kinds and how to detect them. There was one point made by the author of one of these books which is of direct relevance to the point I am discussing. Although fakes can often be made which confuse or actually deceive contemporaries of the faker, the experts, or even the not so expert, of a later age can invariably detect them, whether fraudulent or not because the faker cannot fail to include stylistic or other material not obvious to contemporaries because they are contemporaries, but which stand out a mile to later observers because they reflect the standards, or the materials, or the styles of a succeeding age to that of the author whose work is being faked.[11]

As for the skepticism of the so-called higher critics (or redaction critics) in the liberal theological tradition, it stems from an outmoded methodology (almost universally discarded today by classical and literary scholars and by specialists in comparative Near Eastern studies), and from unjustified philosophical presuppositions (such as anti-supernaturalistic bias and bias in favor of religious evolution).[12] A. N. Sherwin-White, a specialist in Roman law, countered such critics in his 1960–61 Sarum Lectures at the University of London.

It is astonishing that while Graeco-Roman historians have been growing in confidence, the twentieth-century study of the Gospel narratives, starting from the no less promising material, has taken so gloomy a turn in the development of form-criticism that the more advanced exponents of it apparently maintain—so far as an amateur can understand the matter—that the historical Christ is unknowable and the history of His mission cannot be written. This seems very curious when one compares the case for the best-known contemporary of Christ, who like Christ is a well-documented figure—Tiberius Caesar. The story of his reign is known from four sources, the *Annals* of Tacitus and the biography of Suetonius, written some eighty or ninety years later, the brief contemporary record of Velleius Paterculus, and the third century history of Cassius Dio. These disagree amongst themselves in the wildest possible fashion, both in major matters of political action or motive and in specific details of minor events. Everyone would admit that Tacitus is the best of all the sources, and yet no serious modern historian would accept at face value the majority of the statements of Tacitus about the motives of Tiberius. But this does not prevent the belief that the material of Tacitus can be used to write a history of Tiberius.[13]

The conclusion is inescapable: if one compares the New Testament documents with universally accepted secular writings of antiquity, the New Testament is more than vindicated. Some years ago, when I debated philosophy professor Avrum Stroll of the University of British Columbia on this point,[14] he responded: "All right. I'll throw out my knowledge of the classical world." At which the chairman of the classics department cried: "Good Lord, Avrum, not *that!*"

If, as we have seen, the New Testament records are sound historical documents, how good is their testimony of Jesus? This is a question of great importance, since the accounts tell us plainly that Jesus claimed to be nothing less than God-in-the-flesh, come to earth to reveal God's will for the human race and to save human beings from the penalty of their sins. Moreover, the same testimony meticulously records Jesus' post-resurrection appearances, so a decision as to its reliability will also bear directly on our third major question, the historicity of the resurrection.

In a court of law, admissible testimony is considered truthful unless impeached or otherwise rendered doubtful. This is in accord with ordinary life, where only the paranoiac goes about with the bias that everyone is lying. (Think of Cousin Elmo, convinced that he is followed by Albanians.) The burden, then, is on those who would show that the New Testament testimony to Jesus is not worthy of belief. Let us place the Gospel testimony to Jesus under the legal microscope to see if its reliability can be impeached.

Here we employ a construct for attacking perjury that has been labeled "the finest work on that subject."[15] McCloskey and Schoenberg offer a fourfold test for exposing perjury, involving a determination of *internal* and *external* defects in the *witness himself* on the one hand and in the *testimony itself* on the other.[16] We can translate their schema into diagrammatic form thusly:

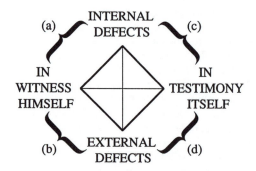

A Construct for Exposing Perjury
Figure 6.2a

(a) Internal defects in the witness himself refer to any personal characteristics or past history tending to show that the "witness is inherently untrustworthy, unreliable, or undependable." Were the apostolic witnesses to Jesus persons who may be disbelieved because they were "not the type of persons who can be trusted"? Did they have criminal records or is there reason to think they were pathological liars? If anything, their simple literalness and directness is almost painful. They seem singularly poor candidates for a James Bond thriller or for being cast in the role of "Spy and Counterspy." But perhaps they were mythomanes—people incapable of distinguishing fact from fantasy? They themselves declare precisely the contrary: "We have not followed cunningly devised fables [Gk. *mythoi*, 'myths']," they write, "when we made known unto you the power and coming of our Lord Jesus Christ, but were eyewitnesses of his majesty."[17]

(b) But perhaps the apostolic witnesses suffered from external defects, that is, "motives to falsify"?

Not all perjurers have committed prior immoral acts or prior crimes. Frequently, law abiding citizens whose pasts are without blemish will commit perjury, not because they are inherently unworthy, but because some specific present reason compels them to do so in the case at bar. Motive, then, becomes the common denominator. There is a motive for every act of perjury. The second major way in which the cross-examiner can seek to expose perjury, therefore, is to isolate the specific motive which causes the witness to commit perjury.[18]

Surely no sensible person would argue that the apostolic witnesses would have lied about Jesus for monetary gain or as a result of societal pressure. To the contrary: they lost the possibility both of worldly wealth and of social acceptability among their Jewish peers because of their commitment to Jesus.[19] Might that very affection for and attachment to Jesus serve as a motive to falsify? Not when we remember that their Master expressly taught them that lying was of the devil.[20]

(c) Turning now to the testimony itself, we must ask if the New Testament writings are internally inconsistent or self-contradictory. Certainly, the Four Gospels do not give identical, verbatim accounts of the words or acts of Jesus. But if they did, that fact alone would make them highly suspect, for it would point to collusion.[21] The Gospel records view the life and ministry of Jesus from four different perspectives—just as veridical witnesses to the same accident will present different but complementary accounts of the same event. If the objection is raised that the same occurrence or pericope is sometimes found at different times or places in Jesus' ministry, depending upon which Gospel one consults, the simple answer is that no one Gospel contains or was ever intended to contain the complete account of Jesus' three-year ministry.[22] Furthermore, Jesus (like any preacher) certainly spoke the same messages to different groups at different times. And suppose He did throw the moneychangers out of the Temple twice: is it not strange, in light of their activity and His principles, that He *only* threw them out twice? (We would have expected it every Saturday—Sabbath—night.) Observe also how honestly and in what an unflattering manner the apostolic company picture themselves in these records. Mark, Peter's companion, describes him as having a consistent case of foot-in-the-mouth disease; and the Apostles in general are presented (in Jesus' own words) as "slow of heart to believe all that the prophets have spoken."[23] To use New Testament translator J. B. Phillips's expression, the internal content of the New Testament records has "the ring of truth."[24]

(d) Finally, what about external defects in the testimony itself, i.e., inconsistencies between the New Testament accounts and what we know to be the case from archaeology or extra-biblical historical records? Far from avoiding contact with secular history, the New Testament is replete with explicit references to secular personages, places, and events. Unlike typical sacred literature, myth, and fairytale ("Once upon a time . . ."), the Gospel story begins with "There went out a decree from Caesar Augustus that all the world should be taxed."[25] Typical of the New Testament accounts are passages such as the following:

Now in the fifteenth year of the reign of Tiberius Cæsar, Pontius Pilate being governor of Judæa, and Herod being tetrarch of Galilee, and his brother Philip, tetrarch of Itoræa and of the region of Trachonitis, and Lysanias the tetrarch of Abilene.

Annas and Caiaphas being the high priests, the word of God came unto John the son of Zacharias in the wilderness.

And he came into all the country about Jordan, preaching the baptism of repentance for the remission of sins.[26]

Modern archaeological research has confirmed again and again the reliability of New Testament geography, chronology, and general history.[27] To take but a single, striking example: After the rise of liberal biblical criticism, doubt was expressed as to the historicity of Pontius Pilate, since he is mentioned even by pagan historians only in connection with Jesus' death. Then, in 1961, came the discovery at Caesarea of the now famous "Pilate inscription," definitely showing that, as usual, the New Testament writers were engaged in accurate historiography.

Thus on no one of the four elements of the McCloskey-Schoenberg construct for attacking perjury can the New Testament witnesses to Jesus be impugned.

Furthermore, one should realize (and non-lawyers seldom do realize) how difficult it is to succeed in effective lying or misrepresentation when a cross-examiner is at work. Richard A. Givens, in his standard work, *Advocacy*, in the McGraw-Hill Trial Practice Series, diagrams ordinary truthful communication and then contrasts it with the tremendous complexities of deceitful communication (figures 6.2b and 6.2c).[28]

Observe that the witness engaged in deception must, as it were, juggle at least three balls simultaneously, while continually estimating his chances of discovery: he must be sure he doesn't say anything that contradicts what his examiner knows (or what he thinks his examiner knows); he must tell a consistent lie ("liars must have good memories"); and he must take care that nothing he says can be checked against contradictory external data. Givens's point is that successful deception is terribly difficult, for the psychological strain and energy expended in attempting it makes the deceiver exceedingly vulnerable.

The wider the angles of divergence between these various images, the more confusing the problem, and the more "higher mathematics" must be done in order to attempt to avoid direct conflicts between these elements. The greater the angle of deception employed, the greater the complexity and the lower the effectiveness of these internal mental operations. If this is conscious, we attribute this to lying. If it is unconscious we lay it to the "bias" of the witness.

If one is lying or strongly biased, it is not enough to simply dredge up whatever mental trace there may be of the event and attempt to articulate it in answer to a question. Instead, all of the various elements mentioned must be weighed, a decision made as to the best approach, a reply contrived that is expected to be most convincing, and then an effort made to launch this communication into the minds of the audience.

The person with a wide angle of divergence between what is recalled and the impression sought to be given is thus at an almost helpless disadvantage, especially if confronting a cross-examiner who understands the predicament.

If the audience includes both a cross-examiner and a tribunal, the number of elements to be considered becomes even greater. The mental gymnastics required rise in geometric proportion to the number of elements involved.[29]

Now, wholly apart from the question as to whether the New Testament witnesses to Jesus were the kind of people to engage in such deception (and we have already seen, in examining them for possible internal and external defects, that they were not): *had* they attempted such a massive deception, *could they have gotten away with it?* Admittedly, they were never put on a literal witness stand, but they concentrated their preaching on synagogue audiences. This put their testimony at the mercy of the hostile Jewish religious leadership who had had intimate contact with Jesus' ministry and had been chiefly instrumental in ending it.

Such an audience eminently satisfies Givens's description of "both a cross-examiner and a tribunal": they had the *means, motive,* and *opportunity* to expose the apostolic witness as inaccurate and deceptive if it had been such. The fact that they did not can only be effectively explained on the ground that they *could not.* It would seem, for example, inconceivable that the Jewish religious leadership, with their intimate knowledge of the Old Testament, would have sat idly by as the Apostles proclaimed that Jesus' life and ministry had fulfilled dozens of highly specific Old Testament prophecies (birth at Bethlehem, virgin birth, flight to Egypt, triumphal entry, sold by a friend for thirty pieces of silver, etc., etc.), had that not been true. Professor F. F. Bruce of the University of Manchester underscores this fundamental point as to the evidential significance of the hostile witnesses:

It was not only friendly eyewitnesses that the early preachers had to reckon with; there were others less well disposed who were also conversant with the main facts of the ministry and death of Jesus. The disciples could not afford to risk inaccuracies (not to speak of willful manipulation of the facts), which would at once be exposed by those who would be only too glad to do so. On the contrary, one of the strong points in the original apostolic preaching is the confident appeal to the knowledge of the hearers; they not only said, "We are witnesses of these things," but also, "As you yourselves also know" (Acts 2:22). Had there been any tendency to depart from the facts in any material respect, the possible presence of hostile witnesses in the audience would have served as a further corrective.[30]

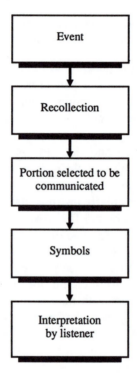

The Mental Process in "Simple"—i.e., Truthful—Communication
Figure 6.2b

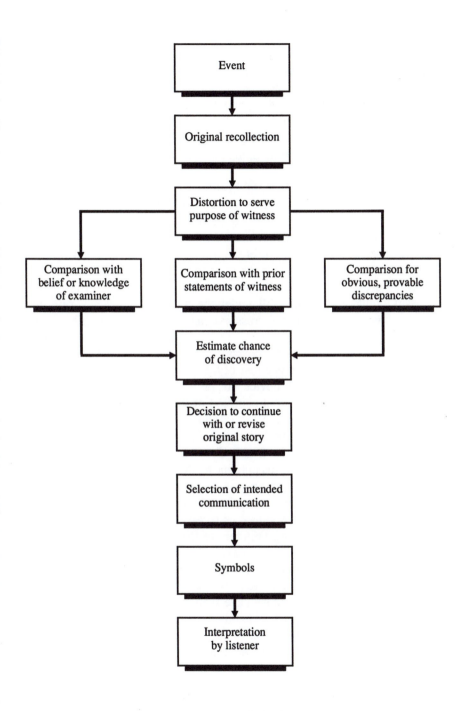

The Lying Witness
Figure 6.2c

We do not waste time on the possibility that the disciples were suffering from insane delusions. First, because the law presumes a man sane, and there is no suggestion in the accounts the Apostles were otherwise. Second, because the point Professor Bruce has just stressed concerning the hostile witnesses applies with equal force to the insanity suggestion: had the disciples distorted Jesus' biography for *any* reason, including a deluded state of mind, the hostile witnesses would surely have used this against them.

The functional equivalence of hostile witnesses with formal cross-examination goes far to answer the occasionally voiced objection that the apostolic testimony to Jesus would be rejected by a modern court as "hearsay," i.e., out-of-court statements tendered to prove the truth of their contents. Let us note at the outset the most severe problem with hearsay testimony: the originator of it is not in court and so cannot be subjected to searching cross-examination. Thus even when New Testament testimony to Jesus would technically fall under the axe of the hearsay rule, the hostile witnesses as functional cross-examiners reduce the problem to the vanishing point.

In the second place, the hearsay rule exists in Anglo-American common law (no such rule is a part of the Continental civil law tradition) especially as a technical device to protect juries from secondhand evidence. Following the virtual abolition of the civil jury in England, the Civil Evidence Act of 1968 in effect eliminated the hearsay rule by statute from civil trials—on the ground that judges can presumably sift even secondhand testimony for its truth-value.[31] In the United States, and in English criminal trials, the exceptions to the hearsay rule have almost swallowed up the rule, and one of these exceptions is the "ancient documents" rule (to which we referred earlier), by which the New Testament documents would indeed be received as competent evidence.

To be sure, the underlying principle of the hearsay rule remains vital: that a witness ought to testify "of his own knowledge or observation," not on the basis of what has come to him indirectly from others. And the New Testament writers continually tell us that they are setting forth that "which we have heard, which we have seen with our eyes, which we have looked upon, and our hands have handled . . . the Word of life."[32]

Simon Greenleaf's summation of the testimonial case for Jesus' life, ministry, and claims about Himself offers a perennial challenge to the earnest seeker for truth.

All that Christianity asks of men on this subject, is, that they would be consistent with themselves; that they would treat its evidences as they treat the evidence of other things; and that they would try and judge its actors and witnesses, as they deal with their fellow men, when testifying to human affairs and actions, in human tribunals. Let the witnesses be compared with themselves, with each other, and with surrounding facts and circumstances; and let their testimony be sifted, as if it were given in a court of justice, on the side of the adverse party, the witness being subjected to a rigorous cross-examination. The result, it is confidently believed, will be an undoubting conviction of their integrity, ability, and truth. In the course of such an examination, the undesigned coincidences will multiply upon us at every step in our progress; the probability of the veracity of the witnesses and of the reality of the occurrences which they relate will increase, until it acquires, for all practical purposes, the value and force of demonstration.[33]

At the heart of the apostolic testimony and proclamation is the alleged resurrection of Jesus Christ from the dead. During His ministry, Jesus offered His forthcoming resurrection as the decisive proof of His claim to deity.[34] Did the Resurrection in fact occur?[35]

First, consider the written records of the Resurrection and of detailed post-resurrection appearances which occurred over a forty-day period.[36] What is important here is that these accounts are all contained in the very New Testament documents whose historical reliability we have already confirmed and are testified to by the same apostolic witnesses whose veracity we have just established. To do an abrupt *volte-face* and now declare those documents and witnesses to be untrustworthy because they assert that Jesus rose from the dead would be to substitute a dubious metaphysic ("resurrections from the dead are cosmically impossible"— and how does one establish *that* in a relativistic, Einsteinian universe?) for careful historical investigation. We must not make the mistake of eighteenth-century philosopher David Hume, who thought he could avoid evidential drudgery by deductively reasoning from the gratuitous premise that "a firm and unalterable experience has established the laws of nature" to the (entirely circular) conclusions: "There must be a uniform experience against every miraculous event" and "That a dead man should come to life has never been observed in any age or country."[37]

Second, we should reflect upon the force of the "missing body" argument of Frank Morison,[38] who was converted to Christianity through his investigation of the evidence for the Resurrection. His argument proceeds as follows: (1) If Jesus didn't rise, someone must have stolen the body; (2) the only people involved were the Roman authorities, the Jewish religious leaders, and Jesus' disciples; (3) the Romans and the Jewish religious leaders would certainly not have taken the body, since to do so would have been against their own interests (the Romans wanted to keep Palestine quiet, and the Jews wanted to preserve their religious influence);[39] and (4) the disciples would hardly have stolen the body and then died for what they knew to be untrue; (5) *Ergo*—by process of elimination—Jesus rose from the dead just as the firsthand accounts declare.

I have shown elsewhere that Antony Flew's attempt to avoid the impact of this argument is unsuccessful.[40] When Flew says that Christians simply prefer a biological miracle (the Resurrection) to a psychological miracle (the disciples dying for what they knew to be false), he completely misses the point. The issue is not metaphysical preference; it is testimonial evidence. No such evidence exists to support a picture of psychologically aberrant disciples, while tremendously powerful testimonial evidence exists to the effect that Jesus physically rose from the dead.

During the last few years, more inventive attempts to explain away the Resurrection have appeared. Schonfield's *Passover Plot* argues that Jesus induced His own crucifixion, drugging Himself so as to survive just long enough in the tomb to convince the fuddled disciples that He had risen.[41] (*Quaere*: How does this square with Jesus' own moral teachings? And does it not leave us with precisely the same problem as to what finally happened to the body?) Von Daniken—who turned to pseudo-scientific writing while serving a prison sentence in Switzerland for embezzlement, fraud, and forgery[42]—"explains" the Resurrection by suggesting that it was the product of a close encounter of the third kind: Jesus was a kind of Martian cleverly dressed in a Jesus suit who knew a few tricks such as how to appear to rise from the dead.

Aren't such hypotheses *possible*? Doubtless, in our contingent universe, anything is possible (as one philosopher said) except squeezing toothpaste back into the tube. But legal reasoning operates on *probabilities*, not possibilities: preponderance of evidence in most civil actions; evidence beyond reasonable (not beyond *all*) doubt in criminal matters.[43] The *Federal Rules of Evidence* defines relevant evidence as "evidence having any tendency to make the existence of any fact that is of consequence to the determination of the action more probable or less probable than it would be without the evidence."[44] Suppose a jury brought in a verdict of "innocent" because it is always *possible* that invisible Martians, not the accused, were responsible for the crime! Judges in the United States carefully instruct juries to pay attention *only* to the evidence in the case, and to render verdicts in accord with it. A guilty verdict in a criminal matter should be rendered only if the jury cannot find any reasonable explanation of the crime (i.e., any explanation *in accord with the evidence*) other than that the accused did it. May we suggest that the tone and value of discussions about Jesus' resurrection would be considerably elevated if equally rigorous thinking were applied thereto?

Can we base ultimates (Jesus' deity, our commitment to Him for time and eternity) on mere probabilities? The analytical philosophers have shown that we have no other choice: only formal ("analytic") truths (e.g., the propositions of deductive logic and of pure mathematics) can be demonstrated absolutely—and the absoluteness here is due to the definitional nature of their axiomatic foundations, as with Euclid's geometry. All matters of fact ("synthetic" assertions) are limited to probabilistic confirmation, but this does not immobilize us in daily life. We still put our very lives in jeopardy every day on the basis of probability judgments (crossing the street, consuming packaged foods and drugs, flying in airplanes, etc.). And the law in every land redistributes property and takes away liberty (if not life) by verdicts and judgments rooted in the examination of evidence and probabilistic standards of proof.

But the issue here is a *miracle*: a resurrection. How much evidence ought a reasonable man require in order to establish such a fact? Could evidence ever justify accepting it? Thomas Sherlock, Master of the Temple Church (owned by two of the four guilds of English barristers, the Honourable Societies of the Inner and Middle Temple) and Bishop of London, well answered these questions in the eighteenth century:

Suppose you saw a Man publickly executed, his Body afterwards wounded by the Executioner, and carry'd and laid in the Grave; that after this you shou'd be told, that the Man was come to Life again: What wou'd you suspect in this Case? Not that the Man had never been dead; for that you saw your self: But you wou'd suspect whether he was now alive. But wou'd you say, this Case excluded all human Testimony; and that Men could not possibly discern, whether one with whom they convers'd familiarly, was alive or no? Upon what Ground cou'd you say this? A Man rising from the Grave is an Object of Sense, and can give the same Evidence of his being alive, as any other Man in the World can give. So that a Resurrection consider'd only as a Fact to be proved by Evidence, is a plain Case; it requires no greater Ability in the Witnesses, than that they be able to distinguish between a Man dead, and a Man alive: A Point, in which I believe every Man living thinks himself a Judge.[45]

Bishop Sherlock is certainly correct that a resurrection does not in principle create any insuperable evidential difficulty. Phenomenally (and this is all we need worry about for evidential purposes) a resurrection can be regarded as *death followed by life*,

D, then L.

Normally, the sequence is reversed, thus:

L, then D.

We are well acquainted with the phenomenal meaning of the constituent factors (though we do not understand the "secret" of life or why death must occur). Furthermore, we have no difficulty in establishing evidential criteria to place a person in one category rather than in the other. Thus the eating of fish[46] is sufficient to classify the eater among the living, and a crucifixion is enough to place the crucified among the dead. In Jesus' case, the sequential order is reversed, but that has no epistemological bearing on the weight of evidence required to establish death or life. And if Jesus was dead at point A, and alive again at point B, then resurrection has occurred: *res ipsa loquitur.*[47]

However, does not the unreliability of eyewitness testimony cast doubt on an event as extraordinary as the Resurrection? Psychologists such as Loftus have pointed up genuine dangers in eyewitness testimony.[48] Nonetheless, as we have already seen, it remains the cornerstone of legal evidence. As for the reliability of identifying acquaintances (the precise issue in the disciples' post-resurrection identifications of Jesus), specialists on the subject agree that "the better acquainted a witness is with a subject, the more likely it is that the witness' identification will be accurate." These same authorities add that "in an eyewitness context, the greatest challenge to the advocate's power of persuasion is presented by the attempt to argue, without support from expert testimony, the unreliability of an unimpeached eyewitness's identification of a prior acquaintance."[49] And this is precisely what we have in the case under consideration: disciples like Thomas provide "unimpeached eyewitness identification" of the resurrected Jesus with whom they had had the most intimate acquaintance for the immediately preceding three-year period.[50] No advocate's "power of persuasion" is going to make a difference to that kind of identification evidence.

Finally, the objection may be offered: even granting Jesus' resurrection, is that fact alone enough to establish His deity and the truth of His claims? Theological presuppositionalists Carl F. H. Henry and Ronald H. Nash tell us that there are no self-interpreting facts,[51] and Calvinists R. C. Sproul and John Gerstner, as well as evangelical neo-Thomist Norman L. Geisler, insist that an independent theistic structure must be established to make any theological sense out of Jesus' resurrection.[52] We profoundly disagree. Even Rat—famous for his leading role in Kenneth Grahame's *The Wind in the Willows*, but hardly an accomplished epistemologist—becomes exasperated with his companion for not recognizing that facts can be self-interpreting:

"Do-you-mean-to-say," cried the excited Rat, "that this doormat doesn't *tell* you anything?"

"Really, Rat," said the Mole quite pettishly, "I think we've had enough of this folly. Who ever heard of a doormat *telling* anyone anything? They simply don't do it. They are not that sort at all. Doormats know their place."

"Now look here, you—you thick-headed beast," replied the Rat, really angry, "this must stop. Not another word, but scrape—scrape and scratch and dig and hunt round, especially on the sides of the hummocks, if you want to sleep dry and warm tonight, for it's our last chance!"

Elsewhere we have argued in detail that facts—historical and other-wise—"in themselves provide adequate criteria for choosing among variant interpretations of them."[53] Philosopher Paul D. Feinberg has defended that case with inexorable logic:

Let us consider an example from recent history. It can be substantiated that some 6 million Jews died under German rule in the second World War. Let me suggest two mutually exclusive interpretations. First, these events may be interpreted as the actions of a mad man who was insanely anti-Semitic. The deaths were murders, atrocities. Second, it might be asserted that Hitler really loved the Jews. He had a deep and abiding belief in heaven and life after death. After reviewing Jewish history, Hitler decided that the Jews had been persecuted enough, and because of his love for them he was seeking to help them enter eternal blessedness. If no necessity exists between events and interpretation, then there is no way of determining which meaning is correct. We would never be justified in claiming that one holding the latter view is wrong. This is both repugnant and absurd. There must be an empirical necessity that unites an event or fact with its correct interpretation.[54]

Beyond this, we merely remind the reader that the very nature of legal argument (judgments rendered on the basis of factual verdicts) rests on the ability of facts to speak for themselves. As a single illustration, taking the leading U.S. Supreme Court case of *Williams* v. *North Carolina* (the "second Williams case"), which stands for the proposition that a divorce on substituted or constructive service in one state need only be given full faith and credit by another state when the parties have acquired a bona fide domicile in the divorcing state. In the course of its opinion, the Court declared:

Petitioners, long time residents of North Carolina, came to Nevada, where they stayed in an auto-court for transients, filed suits for divorce as soon as the Nevada law permitted, married one another as soon as the divorces were obtained, and promptly returned to North Carolina to live. *It cannot reasonably be claimed that one set of inferences rather than another regarding the acquisition by petitioners of new domicils [sic] in Nevada could be drawn from the circumstances attending their Nevada divorces.*[55]

Geisler misrepresents us when he says that we hold that "the resurrection is so bizarre, so odd, that only a supernatural explanation will adequately account for it."[56] In our view there are two compelling reasons to accept Jesus' resurrection as implicating His deity. First, "this miracle deals effectively with the most fundamental area of man's universal need, the conquest of death"[57]—a truth recognized in law by the "dying declaration" exception to the hearsay rule (even the declaration of the homicide victim without religious faith is admissible in evidence, on the ground that one is particularly likely to tell the truth when conscious of the immanence of that most terrible of existential events).[58] If death is indeed that significant, then "not to worship One who gives you the gift of eternal life is hopelessly to misread what the gift tells you about the Giver."[59]

In the second place, there are logically only two possible kinds of explanation or interpretation of the fact of the Resurrection: that given by the person raised, and that given by someone else. Surely, if only Jesus was raised, He is in a far better position (indeed, in the *only* position!) to interpret or explain it. Until Von Daniken, for example, rises from the dead, we will prefer Jesus' account of what happened. And Jesus tells us that His miraculous ministry is explicable because He is no less than God in human form: "I and *my* Father are one"; "He who has seen me has seen the Father."[60] Theism then becomes the proper inference from Jesus' resurrection as He Himself explained it—not a prior metaphysical hurdle to jump in order to arrive at the proper historical and evidential interpretation of that event.

Jesus' deity in itself establishes the truth of the Christian message, over against competing religions and secular world-views. And Jesus' teachings per se, being God's teachings, represent an infallible guide to human life and conduct. But Jesus does more even than this. By His direct statements concerning the Old Testament as divine revelation[61] and by His consistent quoting of it as trustworthy and divinely authoritative in all respects,[62] Jesus put upon it His (i.e., God's) *imprimatur*. By giving His Apostles a special gift of the Holy Spirit to recall infallibly what He had taught them,[63] and, by implication, to recognize apostolicity in others, He proleptically stamped with approval as divine revelation the future writings of Apostles (the original twelve, minus Judas Iscariot, plus Paul—grafted in as Apostle to the Gentiles)[64] and writings by their associates (Mark, Luke, etc.) whose accuracy the Apostles were in a position to verify. As a result, the entire Bible—Old Testament and New—becomes an unerring source of absolute principles.[65]

Two objections may be raised to the argument we have just presented. First, why should the mere fact that God says something guarantee its truth? Second, what if the incarnate Christ was so limited to the human ideas of His time that His stamp of approval on the Bible represents no guarantee of its absolute accuracy?

The first of these arguments is reflected in Descartes's discussion of God as a possible "Evil Genius"—a cosmic liar. But if He were, He would be a divine and, therefore, consummate liar, so you would be incapable of catching Him at it. In short, He would be a better liar than you are a detective. So the very idea of God-as-liar is meaningless—an analytically unverifiable notion in principle. Once you have met God incarnate, you have no choice but to trust Him: as to the way of salvation and as to the reliability of the entire Bible.

The suggestion that Jesus was limited to human and fallible ideas (the so-called Kenotic theory[66] of liberal theology) also collapses under its own weight. On Kenotic reasoning, either Jesus chose to conform His statements to the fallible ideas of His time (in which case He was an opportunist who, in the spirit of Lenin, committed one of the most basic of all moral errors, that of allowing the end to justify the means);[67] or He couldn't avoid self-limitation in the very process of Incarnation (in which case Incarnation is of little or no value to us, since there is then no guarantee that it reveals anything conclusive). And note that if such a dubious Incarnation mixed absolute wheat with culturally relative chaff, we would have no sufficient criterion for separating them anyway, so the "absolute" portion would do us no good!

To meet man's desperate need for apodictic principles of human conduct, an incarnate God must not speak with a forked tongue. And, as we have seen, no divine stuttering has occurred. To the contrary: His message can be relied upon as evidentially established, a sure light shining in a dark world, illuminating the path to eternity.[68]

Notes

[1] Kai Nielsen, "Can Faith Validate God-Talk?" in *New Theology No. 1*, ed. Martin E. Marty and Dean G. Peerman (New York: Macmillan, 1964), esp. 147; C. B. Martin, "A Religious Way of Knowing," in *New Essays in Philosophical Theology*, ed. Antony Flew and Alasdair MacIntyre (London: SCM Press, 1955), 76–95; Frederick Ferre, *Language, Logic and God* (New York: Harper, 1961), 94–104. But see also in part 5 of the present volume philosopher John Hare's endeavor to rehabilitate Christian truth: "The Argument from Experience."

[2] Acts 17:18–19, 22–23, 30–31. This and all subsequent quotations from Scripture in this chapter are from the King James Version of the Bible. Some passages may be paraphrased. The late classical scholar E. M. Blaiklock of the University of Auckland, New Zealand, in delivering the Annual Wheaton College Graduate School Lectures, 21–22 October 1964, on the subject of Paul's Areopagus address, noted that Paul ignored the Epicureans ("the Sadducees of the Greeks"), doubtless because of the intellectual dishonesty into which their movement had fallen, and concentrated on the Stoics, who continued to hold a high view of natural law.

[3] In Acts 17:28 Paul quoted Cleanthes (300 B.C.), *Hymn to Zeus 5*, and/or Aratus (270 B.C.), *Phoenom 5*. Cf. J. B. Lightfoot's essay, "St. Paul and Seneca," in his *St. Paul's Epistle to the Philippians* (Grand Rapids, Mich.: Zondervan, 1953); F. W. Farrar, *Seekers After God* (London: Macmillan, 1906); N. B. Stonehouse, *Paul Before Areopagus, and Other New Testament Studies* (Grand Rapids, Mich.: Eerdmans, 1957); B. Gartner, *The Areopagus Speech and Natural Revelation* (Lund, 1955); and J. Sevenster, *Paul and Seneca* (Leiden: Brill, 1961).

[4] John Warwick Montgomery, "Jesus Christ and History," in his *Where is History Going?* (Minneapolis, Minn.: Bethany, 1972), 37–74.

[5]Cf. John Warwick Montgomery, "Legal Reasoning and Christian Apologetics," in his *The Law Above the Law,* (Minneapolis, Minn.: Bethany, 1975), 84–90; and idem, *Law and Gospel: A Study in Jurisprudence* (Oak Park, Ill.: Christian Legal Society, 1978), 34–37.

[6]Stephen E. Toulmin, *The Uses of Argument* (Cambridge: Cambridge University Press, 1958), 7.

[7]Mortimer J. Adler, *How to Think about God* (New York: Macmillan, 1980), 150.

[8]Jerome Hall, "Religion, Law and Ethics—A Call for Dialogue," *Hastings Law Journal* 29 (July 1978): 1273. We are not persuaded that Job's faith was quite as firm—or as irrational—as Hall suggests, but the reference to Job is in any case an *obiter dictum!*

[9]Montgomery, "Jesus Christ and History"; F. F. Bruce, *The New Testament Documents: Are They Reliable?* 5th ed. (London: Inter-Varsity, 1960); John Warwick Montgomery, "The Fourth Gospel Yesterday and Today," in his *The Suicide of Christian Theology* (Minneapolis, Minn.: Bethany, 1971), 428–65. On the extra-biblical evidence, see C. R. Haines, *Heathen Contact with Christianity During Its First Century and a Half: Being All References to Christianity Recorded in Pagan Writings During That Period* (Cambridge, England: Deighton, Bell, 1923); and Gary R. Habermas, *Ancient Evidence for the Life of Jesus* (Nashville, Tenn.: Thomas Nelson, 1984).

[10]Simon Greenleaf, *The Testimony of the Evangelists, Examined by the Rules of Evidence Administered in Courts of Justice,* reprinted in Montgomery, *The Law Above the Law,* 91ff.

[11]Lord Hailsham (Quintin Hogg), *The Door Wherein I Went* (London: Collins, 1975), 32–33; the theological and apologetic portion of Lord Hailsham's autobiography has been photolithographically reproduced in *The Simon Greenleaf Law Review* 4 (1984–85): 1–67, with editorial introduction by John Warwick Montgomery.

[12]C. S. Lewis, "Modern Theology and Biblical Criticism," in *Christian Reflections,* ed. Walter Hooper (Grand Rapids, Mich.: Eerdmans, 1967), 152–66; Gerhard Maier, *The End of the Historical-Critical Method,* trans. E. W. Leverenz and R. F. Norden (St. Louis, Mo.: Concordia, 1977); and cf. John Warwick Montgomery, "Why Has God Incarnate Suddenly Become Mythical?" in *Perspectives on Evangelical Theology,* ed. Kenneth S. Kantzer and Stanley N. Gundry (Grand Rapids, Mich.: Baker Book House, 1979), 57–65.

[13]A. N. Sherwin-White, *Roman Society and Roman Law in the New Testament* (Oxford: Clarendon Press, 1963), 187.

[14]My lectures and Professor Stroll's are published in Montgomery, *Where Is History Going?* 37–74 and 207–21.

[15]Alan Saltzman, "Criminal Law: How to Expose Perjury Through Cross-Examination," *Los Angeles Daily Journal,* 4 November 1982.

[16]Patrick L. McCloskey and Ronald L. Schoenberg, *Criminal Law Advocacy* (New York: Matthew Bender, 1984), vol. 5, para. 12.01 [b].

[17]2 Pet. 1:16. In vv. 17–18, Peter states expressly that he was with Jesus when He was transfigured (Matt. 17:2; Mark 9:2; Luke 9:29).

[18]McCloskey and Schoenberg, *Criminal Law Advocacy,* vol. 5, para. 12.03.

[19]A point made as early as the fourth century by the historian Eusebius of Caesarea, and reiterated by such classical apologists as Hugo Grotius ("the father of international law"), in "The Resurrection of Christ proved from credible testimony," in his *The Truth of the Christian Religion,* trans. John Clarke (new ed.; London: William Baynes, 1825), bk. 2, sec. 6, 85–88; this section of Grotius's work is photolithographically reproduced

in John Warwick Montgomery, ed., *Jurisprudence: A Book of Readings,* (Orange, Calif.: Simon Greenleaf School of Law, 1980), 327–30.

[20]John 8:44, etc.

[21]"People just do not see things in an identical way when their positions and chances for observation vary. [If so,] the case is a frame up." F. Lee Bailey and Henry B. Rothblatt, *Fundamentals of Criminal Advocacy* (San Francisco: Bancroft-Whitney, 1974), para. 500, p. 240.

[22]John 20:30–31; 21:25. See Edmund H. Bennett, *The Four Gospels from a Lawyer's Standpoint* (Boston: Houghton, Mifflin, 1899); photolithographically reproduced with editorial introduction by John Warwick Montgomery in *The Simon Greenleaf Law Review* 1 (1981–82).

[23]Luke 24:25.

[24]J. B. Phillips, *Ring of Truth: A Translator's Testimony* (New York: Macmillan, 1967).

[25]Luke 2:1. See John Warwick Montgomery, *Myth, Allegory and Gospel* (Minneapolis, Minn.: Bethany, 1974), 11–31, 116–18.

[26]Luke 3:1–3.

[27]See, for example, E. M. Blaiklock, *The Archaeology of the New Testament* (Grand Rapids, Mich.: Zondervan, 1970); and Edwin M. Yamauchi, *The Stones and the Scriptures* (Grand Rapids, Mich.: Baker Book House, 1981).

[28]Richard A. Givens, *Advocacy* (New York: McGraw-Hill, 1980), 13–14.

[29]Ibid., 12.

[30]Bruce, *New Testament Documents,* 45–46.

[31]Peter Murphy, *A Practical Approach to Evidence* (London: Financial Training, 1982), 23–24; cf. George B. Johnston, "The Development of Civil Trial by Jury in England and the United States," *Simon Greenleaf Law Review* 4 (1984–85): 69–92.

[32]1 John 1:1.

[33]Greenleaf, *Testimony of the Evangelists,* 132–22.

[34]Matt. 12:38–40; 16:4; Luke 11:29; John 2:18–22.

[35]I.e., did the resurrection occur in *ordinary* history? We do not deal here with the unverifiable vagaries of "hyper-history" or "supra-history" (as in the thought of Karl Barth and certain of his neoorthodox followers), or with "existential" resurrections (Rudolf Bultmann and the post-Bultmannians). I have discussed elsewhere these modern theological attempts to have one's cake and eat it too: John Warwick Montgomery, "Karl Barth and Contemporary Theology of History," in his *Where Is History Going?,* 100–117; cf. idem, "Faith, History and the Resurrection," in ibid., 225–39; idem, "Luther's Hermeneutic vs. the New Hermeneutic," in his *In Defense of Martin Luther* (Milwaukee, Wis.: Northwestern Publishing House, 1970), 40–85.

[36]Concerning the historical and evidential value of these appearances, see Merrill C. Tenney, *The Reality of the Resurrection* (New York: Harper, 1963); Josh McDowell, *The Resurrection Factor* (San Bernardino, Calif.: Here's Life Publishers, 1981); Richard Riss, *The Evidence for the Resurrection of Jesus Christ* (Minneapolis, Minn.: Bethany, 1977); and Sir Norman Anderson, *The Evidence for the Resurrection* (London: Inter-Varsity, 1966).

[37]David Hume, "Of Miracles," in his *An Enquiry Concerning Human Understanding* (1748); for critique, see C. S. Lewis, *Miracles* (New York: Macmillan, 1947), esp.

chaps. 8 and 13; and John Warwick Montgomery, *The Shape of the Past,* revised ed. (Minneapolis, Minn.: Bethany, 1975), 289–93.

[38]Frank Morison, *Who Moved the Stone?* (London: Faber & Faber, 1944).

[39]Cf. Matt. 27:62–66.

[40]John Warwick Montgomery, "Science, Theology, and the Miraculous," in his *Faith Founded on Fact* (Nashville, Tenn.: Thomas Nelson, 1978), 43–73, esp. 54.

[41]See Edwin M. Yamauchi, "Passover Plot or Easter Triumph? A Critical Review of H. Schonfield's Recent Theory," in *Christianity for the Tough-Minded,* ed. John Warwick Montgomery (Minneapolis, Minn.: Bethany, 1973), 261–71.

[42]Von Daniken had "obtained the money [over $130,000 in debts] by misrepresentation of his financial situation, falsifying the hotel's books to make it appear solvent. A court psychiatrist examined von Daniken and found him a prestige-seeker, a liar and an unstable and criminal psychopath with a hysterical character, yet fully accountable for his acts" (Richard R. Lingeman, "Erich von Daniken's Genesis," *New York Times Book Review,* 31 March 1974, 6.

[43]Probability reasoning is virtually universal in the law: it operates both in common law and in non-common law systems of jurisprudence, and in "civilized" and "primitive" legal systems indiscriminately. See Montgomery, *Law and Gospel,* 35–36.

[44]*Federal Rules of Evidence* 401. This definition was derived from Professor James Bradley Thayer's classic *Preliminary Treatise on Evidence* (1898).

[45]Thomas Sherlock, *The Tryal of the Witnesses of the Resurrection of Jesus* (London: J. Roberts, 1729), 62; Sherlock's book is photolithographically reproduced in Montgomery, *Jurisprudence.*

[46]See Luke 24:36–43.

[47]I have applied proof by *res ipsa loquitur* to the resurrection in my *Law & Gospel,* 35.

[48]Elizabeth F. Loftus, *Eyewitness Testimony* (Cambridge, Mass.: Harvard University Press, 1979); cf. her popular article on this subject in *Psychology Today* 18, no. 2 (February 1984): 22–26.

[49]Edward B. Arnolds, et al. *Eyewitness Testimony: Strategies and Tactics* (New York: McGraw-Hill, 1984), 400–401.

[50]John 20:19–28.

[51]Carl F. H. Henry, *God, Revelation and Authority* (Waco, Tex.: Word Books, 1976), 1:220–23, 230–38, 256–63; 2:313–34; Ronald H. Nash, "The Use and Abuse of History in Christian Apologetics," *Christian Scholar's Review* 1, no. 3 (Spring 1971): 217–26; Ronald H. Nash, *Christian Faith and Historical Understanding,* 2d ed. (Dallas, Tex.: Probe Books, 1989). I have responded to Carl Henry in Montgomery, *Faith Founded on Fact,* xvii–xxv. Paul D. Feinberg wrote a devastating critique of Nash's "Use and Abuse of History" in "History: Public or Private? A Defense of John Warwick Montgomery's Philosophy of History," *Christian Scholar's Review* 1, no. 4 (Summer 1971): 325–31; it is reprinted in Montgomery, *Shape of the Past,* 375–82. Nash's book, *Christian Faith and Historical Understanding* (which, sadly, does not seem to have benefitted in any way from Feinberg's insights), has been critically reviewed by Francis J. Beckwith: "Does Evidence Matter?" *Simon Greenleaf Law Review* 4 (1984–85): 231–35.

[52]R. C. Sproul, John Gerstner, and Arthur Lindsley, *Classical Apologetics* (Grand Rapids, Mich.: Zondervan, 1984); Norman L. Geisler, *Miracles and Modern Thought*, with a response by R. C. Sproul (Dallas, Tex.: Probe Books, 1982).

[53]John Warwick Montgomery, "Gordon Clark's Historical Philosophy," in Montgomery, *Where Is History Going?* esp. 164.

[54]Feinberg, "History: Public or Private?" 379.

[55]*Williams* v. *North Carolina*, 325 U.S. 226, 65 Sup. Ct. 1092, 157 A.L.P. 1366 (italics added).

[56]Geisler, *Miracles and Modern Thought,* 66. Remarkably, Geisler seems entirely unacquainted with my detailed treatment of this issue in my book *Faith Founded on Fact,* 43–73, even though my book was published four years before his.

[57]Ibid., 61.

[58]See, for example, *State* v. *Elliott,* 45 Iowa 486.

[59]Montgomery, *Faith Founded on Fact,* 61.

[60]John 10:30; 14:8–9, slightly paraphrased; cf. Mark 2:5–7; 14:61–64.

[61]E.g., Matt. 4:4; 5:17–19; John 5:39; 10:35.

[62]For example, Matt. 12:38–42; 19:3–6; 24:37–39; Luke 24:25–27.

[63]John 14:26; 16:12–15. Swiss theologian Oscar Cullmann has made much of the apostolic memory as the inspired link between Jesus' ministry and the New Testament scriptures.

[64]Acts 1:21–26; 9:26–27; Gal. 2:11–13; 2 Peter 3:15–16.

[65]See John Warwick Montgomery, ed., *God's Inerrant Word: An International Symposium on the Trustworthiness of Scripture* (Minneapolis, Minn.: Bethany, 1974); idem, *Crisis in Lutheran Theology,* 2d ed., 2 vols. (Minneapolis, Minn.: Bethany, 1973); idem, *Shape of the Past,* 138–45.

[66]From the Greek noun *kenosis,* whose verb form ("empty oneself/divest oneself of privileges") is applied to Christ in Philippians 2:6–8. However, biblical teaching on incarnation has no resemblance to the liberal theological theory of Jesus' fallibility. Theological liberals—typically—developed the theory to have their cake (a divine Jesus) and eat it too (simultaneous rejection of Jesus' conservative view of scriptural authority). Cf. Montgomery, *Crisis in Lutheran Theology,* 1:91–93. It is perhaps worth noting that the well-known passage in the Gospels in which Jesus states that He does not know the hour of His Second Coming (Mark 13:32) is no confirmation of Kenotic theory, for (1) only a single, eschatological item of knowledge is involved, and (2) Jesus' disclaimer of knowledge on this point shows that in His incarnate state He was nonetheless fully aware of the boundaries of His knowledge, and being in control of His knowledge He would not have advertently or inadvertently given false or misleading information when He did make positive assertions (e.g., on the reliability of the Bible).

[67]John Warwick Montgomery, "The Marxist Approach to Human Rights: Analysis and Critique," *Simon Greenleaf Law Review* 3 (1983–84): 51–53, 138–41.

[68]This chapter is reprinted, with slight changes, from chapter 6 of the author's *Human Rights and Human Dignity* (Dallas, Tex.: Probe Books, 1986).

Appendix

Some Concluding Thoughts on Evolutionary Belief

Herman J. Eckelmann

SIR FRED HOYLE HAS ENTERED TERRITORY once that of evolutionary biologists. His purpose is to quantify the actual odds of life springing from non-life by random motions of available matter. He argues that, even if all the oceans were replaced with an optimum prebiotic soup continuously stirred and maintained at ideal temperature, there would not be enough time in the known age of the earth, 4.5 billion years, for the random falling together of atoms to amass the surprisingly large quantity of ordered information we now realize is necessary to specify genetically the replication of a single "simple" cell.

Disdaining artistic intimations of plausible probability, he goes on to calculate the probabilities of our planet Earth producing a cell if all of the planet were such a soup. The probability is still far too small.

Finally, the odds of life happening were worked out for the case of the entire known universe being filled with this prebiotic liquid. The increase in probability brought the odds up to one such cell occurring in $10^{40,000}$ years.[1] This is an enormously longer time than the commonly believed age of the material universe, which is usually held to be in the range of only 1.5 to 2.0×10^{10} years! Others have conceived a froth of an infinite number of bubble universes that cannot intercommunicate and therefore cannot be detected,[2] but only believed in (because they reflect chosen common materialist presuppositions embedded in the mathematical development of the model). The only alternative is *not* that of a young earth and a seven-solar-day creation week.[3]

Evidently the materialist model needs either a much greater mass of prebiotic soup or more time (or both). How much? Ten to the forty thousandth power years—far in excess of the presently believed age of the universe—to account for the development of a single simple living cell with the required high information content in its genetic code against such odds. Hoyle gets past this problem by believing in an everlasting steady-state universe. There's plenty of *time* there. Others try to come up with an infinite froth of bubble universes (plenty of *mass* there).

The idea that just possibly there might be an Infinite Mind as the supplier of such great information somehow escapes serious consideration. How small a chance is represented by $10^{-40,000}$? The argument seems to be that only the infinite age of a steady state universe would allow such infinitesimal odds (of a prebiotic soup at the ideal temperature, constantly stirred, and large enough to entirely fill all space in the known universe) to be played out adequately so as to produce by thermally driven random processes the large and ordered information store necessary to make a single self-replicating living cell.[4] In addition there are the problems relating to the development of all the variety of species.

At this point a remark from Chesterton comes to mind: "It is absurd for the evolutionist to complain that it is unthinkable for an admittedly unthinkable God to make everything out of nothing, and then pretend that it is *more* thinkable that nothing should turn itself into anything."[5] This is a wonderful new gospel. It wants to be believed against all odds—literally. If we were to be able to derive a number that would express the chances of writing history in advance with such accuracy as the Bible does (and as Robert C. Newman describes in this volume and elsewhere[6]) and multiply it by Hoyle's $10^{40,000}$, what would we have? Some would say a much larger than ever reason for recognizing the existence of the truly awesome God of the Bible.

Others might invoke the weak anthropic principle (WAP).[7] But justification for the use of all probabilities under all circumstances would be wiped out equally and everywhere by the WAP. Wherever probabilistic thinking leads, anyone could then claim that it "is only because we happen to have been born into this universe that has succeeded in evolving so as to have happened this way," and yet we all live our lives and do our work constantly using possibility and probability thinking!

The Bible is accredited to us by the fulfilled prophecies conveyed within it. This is not an apology, obviously, for evils done in His Name by strange and evil people in past history or for evils other people may yet perform in the future. Rather, it is a challenge to get to the root of all things by reading thoroughly the Book He has given—His self-disclosure—with an open mind willing to be instructed. The alternative seems to be to believe in an eternally running-down universe being resupplied by the continuous creation of matter out of nothing by nothing at a rate that cannot be detected by experiment.[8]

No one has *ever* observed new matter emerge out of nothing. Yet Hoyle says:

I have a strong emotional dislike for special setups in cosmology. . . . Any suggestion of "initial" tinkering being necessary to explain the most everyday features of our existence seems intensely distasteful to me. . . . The idea I use in cosmological investigations is that all important aspects of the universe are contained within the laws, they are not impressed from outside the laws. This is one of the shortcuts I use. I personally spend no time investigating theories that require special initial conditions.[9]

Is it possible that one can have too high an emotional stake in wanting to have a God-less universe—one that avoids standards of right living and a Judgment Day when all accounts will be balanced?

It used to be fashionable to claim Christianity was only man-made and that it made ego-driven man the center of the universe; evolution was supposed to have dethroned man from this ego trip. Now it is admitted man is very unlikely to be reproduced by evolution should he extirpate himself in a global war. Evolution, we are told, because of its thoroughly random character, might go very differently, or almost not at all, a second time around.[10]

Having been thus demoted, we find ourselves again considered special, a race especially worth saving. Most unlikely to be repeated in an evolutionary sequence, man has been made unique by doctrinaire evolutionists and therefore worth any sacrifice to save!

What good fortune that we have God's Book. Why not make the most of the opportunity for the salvation and life it presents to us?

Notes

[1]Fred Hoyle and Chandra Wickramasinghe, *Evolution from Space* (New York: Simon & Schuster, 1981), 1–33, 130–41; and Fred Hoyle, *Cosmology and Astrophysics* (Ithaca, N.Y.: Cornell University Press, 1982), 1–65.

[2]John Boslough, *Stephen Hawking's Universe* (New York: William Morrow and Company, 1985), 105–15.

[3]See Robert C. Newman and Herman J. Eckelmann, Jr., *Genesis One and the Origin of the Earth* (Downers Grove, Ill.: InterVarsity Press, 1977), 83–88. The authors favor a view that the creation involved six days of God's creative activity. They do not,

however, see the days as consecutive, and they allow for substantial amounts of time between the days.

[4]Cf. Hoyle, *Cosmology and Astrophysics*, 44–61.

[5]George J. Marlin, Richard P. Rabatin, and John L. Swan, eds., *The Quotable Chesterton: A Topical Compilation of the Wit, Wisdom and Satire of G. K. Chesterton* (San Francisco: Ignatius Press, 1986), 113.

[6]See Robert C. Newman's discussion of history written in advance. See also his *The Evidence of Prophecy* (Hatfield, Pa.: Interdisciplinary Biblical Research Institute, 1988).

[7]See Robert C. Newman's discussion of the weak anthropic principle (his chapter on inanimate design in this volume).

[8]Fred Hoyle, *The Nature of the Universe* (New York: Harper & Brothers, 1950), 105–32.

[9]Fred Hoyle, *Galaxies, Nuclei and Quasars* (New York: Harper & Row, 1967), 96.

[10]Cf. Boslough, *Stephen Hawking's Universe*, 115–50, esp. 124.

Contributors

John A. Bloom. B.A. with honors in chemistry (Grinnell College, 1974), M.S. (Cornell University, 1977), Ph.D. (Cornell University, 1980), M.A.R.S. and M.Div. with highest honors (Biblical Theological Seminary, 1983), M.A. (Dropsie College, 1986), Ph.D. candidate in ancient near eastern studies (Dropsie College). Lecturer in Physics, Ursinus College, Collegeville, Pennsylvania; and Director, Bloomsbury Research Corporation, Hatfield, Pennsylvania. Author of articles in the field of biophysics and of research reports for the Interdisciplinary Biblical Research Institute, Hatfield, Pennsylvania.

William J. Cairney. B.A. with honors in biology and chemistry (Rutgers University, 1966), M.S. (Cornell University, 1968), Ph.D. (Cornell University, 1977). Professor of Biology, United States Air Force Academy, Colorado Springs, Colorado. Author of more than twenty professional publications in the fields of hyperbaric oxygen applications, aerospace and environmental physiology, and human factors in aerospace operations.

Herman J. Eckelmann. B.E.E. (Cornell University, 1949), M.Div. (Faith Theological Seminary, 1952). Pastor of the Faith Bible Church of Ithaca, New York. Co-author of *Genesis One and the Origin of the Earth* with Robert C. Newman.

John E. Hare. B.A. (Oxford University, 1971), Ph.D. (Princeton University, 1975). Professor of Philosophy, Calvin College, Grand Rapids, Michigan. Author of *Ethics and International Affairs* with Carey B. Joynt; *Plato's Euthyphro;* "Credibility and Bluff," in *Nuclear Weapons and the Future of Humanity;* and many other articles in philosophy journals.

Allan A. MacRae. B.A. (Occidental College, 1922), M.A. (Occidental College, 1923), Th.B. (Princeton Theological Seminary, 1927), M.A. (Princeton University, 1927), Ph.D. (University of Pennsylvania, 1936). Chancellor and Emeritus Professor of Old Testament at Biblical Theological Seminary, Hatfield, Pennsylvania. Author of articles in theological journals and of the books *The Gospel of Isaiah, An Exegetical Study of Daniel's Prophecies,* and *The Professor Answers.*

Robert C. Newman. B.S. *summa cum laude* in physics (Duke University, 1963), M.Div. (Faith Theological Seminary; 1970), S.T.M. (Biblical Theological Seminary, 1972), Ph.D. in theoretical astrophysics (Cornell University, 1967). Professor of New Testament, Biblical Theological Seminary, Hatfield, Pennsylvania. Co-author of *Science Speaks* with Peter W. Stoner and *Genesis One and the Origin of the Earth* with Herman J. Eckelmann; editor of *Evidence of Prophecy;* author of articles in scientific and theological journals.

John C. Studenroth. B.S. with highest honors in botany (University of Maine, 1969), M.S. in plant pathology (University of Maine, 1971), Ph.D. in plant pathology (Cornell University, 1979), M.A. and M.Div. in theology (Biblical Theological Seminary, 1983). Pastor, Pennridge Community Church, Perkasie, Pennsylvania; doctoral candidate in Biblical Studies, Dropsie College. Author of articles in plant pathology journals.

Garret Vanderkooi. B.A. in chemistry (Calvin College, 1960), Ph.D. in biochemistry (University of Rochester, 1966). Professor of Chemistry and Biological Sciences, Northern Illinois University. Author of numerous research articles in journals of chemistry and biochemistry.

John Warwick Montgomery. To use C.S. Lewis's words, John Warwick Montgomery was brought over the threshold of Christian faith "kicking and struggling." The year was 1949. The place, Cornell University, Ithaca, New York. Hermann John Eckelmann, a persistent engineering student, succeeded in goading Montgomery into religious discussions. Montgomery, a philosophy major disinterested in religion, found himself forced to consider seriously the claims of Jesus Christ in the New Testament in order to preserve his intellectual integrity. After no mean struggle he acknowledged his rebellion against God and asked forgiveness.

Today, John Warwick Montgomery is Professor of Law and Humanities at the University of Luton, England, and Director of the University's Human Rights Centre. During the academic year he teaches in England and practices as a barrister; in the summer he directs his University's annual International Seminar in Jurisprudence and Human Rights in Strasbourg, France. He holds eight earned degrees besides the LL.B.: the A.B. with distinction in Philosophy (Cornell University; Phi Beta Kappa), B.L.S. and M.A. (University of California at Berkeley), B.D. and S.T.M. (Wittenberg University, Springfield, Ohio), M.Phil. in Law (University of Essex, England), Ph.D. (University of Chicago), and the Doctorat d'Universite from Strasbourg, France.

Dr. Montgomery is the author of over one hundred scholarly journal articles and more than forty books in English, French, Spanish, and German. He is internationally regarded both as a theologian (his debates with the late Bishop James Pike, death-of-God advocate Thomas Altizer, and situation-ethicist Joseph Fletcher are historic) and as a lawyer (barrister-at-law of the Middle Temple and Lincoln's Inn, England; member of the California, Virginia, Washington State and District of Columbia Bars and the Bar of the Supreme Court of the United States). He is honored by inclusion in *Contemporary Authors, International Scholars Directory* (editor-in-chief) *Who's Who in America, Who's Who in France, Who's Who in Europe, International Who's Who,* and *Who's Who in the World.*

Index

What is Probe?

Probe Books are published by Probe Ministries, a nonprofit corporation whose mission is to reclaim the primacy of Christian thought and values in Western culture through media, education, and literature. In seeking to accomplish this mission, Probe provides perspective on the integration of the academic disciplines and historic Christianity. The members and associates of the Probe team are actively engaged in research as well as lecturing and interacting with students and faculty in thousands of university classrooms throughout the United States and Canada on topics and issues vital to the university student.

In addition, Probe acts as a clearing house, communicating the results of its research to the church and society.

Further information about Probe's materials and ministries may be obtained by writing to Probe Ministries International, P.O. Box 801046, Dallas, Texas 75204.

OTHER PROBE BOOKS
Strengthening the Christian Mind